C0-AKE-862

Meaning and Geography

Approaches to Semiotics
104

Editorial Committee

Thomas A. Sebeok
Roland Posner
Alain Rey

Mouton de Gruyter
Berlin · New York

Meaning and Geography

The Social Conception of the Region in Northern Greece

by

Alexandros Ph. Lagopoulos
Karin Boklund-Lagopoulou

Mouton de Gruyter
Berlin · New York 1992

Mouton de Gruyter (formerly Mouton, The Hague)
is a Division of Walter de Gruyter & Co., Berlin.

♾ Printed on acid-free paper which falls within the guidelines of the
ANSI to ensure permanence and durability.

Library of Congress Cataloging in Publication Data

Lagopoulos, Alexandros Ph.
    Meaning and geography ; the social conception of the
region in northern Greece / by Alexandros Ph. Lagopoulos,
Karin Boklund-Lagopoulou.
       p.   cm. — (Approaches to semiotics ; 104)
    Includes bibliographical references and index.
    ISBN 3-11-012956-6 (acid free paper)
    1. Human geography — Greece. 2. Environmental psych-
ology — Greece. 3. Semiotics. 4. Regionalism — Greece.
I. Boklund-Lagopoulou, Karin. II. Title. III. Series.
GF581.L34   1992
304.2′09495′6 — dc20   91-43000
                                      CIP

Die Deutsche Bibliothek — Cataloging in Publication Data

Lagopoulos, Alexandros P.:
Meaning and geography : the social conception of the region
in northern Greece / by Alexandros Ph. Lagopoulos ; Karin
Boklund-Lagopoulou. — Berlin ; New York : Mouton de
Gruyter, 1992
    (Approaches to semiotics ; 104)
    ISBN 3-11-012956-6
NE: Boklund-Lagopoulou, Karin:; GT

© Copyright 1992 by Walter de Gruyter & Co., D-1000 Berlin 30

All rights reserved, including those of translation into foreign languages. No part of this
book may be reproduced or transmitted in any form or by any means, electronic or
mechanical, including photocopy, recording or any information storage and retrieval
system, without permission in writing from the publisher.
Printing: Ratzlow Druck, Berlin. — Binding: Lüderitz & Bauer, Berlin.
Printed in Germany.

Θεσσαλονίκη μου, μεγάλη φτωχομάνα,
Εσύ που κάνεις τα καλύτερα παιδιά
...
Θεσσαλονίκη μου, ποτέ δε σ'απαρνιέμαι.
Είσ' η πατρίδα μου, το λέω και καυχιέμαι.

[My Thessaloniki, great mother of the poor,
You who turn out the best kids
...
My Thessaloniki, I'll never deny you.
You are my homeland, I say it and I'm proud.]

Greek popular song by M. Chiotis
Words by Chr. Kolokotronis

Contents

Preface

The research project on which the present book is based was realized largely due to a grant from the Division of Research and Technology of the Greek Ministry of Industry, Energy, and Technology, and a supplementary grant from the Technical Chamber of Greece. Without this financial assistance the book would not have been possible, and this holds a fortiori for the people who participated in the project, directly or indirectly, as primary sources of information or as researchers.

Preliminary bibliographical research for the project took place in 1985 at the University of Denver, Colorado. The main goal of this investigation was to prepare the key technical element of the study, the questionnaire. The active semioticians of space are not many. They are excellent people and friends, but we all have the bad habit of being stubbornly principled, with the result that there are almost as many semiotics of space as there are semioticians. We thought that the broad scope of the present study should contribute to the beginning of a dialogue among us, which is why we wished to relate our questionnaire to those used in previous research projects. At this point, we would like to express our warm thanks to Professor Pierre Pellegrino, who kindly made available to us the questionnaire of his own study on the semiotics of regional space, a study repeatedly referred to in this volume. The same thanks are due to Professor Alain Bourdin, who very courteously gave us access to the questionnaire used by the late Professor Raymond Ledrut in his seminal, sociologically based, study on urban semiotics.

After the feverish time of the field work, the analysis of the data delivered by the interviews, and the preparation of the data for statistical processing by computer, there came a serene period of library research; our aim was to review as far as possible the relevant bibliography. We have the best memories, in the context of this second period, from our stay in 1987 at the Research Center for Language and Semiotic Studies, Indiana University, Bloomington. Not only did the Center offer us all the facilities needed, but its Director, Professor Thomas A. Sebeok, was the first to encourage our effort, and his help has been crucial in getting this book into print. The least we can do here is to express our warmest thanks.

In addition to the authors, the field work team included Ms. Eleftheria Deltsou, graduate student in anthropology; Ms. Ioanna Pandelidou-Spyridonidou, political scientist; Mr. Theodoros Papaioannou, architect-engineer, D.E.A.; and Mr. Dimitris Drakoulis, architect. Ms. Deltsou and Ms. Pandelidou-Spyridonidou also assisted in the analysis of the data from various parts of the interview. Our research collaborators were Dr. Konstantinos-Victor Spyridonidis, lecturer in the Department of Urban and Regional Planning, Aristotle University of Thessaloniki, who greatly contributed to the analysis of the spatial structure of Greek Macedonia and was responsible for the calculation of the indices of Chapter 8; and Dr. Christos Kousidonis, architect-engineer and regional planner, who both analysed some of the data and, most importantly, prepared and executed all our computer programs with the help of the central computer of Aristotle University of Thessaloniki. To all our collaborators we extend our heartfelt thanks for their enthusiastic participation, and our congratulations for having survived more or less unscathed an experience which was at times something of an ordeal. The team was ably completed by Ms. Kalliope Dona, who prepared part of the manuscript, and Ms. Pelagia Limona-Chatzopoulou, who prepared the illustrations for printing.

Certain aspects of the case study have been presented, in different settings and to very diverse audiences, first in Greece, the United States, Germany, and France, and later in Switzerland and Spain. Professor David Lowenthal, Dr. Peter Jackson, and Professor Mark Gottdiener were kind enough to read a first draft of the introductory chapters and to provide us with helpful comments and suggestions. Professor Ioannis Hasiotis of the Department of Modern History, Aristotle University of Thessaloniki, kindly read and commented on the section on the history of Macedonia. To all our friends, colleagues, and family members who put up with us during the writing of this volume we also extend our thanks - and our apologies.

As will be clear to the reader, this book has evolved as a continuous interplay between theoretical analysis and the elaboration of empirical data. One of our aims was the presentation and systematization of these data, and from this point of view the book may be considered as a research monograph. But we also had a second, equally important goal: to reason from the specific to the general, from the case study to a theoretical conception of the semiotics of macro-environments. Theory stands at the two ends of our enterprise, as the indispensable context for the realization of the case study and as the generalizations based on the data from the latter. In such an enterprise, theory and data are equally valuable.

Theoretical knowledge is acquired privately, our data were gathered among real people. Our book was born from the support and participation of these subjects of semiosis. The willing assistance of the relevant agencies, principally the local authorities in the settlements of Ormylia and Axioupoli, and of certain key persons was the necessary precondition for the preparation and carrying out of the field work. In this context, we would like to express our thanks to Mr. Giannis Tsamardas, former President of the Community of Ormylia, and Mr. Dimitris Lelegiannis, whose coffeeshop we can warmly recommend; Mr. Theodoros Tongelidis, former Secretary of the Municipality of Axioupoli, who knows personally at least three generations of his fellow Axioupolitans; and Mr. Konstantinos Vafidis, practicing architect in the city of Veria. But most of all we feel grateful to the 144 persons who opened for us their houses and their hearts, and did their best to respond to our intricate and tortuous questions. Without their help, this book would quite simply never have existed.

Part I. Theory of space: Geography, semiotics, and Marxism

Space that has been seized upon by the imagination cannot remain indifferent space subject to the measures and estimates of the surveyor. It has been lived in, not in its positivity, but with all the partiality of the imagination .... the house image would appear to have become the topography of our intimate being.

Gaston Bachelard, *The poetics of space*

Chapter 1. Objectivism and subjectivism in spatial studies

1. The sphere of spatial studies

Social space and spatial theory have been the concern of varied scientific domains. One privileged domain is human geography, which for more than a century in its contemporary form, and in spite of the multitude of divergent approaches it encompassed in its recent history, has set as its aim the study of geographical space. The other principal domain producing spatial theory, which like geography has a long prehistory of systematic writing, is architecture, in which theory-making has been closely related to professional practice (whence its frequently normative character). These two domains overlap to a limited extent only, given that architecture traditionally has been, and still is, focused on individual buildings and groups of buildings, while geography is usually oriented toward wider-scale spatial phenomena. In spite of its efforts, architectural theory does not seem able to be of more than mediocre help in the study of wider spatial scales, since it approaches them analogically by extrapolating from its findings within its own sphere of pertinence.

This was not the case with the Chicago school of urban sociology, which in successive waves beginning in the second decade of our century came to challenge the primacy of geography in the analysis of urban space. The field called human ecology thus created, which was based on analogies from plant and animal ecology in addition to geography, was active for about half a century before retreating from the scientific arena, leaving some influences and echoes behind. During this period of the late sixties and early seventies there was an increasing discontent among geographers with the mainstream positivist and quantitative new geography which dominated the field, paralleled by an increasing awareness of the social context of geography as an institution and its sociological context as a science (see also Gregory 1978: 49-50). The reaction to positivist geography, nourished by the new ideology of the sixties, was brought into sudden prominence by the events of May 1968 in France, which are connected with the names of two major Marxist theoreticians of space, the philosopher Henri Lefebvre and the sociologist Manuel Castells. The result was the creation for the first time of a Marxist geography, first in France, and then in Britain and the United States.

A less political reaction to positivist geography which also appeared during the sixties, though it had earlier roots, was oriented toward the subjective meaning of space. This reaction took two very different forms. The first, which has been called the humanistic approach, diverged radically from the positivist paradigm and was - and still is - strongly inspired by phenomenology. This approach is not internally unified, either in respect to the particular status of the geography it proposes in relation to mainstream geography, or in respect to methodological questions, but it nevertheless acquires a character of its own through its phenomenological awareness of the meaning of environmental experience. We can date the first explicit statements in humanistic geography from about the mid-seventies (Relph 1981: 131-134, 142-143).

The second, the analytical behavioral approach, continued to be founded on positivist premises (a relation which was to weaken in the years to come) but operated a radical revision - even inversion - of the traditional positivist stance. The cornerstone of positivism, as well as its precursor empiricism, is that knowledge is based on the observation of an exterior objective reality and the facts and events taking place in it. The inversion made by analytical behavioral geography consists in the replacement of the study of exterior facts with that of conceptual facts. Instead of describing and explaining urban and regional organization, movements and transformations as deriving from material factors, it derives them from conceptual factors. But while it is true that behavioral geography operated this radical shift on the epistemological level, we should be aware that in the history of human geography the shift evolved to a certain degree logically from discontent with the previous state of locational analysis (cf. Cox 1981: 257-258).

This new orientation within the positivist tradition is not unique to geography, nor does it lack a wider epistemological background. A direct parallel to behavioral geography can be found earlier in French structuralism, notably in the work of one of its founders, Claude Lévi-Strauss. Lévi-Strauss' epistemology springs directly from logical positivism, though it is also influenced by Kant. He considers social anthropology as a branch of semiotics, the study of sign systems and sign processes. The aim of anthropology would be the study of cultural communication systems. Natural and social reality is apprehended through the mediation of the structure of the human senses and the brain, and, given that the conception of reality constitutes a whole, we can conclude that there must be a unified semiotic coding system located in the human mind. Lévi-Strauss' structural anthropology, in its implied reduction of the whole range of social phenomena to systems of communication only, thus operates within positivism a reversal curiously similar to the one performed by behavioral geography. But structural anthropology also implies the reduction of the cultural and historical variety of these systems to allegedly innate and uniform, hence a-historical and universal, laws of the human mind. According to Lévi-Strauss, the structure of these universal semiotic laws derives from the structure of the human brain through the mediation of the structure of language (see Lévi-Strauss 1958: 28, 49, 67, 78-82, 105-108, 224-225; see also Lagopoulos 1986: 223-225). This second form of reductionism, from the cultural and historical to the biological and universal, is also characteristic of behavioral geography, as we shall see in Chapter 2 below.

The dominant position given by Lévi-Strauss to language follows directly from his neopositivist epistemological background. For the logical positivists of the Vienna circle, the aim of philosophy is the critical analysis of language and its meaning, since reality as a whole is not accessible to us, and what we can know about reality exists in language. Lévi-Strauss applied this principle in the domain of social anthropology, simultaneously considering that language is not only the vehicle of universal structural laws, but also the form of their manifestation in social reality. Logical positivism opened the way in the positivist tradition for the study of systems of communication and offered a common background for structuralism and geography. In their turn, these two domains brought something new to logical positivism, through the shift from the positivist interest in language as a means for understanding exterior reality to the focusing on signification in its own right.

Structuralism and behavioral geography both have their sources of inspiration. The direct source of Lévi-Strauss is structural phonology, the foundation of which is associated with the names of N.S. Troubetzkoy and Roman Jakobson, both working within the tradition of the structural linguistics of Ferdinand de Saussure (1857-1913). Here we have the major source of contemporary semiotics, the discipline which took up Saussure's (1971: 33) project of creating a *sémiologie*, "une science qui étudie la vie des signes au sein de la vie sociale" ['a science which studies the life of signs within society'], and which bears the strong imprints of Lévi-Strauss' structuralism. In the magnetic field of Lévi-Strauss' interests space was also pulled in, to the extent that he turned toward the analysis of settlement space in relation to cultural systems of meaning. Beginning in the mid-sixties the example of Lévi-Strauss was followed by other researchers, with as a result the creation of a specific branch of semiotics, the semiotics of space, a branch which up to today has remained peripheral to spatial studies as a whole. While European semiotics thus has had a certain impact on spatial studies, the influence of American semiotics in this sphere has been extremely limited and, ironically, manifested on European soil in the form of the small circle around Max Bense in Germany.[1]

If Saussure's structural linguistics lie behind French structuralism and semiotics, the basic theoretical concepts and techniques of behavioral geography were borrowed from two different sources of unequal size. The first is almost a one-man source, the city planner Kevin Lynch, whose seminal study *The image of the city*, first published in 1960, had a strong impact on both behavioral geography and environmental psychology. Lynch himself states that the theoretical framework of the research underlying the book was the product of his cooperation with the painter Gyorgy Kepes, the link of Lynch with the economist Kenneth Boulding, author of *The image*, published in 1956 (Canter 1977: 22).

Environmental psychology is the second, and major, source of behavioral geography. The central trend of environmental psychology borrowed its theoretical presuppositions from cognitive psychology, while the field took shape from the beginning through real-life research - as opposed to the controlled laboratory conditions of mainstream experimental psychology - oriented toward practical issues. Architectural psychology of the late fifties and early sixties can be considered as the first phase of environmental psychology. The research objects of architectural psychology were the expectations of the future users of the new projects built following the massive reconstruction plans prepared after World War II, and the reactions of the actual users to their architectural environment. Since the late sixties environmental psychology has been oriented towards a wide set of issues. They include a multiplicity of issues addressing a larger environmental scale, such as cognitive mapping, and environmental attitudes, beliefs, and assessments, such as landscape quality and preferences; consumer attitudes and behavior; significative spatial behavior studied by proxemics; the consequences of action on the ecological environment, and the impact of the ecological and the built environment on behavior and physiology. It should be noted that during this phase environmental psychology has been strongly planning-oriented (Canter & Craik 1981: 2-4; Stokols 1978).

2. The unbridged dichotomy of spatial studies

The preceding brief excursion into the sphere of spatial studies does not attempt to be exhaustive, since in such a case other fields should also be addressed, such as spatial economics and the normative models of urban and regional planning. Its aim was the presentation of the larger context in respect to which the study of the conception of regional space can be approached. There is, in our opinion, a fundamental epistemological weakness which to a greater or lesser degree characterizes all the available approaches to the study of space, namely the division between what we would like to call subjectivist and objectivist approaches. As we shall argue in this section, these two viewpoints on space have evolved in a parallel and antagonistic manner within the sphere of spatial studies. We shall concentrate here on the various trends of the subjectivist viewpoint, though we shall also make references to the objectivist whenever we feel that it might help as a contrast, since the subject of our own research can be considered as more closely related to subjectivist approaches. As we shall argue, however, there is a need for a holistic paradigm on the basis of which to treat the issue of environmental representations. We believe that our own social semiotic approach is situated within such a paradigm.

There is a strong dividing line running through spatial studies, whose traces can be detected as far back as the early French school of *géographie humaine*, the ancestor of humanistic geography introduced by Vidal de la Blache at the turn of the century, but which first became apparent in connection to the historical evolution of the school of human ecology. We can discern in the latter four major approaches, which can be grouped in two broad trends. The older approach in the dominant trend coincides with the roots of human ecology and can be called "classical" or "orthodox" ecology. For this approach, society is composed of two different levels of organization, the "biotic" level and the "cultural" level, including social communication and conventions, which depends on the former but also exercises some influence on it. The crucial biotic level is based on a fundamental mechanism, operating in the whole realm of nature - not only in human societies but also in animal and plant communities - namely competition between the members of a group; thus, the interrelations within a group acquire the character of a natural economy. Human society would be founded on the competitive cooperation of its members, hence on a pre-social reality shaped by unconscious adaptations taking place during the struggle for survival. Classical ecology is not only a theory of society, but also a theory of space. One aspect of the struggle for existence would be the struggle for space, and there is a series of suggested primary and secondary bipolar ecological mechanisms of universal value, which mediate between competition and spatial organization (see Park 1936; Theodorson 1961: 3-4).

This short account of the fundamental theoretical premises of classical ecology brings to the foreground its two main epistemological characteristics. First, it shows its reductionist character, because society and social processes are seen as reducible to bioecological processes, the form of reductionism known as social Darwinism. We find here an interesting and unexpected parallel with Lévi-Strauss' structural anthropology, to the extent that in both cases we find the same reduction from human society to nature. At this point the views diverge, the human ecologists locating the ultimate explanation in the natural ecological relations between human organisms, while the structuralists look for it in the equally natural biological structure of the individual brain. Because biological factors are material factors, classical ecology has been considered as materialist. The other characteristic of classical ecology which follows from our discussion is the secondary role of the non-material factor for the constitution of society and space. This factor, the cultural level, is derivative and thus of secondary importance, although it is accorded certain functions, for example, in social change; the study of the cultural factor is not included in the interests of human ecology.

After an extended barrage of criticism, the classical position in human ecology was extensively modified and replaced by three distinct approaches, two of which can be grouped together with the classical school as part of the dominant materialist trend in human ecology which emphasizes the material factors operating behind spatial organization. Social area analysis, the most recent of the two, totally neglects cultural and ideological factors, while the "neo-orthodox" approach makes some room for culture and ideology, as did classical ecology, but shows no real interest in their connections with space (cf. Theodorson 1961: 129-132).

On the other hand, the "sociocultural" or "voluntaristic" approach, the second broad trend in human ecology, is exclusively focused on this connection and replaces the study of material factors with that of attitudes, values, and feelings, that is, ideology. Thus, for example, Firey (1945) and Jonassen (1949) attempt to explain the social organization of urban space (Firey also studies land uses) in terms of the ideological choices of community members and the incidences of these choices on their actual locational processes, a causal succession which we shall encounter again in human geography.

The polarization between the materialist and the sociocultural approach, that is, between the explanation of spatial organization by material or by ideological factors - in short what we called the objectivist and the subjectivist model in spatial studies - that became manifest with human ecology was to haunt spatial studies until today. This split divided human geography, the main locus of spatial studies, in two opposed camps. The objectivist field in human geography covers two broad epistemological orientations, the one taking as the object of geography the relation between man and nature, and the other, new geography, defining this object as the spatial organization of human activities on the surface of the earth. In studying the man-environment relation geography adopted different viewpoints, one of which, environmental determinism, arrived at the same extreme as social Darwinism in human ecology, maintaining that the crucial factor accounting for geographical organization is the natural environment. There also appeared a more composite view, associated with the school founded by Vidal de la Blache and related to subjectivism, which weakened the role of the natural factor by including in geographical explanation the human freedom of acting upon nature. *Géographie humaine* thus to a certain extent takes into account the ideological factor and its relation to space, something that is totally lacking in environmental determinism.

It is equally lacking in the new geography, which operated a second reduction beyond the reduction of society to its material aspect only. New geography, following the positivist principle of pertinence, that is, the exact delimitation - and isolation - of the object of research, considers that the epistemological object of geography is geographical space as such. In all the social sciences, the application of this principle without the necessary balance of some complementary principle allowing for the introduction of connections with other research objects has led to an untenable fragmentation of scientific knowledge and scientific fields. New geography is no exception to this rule, since it took the position that geography should formulate only morphological, specifically spatial laws of universal validity, in contrast to the systematic social sciences which would formulate the process laws of society independently from that society's geographical manifestation. This kind of geography seeks for its universal and naturalized laws in geographical space as such, seeing it as a natural, not social, reality. Its viewpoint is thus comparable to the explanation of spatial organization through recourse to ecology attempted by the human ecologists, or through recourse to the structure of the human brain if we follow the structuralists.

Reactions to the new geography, as we saw in the previous section, took the form of Marxist, humanistic, and behavioral geography. While the first was drawn into the objectivist model, the two other forms of geography attempted to remedy the lack of the ideological factor in geographical explanation through the adoption of - unfortunately, purely - subjective principles. One of the precursors of subjectivism in human geography, John K. Wright, pleads for the exercise of "realistic subjectivity" and imagination on the part of geographers. Geographers should not only rely on their mastered subjectivity, but also show a special interest in "geosophy", the "study of geographical knowledge", which plays for geography the same role that historiography plays for history, and studies the subjective conception of geographical space by all kinds of people, including geographers.[2] Wright does not reject mainstream "scientific geography", but he leaves undeveloped the question of the epistemological relation between scientific geography and his geosophy, with the exception of his remarks that geosophy offers mainstream geography a larger context and helps us to better understand its relation to and production from history and culture (see Wright 1947: 5-7, 11-14). As we shall see below, this inability to relate the objectivist and the subjectivist models marks the whole of the sphere of spatial studies.

Humanistic geography approaches geographical space in a similar manner. According to Ley and Samuels (1978: 5, 11), humanistic geography places at the center of human geography the human subject, the human condition, and meaning; thus anthropocentrism would be its primary concern. But even in respect to this very fundamental theoretical, or rather philosophical, starting point the heterogeneity of this brand of geography surfaces, since Relph, borrowing from Heidegger, rejects Western scientific humanism and its anthropocentrism aiming at the domination of nature, and argues for the practice of "environmental humility", marked by respect for the individuality of communities and landscapes (Relph 1981: 156-157, 189-191).

In spite of their divergence, the humanistic geographers meet in their use of a fundamental concept, place, as opposed to space. Space would be an abstract and neutral way of indirectly and conceptually understanding geographical entities, while the transformation of space into place presupposes the direct and intimate experience of concrete space in consciousness and its investment with meaning, value, and feeling. This existential recuperation of space contains and makes accessible the original inner structure of space. Not only is place, according to humanistic geography, experienced (we would say consumed) in this manner, that is, as a meaningful entity, but it is also produced in the same context. In this production process, human thoughts and feelings are materialized in the built urban or architectural environment, which is shaped after them (see Tuan 1977: 5, 17; Saarinen & Sell 1980: 531).

Undoubtedly, humanistic geography touches upon a very real dimension of geographical space, so it would be unfair to criticize it on the grounds that it is preoccupied with an object of no pertinence for spatial studies. Its weaknesses for us lie elsewhere. The phenomenological paradigm underlying humanistic geography offered the latter a philosophical view of man in the world rather than a systematic way of investigating the universe of meaning in its relation to space. On this point, Pickles (1985) would counterargue that consistent phenomenology is able to lead to a harmonic coexistence of philosophical or transcendental phenomenology, which he sees as the foundation of a scientific philosophy, with the sciences, which he sees as derived from this foundation. One such science would be "phenomenological geography", which he distinguishes from "geographical phenomenology", i.e., humanistic geography. For Pickles, scientific approaches are nothing more than abstractions from and formalizations of everyday practical experience, and both the former and the latter are the subject matter of phenomenology. His main effort is directed toward the foundation of a science of geography that would be a science of human spatiality, grounded in phenomenology and studying both place and space. Pickles even makes a gesture of good will toward Marxism, a gesture which, however, remains on the level of wishful thinking since his paradigm does not allow for the social production of meaning (cf. Pickles 1985: for example, 5, 67, 73-79, 94, 154-157, 169-170).

Beyond this attempt at synthesis, the question of the epistemological marriage between the phenomenological approaches to geography and the rest of geography remains unanswered. Humanistic geography is, if anything, contrasted to the mainstream trend: in Relph's (1981: 138-142) view, for example, his geography is a counterbalance to non-subjectivist "scientific geography", bringing to the forefront subjective experience. This does not advance the synthesis of the two approaches to geography one step beyond the views of Wright in 1947.

Another problem with phenomenology is its very philosophy of knowledge. Phenomenology believes in a dialectical synthesis between the subject and object of knowledge, between nonsensual subjective elements and sense experience, and thus rejects both pure objective and pure subjective knowledge. We would suggest that this thesis is rather rhetorical and that in reality phenomenology is interested in the movement of consciousness beyond the subject to embrace the object, i.e., in the subjective experience,[3] thus turning its back on dialectics and rendering itself liable to integration into idealist paradigms. Parallel to this putting aside of the materiality of the object of knowledge, phenomenology, and humanistic geography, also ignore the material social preconditions of knowledge, ideology, and of course of the production of geographical space (see also Gregory 1978: 146; Cox 1981: 265-267). Also, while their orientation sensitizes the humanistic geographers to the cultural aspects and the individuality of places, as the example of Relph showed us, it can also lead them to make pronouncements about the human condition in general and its allegedly universal aspects. Thus Yi-Fu Tuan (1977: 5-6), while accepting the realization of specific values in a cultural context, gives predominance to what he considers as universal human dispositions and capacities, which would be an "animal heritage"; culture, for him, has the secondary function of "emphasizing" or "distorting" them (cf. Pickles 1985: 155-157). We recognize once more, this time in the heart of phenomenology, the favorite explanation of space by ultimate reference to nature, embodied for Tuan in the individual human body.

This conceptual framework and the weaknesses of phenomenology and humanistic geography make it difficult for us to share the enthusiasm of Ley and Samuels (1978: 9) when they assert that humanistic geography aims at the reconciliation "of social science and man", of "objectivity and subjectivity", as well as of "materialism and idealism". It seems evident that the kind of materialism we should look for in respect to society and its relation to geographical space should be a sociological materialism, and humanistic geography has not proved particularly efficient on this matter (see also Cox 1981: 265-267).

In spite of its different founding paradigm, behavioral geography shares with humanistic geography the fundamental epistemological position that geographical space is the outcome of subjective processes. According to behavioral geography, the mind through its psychological processes realizes a subjective representation of the external world; this representation is achieved by observing the world and selecting and structuring incoming information. These processes are inseparable from attitudes, values, emotions, desires, and motives, as well as perception, sensations, cognition, and learning. This group of psychological factors, leading to the formation of our image of and perspective on the world, is the context within which occur the mental processes focused specifically on environmental information, the cognitive mapping processes, the output of which are mental or cognitive maps. When spatial choices are faced, these processes are conjoined with decision rules, deriving from the same group of psychological factors. Finally, evaluations and spatial choice decisions would be the cause of overt spatial behavior, one aspect of which is to cause objective spatial structures to change, the other aspect being spatial movement. For this point of view, mind is the mediator in the interaction between man and his environment, in the double sense of being the basis of the subjective representations of external space, the mental map, and of underpinning, in the form of this representation, the use of space through movement and the alteration of existing spatial conditions and morphology; in the context of this double mediation, the mind also mediates between the environment and the behavior occurring in it (Burnett 1976: 25-26; Golledge & Stimson 1987: 11-13, 38-39; Downs & Stea 1977: 1-29, 58).

We hope that the preceding discussion has lent support to our view concerning the crucial dichotomy within spatial studies between objectivism and subjectivism. The semiotics of space and environmental psychology have not suffered a similar split, not because they were able to surpass it, but because, due to the context within which they were shaped (respectively, the theory of signs and sign processes, and mainly cognitive psychology) they take for granted an exclusive reliance on the subjectivist model.

The two models, objectivist and subjectivist, follow two parallel courses, but as we saw they may and frequently do intersect, not in a common source but on a common ground. This common ground has two interrelated aspects: its natural, usually biological character which proffers itself for the formulation of universal regularities, and its reductionist function which follows from this naturalism. This reductionist insistence on founding society, ideology, and space on natural laws seems to be due to a misleading identification of the human with the natural sciences, reflecting a by now obsolete inferiority complex of the human sciences, a relic of the insecure times when they were trying to convince the scientific community of the seriousness of their intentions by having recourse to the supposed objectivity of the natural sciences and natural laws.[4]

Naturalism and biologism pervade spatial studies incessantly in all its branches and in insidious ways; they also occur in behavioral geography, as can be seen for instance in the positions of Downs and Stea. Although Downs and Stea (1977: 5, 20, 30-36, 172-176) mention in passing that they are exploring an as yet unknown interdisciplinary area situated somewhere between the current social sciences, they then proceed to follow the same reductionist path when they assert that cognitive mapping is the means for all mobile animals, including man, to solve spatial problems, and that it is the solution to these problems that causes overt spatial behavior. Cognitive mapping ability would be an adaptive mechanism securing spatial survival, and have its physical locus mainly in the right cerebral hemisphere (see also on this last matter Chapter 5, Section 2, on the sociology of environmental conception). What becomes clear in this line of argument is its Popperian inspiration, in the context of which the authors' cognitive mapping is related to Popper's theory-making and the latter's concept of survival is geographically specified as spatial survival.

Objectivism and subjectivism are both convincing in that they both propose a legitimate object for spatial studies. What is problematic thus does not pertain to their object, but to the partiality of each approach and the reduction to naturalism which both approaches usually effect. This dichotomy and reductionism in spatial studies made it urgent, on the one hand, to bridge the gap between objectivism and subjectivism, and on the other, to disengage from the naturalist explanations of space and social phenomena in general, at least from the point of view of the human sciences, that is, to achieve what *géographie humaine* was not able to do. This is what Marxist geography set out to accomplish.

Historical materialist epistemology indeed incorporates these two aims in their general form in its very foundations, and has connected them directly or indirectly to space since the time of its founders. In the late sixties this connection was revived by the presursors of Marxist geography, Lefebvre and Castells. For historical materialism, consciousness and ideology are neither the primary factor shaping society, nor are they independent from material social praxis. Indeed, any emphasis on the primacy, or even exclusivity, of ideology would for Marxism imply a direct or indirect inprisonment within idealism, since any approach following such a line of thought with difficulty avoids situating the source of ideology either in a divine spirit or in biological "human nature" (cf. also Blaut 1984: 149-156). For historical materialism, ideological practices are built on, and in the last analysis depend on, material practices (see also Boklund & Lagopoulos 1984: 432), and the fundamental social relations, the relations of production, are constituted independently of the will of social subjects. Subjects are not "human", i.e., biological, subjects in general, but specific social and historical subjects. This view of the individual overcomes the duality between individual and society, since society emerges from a whole of interacting individuals, and the individual acquires his/her being in connection to society and through social practices. As man is a social subject, so space is a social and historical product, produced by social processes and regulated by the historically specific rules governing them. Thus, for historical materialism, nature as the foundation for social phenomena is replaced by society; a social structure always intervenes and mediates between biological nature and all social phenomena.

However, historical materialism has also been accused of reductionism, because of its tendency to see the whole of society as reducible to economic processes. This critique is not unjustified when it is addressed to the dogmatic "orthodox" variant of Marxism according to which society, ideology, and space can be seen as simple reflections of the economic structure. But it is surely unfair when applied to either the writings of Marx and Engels, or contemporary Marxism. Current Marxism conceives of these phenomena in terms of production from, not reflection of, socioeconomic processes; socioeconomic processes are general social processes, as opposed to simply economic processes or naturalized and pseudoautonomous factors such as technological development (one of the influential themes of ecological materialism). The production of ideology or space from the socioeconomic processes is not a direct reflection but involves a series of mediations, and these two social components are conceived as relatively autonomous, able to function at the very heart of the socioeconomic processes which produce them.

The contributions of Lefebvre and Castells to spatial theory operate within this epistemological framework. Castells (1975: 166-171, 218,

221, 231-233, 273-280), following Althusser, believes that the nucleus of social structure is composed of the interrelation between three fundamental components of society, namely a socioeconomic component, which is in the last instance determinant and which incorporates the class struggle; a political component; and an ideological component. Each one of these components, in its relation to the others, is manifested in urban space, which is the specific area of interest of Castells. He presents a general theory of the production of urban space, in the context of which he conceives of ideology - in the form both of general ideology and the ideological sub-systems evolving specifically around the morphology of built space - as articulating with this morphology, the two of them constituting a "symbolic structure".

A similar holistic view on space is present in the work of Lefebvre (1974: 42, 48-57). He relates urban space to three processes. The first process includes the spatial practices producing and reproducing society in space. Then there is a second process, which has as its starting point codes and signs generated by the material relations of production, with an important impact on urban morphology. The third process is the experiential appropriation of an already existing space, which is accomplished by individuals with the help of a subjective code and which has only a limited influence on urban morphology. Thus urban space for Lefebvre is an ideological structure, but this is neither its only nor its essential quality, since this structure is supported by the materiality of space.

In spite of this synthesis of the objectivist and subjectivist models offered by Lefebvre and Castells, Marxist geography has been only marginally preoccupied with the function of ideology in relation to space. Perhaps one reason for this has been a desire to critically address a previous state of affaires by remaining on the same grounds; another reason could be the lack of persuasiveness of the subjectivist approach. But the choice of Marxist geographers also followed from the internal structuring of the historical materialist paradigm. This paradigm is not functionalist, in the sense that it is not composed of equivalent components interacting on the same level; on the contrary, its components as we saw belong to different hierarchical levels. Primacy is given to the socioeconomic processes, and it is these processes which have been favored by Marxist geographers. If Lefebvre and Castells show Marxist geographers the way to enlarge their conceptual framework to include ideological phenomena, there have also been pro-Marxist pleas for a parallel broadening of subjectivist geography. There have thus been two inverse and complementary movements, the one within Marxist geography aiming to give the subjectivist approach the place it deserves in Marxist theory, and the other following from the critique of subjectivist geography and arguing for its extension in a Marxist context. Clearly, both movements spring from and converge in the historical materialist paradigm.

Chapter 2. Society, space, and meaning

1. Behavioral geography: A problematic area

We hope the preceding discussion has helped to clarify our uneasiness when we tried, in the introduction to Section 2 of the previous chapter, to relate the present study of the conception of regional space to the main tendencies in spatial studies. On the one hand, we adopt a viewpoint on space akin to subjectivism, but on the other we are critical of the subjectivist paradigms and search for a holistic context in historical materialism. We understand that our dissatisfaction with current subjectivist approaches is a strong position which obliges us to some further clarifications. Below, we shall concentrate on the most scientific and elaborated version of subjectivism, behavioral geography, and use the discussion as an introduction to our own views, which will be presented in the next chapter.

As we saw, the cornerstone of humanistic and behavioral geography, as well as of environmental psychology, is the belief that spatial behavior and its spatial products are caused by subjective processes. This is also the case with an approach such as that of Bunting and Guelke (1979: 455-456, 460), who try to modify this position by observing that we should not expect a direct and simple relationship between the cognitive behavior studies by geographers and overt behavior, since geographers study only the passive aspects of their subjects. We would like to examine further the presuppositions, implications, consequences, and real meaning of this position. To begin with, it implies a fundamental negative proposition, namely that there are no other major processes, of whatever kind, able to influence behavior and space. This proposition is simply false, not because we believe it to be so, but as demonstrated by the very dynamics of geography: for most geographers, whether they are objectivists or subjectivists, objectivist geography does not seem to by preoccupied with imaginary issues. This situation is attested by the pro-Marxist tendencies within subjectivism, but also by other tendencies coming from different directions. We already referred to the ambitious views of Ley and Samuels that humanistic geography is aiming at the synthesis of what we called subjectivism and objectivism. A similar attitude can be found in behavioral geography.

Behavioral geographers, as we can see from the account given by Reginald G. Golledge and Robert J. Stimson (1987: 186, 194-197), discovered something which does not seem to preoccupy humanistic geographers, the fact that spatial behavior takes place in the context of constraints of different kinds and degrees, and that these constraints are critical for the explanation of behavior. Due to these constraints, the geographical subject is frequently not able to actualize his or her preferences and thus often has no free choice (see also on this point Blaut 1984: 150, 157). Following Golledge and Stimson, the existence of these constraints is related to the subject's socioeconomic position, which they do not seem to consider as a subjective fact; the decision-making process and the behavior resulting from it are influenced by "objective variables". However, this movement of goodwill in respect to the objectivist approach does not find any theoretical expression in their model which we presented in the previous section, and leads to an unsolved epistemological contradiction which could be formulated as follows: either spatial environment and overt spatial behavior are mediated by "mind" alone, as the authors maintain when they present their theoretical model, or mind *and* the environment are both seen as mediating between environment and behavior, as implied by their statements quoted above.

It is not fortuitous that this contradiction appears in the behavioral approach, given its psychological origin which structurally predisposes it to be subjectivist and individualistic (cf. Gottdiener & Lagopoulos 1986: 7, 9-12). These two attributes together are founded on what James M. Blaut (1984: 154-155) calls psychological reductionism in the form of psychologism, one variant of which would be the "cognitive positivism" of behavioral geography. Behavioral geography is indeed marked by several interrelated "-isms". For Blaut (1984: 156), the individualistic background of the behavioral approach causes it to "ascribe causal efficacy to human individuals and not to human collectivities; more completely: to isolated individuals and not to social systems like communities, cultures, and states. This leads to a blindness toward all causes of environmental behavior which are external to the individual." Following Blaut, individualism fails to take into account both the internalization of culture and its effect as an external factor on behavior. It makes the mistake of trying to bypass society and culture, and in spite of that to study more general systems, such as the social, the economic, and the political, through the reduction of these systems down to the level of the individual. Cox (1981: 261-262) also acknowledges this critique, but he feels there are no epistemological obstacles to the integration of society into behavioral geography, a position that we cannot accept for the reasons explained below.

Blaut (1984: 150-152, 158) believes that, due to its individualism, subjectivism in geography can find its legitimation only as a micro-geography, a psychogeography studying the spatial behavior of the individual with its psychological characteristics, able to approach from below certain macro-geographical problems. However, subjectivism can never deal with material processes, at least on the epistemological level, a fact noted by Cox (1981: 263, 265, 267-269) in his Marxist critique of humanistic geography. For this author, while humanistic geography challenges the positivist separation of subject and object (for example, the spatial environment) effected by behavioral geography, on the sound grounds that an object is always an object for a subject, it does not realize, on the other hand, that the object is also the condition for the realization of the subject, thus missing the dialectical relation between the subject and the material world formulated by Marxism. As we can see, this critique of humanistic geography is quite parallel to our own critique of phenomenology.

The subjectivism and individualism of the behavioral approach draw with them two other characteristics, naturalism and universalism. The standard terminology of behavioral geography includes terms such as "cognitive representation", "cognitive map", "mental image", "human mind", "memory", "information processing", "brain". Thus, "Cognition refers to the way information, once received, is stored and organised in the brain so that it fits in with already accumulated knowledge that a person has, and with his/her values" (Golledge & Stimson 1987: 38). Or, "the cognitive map may be conceived of as a mental representation of the properties of and the components in the everyday large-scale environment that is supported by internal structures of short-term and long-term memory" (Gärling, Böök & Lindberg 1984: 19). This kind of conceptualization, of obviously psychological origin, naturalizes and thus universalizes thought processes and contents, reducing social being to a general "human" nature operating at an infra-social, biological level and accompanied by innate attributes (see also Blaut 1984: 152, 156-158), while simultaneously removing geography from the social sciences and perpetuating the search for laws of universal validity (see also Ley 1981: 215-217; Cox 1981: 263-265).

Of course, these observations concern the epistemological background of behavioral geography; it could seem that they are contradicted by the scientific practice of the field, which has frequently been oriented toward the search for group - that is, social - views on the environment (as is also true of environmental psychology). But the real contradiction lies in the inability of this "social" line of research to articulate epistemologically with the founding individualistic model of behavioral geography, a problem which, in its general form of an inability to account for cultural and material social factors external to the individual as we already pointed out, lies behind the very low explanatory power of behavioral geography (cf. also Downs 1981: 113) and the characteristic trend of the field away from geographical explanation and toward the more secure study of the geographical subject (cf. also Bunting & Guelke 1979: 452, 455).

The all-encompassing characteristic of the behavioral approach, however, is its psychologism, shaped mainly under the influence of behaviorism. The epistemological aim of behaviorism was in the past and continues to be the study of psychological phenomena through the objective analysis of behavior, a view founded on positivism and combined with the axiomatic goal of turning psychology into a natural science. For contemporary behaviorism, the external environment or the internal biological processes are the cause of the emergence of stimuli which, after their processing by the cognitive apparatus of the organism, provoke certain behaviors as a response. The evolution of behaviorist thought led it to accept the concept that the organism is endowed with goals and purposes, which were rejected by classical behaviorism. This kind of relation between organism and environment allows the organism to adapt to the environment and thus secures its survival. For behaviorism, therefore, both our representations and our overt behavior are reduced to a biological survival mechanism. We saw that this was exactly the interpretation of the cognitive mapping ability offered by Downs and Stea.

But, if the psychological and biological explanation of spatial representations is reductionist, the task of geography should be to search for a sociological explanation of such representations. This attempt can be greatly advanced by the views of the French sociologist Raymond Ledrut. Ledrut (1973: 26-29, 113) criticizes Lynch on grounds similar to those of our own critique of behaviorism. He observes that Lynch holds a psycho-biological view of the urban "image" and that he relates this image, which would underlie spatial behavior, to the general function of the adaptation of an individual to his environment. In this manner, he writes, men are in a situation not very different from that of animals, and for both men and animals their environment should be understood as a "territory". For Ledrut, Lynch is not mistaken, but what he studies is both partial and derivative. The act of dwelling in a place goes beyond simply having a territory, adaptation does not cover the whole of apprehension, and spatial behavior is less than spatial practices.

We cannot agree with Ledrut's compromise in accepting the behavioral approach to urban representation even as a lower-level reality, as is evident from our previous discussion. But in justice to Lynch, we should point out that he too is aware of the existence of another level in the urban "image", that of meaning. Ledrut also acknowledges this fact when he considers pertinent the three main components of the urban image that Lynch defines, identity, structure, and meaning. Thus, the critique that Ledrut addresses to Lynch does not concern the absence of the level of meaning in his approach, but the underestimation of meaning and the independent treatment of the two other components. Here, Lynch's concept of *legibility* plays a determinant role. Legibility, or imageability, for Lynch would be both the morphological quality of a city or physical object in general which gives it a high degree of probability of creating a strong image in any observer, and the corresponding quality of the image or representation of the object or city. Thus, legibility relates both to the physical environment and to the subjective components of identity and structure. And it is precisely legibility which Lynch placed in the center of his interests (Lynch 1960: 2-3, 9). This delimitation of the research object could be due simply to a legitimate practical decision to limit the scope of his research, but this is not the case, because it in fact follows from a theoretical position. For Lynch (1960: 4), a legible physical setting and image "may serve as a broad frame of reference, an organizer of activity or belief or knowledge" and further "can furnish the raw material for the symbols and collective memories of group communication." It is Lynch's emphasis on legibility that Ledrut (1973: 25-26, 111-113) rightly denies. He aims to operate a reversal, by privileging symbolism and connotative semiotics, and arguing that, while legibility and meaning are inseparable, it is the former which follows from the latter: "Non que l'identité de l'image et sa structure soient oubliées, car pourrait-il y avoir signification sans identité et sans structure de l'image...? Toutefois c'est par rapport à la signification, au symbolisme que l'identité et la structure sont ici definies et recherchées" ['Not that the identity of the image and its structure are forgotten, since there could be no meaning without the identity and the structure of the image... But it is in their relationship to meaning, to symbolism, that this identity and structure are here defined and explored']. In this manner, the legibility level of urban representations is not, for Ledrut (1973: 27-28, 113, 311-312), neutral and technical, but charged with social meaning, that is, ideology; the urban image, following from social practices, would secure our anchoring in the world (cf. Gottdiener & Lagopoulos 1986: 11-12).

The reversal of perspectives effected by Ledrut is full of consequences, in the sense that he opposes to the biological interpretation of urban representations a sociological one. The sociological perspective invalidates the behavioral model in geography, in spite of Ledrut's efforts to rescue it by attributing to it a limited explanatory power. It calls for a new model, in which the unit is not the individual and his/her "mind", and the group is not seen as a sum of individuals, a sociological perspective which is implicit in the geographical (and psychological) studies focusing on social groups, but which has not proved able to question the epistemological foundations of behavioral geography. Such a sociological perspective can only be accommodated within the framework of a sociological theory of social groups and their representations. Otherwise, we shall continue the epistemologically circular movement between the universal mind of an individual, which as such mirrors the general, and what is each time considered as a general image, which follows from the sum of identical, because universal, individual images. It is in this vicious circle that Lynch's "public image" is trapped, an image that would be a "mental picture" common to many or even all of the inhabitants of a city (Lynch 1960: 7, 15, 46, 156; cf. Golledge & Stimson 1987: 97).[5] This concept of the public image also shows the kind of inachieved synthesis of sociology with behavioral psychology observed in the geographical studies using social groups. The social group bearing the public image is here, for better or for worse, the city, a sociological perspective on representations, but what is primarily at stake are the hypothetical common elements of the representations, presumed to fulfill a biological function. For behavioral geography, the social group is constructed *en passant* in between the individual and the universal, while the universal individual is also a unique individual, and the only unit epistemologically defined (cf. Golledge & Stimson 1987: 39, 197, 311).

A first step in moving away from the behavioral model is to accept the specificity of the environmental representations of pertinent social groups, and such a stance was adopted by Amos Rapoport (1976). Rapoport stresses the relativity of "environmental cognition" and its "cultural" and "subcultural" foundations, and differentiates the conceptualization of environmental cognition in his cognitive anthropological approach from that in the psychological approach. While the latter would stress knowledge of the environment, cognitive anthropology conceives of cognitive processes as aimed at making the environment and the world meaningful, and this view implies a cross-cultural and comparative material; the main characteristic of the cognitive processes is that they are taxonomic processes imposing classifications upon the conception of the world. Appleyard (1979: 143-144, 148-152) converges with Rapoport in emphasizing environmental symbolism and its variation in accordance with social groups. The physical environment has for Appleyard a social, or political, meaning, as, for example, when it connotes individual or group identity, or power, beyond the characteristics studied by environmental psychologists; on the basis of his account of these characteristics, we can relate them to Lynch's legibility (cf. also Bunting & Guelke 1979: 453-454, 458, 461).

Thus, for Rapoport, the psychological view would be a special case of the more general and important anthropological, while the meanings we ascribe to the world vary more than our knowledge of it. By this last statement we should understand that "meaning" is culture-specific, while "knowledge" species-specific, and this view draws us back to the behavioral model in an extended version. It is our representations that would underlie our behavior and the production of built space, but these representations are not produced by the interaction between "organismic" and environmental factors alone, as in the psychological view, but are explained according to a "three-element model" - manifestly of a functionalist and systemic nature - which also includes culture. Culture, far from contesting the behavioral model, is simply superimposed on it, with the result that the individual is seen as an "adaptive" and "goal-seeking" organism able to structure the world culturally.

Rapoport is trying to move away from the behavioral model, while Ledrut moves marginally towards it. Though both see meaning in its cultural setting and both give priority to the deeper layers of meaning, they nevertheless diverge in that Rapoport uses as his starting point the behavioral model to which he adds culture, while Ledrut tries to incorporate the behavioral model in his movement down from social ideology. And in these opposite movements the two authors arrive at a different conception of the nature of meaning. Meaning for Rapoport has a dualistic nature, since some level of meaning is inescapable as a universal product of the ecological conditioning of man, while some other level is relativized in its cultural specificity; in this manner, Rapoport introduces the problem of universals of meaning. On the contrary, for Ledrut meaning is of a unified nature, since even its most biological level is socially shaped; in his case the ecological function of man seems to offer merely a context of secondary importance, within which evolve representations originating, not in this context, but from a superior level of meaning, itself dependent on social practices.

We would not like to reject the possibility of operating with individual meaning and behavior, and by extension a legitimate scientific field such as psychology, nor the orientation of this kind of approach toward geographical matters. Independently from our discontent with the behavioral model, this orientation can lead to useful considerations, provided that it remains on its own level of pertinence, that which following Blaut we might call psychogeography *strictu sensu* - and which might be better considered as environmental psychology - without aspiring to extrapolations outside this level. Neither do we deny the legitimacy of the physiological psychological approach to cognition and cognitive processes, in so far as it again remains on its own level of individual mechanisms and is not used to account for contents - at least beyond those meanings which the existence of universals of meaning, if proved, would be able to accommodate - or as the main framework for the explanation of macrophenomena. What we plead for, then, in the study of geographical phenomena is a higher-level sociological perspective oriented toward the study of geographical space, as opposed not only to the behavioral and the behaviorist model, as we already observed, but to any kind of psychological model. It seems to us imperative to operate with social groups and their representations, and this is the crucial meeting point between the differentiated views of Blaut, Ledrut, and Rapoport. Once we adopt this point of view, we realize that we cannot proceed in the macro-geographical study of space without a theory of the forces structuring historical social groups and of the production of their representations. It is here that historical materialism enters the scene, and views such as those of Lefebvre and Castells seem able to offer some crucial guidelines for geographical research.

An alteration in theoretical perspective such as the one proposed here implies by definition a change in research context, objects, and priorities.

While there are studies in behavioral geography oriented toward the conceptual structure of the environment, an important part of this geography deals with Lynch's legibility level of spatial representations, and the degree of correspondence of this level to external spatial organization, an issue which is conceptualized as the accuracy of these representations when compared to topographical maps. In this interest the prescriptions of the behavioral model seem to converge with the geographical habit of map-making. Concepts such as "accuracy" and "cognitive distance", as well as elaborate techniques for the cartographic representation of "mental maps" become central to this line of research.

There are obvious limitations to this approach, the most important being the isolation of legibility from its wider causative ideological context and thus the neutralization of subjective space, as pointed out by Ledrut, which is equivalent to the technocratic treatment of our inner world (see also Appleyard 1979: 144). Legibility is not a reflection of physical forms, since it presupposes their symbolic investment, as Pocock and Hudson (1978: 32-33) also note. Accuracy is surely interesting at some level of research, but it becomes doubtful when the subjects are forced counter-intuitively to conceptualize crow-flight distances because this is the way the geographers are able to do their mapping; it becomes partial and deforming when the divergence of conceptual geometry from the topographical map is labelled "distortion", "disturbance", and "bias", while the tendency to coincidence of the former with the latter acquires a normative status and this "stable state" spatial conception is outrageously equated with coherence of representation, thus privileging a certain aspect of the representation at the expense of its total meaning (Golledge 1978: 81, 87, 91, 95); and finally, it becomes scientifically and politically suspect when it is promoted to the level of interpretative tool: "it is the variations in the accuracy of these cognitive orderings that will furnish some explanation of the variations evident in the behavior of different people in the same environment" (Golledge & Stimson 1987: 39). The concentration on the legibility characteristics of spatial representations results in the privileging of the physical environment (built space - cf. Gottdiener & Lagopoulos 1986: 6-8), as distinguished from other aspects such as the social, economic, or political environment, a restriction which at least should be made explicit.

Things, of course, are not quite as monolithic as this critique implies, as already suggested and witnessed by the study of subjective preferences and choices. But the main orientation of behavioral geography is the one described above. The problems with this mainstream line of research did not pass unnoticed and there have been voices from the interior of the movement, on the part of psychologists and planners, pleading for the incorporation of the symbolic meaning of the environment (see on this point Spencer & Dixon 1982: 374-375), and thus converging with the critiques of Ledrut and Rapoport. As is manifest these views also accord to a certain degree with humanistic geography. The whole of this multifaceted opposition seems able to exert some influence on behavioral geography, as indicated, for example, by the project by Spencer and Dixon (1982) aiming at the study of the affective investment of urban space.

Humanistic geography, on the other hand, cannot by any means be accused either of technocracy or of neglecting feelings. But its strength proves also to be its weakness, because it is exactly the emphasis on experience and the lived dimension of space as a whole that becomes so exclusive that it underestimates the descriptive level of spatial representations, what is for semiotics the denotative level; the importance of a whole set of conceptual dimensions, such as the social, the economic, and the political; and, as a consequence, the richness of environmental representations, and notably global spatial patternings and ideological structures.

2. The analysis of meaning

Behavioral geography borrowed from cognitive psychology two main modes of operating with meaning, which are, as we shall see, compatible. The first mode is borrowed directly from George A. Kelly's "psychology of personal constructs". For Kelly (1963; see also Bannister & Fransella 1986: 21, 30-31, 38-39), men (and the lower animals) look at the world through patterns they create, patterns which are not merely a response to the environment but an active representation or construction of external reality with the function of anticipating future events and assessing the accuracy of the forecast. He sees his psychology, which he considers as a behaviorism with active subjects, as one of individual differences, but asserts that there are widely shared public systems of these patterns. He calls these patterns "personal constructs", a concept related to both cognition and emotions. The fact that all men equally are motivated to make forecasts would show that the layman is a miniature scientist.

Kelly defines the personal constructs on the basis of the theoretical opposition *similarity* vs. *contrast*. He arrives at this opposition by observing that a person anticipates events by locating their similarities, and that he chooses a construct in respect to which he considers two phenomena as similar and a third phenomena as contrasting to the first two. Consequently, the construct is composed of two psychologically, not logically, contrasting poles. The definition of the construct and its opposed poles presupposes a comparison between at least three phenomena, but any number of phenomena may correspond to the poles of a construct. Kelly derives his psychological methodology from this theoretical presupposition for the definition of a construct, the minimal context of three elements, since his "repertory grid test" consists of comparisons within triads.

The constructs are organized into an individual hierarchically structured system, including multilevel ordinal relationships between a finite number of constructs. The construct system is not stable, but evolves with the addition of new constructs, an evolution constrained by the existing system itself. As a result, the construct system is not a harmonious whole, but includes incompatible constructs.

Kelly's theory and methodology have been applied to the study of the environment. Indeed, Harrison and Sarre (1971:365 and 1975: 56) consider it as almost "a ready-made approach to the study of environmental images" and comment, after applying the method in two case studies, that it "may well prove to be more successful in this respect [i.e., in revealing the links between urban image and behavior] that alternative methodologies."

Although Kelly accepts that a construct can be a graduated scale, his emphasis is on bipolarity, which he considers as the state of the basic constructs of a system. On this point Charles E. Osgood (1952) adopts a somewhat different attitude. As the title of his article indicates, Osgood is preoccupied with the nature and the systematic analysis of meaning. He writes that the approach sprang from research on synesthesia, and he envisages it as the application of experimental semantics in psychology, while his interest is turned toward social stereotypes. After reviewing briefly some of the main theories of meaning, Osgood proposes his own theory, as well as a method of operating on meaning, set against a background of similar studies.

The analysis of meaning can be effected, for Osgood, with the help of the "experiential continua" which people use for the description or judgment of a concept, and which represent different ways according to which the meaning of the concept can vary. The experiential continua evolve between two polar adjectival terms, and can be accurately analysed according to a scale, formed a priori with seven gradations, which renders both the direction and intensity of the description or judgment. To each concept corresponds a limited number of these semantic scales, which as a whole constitute its semantic space. Osgood observes that different continua can be functionally equivalent, with the result that they can be represented by a single factor, and that a limited number of factors is able to differentiate the meaning of different concepts, whence he calls his approach to meaning "semantic differential".

There has been an impressive number of studies aiming at the definition of the factors underlying judgments, both at the intra-cultural and the inter-cultural level. This literature tends toward the ambitious conclusion that, on a more general level of analysis, three major factors underlie all judgments in human thought in general: in order of importance, Evaluation, Potency, and Activity - the EPA structure; several other factors of secondary importance also appear. The studies further indicate that there are more specific cases in which the EPA structure is restructured to a greater or lesser degree: thus, the EPA structure can be expanded through further elaboration of the original factors or the addition of new factors; factors may be subtracted; or a combination of these modifications can occur; or there may be changes in the hierarchy and internal composition of the original three factors (see, for a discussion of these points, Osgood, Suci & Tannenbaum 1975: 31-75, 325-327; Heise 1969: 412-418). As we see, then, the semantic differential has turned out to be one more search for a universal human nature. But while Lévi-Strauss was looking for the universal in structures, the semantic differential is focused on contents.

As becomes clear from this discussion, Kelly's repertory grid and Osgood's semantic differential can be combined without major obstacles, and indeed they have at times been combined in behavioral geography. Of course, these two methodologies do not exhaust all the methods used in behavioral geography for the study of meaning, as the analysis of sketch maps reminds us, but they provide the main viewpoint on the structuring of meaning used by geography. It is of some interest to note that after so many years of accumulation of studies and intense discussion on technical matters, the main points of the two approaches just presented have not been developed much beyond their original form.

Our study is aware of these approaches, the methodologies and techniques used in behavioral geography, the issues discussed there, and the subjectivist approach in general, as we hope the present book will show. We do not intend to reject the important accumulated knowledge in these areas. But as our previous discussion has demonstrated, we also adopt a critical stance toward subjectivism; we feel that any approach to the meaning of space which takes as its starting point individual psychology is inadequate to the study of the social conception of space, and we believe that historical materialism offers a holistic sociological view, opposed to the individualistic epistemology of behaviorist psychology. As we already observed, historical materialism, in addition to a theory of society, can provide geographers with a theory of consciousness and ideology, i.e., meaning. The handicap with Marxism, however, is that it may provide a sound theory *on* culture, but it is of rather limited usefulness for the in-depth analysis of cultural systems themselves. What is needed, then, is an extension of Marxist theory which would allow it also to embrace a theory *of* culture and meaning.

With this perspective, one possibility would be to combine Marxism with the approaches to meaning used by behavioral geography, some of which were presented above. There are three major drawbacks to this line of thinking. The first follows from the very psychological origin of these approaches, that does not allow sociologically acceptable generalizations from the partial and individual to social groups and society (cf. Hudson 1980: 355). The second drawback is analogous to the problem we noted in the case of Marxism above, namely that the aim of the more technical analysis of meaning offered by psychological theories is not the construction of a systematic theory of meaning but to contribute to the needs of psychological analysis, which thus define the kind of semantic analysis to be pursued. The third drawback is related to this limitation: at the time of Kelly and Osgood the field of semantic theory itself was already considerably richer that that part of it which they found useful to their purposes, and this is even more true of semantics today. The current development of semantic theory has also been accompanied by the blossoming of structuralism and semiotics, not to mention post-structuralism and deconstruction, all of them approaches to the phenomena of communication and meaning which we can group together under the label of semiotics. This is why it seems to us reasonable, in studying conceptual systems and representations of any kind, to turn to the latest developments in the theory of meaning, or more accurately the theories of meaning.

There are tendencies within semiotics which would link the study of meaning with biology and the natural sciences. Thus, Thomas A. Sebeok (1975) is sympathetic to a synthesis of semiotics with ethology in the form of zoosemiotics, and considers semiosis as a "universal, criterial property of animate existence". However, it should be clear by now that our own approach is oriented towards the integration of semiotics with the social sciences, and we believe this is the pertinent perspective from which to approach the study of semiosis in society.

There are two major traditions in semiotics today, the European Saussurean tradition and the American tradition following Charles Saunders Peirce, and there are different tendencies within both of them. The question for our own approach is, then, how best to integrate semiotics with Marxism and the Marxist theory of ideology, and more specifically with a Marxist approach to geographical space and its meaning. Chapter 3 below revolves around the second issue. As to the first issue, this is not the place to elaborate on the epistemological problems arising from such an attempt (the interested reader is referred to Lagopoulos 1988). What follows will therefore be a very brief and, of necessity, somewhat oversimplified presentation.

There is a fundamental and ultimately irreconcileable difference between the paradigms underlying historical materialism and semiotics. The former gives priority to the social and historical dynamic and the material socioeconomic processes composing it. It sees the production of semiosis as springing mainly from these processes, and seeks to define the regularities of that production in sociohistorical terms. Structuralism, as we saw, is founded on logical positivism, which on the contrary detaches semiosis from sociohistorical processes and attempts to formulate its regularities in universal terms. These epistemological traits derive directly from the ancestor of logical positivism, the positivism of Auguste Comte, on which it can be argued that Saussure, the founder of European semiotics, constructed his linguistic theory. European semiotics thus spring from the positivist tradition. However, there are also frequently signs in European semiotics of another underlying paradigm, of lesser importance and quite opposed to the positivist one, namely neo-Kantian idealism. This same paradigm, together with empiricism, animates the Peircean *semeiotic*.

The conflict between the epistemological premises founding historical materialism and semiotics takes concrete shape in the basic concepts used in the two domains. Semiotics operates principally with the static concepts of structure and system, while Marxism emphasizes the structuring processes and the functioning of systems. Semiotics uses the law of pertinence to isolate the study of signifying practices and the systems of signification from socioeconomic processes, Marxism immerses these practices and systems in material processes in an attempt to understand and explain them as one of the aspects of society as a whole. Semiotics is obsessed with synchronicity, with the study of systems in their immobility; Marxism is oriented toward historically and sociologically moving realities.

Under these circumstances the articulation of semiotics and Marxism is not an easy task, and can in no case be derived from a simple putting-together of the two domains. It will have become clear from the previous discussion that we envisage this articulation as the epistemological integration of semiotics within Marxism, something that calls for the derivation of the fundamental premises and concepts of semiotics from Marxist epistemology. There are of course historical precedents for such a task, as witnessed by the development of sociolinguistics. We believe, however, that the landmark for this synthesis is the work effected by the circle around M.M. Bakhtin in the Soviet Union in the twenties (see Volochinov 1977 and Medvedev & Bakhtin 1978). In the same direction evolves the work of such authors as Lucien Goldmann (see, for example, Goldmann 1970), Ferruccio Rossi-Landi (1983), Maurice Godelier (1978), and Pierre Bourdieu (1977). For all these authors, the articulation of semiotics and Marxism is worth the attempt despite the inherent difficulties, because semiotics offers a complete, and complex, theory of meaning, a theory which would enable a Marxist approach to analyse cultural phenomena with the required sophistication.

Not all trends within semiotics are equally resistant to a sociologically informed approach to cultural systems. The main concepts animating Peircean pragmatism do not lend themselves to integration into a sociohistorical perspective. The case with the Saussurean tradition is rather different, as we can see from the work of Saussure himself (1971), who flirts with sociology and history though he does not use either systematically. For Saussure the central object of linguistics, treated by descriptive, static (synchronic) linguistics, is language as a multi-dimensional system of signs, what he calls *langue*. The systemic nature of *langue*

follows from the fact that the meaning of each element is defined rela-
tionally through its difference from all the other elements of the system.
We can recognize in this conception of language the organicist conception of society advocated by Comte. *Langue*, according to Saussure, is
supra-individual and constitutes a social system, but should be studied
autonomously. In this manner, linguistics is in practice cut off from
sociology.

If *langue* is the abstract aspect of language, *parole* is *langue* in action,
as realized in the speech of concrete individuals. *Parole* introduces innovations which, when generalized and thus socialized, provoke changes in
the system of *langue*, but the nature of these changes is independent from
the nature of the innovations. The reason is the systemic character of
langue, which causes any changes introduced into the system to be
adapted to its other elements. Since for Saussure the linguistics of *parole*
is part of the history of language, the epistemological conclusion from
this position is that the system of *langue* is unrelated to its history.

What is lost of society and history from the proper field of linguistics,
Saussure tries to recuperate in his "external linguistics". The object of
the latter is the influence on the system of *langue* of factors in the history
of civilization, political history, internal politics, and institutions. Saussure stresses the fact that this field is alien to the internal constitution of
the system. Thus, once more the system remains uncontaminated by social and historical factors; no way is found to bring them into the heart of
linguistic, and by extension semiotic, theory.

In spite of these oscillations to and from sociohistorical realities, Saussurean linguistics and European semiotics in general are more open to the
social sciences than is the American tradition in semiotics, as shown by
the fact that syntheses were attempted between Marxism and the Saussurean tradition of semiotics. One of the main reasons lies in the very
analysis of the composition of the sign as effected by Saussure. For him,
the sign is conposed of a signifier (what Louis Hjelmslev calls the "form
of the expression") and the related concept, the signified (what Hjelmslev
calls the "form of the content"). The linguistic form is carried by a material substance (the substance of the expression). Of special interest to a
sociological perspective, however, is the Saussurean concept of an amorphous substance of thought (substance of the content), by the subdivision
of which the linguistic signifieds are derived. Hjelmslev (1971: 44-76)
identifies this substance (or rather, that level of it which is immediately
connected to the semiotic system) with the social value system, a concept

akin to the Marxist concept of ideology. But the concept of the signified can also find a direct sociological expression: Umberto Eco (1976: 66-67) defines the signified as a cultural unit, and Roland Barthes (1964: 131) calls the connotative level of the signified "a piece of ideology".

Semiotics is a powerful tool - the most powerful tool we possess - for the in-depth analysis of ideology, culture, and the systems of meaning. It studies the universe of signs and its structure in all their aspects and complexity. It can study the articulation and classification of signifiers; penetrate into the phenomenon of perception; analyse in detail the structure of conception; describe the direct, denotative meaning of semiotic messages; discover the ideological presuppositions of scientific modes of discourse; explore the hidden, connotative meaning of cultural texts and together with this their fundamental value systems or world views; formulate the surface and deep structures of these texts; read them in terms of both individual psychology (normal or pathological) and social systems; and, in integration with Marxism, lead to a powerful theory of cultural phenomena incorporating social and historical dynamics. Semiotics offers not only a theory of meaning, but has also elaborated methods for operating on meaning and qualitative techniques for detailed analysis. Our attempt to articulate semiotics with Marxism, although focused on geographical space, thus has the wider ambition of providing a Marxist theory of meaning, a materialist social semiotics applicable to all cultural signifying systems.

Chapter 3. A materialist social semiotics of space

Our critical comments in the previous chapters contain the nucleus of the approach we are here proposing to the study of spatial representations, in the sense that our critique of existing approaches led to a set of interrelated positive propositions. We expressed our discontent with the subjectivism of the behavioral model in geography and asked for a holistic approach articulating subjectivism with objectivism. We rejected the individualist, naturalist, and universalist assumptions of the same model and proposed instead an historically sensitive sociological theory. We objected to a technocratic isolation of the descriptive level of spatial representations from their deeper, and causative, layers of meaning which results in interesting, if slippery, trivialities. And we proposed historical materialism as the epistemological paradigm able to guide geographical research on spatial representations as well as the whole sphere of spatial studies.

There is no need here to present the reader with a general introduction to historical materialist theory, and we shall limit ourselves to the brief comments already made above and the discussion concerning social classes in the section on the sociological characteristics of our research corpus in Chapter 5, Section 3. But if historical materialism, as we believe, is able to provide the epistemological framework for the subjectivist study of space, it does not in its present state cover such an enterprise in all its extent (as we saw above). The study of the processes concerning the conception of space from a Marxist perspective presupposes two interrelated mediating levels, which should be seen as relatively autonomous specifications of the general theory, effected with the help of the two scientific fields of social geography and the theory of meaning. We would argue that the study of the relationship between conceptual space and external space must necessarily pass through the articulated whole of a Marxist geography and a Marxist theory of meaning, an articulation which in its general lines preoccupied Lefebvre, and in a more analytic manner Castells. We propose, then, to concentrate on this articulation, emphasizing the component of meaning, given the kind of material we shall be concerned with in this study.

The fundamental concepts for the study of this articulation seem to us to be provided by Marx's analysis of the circulation of capital. For

Marx, this circuit evolves in three stages. The first stage is a circulation process in the end of which money is transformed into - i.e., used to purchase - the commodities necessary for production, such as the work force and raw materials. The commodities thus acquired are consumed in the second stage, production, which is thus characterized by productive consumption. Societies as a whole organize the production stage in different ways, depending on the level of development of their productive forces and on their relations of production (roughly equivalent to their social structure); the specific manner in which the complex of forces and relations of production are articulated determines the mode of production of a society. After the stage of production, the third stage is again a circulation process, during which the produced commodities are transformed in the market into money, that is, are purchased for "individual" comsumption by the consumers who use the commodities in securing their own reproduction (Marx 1976, II: 27-57). In addition to commodities there is another kind of product, services, which are not physical products, but are produced in the process of circulation and consumption.

It is our contention that Marx's economic model of the circuit of capital is only a specification of a more general social model regulating all societies and all levels of social practices. If we focus, in the context of the general model, on the production of space, we observe that there are specific production systems of space, representing specific channellings of the global production system of a society toward different kinds of space, such as physical, economic, social, or political space. These specific production systems are moved by a specific orientation of the whole complex of the social relations of production and the productive forces, and perform an alteration of geographical space which results in different forms of organized or constructed space. The systems of the production of space are animated by social actors, occupying different socially determined positions within them and including the professionals of space, architects and planners, and can be set in motion by either private or public agents, such as the state.

The same complex of the relations of production and the productive forces which gives the whole of society its general shape, also shapes culture and consciousness. For Marx and Engels (1975: 43-44, 50-51, 62-63, 87), man produces himself while producing, through his engagement with material praxis. Labor, consciousness, and language appear simultaneously, phylogenetically: language is practical consciousness, it is the product of interaction with others, and language and consciousness are consequences of social labor. Man produces himself as a social being, and in consequence his individual consciousness and language competence are also, and mainly, social. This view allows for the transition from the social to the individual level and the articulation of psychology with sociology. Language, consciousness, and culture in general, which we understand here as the whole complex of signification and communication processes and systems in a society and their interrelations, are founded on material practices.

Four points should be stressed, however, in order to avoid misunderstandings. First, this account of the production of meaning does not imply that meaning appears later in time than material practices. Both are *simultaneous*, because they are interwoven, and man is a totality that cannot be split into an acting man and a thinking man. Second, given this totality, meaning is not only shaped, but also shaping, even if these two movements are of unequal weight. This dialectic of meaning indicates that cultural systems preserve a *relative autonomy* vis-a-vis material practices. Cultural systems cannot be considered as entirely autonomous, since they originate and occur within a social ideology which is produced by and which functions within the material processes of production. But simultaneously, cultural systems acquire an original dynamics and regularities of their own which are thus not directly deriveable from material processes.

Next, the opposition between material and signifying practices does not imply that the latter are somehow non-material or that meaning, language, and the cultural systems in general are of a ghostly nature. Cultural systems do not exist without a material vehicle, whether it is sound waves, graphic representations, behavior, or the built environment. Their materiality is obvious to a greater or lesser degree depending on their vehicle, and their specificity resides in that, even when they are attached to a material vehicle which also serves other, material, functions, their own function nevertheless remains signification. Thus signifying processes and systems are also material, but they have a function different from, and in addition to, their material function. This materiality of signifying systems did not escape the attention of linguistic and semiotic theory. Language, for example, is for Saussure (1971: 155-156) carried by the phonic substance, and Hjelmslev's (1971: 59-63) "substance of the expression" of language and of all semiotic (that is, signifying) systems is also materially shaped. Finally, the last point we should like to stress is that meaning, exactly because of its social origin, is differentiated in the interior of a society in accordance with the significant differentiation of social groups, which in class societies tends to be that of social classes.

We can see why, from the perspective of historical materialism, terms such as "human mind", "cognition", and "mental image" would neutralize the social origin of our representations, their social and historical specificity, and their differentiated, even conflicting, contents. It instead proposes the alternative terms of "ideology" and "world view" (*Weltanschauung*). The concept of ideology is not without ambiguities in Marx, and extends from the overtly pejorative sense of false and mystifying consciousness which inverses social reality to the sense of all cultural products, including the human sciences, and all psychological aspects of class or socialized individual consciousness. Marx himself excludes from ideology the supposedly objective exact sciences, Marxist political economy, and proletarian ideology, which he sees as interchangeable with Marxist political economy (cf. Gurvitch 1966: 52-57). We are rather sceptical on this objectification of these domains, since we cannot see how it is possible for them, as social and historical phenomena, to escape some regulation by value systems. We would nevertheless accept that there is a differentiation between spontaneous representations and scientific operations, a differentiation which is not absolute since both are regulated, though to a different degree, by values, and which should not be thought of as bipolar, but as the two abstract extremities of a continuum. This differentiation is found in semiotics in the form of the distinction between the non-scientific denotative and connotative semiotics, and the scientific metalanguages (Hjelmslev 1961: 113-114, 119-121, 125; Barthes 1964: 130-132). For us, "ideology" is equivalent to "culture", and we consider that all cultural practices are activated by the universe of signification - which may also be called ideology - which is each time a socially determined specific *conception* of the world.

When the conceptual world is approached in this manner, it becomes extremely difficult to accept the biological interpretation of conceptions as a survival mechanism. Theory must thus provide an alternative interpretation of representations as having *social* functions. One obvious and general function of our conceptions and the cultural systems of which they are a part is that they signify and are used for social communication. But there is also a less obvious general function, relating to the dominant ideology of a society, which is to secure the reproduction of that society without any alteration of the existing social structure, that is, of the relations of production. In order to achieve this end, the dominant ideology functions as an instrument of power. There are also more specific functions of the conceptions of the world, which have repercussions on their interior organization, and which Godelier (1978: 172-173) defines as: representing an aspect of reality; interpreting, which is inseparable from representation; organizing the relations of men with each other and with nature, on the basis of the two preceding functions; and legitimating or questioning these relations.

To come back to the systems of the production of space, as they are set in motion by the specific form that the fundamental socioeconomic processes take when channelled toward space, they are also animated by their own specialization of the general conceptual systems. It is not strange, then, that we find in these systems producing space the above-mentioned functions of all conceptual systems. As Ledrut (1973: 29) observes, "Les images ont des fonctions sociales: il y a des images conservatrices et des images utopiques" ['Images have social functions: there are conservative images and there are utopian images']. Space is produced by a particular convergence of the apparatus of material production with that of conceptual production (that is, signifying or semiotic production, since the conceptual systems are vehicles of meaning). Because of this double nature of the process of the production of space - and of all production processes in society - it is possible, from the point of view of meaning, to consider the apparatus of material production as "exosemiotic"; the same concept may also be applied to the material practices producing the spatial conceptions that animate the semiotic production of space. This production ends in giving meaning to organized or constructed space. Space, then, is both a material system and a cultural system; the two systems are intricately related, but the material is primary and the materiality of space is the *sine qua non* presupposition for the manifestation of the cultural system. Thus, we find that at the end of the production process a new exosemiotic reality has been produced. This approach to space invalidates any claim on the part of subjectivism to account exclusively for spatial organization and form.

Cultural products, much like commodities, are integrated into a production-consumption circuit. If we consider space as a cultural product, then in terms of communication theory there is a sender and a receiver of the spatial message; or, in semiotic terms, an addresser and an addressee; or, in Marxist terms, a producer and a consumer of the message. They can be seen as individuals, but also, and mainly, as social groups. They both belong to a structured market of symbolic relations, itself produced by material processes, a market which is not neutral but structured by power relations, and in which space as a cultural product circulates (cf. Bourdieu 1977). This semiotic and communicational view of space is similar to the one adopted by Appleyard, though it pays more attention to the material prerequisites of the cultural dynamics of space. As the production of space, the consumption of space is also twofold, material and conceptual or semiotic. Space is materially used and simultaneously culturally appropriated, consumed. It is not necessarily true that the conceptions in consumption will coincide with those in production, at least in modern societies. On the contrary, the existence of differing and antagonistic subcultures is frequently the cause of an asymmetry between conceptions in consumption and production. It is also the cause of inconsistencies within consumption or production. Differences between social groups are not the only cause of differentiation between conceptions: a substantial temporal distancing between the moments of production and conception can have a similar effect, due to the historical evolution of conceptions.

Our account of the generation of meaning shows that meaning and its modalities arise in relation to the social differentiations occurring in production. We believe that consumption is mainly structured by production, and that the social classes and groups remain stable throughout the production-consumption circuit, that is, that the classes and groups produced in production remain the same also in consumption. Thus, the differentiation of meaning in production is also that of consumption. But this holds for the *general* ideological tendencies; meaning takes more specific forms in the interior of the different production processes. Due to that fact, a consumer group can conceptualize a spatial product differently from the producer group, even if the two groups are socially similar, and this adds to the asymmetries between production and consumption. In spite of the existence of such asymmetry, the coincidence, on a more general level of meaning, of the conceptions in production and consumption for the same social groups, and the fact that conceptions in production are also oriented toward future consumers, shows that we should not differentiate too sharply the messages at the two extremes of the spatial communication systems. We could envisage an even more general level of meaning than the one corresponding to social groups, in which case we would be dealing with the overall universe of meaning of a society. While this very general level of meaning reveals the consensual foundations and the general outlook on the world of a whole society, it on the other hand conceals differences within the society by neutralizing them, and is thus not very useful for the study of specific conceptions of space.

The semiotic production and consumption of space are not passive processes. Both are active processes created by the social labor of semiotic workers operating on and with signs (cf. Eco 1976: 151-158). The semiotic consumption of space is not a reflection of external realities, but is founded on this active semiotic labor, which re-constitutes reality by selecting, organizing, and interpreting signs. The active semiotic investment of space by an historical subject is literally an act of appropriation and recuperation, something that, as we saw, behavioral geographers are coming to realize but frequently do not seem able to confront.

With this discussion on the conceptual consumption of space we arrive at the subject of our own study. Using as background the debates within the domain of spatial studies, we have moved critically through it to achieve a gradual definition of our own approach, as approach which is simultaneously a position and an opposition to currently available subjectivist approaches. Our approach is founded on historical materialism, but also attempts a synthesis with the theory of meaning developed by semiotics, a synthesis which takes the form of the integration of semiotics within the epistemological and theoretical framework of historical materialism. We would like to call this approach to cultural processes and systems a *materialist social semiotics*. The aim, however, of this book is not the construction of a social theory of semiosis. This construction was a necessary stage in the development of a geographical theory of spatial meaning (and practices) or, from another point of view, a semiotic theory of space with solid sociological foundations.[6]

In connection with a Marxist theory of geographical space, we feel that a *social semiotics of space* has a significant contribution to make to the study of the conception of space. We propose to erect this domain on a sociological theory, historical materialism, instead of on a psychological and individualistic theory, behaviorism, and similar theories which are not sociologically and historically sensitive. Within this sociological context, we propose the virtualities of semiotics as a theory of social (and individual) signification and communication, instead of cognitive psychology. We believe the results of this study will convince the reader that our choices are justified.

Part II. Society, space, and meaning

ἔνθα δ'ἄν ἀργικέρωτας ἴδῃς χιονώδεας αἶγας
εὐνηθέντας ὑπ'ἠῶ, κείνης χθονὸς ἐν δαπέδοισι
θῦε θεοῖς μακάρεσσι καὶ ἄστυ κτίζε πόληος·

[Where thou shalt see white-horned goats, with fleece
Like snow, resting at dawn, make sacrifice
Unto the blessed gods upon that spot
And raise the chief city of a state.]

The Oracle of Delphi describing to King Perdikkas of
Macedonia where to found his capital city of Aigae -
city of goats (Diodorus of Sicily, Bk. VII. 16)

Chapter 4. Land and people

1. The history and geography of Macedonia

The field work on which this study is based was undertaken in the summer of 1986 in four settlements in the region of Central Macedonia: Thessaloniki, Veria, Ormylia, and Axioupoli. These settlements were selected after careful consideration of both Central Macedonia and the larger region to which it belongs, the whole of Greek Macedonia. The process of selection of the settlements will be explained in the next section of this chapter; here, we will only attempt to place them in their historical and geographical context.

Thessaloniki, the capital of Northern Greece, is situated in a strategic position at the bottom of the Thermaïc (or Thermaïkos) bay and on a wide plain extending from Mount Vermion and the Pieria mountains in the west to beyond the borders with Yugoslavia in the north, and to Mounts Vertiskos (Bertiskos) and Cholomon in the east; Mount Cholomon acts as a barrier between Chalkidiki and the rest of Macedonia.[7] Veria is at the westernmost edge of this plain, in the foothills of Mount Vermion, and on the Aliakmon (Haliakmon) river. Of the two other settlements, Axioupoli is situated north of Thessaloniki and Veria, just to the east of Mount Païkon on the Axios river, while Ormylia is southeast of Thessaloniki and south of Mount Cholomon, close to the edge of the main body of the Chalkidiki peninsula just before it branches into the three "fingers" of Kassandra, Sithonia, and Mount Athos (see map, Figure 1).

We considered it useful, before the discussion of the contemporary characteristics of Macedonia and the research settlements, to give a brief historical review of the region, and this for many reasons. To begin with, we felt that the historical context of the region is able to provide the contemporary situation with some depth and transmit something of the flavour of the place. But it is also the case that many peculiarities of contemporary Macedonia can be explained on the basis of historical factors. Then, the history of the region allows for references to the research settlements or the areas where they are located, thus offering the reader a first acquaintance with the study. And finally, various phenomena which

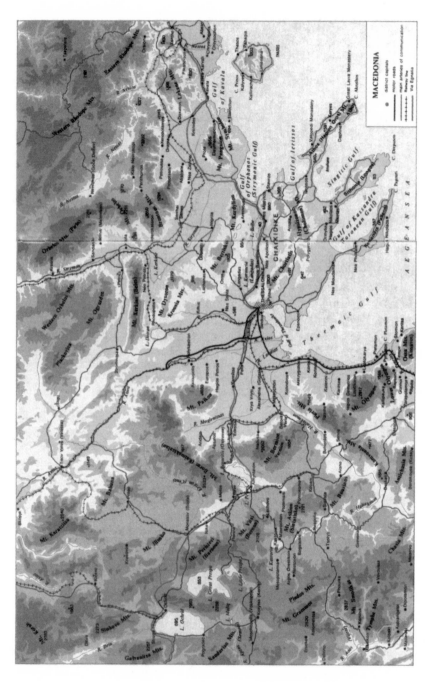

Figure 1. Macedonia and surrounding area (Sakellariou 1982: 14-15).

are the outcome of a long history were proved to have been recuperated by our subjects as part of their regional ideology.[8]

The name Macedonia has historically been used to refer to a region located roughly between the Pindos range to the west, Mount Olympus and the Kamvounian mountains in the south, the delta of the Nestos river and the Rhodopi mountains to the east, and including in the north the Axios river basin roughly as far as the modern Yugoslav city of Titov Veles (former Velessa). In the 3000 years of its history this region has changed hands many times, and the boundaries of "Macedonia" in any given period have varied greatly. Parts of what was at one time or another called Macedonia are now incorporated into the modern states of Greece, Yugoslavia, and Bulgaria, and the northwestern frontiers of the region are in the border areas between Greece, Yugoslavia and Albania. The core of the region of Macedonia, both historically and geographically, are the river basins of the Aliakmon, the Axios (Vardar), and the Strymon rivers, and the surrounding mountain slopes and coastal plains (see map, Figure 1).

The landscape of Macedonia is perhaps best described as fragmented into a succession of mountains and relatively isolated valleys. The lowlands of the central Macedonian plains, where the four great rivers of Gallikos, Axios, Loudias and Aliakmon have for millennia left their deposits, were until the early twentieth century swampy wetlands inaccessible to cultivation or inhabitation; the coastline of the Thermaïkos bay ran during antiquity as far inland as Pella and Yannitsa. Wetlands also covered much of the Strymon river basin, and the shores of most of the large lakes were swamps. The fertile fields in these areas today are the result of extensive, costly and difficult drainage projects undertaken largely in the early years of this century.

The climate of the region is more continental than mediterranean. The olive tree is cultivated only along the coast south of Katerini, and on the Chalkidiki peninsula and the island of Thasos; in inland Macedonia it is extremely rare. The climate is wetter, and the winter temperatures colder, than in southern Greece. The traditional crops of grains, beans, legumes and tobacco have in recent years, with the advent of irrigation, been supplemented with fruit trees and market gardens. Sheepherding and goatherding were for centuries the principal form of economy of the mountainous areas, though they are today of less importance; cattle were (and are) raised in the plains. The extensive forests which once formed an important economic resource for the kingdom of Alexander the Great have receded due to grazing and woodcutting, though there are still large forested areas in the mountains. Mining has been important since antiquity in Chalkidiki and on Mount Pangaion.

Communications between Macedonia and the Thessalian plain to the south run through the narrow passes of Tempi (between Mount Olympus and Mount Ossa, where the river Peneios has cut a narrow gorge to the sea) or Sarandaporos (between the Kamvounian and Pierian mountains, through the town of Servia, and then to Kozani or Veria). To the west the Pindos mountains, the southernmost extension of the Dinarian Alps, present great difficulties to road construction even today. The ancient Roman highway between Constantinople and the harbour of Dyrrachion (the modern Albanian city of Durres) on the Adriatic, the Via Egnatia, ran from Thessaloniki west to Edessa, then south of Lake Vegoritis (Begoritis) through Amyntaio and northwest to Monastir (Bitola in Yugoslavia), and from there north of the Prespa lakes and Lake Ochrid through Achris (modern Yugoslav Ochrid) and west to the coast; the same route is still one of the two highways that connect Albania with the outside world. Communications are easier along the Axios and the Strymon river valleys toward the north, but in the east and northeast the Rhodopi mountains on the Greek-Bulgarian borders present a very effective barrier to travel even today. The ancient Via Egnatia, continuing east from Thessaloniki, followed the valley of Lakes Agiou Vasiliou (Koroneia) and Volvi (Bolbe) across the Chalkidiki peninsula, used the valley of the Strymon and two of its tributaries to bypass Mount Pangaion to the north, and then ran along the foothills bordering the coastal plains to avoid the swamps of the Nestos river delta and the wetlands of the Thracian coast. The Chalkidiki peninsula throughout much of its history remained to a large extent isolated from the rest of Macedonia, and the inhabitants of its long and winding coastline found it easier to communicate with the areas south of Mount Olympus by sea.

Macedonia has been inhabited since prehistoric times. Permanently inhabited sites supporting a population of farmers and husbandmen are found beginning with the early Neolithic period (approximately 6000 B.C.). The material remains of these sites would relate their inhabitants culturally to the Central European neolithic culture which extends throughout the southern Balkan peninsula, from Thessaly to the Danube. The earliest mention of a tribe called Macedonians is by Hesiod (Fragment 7), who situates them in the Pierian mountains. It is not unequivocally clear from the sources who the Macedonians were. The interpretation most generally accepted is that they were an Indoeuropean people, probably a Greek-speaking tribe related to the Dorians, though some scholars have related them to the Illyrians. In either case, they were not the only people in the area: other Greek, Illyrian, and Thracian tribes, as well as, possibly, remnants of older populations, were also settled in the wider area of Macedonia.

The Macedonians, originally nomadic shepherds, seem to have settled in the plains northeast of the Pierian mountains, expanding north along the foothills of Mount Vermion and south along the eastern foothills of the Pierians and the coast. The first king of the Temenid dynasty, Perdikkas I, founded his capital, Aigae, on the site of the modern town of Vergina close to Veria. The Temenid kings profited from the Persian Wars (513-477 B.C.) by allying themselves with the Persians and extending their rule up the Axios river and the plains of the upper Aliakmon, and later to the west bank of the Strymon river including the gold mines of Mount Pangaion, but with the withdrawal of the Persians this expanded kingdom fragmented into its constituent parts until Philip II became king in 359 B.C. With a series of successful campaigns, alliances, and marriages, Philip recovered these territories and annexed the Athenian colonies in Chalkidiki; through diplomacy and war, at the time of his death in 336 B.C. he had effectively made the southern Greek city states into a Macedonian protectorate.

When the Macedonians first appear in the writings of their southern neighbors, they tend to be seen as provincial, backward and archaic. During classical times the Macedonian aristocracy obviously preferred the culture and learning of Athens, and Philip II apparently adopted the Attic dialect as the language of official state documents and assured an Attic education for his son Alexander. Upon Philip's death Alexander succeeded in maintaining the Macedonian position vis-a-vis the southern Greek city-states and, apparently following his father's scheme, set out to conquer the Persian empire as the leader of a joint Greek and Macedonian army. His spectacular conquests in the east do not seem to have affected his homeland of Macedonia, which he had placed under the governorship of his friend Antipater. Alexander's death in 323, however, led to struggles over the succession in Macedonia; in the border areas, tribes subservient to Philip seem to have reasserted their independence. Eventually the expanding power of Rome brought the Romans into contact with Macedonia, and the military activities of the last Macedonian king led the Romans to "stabilize" their eastern borders by defeating him and annexing the kingdom of Macedonia in 168 B.C.

The boundaries of the Roman province of Macedonia were in the beginning considerably wider than those of the former kingdom. In the west it reached to the Ionian sea, incorporating southern Illyria; in the east it apparently included all of Thrace; north and south its boundaries expanded with the Roman conquests in the Balkans toward the Danube and the Black Sea. Roman administrative changes were not uncommon, however, and in later centuries the area was divided in several different ways. The province participated in the historical developments that marked the Roman empire; in 49 A.D. Paul the Apostle preached the Christian gospel for the first time on European soil in Philippi and in the Jewish communities of Thessaloniki and Veria.

Macedonia achieved a more central role with the division of the empire. With the foundation of the eastern capital of Constantinople, Thessaloniki gradually became the second city of the eastern empire and capital of the Balkans. Maximianus Galerius, member of the Tetrarchy under Diocletian and emperor from 306 to 311, made Thessaloniki his capital and built a huge palatial complex in the city, including a hippodrome and a triumphal arch. Constantine the Great used Thessaloniki as a base for military operations, and other emperors often stayed in the city or used it as headquarters during military campaigns, which were frequent; the pressures of the major population movements which crossed Europe from east to west beginning in the period of the late Roman empire were particularly strongly felt in Macedonia.

Attacks by Gothic tribes in Macedonia began in the late fourth century and only ceased when the Goths moved on to Italy in 497. Early in the sixth century Slavs and Huns passed through the Balkans toward Thessaly; Bulgars and Koutrigours attacked Thessaloniki unsuccessfully in 540, and almost every year saw raids and plundering expeditions. The Macedonian cities were fortified and remained relatively safe, but the countryside was repeatedly plundered. No permanent settlements seem to have been made, however, until the Avar and Slav invasions of the seventh century. Then, while the emperors of Byzantium were occupied in wars with Persia, the Avars and their allied Slavic tribes overran the empire's Balkan territories and attempted repeatedly to take Thessaloniki. The Slavic tribes during the course of the century made themselves independent of the Avars and settled in small groups in Macedonia and Thessaly, the first of many Slavic groups which have settled as a result of invasions or peaceful migration in what is now Greek Macedonia. Settlements of bands who acknowledged their allegiance to the emperor was accepted by Byzantium, and this seems to have been the form of settlement in Macedonia, though further north there was a Slavic state independent of the empire. The weakening of the Avars, however, apparently allowed Bulgar tribes to move south, and by the late seventh century they were exerting pressure on the Byzantine territories in the Balkans.

The Bulgarian threat dominated Byzantine policy and political developments in Macedonia and the Balkans for some 400 years. Beginning in the late seventh century the empire made determined efforts to assimilate the settled Slavic population by peaceful or forceful means, moving populations from one area to another and above all supporting systematic missionary activity among the Slavs and Bulgars. The missionaries Cyril and Methodius, who in the mid-ninth century christianized the Slavs of Moravia, created an alphabet for the Slavic language, and were responsible for the first written texts in that language (translations of the Bible, and liturgical and theological works), were born the sons of a Byzantine army official in Thessaloniki and apparently knew the Slavic language from childhood. When upon their death the Byzantine clergy had to leave Moravia, their student and successor Clement (also from Macedonia and also apparently bilingual) returned to establish a school for the education of Slavic-speaking clergy in Ochrid which seems to have been very successful in spreading Byzantine learning and culture as well as the orthodox Christian religion. Clement became the first bishop of Ochrid shortly after 893; his hymns and prayers in Slavonic are considered the first original literary compositions in that language.

The christianization of the Slavs and Bulgars appears to have been completed by the late ninth century, and the pacification of the area allowed for a blossoming of economic life in Macedonia. Thessaloniki was a crucial commercial center, with its position on the crossroads between the Via Egnatia and the trade route from the north Aegean up the Axios to Belgrade and from there along the Danube toward Russia, the Crimaea and the Caucasus; through the harbour of Thessaloniki passed all the trade from the shores of Asia Minor and the Byzantine and Arab port cities of the Middle East towards the Balkans and vice versa. The Fair of Saint Demetrius, held each year at the end of October, attracted merchants from as far north as Russia and Celts from beyond the Alps, and displayed wares from all over the Mediterranean and north Africa. This economic wellbeing was reflected in a lively cultural life. Especially the flourishing ecclesiastical art and architecture, beginning in Thessaloniki as early as the eighth century, has left a wealth of churches and monasteries which mark the cityscape even today.

When in 893 Symeon became tzar of Bulgaria he began a series of campaigns to enlarge his state. Though this expansion was shortlived, another effort was made by tzar Samuel in the late tenth century. Samuel began his military operations shortly after 976 from the area around lakes Ochrid and Prespa, took Veria in 989, and apparently controlled the countryside as far east as the straits of the Dardanelles, though Byzantium retained control of the two major Macedonian cities of Serres and Thessaloniki. Not until 1014 did the Byzantine emperor Basil II succeed in winning a decisive victory over the Bulgarian army, which he then destroyed with coldblooded brutality. But the defeat of the first Bulgarian empire did not bring a lasting peace to Macedonia, which was the scene of repeated battles (Bulgarian risings, Byzantine civil wars, invasions by Norman crusaders) throughout the eleventh and twelfth centuries. In 1185 a campaign by the brothers Petros and Asen resulted in the establishment of a new Bulgarian state, which Byzantium was forced to recognize, between the Danube and Mount Balkan (Skardos) north of Skopje; this second Bulgarian empire (or "empire of the Vlachs and Bulgars", since the Asenids were apparently of Vlach origin) rapidly expanded to lay claims to Thrace and to include much of northwestern Macedonia, Pelagonia (the Erigon river basin), the mountainous areas above the lakes of Ochrid and Prespa and, briefly, large areas of central Greece as well.

This is also the period of the foundation of the monastic communities on the Mount Athos peninsula in Chalkidiki and the development of the whole peninsula into a kind of independent religious state, a fact which was to have significant impact on the history and culture of medieval Macedonia and especially of Chalkidiki. In 883 Basil I prohibited access to the area by the local population of nearby villages and forbade state officials to disturb the monks; the first grants of income from landed estates were given to the monasteries in 956. The unified charter of the "Holy Mountain" was signed by the emperor John Tsimiskes in his own hand in 971. Major monastic churches were built here during the eleventh and twelfth centuries. Churches were also built in the cities, not only in Thessaloniki but in many of the smaller Macedonian cities as well: Veria, Edessa, Kastoria, Prespa, Serres, Meleniko. The models for art and architecture are usually found in Thessaloniki, which transmits influences from the capital of Constantinople, or in the northwestern center of Ochrid.

When in 1204 Constantinople was taken by the army of the Fourth Crusade and the Byzantine state temporarily disintegrated, Macedonia was made part of the "Kingdom of Thessaloniki" given in feoff to Boniface, marquis of Montferrat. But the Franks soon discovered that the real power in the area was still the Bulgarian tzar, who with an army of Vlachs and Bulgars took Thrace, Serres, Veria and Philippoupolis (modern Bulgarian Plovdiv); having conquered all the countryside, he laid siege to Thessaloniki, but died in 1207 before he could take the city. At his death strife over the throne fragmented Bulgaria. The Despotate of Epirus, ruled by a Byzantine noble family, gradually extended its territory into Macedonia, from Ochrid and Pelagonia in 1216 to Serres in 1221 and Thessaloniki in 1224, but lost most of it to John Asen II of Bulgaria in 1230. In 1246 the reconstituted Byzantine state whose capital was at Nicaea retook Thessaloniki and the rest of Macedonia up to Skopje and Meleniko, though the emperor had to fight the Bulgarians and the Despotate of Epirus repeatedly to keep the territory. Constantinople was retaken in 1261.

During this period there are occasional references to "Serbian and Albanian lands" in the northwest, and with the decline of Byzantine power the newly founded Serbian state expanded. In 1282 the Serbs under Stefan Milioutin took Skopje and areas north of Ochrid and Prilapo (modern Yugoslav Prilep); in 1334 under Stefan Dusan they momentarily descended as far as Thessaloniki; in 1345 Dusan had conquered Edessa, Kastoria, Florina, and Serres and was proclaimed emperor of Serbia and Romania; and at the time of his death in 1355 the Serbian empire covered most of Epirus and Macedonia up to the Nestos river, except for Thessaloniki and Chalkidiki. The weakening of Byzantium also led to civil unrest. In 1308-1309 the Catalan Company of mercenaries plundered in Thrace and Chalkidiki, including Mount Athos. The Zealot controversy led to a Zealot "takeover" in Thessaloniki which controlled municipal government between 1342 and 1350.

During the later fourteenth century the Turks, who had first settled on European soil at the invitation of one of the parties involved in the civil strife of Byzantium, gradually advanced westward across the Balkan peninsula. The governor of Thessaloniki, Manuel Palaeologus, after 1371 managed to extend his power over Macedonia from the Nestos river to Mount Vermion and to hold many of the Macedonian cities for about a decade, but after 1383 they fell rapidly to the Turks; Thessaloniki finally surrendered in 1387 after four years of siege. Manuel, who became emperor of Byzantium in 1391, was able to regain the Macedonian cities briefly 1402-1421 as the Turks struggled with the Mongols of Tamurlane; he entrusted the defense of Thessaloniki to the Venetians, but since they were not popular with the citizens there was little enthusiasm for battle when Sultan Murat II laid siege to and took the city in 1430. The capture of Thessaloniki marked the final end of resistance against the Ottoman conquest of Macedonia.

The Macedonian cities, especially Thessaloniki but also lesser cities such as Veria, Kastoria, Serres, Drama, Ochrid, remained economically important during this period of instability. Behind the walls of their fortifications, crafts and trade nourished a small but significant middle class, and the large landowners of the aristocracy now more than ever preferred to live in the cities rather than on their estates exposed to raiding and plunder. All attempts of the state to limit the powers of the large landowners ended in failure. Among the largest estates were those of the church, and huge expanses of land in Macedonia, especially in Chalkidiki and around Veria, Thessaloniki, and Serres were owned by monasteries. With the fall of Constantinople to the crusaders cultural life had moved to peripheral centers, and Macedonia benefitted from an influx of intellectuals; Thessaloniki retained its libraries while Constantinople was plundered. Churches continued to be built and decorated in Thessaloniki, Veria, Ochrid, Kastoria, Serres, and other Macedonian cities, and a certain stylistic detachment from Constantinople is evident in art and architecture in the provincial areas, with the development of more local schools.

The Ottoman conquest had consequences for Macedonia deeper and more farreaching than perhaps any other event in its history. At the time of the Ottoman conquest the inhabitants of Macedonia were all orthodox Christians with the exception of a small Jewish community. Linguistically they were divided into four language groups, Greek, Vlach, Slavic (the Slavic language of Macedonia is a south Slav dialect related to Bulgarian), and Albanian. The Greek community had been present since antiquity; the Vlachs were descendants of a Latinized population which had settled in Macedonia; and the Slavs were descendants of the Slavic-speaking settlers and invaders who had arrived beginning in the late sixth century. With the Ottoman conquest another group, Muslim in religion and Turkish in language and culture, arrived in Macedonia. In Thessa-

loniki and Monastir, there was also a great increase in the Jewish population (see below). The Turks actively encouraged subject populations to
accept the Muslim faith, which gradually led to assimilation of Turkish
culture and language, though when whole groups or areas became Muslim they often retained their local language and culture for centuries - as
was the case with the Albanians, for example. All these groups, during
the four and a half centuries of Ottoman rule, could move freely within
the huge Ottoman empire.

Turkish colonization in Macedonia took place throughout the fifteenth
century, and displaced subject populations from the plains to the less
fertile mountainous areas or to the isolated Chalkidiki peninsula. Jewish
settlers, exiled from Spain, Sicily, Italy, Portugal, and Provence, came in
waves starting around 1470 and continuing up through the early sixteenth
century. Vlach-speaking peoples from the region of Agrafa and the Ache-
loos river (the western slopes of the central Pindos range) moved into
Macedonia beginning toward the end of the sixteenth century and settled
around Thessaloniki; in 1605 they made up half the Christian population
of the city. Beginning in the seventeenth century and continuing up to the
early 1800s, Greek and Vlach villagers from Macedonia emigrated north
to the urban centers of the Ottoman empire and beyond; other settled in
the Macedonian towns. Bulgarian labourers moved south into Macedonia
(for instance to the mines in Chalkidiki) looking for work. There are also
nomadic Gypsies in Macedonia, as elsewhere in the Balkans. Thus, the
mixture of ethnic and linguistic groups which was already present in
Macedonia since Byzantine times was further complicated during the
nearly five centuries of Ottoman domination. It has left such an indelible
imprint on the composition of the population that it is (as we will see) a
significant part of regional ideology in the area even today, although few
ethnic differences are in fact perceptible in everyday life in present-day
Greek Macedonia.

Ottoman law and administration distinguished only between the faithful
(Muslims) and the infidels, among whom it differentiated Christians and
Jews; it recognized no ethnic or linguistic groups. All the old inhabitants
of Macedonia were referred to as "Roum", Romans. Their common fate
and religion tended to bring Greeks, Bulgars, Albanians, Serbs and
Vlachs together. Though each ethnic group was certainly well aware of
its own identity, they apparently felt little need at this time to formulate
this identity in political terms; national consciousness was at first an af-

faire of a few Grecophone intellectuals, which only very gradually spread among the merchants and craftsmen in the cities.

The Christian population was concentrated primarily in the old Macedonian cities, and after the mid-sixteenth century the flourishing Jewish population of Thessaloniki also emigrated to other Macedonian towns. New towns were founded in the mountains or foothills (Naoussa, Siatista, Kozani) by Christian settlers displaced by the conquest, and on the plains in connection with Ottoman administrative needs (Yannitsa). There were large Muslim populations in certain cities (Veria, Serres, Stromnitsa, Edessa, Monastir), though the smaller towns of western and central Macedonia were primarily Christian. With the migration to the cities in the eighteenth century, the Christian urban population grew in relation to the Muslims.

Theoretically, all conquered lands under Ottoman law belonged to the sultan, and no infidel could hold absolute property rights over land. In the early days of Ottoman rule some Christian landowners seem to have become Muslims in order to be able to keep their lands; the monasteries especially were in a difficult position, though by the late sixteenth century they had managed through the payment of large sums of money to acquire the same property rights as Muslim religious foundations. But as the pace of Ottoman expansion slackened and stopped in the seventeenth century, the loss of income from new conquests led to attempts to intensify the exploitation of the subject population. The exploitation often drove the farmers to become outlaws, joining bands of robbers in the mountains; to control the outlaws, the Ottoman authorities established *armatolikia*, bands of armed men under their own captain charged with keeping the peace in mountainous areas. Many of the *armatoli* had more in common with the outlaws than with the Turks, and might make common cause with them on occasion. The weakening of the central administration also led to more high-handed and arbitrary behaviour on the part of local authorities. Local governors occasionally established themselves as warlords with private armies, exploiting the populace in much the same way as the other robbers.

In addition to the traditional crops of grains, beans, legumes, flax, fruit, and nuts, Byzantium had introduced the cultivation of the silkworm in Macedonia. The Ottomans brought tobacco; rice, maize, and cotton were gradually added. But as exploitation of the farmers increased, arable lands in the exposed plains were often abandoned as the settlers escaped to the more inaccessible mountain regions, where sheep- and goatherding were common in addition to farming.

Commerce, especially long-distance trade with Europe, in the early centuries of Ottoman rule was almost exclusively in the hands of the Jewish community of Thessaloniki, and spread with their migration to Veria, Monastir, and Kavala. Greeks gradually began to participate by selling products of crafts and manufacture, and Turkish landowners by selling excess farm produce and by moneylending. By the seventeenth century Greek merchants controlled most of the inland trade; during the second half of that century the Jews of Thessaloniki suffered severe setbacks from wars between their commercial ally Venice and the Ottomans, and from a messianic movement that fragmented their community. By the early nineteenth century, two-thirds of commerce in Thessaloniki was in Greek hands, but commerce during the later centuries was plagued by the complex and irregular Ottoman tariff system, the greed of persons in positions of authority, the systematic bribery required to make the bureaucracy function, the insecurity of roads, and the attacks by robbers and pirates.

The Christian population of Macedonia never seems to have quite given up hope of being freed from Ottoman rule. Each international conflict between the Ottoman empire and a European power led to small-scale conspiracies and rebellions. But more serious resistance against the Turks began among the Christian population of Macedonia in the eighteenth century, with the growth of the concept of the nation-state. The most important role in the development of national consciousness was played, though at first quite unintentionally, by the Christian schools. Cosmas of Aetolia, monk of Athos and scholar of Constantinople, criss-crossed Macedonia and Epirus from 1759 to 1778 founding schools in the countryside to counteract conversions of Christians to Islam; it is said that his activities brought about the founding of 10 secondary and 200 elementary schools. These schools originally all offered instruction in Greek, though they were open to Christians of all ethnic groups; there had also been an extensive Jewish school system during the sixteenth and seventeenth centuries, but it declined with the reduced influence of the Jewish community in later centuries.

The growing political unrest of the various ethnic communities is probably directly related to their increased commercial role and consequent economic security. Eighteenth-century private homes in many Macedonian cities (Veria, Siatista, Kastoria, Kozani, Florina, Thessaloniki) show impressive evidence of this in their splendid architecture. These mansions still constitute a striking element of the city-scape wherever the accidents of modernization have allowed them to survive, and as our study found, they form part of the conception of space by the inhabitants, who are at times rather ambivalent about how these remnants of the Ottoman past should be considered.

The nineteenth century brought the founding of the first national states independent of the Ottoman empire in the Balkans (see map, Figure 2). The Greek war of independence (1821-1827) was accompanied by risings in Macedonia, but a revolt in Chalkidiki in 1821 and rebellions on Mount Olympus and Mount Vermion in 1822 were suppressed, and the civilian population suffered brutal reprisals. The new Greek state, as soon as it had established diplomatic relations with the Porte, opened consulates in Macedonia and actively though secretly encouraged nationalist movements. Repeated romantic uprisings took place during the first half of the century, and armed bands of outlaws (as well as the armatolikia) were ready to take action as soon as an occasion appeared. But the church and the schools remained the main vehicle for the spread of nationalist sentiment; Grecophone and Vlachophone emigre merchants from Macedonia who had successfully established themselves in the major cities of Europe and the Middle East founded and supported dozens of schools in their home towns and villages.

The Russo-Turkish war of 1853 was catalytic for the Serbian and Bulgarian nationalist movements. In 1861 Russia opened a consulate in Monastir to actively support Slavic propaganda in that area. A Principality of Serbia had existed since 1815; it was recognized as an independent state in 1878. At that time Bulgaria was also recognized as an autonomous principality technically under the sovereignty of the sultan. But long before statehood, the Bulgarian nationalists, like the Greek state, laid claims to parts if not all of Ottoman Macedonia in the name of the liberation of their ethnic brethren. All ethnic groups, Serbs, Vlachs, and especially Bulgarians, founded schools offering instruction in their own languages in support of their various nationalist movements. Though Macedonian freedom fighters often saw their struggle in terms of a pan-Balkan alliance of oppressed peoples, the Balkan national states and the European powers who had interests in the area clearly had other aims in view, and when not in temporary alliance against a common enemy, were openly competitive in their claims.

Figure 2. National boundaries in the Balkans around 1900.

The Greek government in Athens, which may not have been clearly aware of the ethnic composition of the population in Macedonia, apparently assumed that all orthodox Christians were Greek in culture and sentiment, whether they spoke Albanian, Vlach, or Slavic. Thus, the successful campaign of Bulgaria for a national church independent of the Patriarchate of Constantinople was felt by the Greek government to be a dastardly political trick. But the possibility of a liturgy in their own language and priests from among their own people was attractive to many Slavic-speaking parishes in Macedonia, who eagerly voted to belong to the Bulgarian Exarchate after 1870 when they were given a choice by the Ottoman authorities.

Macedonia was not a recognized administrative unit in the Ottoman empire. The area which in the late nineteenth century was referred to as Macedonia, and to which all the neighboring Balkan states laid claim, included the two administrative districts (vilayets) of Thessaloniki and Monastir, i.e., what is today Greek Macedonia (see Figure 3), and extended to the north into what are today the Yugoslav Republic of Macedonia and Bulgarian Macedonia. It was thus significantly larger than the ancient Macedonia of the mid-fifth century B.C. (about three times as

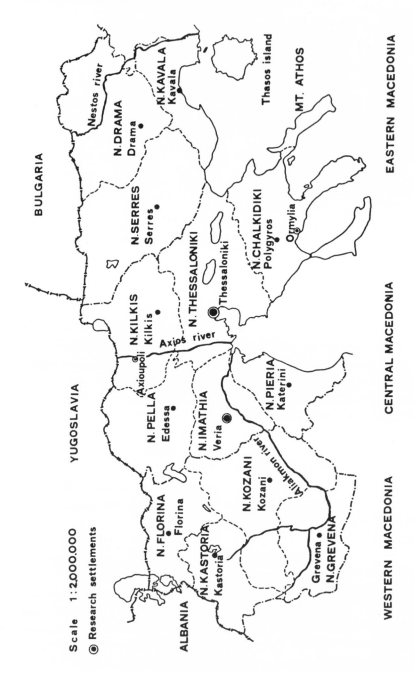

Figure 3. Administrative divisions of Macedonia.

large), since in the intervening centuries it had come to include large territories mainly to the north and east of the ancient kingdom.

It is exceedingly difficult to determine the ethnic composition of this area toward the end of the nineteenth century. Linguistically, Slavic seems to have been the predominant language north of a line running roughly from Ochrid north of Monastir and Stromnitsa to Meleniko and Nevrokopi. Greek was dominant from Mount Olympus and the Pindos range to Kastoria, and from the coast up to the area just north of Veria, Thessaloniki, Serres, and Drama. In between, Christian and Muslim communities speaking Slavic, Greek, Vlach, Albanian, and Turkish lived side by side (one of our research settlements, Axioupoli, is located in this linguistically mixed zone of the late nineteenth century). The Slavic speakers were numerically stronger, but the ethnic identity of the Christian population proved very difficult to determine, and here the appearance of the independent Bulgarian Exarchate was a crucial factor, both in swaying the allegiance of the local population and in the propaganda of the European powers who, for reasons of their own, supported the one or the other party in the conflict. Among the Vlachs Greek national consciousness was traditional, and after 1870 they systematically chose to remain under the Patriarchate of Constantinople. The Slavic-speaking population of north and northeastern Macedonia chose the Bulgarian Exarchate or occasionally, in the northwest, an alliance with Serbia. Toward the end of the nineteenth century Romania also actively prozelytised among the Vlach population in Macedonia and Epirus, though without much hope of putting forth claims to Macedonian territory. In the constant sporadic armed struggles, guerilla warfare, political crises and wary alliances of the late-nineteenth-century Balkan peninsula, the struggle for Macedonia was won, in spite of all, primarily through the schools: Bulgarian influence extended, through the founding of schools and the Bulgarian Exarchate, toward Meleniko and Nevrokopi; Greek influence remained strongest in central Macedonia.

Around 1900 the situation in Macedonia was effectively one of civil war on all fronts, with armed guerilla bands, clandestinely supported by both the Bulgarian and the Greek government through semi-official organizations, fighting each other, the civilian population, the Turks, and the Albanians who often served as mercenaries for the Ottoman authorities. In 1898 the Bulgarian government announced its support for an independent state of Macedonia; this position, the official goal of the Bulgarian-influenced Internal Macedonian Revolutionary Organization

(IMRO), was received by the Slavo-Macedonians rather more enthusiastically than Bulgaria had intended, and "wings" supporting a Bulgarian and an independent Macedonia developed within IMRO. But the Young Turk movement (which started in Thessaloniki) forced the Ottoman authorities in 1908 to attempt to end the anarchy in Macedonia, and their promise of equal civil rights persuaded the Christians to temporarily stop slaughtering each other. With the Balkan War of 1912-1913 there was a dash for territory by the armies of Greece, Bulgaria, and Serbia which effectively set the boundaries of these three states in Macedonia roughly where they are today. Thus, in 1913 the territorial struggle in Macedonia was in fact over, though none of the parties involved would have accepted this; claims and counter-claims continued to be hotly debated and fought over up to World War II and beyond.

The idea of an independent Macedonia has had a curious ghostlife after World War II, when the Yugoslav communist party revived it as part of a projected Balkan federation of autonomous communist regions along the lines of the present-day state of Yugoslavia. The notion was (and to a certain extent still is) enthusiastically supported by Yugoslavia, and more reluctantly by Bulgaria and the Greek communist party. But the Greek government rejected it out of hand, and in the postwar years it was quietly dropped by all except the autonomous Yugoslav Socialist Republic of Macedonia, where occasional protests are still organized in support of the "oppressed" Macedonians. The result is that the issue of the history and ethnic composition of Macedonia has retained a political sensitivity out of all proportion to its present-day reality.

One last major movement of populations in Macedonia occurred in connection with the Greco-Turkish war of 1921-1922. After this ultimate defeat of Greek irridentist ambitions, much of the Greek population of Asia Minor fled to the Greek mainland. The settlement of the Treaty of Lausanne in 1923, which provided for a compulsory exchange of populations between the two countries, resulted in an influx of about 1.5 million Greek refugees (equal to one-fourth of the total population of the country at that time). A similar agreement with Bulgaria in 1919 had also brought about a (voluntary) exchange of populations but on a much more reduced scale. The impact of the exchange of populations was felt particularly strongly in Macedonia and Thrace. During the 1919-1924 period some 360,000 Turkish and Bulgarian refugees left Macedonia (which in 1920 had a total population of about 1,090,000). Of the Greek refugees from Asia Minor, about 640,000 were settled in Macedonia, mostly in small agricultural settlements in the plains, though an important proportion were also settled in suburbs to the cities. These refugee settlements have retained a sense of identity up to the present day. All the research settlements were in some sense marked by the influx of refugees. Axioupoli is a refugee settlement; next to Ormylia lies the refugee settlement of Vatopedi, which is part of the same local community as Ormylia; next to Veria and today part of the city is the refugee settlement of Promitheas; Thessaloniki had an influx of refugees close to one-third of the city population.

The consequences for Macedonia of its late integration into the three neighboring states in 1913 were not unequivocally positive. The economy of the region had been destroyed by the long period of strife. New national borders cut the particularly the urban centers of Greek Macedonia off from their traditional hinterlands, and from their role in the network of Balkan trade routes; this was especially damaging for Thessaloniki, but also for the smaller Macedonian manufacturing centers such as Veria, Edessa, and Naoussa. Athens with its port of Piraeus was the economic and administrative center of the Greek state. After 1913, the objective difficulties in the reorientation of its commercial ties which Thessaloniki encountered were exacerbated by its new subordinate position vis-a-vis Athens. The concentration of economic activities and political decision-making in Athens is felt even today in Thessaloniki and Northern Greece as an encroachment by Athens and the south on their traditional roles, and an unfair dependence. Our research, as will be apparent below, brought out this solidarity of the north with Thessaloniki and the hostility to Athens.

After World War II all of Greece, including Macedonia, has been subject to a decline in population in the countryside and rapid urbanization in a relatively few urban centers, Thessaloniki among them. Intense building activity reshaped the city almost completely after 1960; in our study, old residents complain of disorientation and are nostalgic for the city of their childhood. Notable growth in the sixties, and a real boom in the seventies, also affected Veria, where some research subjects expressed conflicting feelings about the need for modernisation and the desire to retain the familiar forms of the individual and collective past.

In both Veria and Thessaloniki there has been an influx of population from the countryside, usually employed in industry and manufacture. The distinction between "old" and "new" residents and neighborhoods appears in several ways in our study, especially in the case of Thessaloniki.

The effects of this dislocation and of the rapid shift to a capitalist urban economy has clearly been a homogenization of the urban population, effectively erasing ethnic differences which in a more traditional environment might have survived; we were told repeatedly that there are no longer any (ethnic) differences between social groups, but that there used to be in the recent past.

But even in the countryside ethnic identity has become largely an object of folklore. Where differences persist, there is reason to believe that they have been reinforced by other distinctions: in Chalkidiki the refugee settlements, which are often located on the coast, were quick to capitalize on touristic development, a fact for which they are both admired and resented by the "locals", for example in Ormylia. Tourism has acted as a supplement to the agricultural economy in Chalkidiki and other coastal areas of Macedonia, enabling the smaller settlements to a certain extent to resist the depopulation that characterises the countryside as a whole. Inland areas, particularly those that are at a distance from the national highways, have been less able to benefit from tourism. Thus, the area around Axioupoli is having serious trouble retaining its population. Axioupoli itself, which functions as a local commercial center, is surviving fairly well, but the mountain villages around it are declining. Thus, the four settlements we selected for our study represent four rather different situations with respect to settlement size and regional economic development in Central Macedonia, as will be clear also from the discussion in the following section.

2. The research settlements and the regional context

The four research settlements were selected as part of, and representative of, the social and geographical organization of the region of modern Greek Macedonia. The selection was effected on the basis of a group of three criteria which represent a combination of the geographical and the sociological viewpoints and which we will call regional criteria. In this section we present these regional criteria together with data on the contemporary geographical organization of Macedonia; by applying the regional criteria to these data, we arrived at our choice of the research settlements. It is clear, however, that the definition of the settlements is not in itself enough to indicate the research subjects in each settlement, and for this reason the regional criteria were supplemented with a group of purely sociological criteria independent from geographical considerations. The sociological criteria and data will be discussed in the next chapter.

The purpose of the regional criteria was to lead to a selection of settlements differing in such a degree that it could be supposed that their differences would influence the ideological conception of regional space. We used two major criteria, of a mixed sociological and geographical nature, and a third of lesser importance, all of which were explicit from the start of the research project. The first major criterion is related to the city-country opposition, an opposition of prime importance to Marxist theory. As Marx and Engels observe (1970: 43), "The division of labour inside a nation leads at first to the separation of *city* and *country* and to the conflict of their interests." This opposition may tend to take new, less obvious forms in countries of advanced capitalism, but in Greece, which is a developing country, it holds a prominent position economically, socially, and demographically. The importance of the city-country opposition in Greek society led us to select two representative settlements from each of these geographical categories.

The second major regional criterion concerns the hierarchical structure of the regional settlement network. This settlement hierarchy can also be seen as a series of relations of conflict and complementarity between settlements occupying different positions in the network, and seen from this angle it can be considered as an extension of the city-country opposition. We felt that the inhabitants of settlements in different hierarchical positions in the settlement network were likely to view regional space from different points of view, and thus to conceive of the region differently; thus, our hypothesis was that the settlement hierarchy, a central issue for geographers and planners, would be important for the study of the conception of regional space as well. We therefore wished to include one large city, one medium-size city, and one large village (all these terms are to be understood with reference to modern Greek conditions).

We were interested in locating settlements of this nature within Greek Macedonia, which was defined from the beginning as a wider research area representative of Northern Greece. Since certain statistical data are not available for settlements but only for the nomoi, we complemented contextually the data for the Macedonian settlements with data for the nomoi. The *nomos* (plural *nomoi* or *nomi*) is an important regional administrative unit in Greece, comparable in some ways to the French *département*. There are thirteen nomoi in Macedonia, and together with the three nomoi of Thraki (Thrace) they constitute Northern Greece. Macedonia is divided into three parts, Western, Central, and Eastern Macedonia. Western Macedonia is composed of the nomoi of Kastoria, Florina, Kozani, and Grevena; Central Macedonia includes six nomoi, namely Pella, Imathia, Pieria, Kilkis, Thessaloniki, and Chalkidiki; and Eastern Macedonia contains the nomoi of Kavala, Drama, and Serres (Figure 3). The geographical analysis of Macedonia, which we present here in a very abridged manner, was used as the background for the selection of the research settlements, which as we shall see were finally chosen from Central Macedonia. We were interested in the main economic and demographic characteristics of the thirteen nomoi of Macedonia, and to this purpose examined the data for the nomoi presented in Table 1 below. These are the change in population from 1971 to 1981, the degree of urbanization of the nomos in 1981, and the composition of employment in the three main sectors of the economy in 1981.

On the basis of Table 1 it is possible to derive a typology of the demographic dynamics, and the urban or rural character, of the nomoi of Macedonia, and hence a typology of their level of development. At the head of the list, as we would expect, is the nomos of Thessaloniki, with a large population increase (22.7%), a high degree of urbanization (urban population 81.0%), and a very low level of employment in the primary sector (10.2%). Thus, the nomos of Thessaloniki is a dynamic and developed nomos, with emphasis mainly on the secondary and tertiary sectors, characteristics which derive directly from its capital city of Thessaloniki. The nomos of Thessaloniki is followed by the nomoi of Kavala, Kastoria, Kozani, and Imathia, all of which show an important population increase, a medium degree of urbanization (with the exception of Imathia which has a relatively high degree, 52.4%), and a low presence of the primary sector, again with the exception of Imathia which has a medium level of employment in the primary sector (43.1%). These nomoi, then, show positive demographic development and a mixed rural and urban character, hence they can be classified as developed. A similar mixed character is also shown by the nomos of Drama, which however has a low population increase, and that of Pieria, which has a more rural character. The last group is composed of the nomoi of Grevena, Serres, Florina, Kilkis, Pella, and Chalkidiki, which are predominantly rural in character. The demographic evolution of these nomoi varies from slightly negative to fairly positive, with the higher rate of increase in Chalkidiki (7.0%) and the lowest (-3.3%) in Serres and Kilkis. Grevena and Chalkidiki are the only nomoi in Macedonia without any urban settlements. All these characteristics are indicative of the low degree of development of the nomoi in the last group.

Table 1. Demographic and economic characteristics of the nomoi of Macedonia (based on National Statistical Service of Greece 1972, 1977, 1982, 1984, and 1985).

Nomos	Population change, % 1971–1981	Degree of urbanization* 1981			Employment, % 1981		
		urban	semi-urban	rural	pri-mary	second-ary	terti-ary
Florina	0.3	24.3	6.6	69.1	54.7	20.4	24.9
Grevena	3.2	0.0	33.6	66.4	47.6	26.7	25.7
Kastoria	16.3	39.3	11.9	48.8	27.1	53.0	19.9
Kozani	8.4	35.7	12.5	51.8	31.2	42.3	26.5
Chalkidiki	7.0	0.0	44.2	55.8	37.8	33.2	29.0
Imathia	13.2	52.4	6.9	40.7	43.1	29.5	27.4
Kilkis	−3.3	15.0	15.6	69.4	51.0	26.2	22.8
Pella	5.0	30.8	16.0	53.2	59.1	20.3	20.6
Pieria	16.5	36.2	19.7	44.1	51.8	22.8	25.4
Thessaloniki	22.7	81.0	9.8	9.2	10.2	42.5	47.3
Drama	4.1	40.8	20.2	39.0	42.5	28.8	28.7
Kavala	11.2	41.0	16.1	42.9	35.6	32.0	32.4
Serres	−3.3	23.2	19.2	57.6	59.9	18.2	21.9
Macedonia	12.2	51.6	14.3	34.1	32.3	33.8	33.9

* Urban: population in settlements with more than 10,000 inhabitants
Semi-urban: in settlements with 2,000–10,000 inhabitants
Rural: in settlements with less than 2,000 inhabitants.

Of all the nomoi of Macedonia only the nomos of Thessaloniki includes a metropolitan city, a settlement rank we felt it useful to include in our study. By selecting the nomos of Thessaloniki, we simultaneously selected the only fully urbanized nomos of Macedonia. It was then logical, though not obligatory, to select the medium-size city from the second group of nomoi and the two large villages from the last group.

Here we introduced the minor regional criterion used to define the research settlements. We wanted the settlements if possible to occupy opposed geographical positions, with the aim of defining settlements with an important heterogeneity in their physical and natural environment, so that the regional ideology of the inhabitants would refer to different types of settlement networks and different natural surroundings. This geographical and topological criterion can be applied in two different cases, one in which the settlements selected are largely independent from each other, and the other where they are, directly or indirectly, rather closely connected, thus belonging to the same wider geographical unit. A look at the groups of nomoi shows that we can arrive at a rather closely connected set of settlements by choosing from the nomos of Imathia and the nomoi of Chalkidiki and Kilkis; in fact, Imathia, the southern part of Kilkis, and the northwestern part of Chalkidiki are all strongly connected to the Thessaloniki metropolitan area (Kousidonis 1983: 220-247). This criterion of selecting settlements belonging to the same polarized region occurred a posteriori and was used, together with the topological criterion, to help us define settlements geographically heterogeneous but nevertheless not independent from each other.

The definition of the specific research settlements was constrained by these considerations, and based on the population statistics for 1971 and 1981 for all settlements of Macedonia with a population of more than 2,000 inhabitants and the rate of demographic growth of these settlements between 1971 and 1981 (National Statistical Service of Greece 1972 and 1982). As we saw, the selection of Thessaloniki was empirically given. Its metropolitan area in 1981 had a population of 706,180 inhabitants and the rate of population growth for the 1971-1981 period was 26.7%, among the highest in Macedonia. The same is true for Veria, capital of the nomos of Imathia, which has a rate of growth of 25.6%, but a much lower population, 37,087 inhabitants, representing the lower range of medium-size cities in Greece. Given the general character of development of Imathia and the demographic growth rate of Veria, it can be assumed that the city is a dynamic, economically wealthy settlement, a hypothesis that will be corroborated below by statistical data and that corresponds to our empirical impression during field work.

Thessaloniki and Veria being the two urban settlements selected for our study, let us now introduce the two settlements which were considered representative of the category of large villages. The first is Ormylia in Chalkidiki, with a population of 2,780 and a growth rate of 6.1%, which is a medium rate for the large villages of Macedonia. The second settlement, Axioupoli in Kilkis, presents similar characteristics, with a population of 3,229 and a lower rate of growth, 2.3%. Ormylia is rural, in the image of Chalkidiki, and shows a comparable demographic development, while Axioupoli has a very low growth rate and rural character like the nomos to which it belongs, and as we shall see acts as a local service center for its area.

Below, we present briefly each of the four research settlements (see Figure 3) before going on to the discussion of the sociological criteria employed in defining the research subjects.

Thessaloniki metropolitan area. Thessaloniki is the second largest city in Greece (the first city, Athens, in 1981 had approximately 3 million inhabitants). Thessaloniki has had a remarkable development as a modern city over the last 25 years, as can be inferred from the fact that between 1961 and 1981 its population almost doubled. One result of the spatial expansion accompanying this growth was that many previously independent villages around the city have been incorporated into the metropolitan area. Thessaloniki functions as an economic center for all of Northern Greece.

It is possible to see the economic structure of the city from unpublished statistical data on employment provided by the National Statistical Service of Greece for the years 1978 and 1984. Employment in the secondary sector amounted in 1978 to almost half of the total employment in the city (the primary sector, construction, and certain services are not included), a ratio much higher than the corresponding ratios for the three other settlements and indicative of the industrial character of Thessaloniki. The share of employment in commerce was 35.6%, while the share of employment in transport activities is significant (9.0%), revealing the role of the city as a transport node; it should not be forgotten that Thessaloniki has been a port city since antiquity. In 1984 the distance between the secondary sector and commerce had increased further, showing a further accentuation of the industrial character of the city.

Geographically, industrial activities are scattered all over the city, but the main industrial concentrations are located in the western part of the city and beyond it. This western section also shows a heavy concentration of low income, working class inhabitants. On the other hand, the adjacent central part, including the central business district, while not socially homogeneous, is characterized primarily by higher income categories. This central section, squeezed between the sea and a hilly forested area to the north, has developed linearly along the shore; we will have occasion to note the semiotic importance of this area in our discussion of the regional conception of the inhabitants of Thessaloniki (Chapter 6, Section 2).

Veria. The historic Macedonian town of Veria is located in the eastern foothills of Mount Vermion, on a plateau overlooking a wide plain through which the Aliakmon river flows east to the sea. The city is the capital and main economic pole of Imathia and its catch area seems to cover all the central part of the nomos. While in 1978 the share of commerce in total employment was slightly higher (39.9%) than that of the secondary sector (35.5%), this situation was dramatically reversed by 1984, when the secondary sector exceeded commerce by 70%. These data corroborate our initial assumption concerning the economic wealth of the city. Two further indices of its dynamic economy are the share of transport, which in 1978 accounted for 12.3% of total employment - more than the corresponding ratio for Thessaloniki and far above the ratio in Ormylia and Axioupoli (2.0%) - and the share of banking and finance (8.2%), which is twice that of Thessaloniki. In spite of these developmental trends, the scale of the phenomenon should not escape our attention: total employment in Veria in 1978 amounted to 4,510 persons as compared to 118,113 in Thessaloniki.

Ormylia. In contrast to the two cities, the catch area of Ormylia is extremely limited. The settlement was dominated in 1978 by commercial employment (67.9% of total employment), while in 1984 employment in the secondary sector acquired a somewhat greater importance. Beyond the secondary sector and commerce, the share of each of the other economic activities is unimportant. The total employment amounted to only 196 persons, a number indicative of the strongly agricultural orientation of Ormylia (employment in the primary sector is not included in these figures for total employment, as we noted earlier).

Ormylia is located not far from the sea and thus tends to be integrated into the zone of touristic development of southern Chalkidiki. The result is the appearance of pressures from tourism, mainly on the traditional agricultural activities. Mining, another traditional activity in Chalkidiki, provides employment in a neighboring settlement for some of the inhabitants. The settlement is on a small plain surrounded on three sides by higher ground and open to the sea to the south.

Axioupoli. Axioupoli, one of the refugee settlements of 1928, differs from Ormylia in that it has a catch area of some importance. Axioupoli shows a dramatic inversion similar to that in Veria of the relation between commerce and the secondary sector. Indeed, while in 1978 the share of commerce (45.1%) was ahead of that of the secondary sector (36.1%), in 1984 the secondary sector was more than five times greater than commerce. At the same time, the share of banking and finance was in 1978 three times higher than in Thessaloniki (12.7%). If finally we take into account the fact that total employment in the settlement in 1978 equaled 379 persons, a number twice as high as that for Ormylia which has a total population comparable to that of Axioupoli, and in 1984 it was over 700 persons, we can see that Axioupoli is much less rural than Ormylia and in fact functions as a service center for a wider rural area.

This situation needs some further clarification. The inversion of the relation between commerce and secondary sector in Veria was combined with a high rate of population increase, and these two facts together point to the dynamic economic development of the city. But in Axioupoli the inversion of this relation seems to demand a different interpretation, given the small size and very low rate of population growth of the settlement. What has probably happened is a shift of the same population away from the primary sector and towards traditional manufacture, which is not an exclusive type of employment but allows for the combination of the new economic activity, which gradually has become dominant, with agricultural pursuits. Under these conditions, the shift to the secondary sector indicates a tendency for the economy of the settlement to transform, a tendency which, however, at least for the moment, is less radical than it appears and has not deprived Axioupoli of its rural character.

Geographically, Axioupoli lies on the west side of a plain below Mount Païkon, which forms the limit of the plain to the west, and almost in contact with the Axios river, which forms the limit of the area to the east. The river traditionally constituted a barrier between the settlement networks on the east and west side. Opposite Axioupoli on the other side of the river, at a very small distance from Axioupoli, the town of Polykastro with more than 5,000 inhabitants functions as a service center of a higher order.

Chapter 5. Corpus, sample, and sociology

1. The semiotic corpus and the statistical sample

Our regional criteria allowed us to define the research settlements, and the selection of these settlements was the first step toward the definition of the research subjects. But further specifications were needed for the definition of the specific social profiles according to which to select the research subjects among the inhabitants of the settlements. Both the sociological criteria used and the social profiles derived from them will be discussed in the present chapter. The research subjects provided us with the interviews which constituted the object of our analysis.

At this point two issues emerge. First, this manner of operating is not the only one possible; there is another method used in the human sciences, including semiotics, the field which we focus on in this study. Secondly, the research material can be approached and treated in two very different ways, something rather disconcerting for a researcher in the human sciences. We considered it important to discuss these issues in the initial section of this chapter, because of their general epistemological interest and because our own view on them forms part of the epistemological foundation of our study.

The historical development of semiotics is linked to a qualitative approach to semiotic data; this is true of both the methodological and the technical operations performed on the data. Within this context, semiotics delimits its subject and object of analysis on the basis of the concept of the *corpus*, as opposed to that of the *sample*, used, for example, in analytical behavioral geography and environmental psychology. The corpus, like the sample, is a flexible unit and can extend from a collection of sentences to a book by an individual author, to his complete works, to the variants of a myth, or to the whole of a semiotic system of a particular period. For Greimas and Courtés (1979: 73), the corpus in descriptive linguistics is defined as "a finite set of 'enunciates' [utterances], constituted in view of [semiotic] analysis that, once effected, is considered to account for them in an exhaustive and adequate manner." The same authors point out that for generative grammar the corpus is limited and supposed to be representative of the whole studied, and that the criteria of exhaustiveness and adequacy, which refer both to the rules for the constitution of the corpus and to the analytical procedure, are replaced in generative grammar by the more or less intuitive criteria of grammaticality and acceptability. For the same authors, the extension of the concept of corpus beyond linguistics leads to a corpus which is neither closed nor exhaustive but only representative, and to a corresponding model which is only hypothetical (Greimas & Courtés 1979: 74).

There is nothing intrinsic in the nature of the corpus preventing quantitative operations, but such operations are not usually performed due to the theoretical integration of the concept of the corpus into the structural-semiotic paradigm. It is rather intriguing to note that, though the corpus is a central concept in semiotics with, as we shall see, far-reaching consequences, the semiotic bibliography does not discuss the theoretical presuppositions for the constitution of a corpus. One exception are Greimas and Courtés (1979: 74-75), who propose two ways to construct a well-formed corpus: statistical sampling, and saturation of a model, i.e., beginning with an initial model constructed on the basis of an initial corpus, one arrives at a final model after a series of new applications.

Given these characteristics of the corpus, the concept of the sample can be considered as historically opposed to that of the corpus. The sample is a statistical entity, constructed according to a systematic procedure in order to be subjected to quantitative operations. While semioticians do not seem to be sensitized to the idea of a well-formed corpus, the number of works on sampling indicate the concern of the statistical approaches in the social sciences to secure the representativeness of the sample, i.e., the possibility of using it as a basis for scientifically meaningful and valid generalizations.

This opposition between the qualitative structural and the quantitative statistical approach is put forward by Lévi-Strauss (1958: 311-317) in his discussion of the opposition between "mechanical" and "statistical" models. Both types are, according to the author, structural and both study one particular case each time. The only difference between them would be that, when we compare the scale of the model with that of the phenomena under study, the constitutive elements of the mechanical model are of the same scale with these phenomena, while the elements of the statistical model exceed the scale of the phenomena. Thus, the marital rules in primitive societies are represented as mechanical models referring to individuals distributed in kinship classes or clans, while the different types of marriage in modern society depend on more general factors and the regularities which can be observed in them are based on statistical data. Lévi-Strauss, following Émile Durkheim, believes that the corpus for the construction of a mechanical model should be limited to a small number of cases, the in-depth analysis of which can lead to pertinent generalizations. Thus, Lévi-Strauss and Noam Chomsky agree on the principle of the construction of the corpus, and both apply the method of saturation for the construction of their models. On the other hand, the corpus of a statistical model is, for Lévi-Strauss, very vast. Extending the opposition of mechanical versus statistical to the concept of time ("mechanical" time: reversible, non-cumulative, non-historical; "statistical" time: non-reversible, oriented, linked to evolution), Lévi-Strauss relates social anthropology and ethnography to the mechanical model and "mechanical" time, and sociology and history to the statistical model and "statistical" time. It is on "mechanical" models that the work of Lévi-Strauss in anthropology has been exclusively focused and it is this kind of model that has come to dominate semiotics through the influence of Lévi-Straussean structuralism.

It is not only the structural-semiotic paradigm which is opposed to statistical analysis. A similar attitude is built into the field work methods of social anthropology, where data are gathered through selected informers and through the observation of the anthropologist. The extreme case of this qualitative gathering of information is full-scale participant observation, where the researcher participates fully in the life of the group he is studying.

Many of the traditional disciplines that form part of the human sciences and in which the influence of structuralism was felt, such as literary studies or art history, are accustomed to working with a corpus defined by more or less subjective criteria and find quantitative analysis quite foreign to their habitual methods of operation. The tension between qualitative and quantitative analysis appears within the domain of psychology, and is discussed by Mostyn (1985: 115-117, 120-124, 136) with reference to content analysis. Mostyn presents the major differences between quantitative and qualitative approaches in psychology in the form of a set of binary oppositions: interpretation vs. analytical description; expansion vs. refinement of existing data; low vs. high reliability; resistance to vs. possibility of validation; use of interviews with open-ended questionnaires vs. use of structured questionnaires allowing for short or fixed-alternative answers; interview length: more than an hour vs. rapid completion of the questionnaire; small sample (less than 100 persons) vs.

large sample. The author concludes, however, that both approaches are useful, and that they are more similar than different.

The split between the qualitative and the quantitative approach also appears in geography, with the study of the subjective experience of space. Thus, contrary to the quantitative techniques of analytical behavioral geography, the humanistic geographical approach tends to rely on the hermeneutic treatment of ample empirical material. The problem of the differentiation of the two approaches reappears in the interior of humanistic geography, as is well illustrated by the 1978 volume edited by Ley and Samuels. In their discussion of the papers on methodological issues (Ley & Samuels 1978: 13-14), the editors deal with this problem and present the range of answers to it found in the volume. It is relatively easy to distinguish the nucleus of the theory and methodology of humanistic geography in this discussion. First, the phenomenological approach to the geographical material, that is, the understanding (*verstehen*) of this material, the recuperaion of and immersion in it on the part of the researcher as a subject; through this interplay between subject and object, deep insight into and understanding of the material can be achieved, and the informed judgment and interpretive capabilities of the researcher exercised. Then, participant observation as the fundamental field work method, allowing for penetration into the subjectivity of the other. Finally, the interest in the in-depth analysis of a limited material, rather than quantitative analysis of a statistical sample. It is interesting also to note that one of the papers argues for an ad hoc, limited and local use of quantitative techniques.

This theoretical and methodological nucleus is not just characteristic of humanistic geography, but is at the core of the phenomenological paradigm. Though the latter overlaps with the structural-semiotic paradigm with regard to the qualitative approach to the research object, the resemblance of these two epistemological paradigms is far from close. Indeed, the semiotic paradigm shares with positivism an analytical, detached and supposedly value-free attitude toward the research object, diametrically opposed to the belief in a dialectical relation between object and subject claimed by phenomenology and historical materialism (Lagopoulos 1986: 220-221).

Neither humanistic geography nor semiotics offer any firm grounds for the constitution of the corpus. This methodological gap is problematic, since the constitution of the corpus is crucial for the credibility of the results, in a manner exactly parallel to the incidences of the sample on statistically-based conclusions. The corpus of humanistic geography and semiotics can correspond to a predefined combination of a subject (or group of similar subjects) of study and an object of study, i.e., it can be non-comparative in character, as can also be the case with the sample. But it can also be concerned with more than one heterogeneous subject or group, in which case it becomes comparative. We can distinguish within this context two possibilities. According to the first possibility, the researcher predefines on empirical grounds the subjects he/she intends to study. According to the second possibility, however, the corpus is selected in view of the discovery of its internal differentiation, a process that implies the a posteriori definition of the subjects. In the two first of the above three cases there can be reason to question the selection of the subject or subjects respectively. As to the last case, things are usually slippery, since the research subjects are localized and defined through the corpus and since there are no firm criteria for the constitution of the corpus. But even when such a corpus happens to be well-formed, the fact remains that subjects are always defined a posteriori through the mediation of the corpus. To the extent that the corpus includes a universe of meaning, the subjects arrived at on this basis are discursive subjects, and can thus be considered "semiotic" subjects.

This latter case does not occur in the current procedure of sociology and analytical behavioral geography. The groups of research subjects in these areas are always predefined, as in the first two cases above, and indeed frequently according to stricter sociological criteria. The sample is constituted after and on the basis of the selection of these groups. We do not have semiotic, but "sociological" subjects. The result is that these subjects are not defined on the basis of their ideological properties, as are the semiotic subjects, but according to criteria referring to their material characteristics, such as social class, gender, or age.

While in the present study we conceptualize the material gathered during field work as a semiotic corpus, we at the same time constructed it as a stratified sample, extracted from predefined types of social subjects. Our decision to make this kind of selection is due to the primacy given by Marxist theory to material factors in the interpretation of social phenomena, including ideology. Our preference, on the other hand, for the analytical as opposed to the phenomenological approach follows, to give only the negative part of the argument, from our discomfort with the phenomenological paradigm. As we have already seen, both phenomenology and historical materialism reject the positivist bias toward absolute objectivity and believe in the relativity of knowledge. But from this common ground the two paradigms depart in opposite directions. In spite of its dialectical starting point, phenomenology gives its attention almost exclusively to the subjective recuperation of reality, leading, for example, in humanistic geography to idiosyncratic studies whose reliability is at best very difficult to assess. We firmly believe that the Marxist concept of a relative, historically bounded objectivity can prevent the continuous subjective intervention of the researcher throughout the research process and thus tends to limit the subjective factor to the basic research premises. The sociohistorical approach of Marxism to the research subject, who is seen as socially constituted, protects one from a priori universalist claims such as those appearing in the phenomenological tradition: for example, Tuan (1977: 5-6), discussing the experience of place, accepts that it is culturally bounded, but emphasizes its supposed transcultural traits which for him correspond to the human condition in general.

In spite of their positivist affiliations, elements of the analytical behavioral approach have been incorporated into our own method when we felt that the incompatibility of the two paradigms could be overcome by the integration and absorbtion of the behaviorist elements within a wider Marxist framework. This integration was facilitated by the fact that recent behavioral research is to some extent distancing itself from classical positivism in a direction in some respects converging with Marxism, as well as phenomenology and semiotics (cf. Golledge & Stimson 1987: 8-9). Likewise, a synthesis was attempted between the analytical operations effected on the sample and the semiotic operations accompanying the corpus, in an attempt to combine the two concepts of sample and corpus.

Our concern for the meaningful constitution of this sample-corpus first led us to familiarize ourselves with its context, historically and geographically; we have already presented these aspects to the reader in a previous chapter. Another important aspect of this context, its sociological configuration, will be presented together with the sociological characteristics of the corpus in Section 3 below. To substantiate the selection of these characteristics as relevant for our study, a review of the current literature on this topic will be helpful.

2. The sociology of environmental conception

There is a vast literature concerning the influence of membership in different social groups on environmental conception, and it will be useful for the reader if we present the main issues involved in it as background to the selection of our own criteria. Evans (1980) presents a concise review of the existing literature and an empirical classification of the studies on spatial conception in real-life situations according to the factor whose impact on spatial conception was studied each time. He defines five factors: class and culture; gender; age; familiarity; and physical components of the environment.

Concerning the first factor, Evans feels that the influence of class and culture on spatial conception is not yet established, and is inclined to transform it into travel mode (cf. Appleyard 1970: 113-114 for differences in sketch map type and extension between bus and automobile travellers) and extent of spatial activity patterns. On the other hand, there are studies inversing this view and arguing, for example, that travel mode depends on class position. Further, a study by Goodchild (1974), while far from definitive, nevertheless points to the existence of class differences in conceptualizing urban space. A similar conclusion is reached by MacKay, Olshovsky and Sentell (1975: 31), who find a relation between the socioeconomic characteristics, as well as the location, of supermarket customers and their cognitive distances. In the same line, but with a much broader scope, Ledrut (1973: 379-382) correlates socioprofessional categories with general ideological models of apprehending the urban. As for the influence of culture, Rapoport (1976: 231) pleads from the standpoint of cognitive anthropology for a comparative, cross-cultural approach to spatial conception. For this author, phenomena such as travel mode and behavioral space are culturally determined.

Evans discusses the material derived from the studies on the influence of gender on spatial conception and concludes that there are few sex differences; even when such differences appear, he feels, they can often be attributed to a factor other than gender, namely the extent of spatial activity patterns again. But this conclusion simply transfers the problem somewhere else, since it is difficult to imagine this as the first causal factor. A more plausible explanation would be, on the contrary, that the activity spaces of males and females differ as a result of their social roles (cf. Brown & Broadway 1981: 316). This is not, however, the view taken by Harris (1978), who, without rejecting social influences, considers the biological factor as fundamental for the differentiation of gender activity patterns. Harris believes that a genetic, more specifically hormonal, factor underlies the differences - favouring the former - between male and female children in respect to their physical activities of exploration of and movement in the environment, as well as strength, dominance, and object manipulation, which he considers as crucial for the development of spatial and geographical activity.

Harris discusses the general issue of gender difference in spatial ability and expresses the view, based on psychological and biological sources, that although this difference is biologically determined, the related biological factors act as predisposing, not obligatory, conditions, while culture may act as a constraint. According to the same author, gender difference in spatial ability would be caused by three biological factors, one of which is the genetic factor mentioned above explaining the greater interest and aptitude of males for physical activity. The crucial factor, however, which is also genetic and hormonal, would amount to gender differences in the lateralization of the cerebral hemispheres and thus differences in the neurological specialization of the latter. Males would show greater cerebral lateralization and right hemisphere specialization, while the functioning of this hemisphere is probably less efficient for females. It is precisely this hemisphere which is responsible for visuospatial functioning and spatial coding. Finally, another factor would follow from language lateralization gender differences and relate to the genetic and neurological predisposition of females to rely more, and earlier, on the left hemisphere and thus be superior in linguistic rather than spatial coding, and to the fact that males use linguistic coding less than females. This difference points, for Harris, to inferior female spatial ability, because language is not usually suitable for spatial analysis. He believes that lateralization during childhood has the effect of starting for girls an intellectual development different from that of boys, marked by the preferential processing of the linguistic code, a difference which also influences adult performance. Gender differences in lateralization are manifested during childhood and persist throughout adulthood, when maturation processes cease to exist. On the whole, the aggregate result of the three biological factors is that males tend to be superior in spatial ability in the ages between 4 and 6, are clearly superior in the ages around 10, and consistently later in adulthood.

Ward, Newcombe and Overton (1986), on their part, find certain gender differences in direction giving, differences which they attribute to stylistic preferences and pragmatic choices rather than to differences in competence and underlying forms of spatial conception. Brown and Broadway (1981: 321-324) conclude that the accuracy of regional cognitive distances is explained, but only to a modest degree, directly by gender, as well as by automobile mobility and spatial interaction (the proportion of settlements visited), and indirectly by location in settlements of different ranks in the settlement network. Also on the matter of gender, Spencer and Weetman (1981: 381) studied the development during a three-month period of the type and degree of structuring of sketch maps elicited from first-year college students arriving in an unfamiliar area. They conclude, among other things, that the type of certain sketch maps is mainly influenced by gender. On the other hand, Spencer and Dixon (1983: 380) made a longitudinal study of the affective reaction of first-year students to the urban elements of their choice from the city where their university was located, and found that the affective relation to the city was not influenced by gender or mobility.

Returning to Evans' classification, another category of studies derives from the consideration of age as the factor influencing the conception of space. There is a strong emphasis in this category of studies on the ontogenesis of spatial conception, i.e., on its developmental nature accompanying the biological growth of the child, and thus it is closely related to the views of Jean Piaget. Given the sociological orientation of the present study, the ontogenetic dimension in the conception of space, interesting as it is, does not constitute part of our research program. The result of such a decision is to limit the selection of research subjects to individuals over twelve years old, the age at which the whole developmental process has come to an end. A further constraint on age seems to follow from Harris' account of the maturation process related to the cerebral hemispheres, which comes to an end in adulthood. The developmental bibliography aside, the material discussed by Evans gives some attention to studies of adolescents and the elderly which seem to reflect psychological rather than sociological interests, given the position of these two age groups at the two extremes of the age spectrum after the end of the developmental process. While the intermediary range of this spectrum is underrepresented in Evans' account, age has been studied as a factor of differentiation in environmental conception. It is used, for example, by Lyons (1983), who studied groups covering an important range of the age spectrum (from 8 to 67). Lyons concludes that age as such, or age in combination with gender or natural residential environment, is a significant factor in explaining differences in landscape preference.

Another factor in Evans' classification is familiarity with the environment recalled. It is clear from his review that an important part of the studies oriented toward the effects of familiarity deal with the issues of development in the type and structuring, accuracy, and characteristics of the elements of, spatial representations, and it is thus directly comparable to the ontogenetic studies. The rest of the studies on familiarity evolve around the existence of differences between spatial representations in respect to similar issues, without emphasis on developmental trends. Thus, Spencer and Weetman in the study mentioned above (1981: 380-383; also Murray & Spencer 1979: 388-389) arrive at the conclusion that, while some development in the type of sketch maps can be detected for more complex environments such as a city, and while there is a diachronic increase in the number of the map elements though without any change in their proportion, the main factors influencing map type are the kind of task demanded of the subjects and their gender.

The current measure of familiarity is the length of residence in an area. With this measure, one of the extreme cases of familiarity is that of the tourist. Thus, Pearce (1977) studies the sketch maps of tourists visiting a city for the first time, in respect to their elements and accuracy, and according to the length of stay (two or six days), as well as the gender and the location of the tourists. Spencer and Weetman (1981: 380-381) observe that a period of eleven weeks was enough for the majority of their subjects to show a type and degree of structuring of their sketch maps similar to those displayed in their home maps. Spencer and Dixon (1983: 379) write that the nucleus of the affective relation of new residents to their city was stabilized after only three weeks. Appleyard (1970) finds some difference in sketch map type for residents living in the city he studied for a period under one year as contrasted to more than one year of residence; the newcomers' maps were more restricted than those of the older residents. Evans hypothesizes that map accuracy improves diachronically and reaches its final state within approximately a year. He believes, however, that familiarity measured in time periods should be complemented by another familiarity measure, namely the extent of the spatial activity patterns.

The last factor discussed by Evans are the physical components of the environment, a criterion which is not sociological in nature. He examines the influence of these components under two headings, environmental structure and landmarks. Environmental structure refers to the street pattern and the overall organization of the city. The former is discussed in respect to its influence on the accuracy of the sketch maps of urban space, and the latter as to the spatial orientation patterns. As for landmarks, in the studies referring to adults the landmarks considered are urban and are examined as to their nature, physical features, use, visibility, and distance. Evans draws conclusions on their influence on recognition, recall, and (re)location accuracy, but he also thinks that environmental cognition is related to the social meaning and symbolism attached to places. In a similar line, Lyons (1983: 489-491) is reluctant to accept the explanations of landscape preference that see such preference as following exclusively from the physical characteristics of the landscape. According to her, the allegedly universal responses to landscapes valuable per se - for example, landscapes of "natural scenic beauty", landscapes with running water, or landscapes of a "park-like" character - are misleading and preferences diverge according to the social background of individuals. We would add that the view deriving landscape preference exclusively from the physical characteristics of the landscape is related to the so-called "realistic" theories of aesthetics, where the quality of being aesthetic is attributed to the object itself and the participation of the subject in the aesthetic experience is ignored, a position which is scarcely convincing.

We should finally mention a factor which may influence, not environmental conception as such but one of its possible and frequently used vehicles, namely the sketch map. This is the graphic ability of the subject, more specifically his or her cartographic skills in expressing spatial conception. Murray and Spencer (1979: 390-391), for example, detect an influence of graphic ability on the richness and on certain characteristics of the elements of sketch maps. Indeed, the interference of graphic ability, as an external factor, with the other factors influencing sketch mapping has been a source of criticism of conclusions based on this mapping technique. The concept of "graphicacy" has been used to cover this graphic ability, but also the ability to perceive and recall the characteristics of spatial situations. Murray and Spencer (1979: 388-389, 391) find a very weak influence of this second factor on the characteristics of sketch maps just mentioned. They find, on the other hand, that both these characteristics and the types of the maps are related to the degree of mobility.

3. The corpus and its sociological characteristics

Let us now pass to the sociological criteria of the present study, which, as we saw, together with the regional criteria led to the definition and stratification of the research subjects. We considered as a fundamental criterion for the definition of our corpus the division of society into classes, the central concept of Marxist social theory. Social classes have for Marxism not only a central sociological role and a specific sociological position, but also a semiotic character. Classes cannot be reduced to socioprofessional or income categories, or to education, as is usually done in geographical studies. Classes are defined by their position in the process of material production and hence by their relation to other classes. In order to define this position, and thus the classes of a specific society, Marxism uses the concept of the social relations of production, which can be broken down into two interrelated concepts, the concept of the social division of labor and that of access to and appropriation, including economic ownership, of the means of production and the social product.[9]

For Marx, the social division of labor implies in capitalism the fragmentation of capital between different owners, the fragmentation between capital and labor, and between different forms of ownership. Thus, the social division of labor implies the division into broad economic branches and their subdivisions, and hence the separation of professions. The first fundamental, broad and developed division of labor is the division into industrial and commercial as opposed to agricultural labor (a division which corresponds for Marx to the first division between intellectual and manual work), whence the separation between city and country. We already referred to this separation, which we used as our major regional criterion for the corpus. The further development of the division of labor leads for Marx to the separation of commercial and industrial labor; later, we might add, to the appearance of the service sector.

While these concepts refer to the material factors defining social classes, classes are not only materially composed. A class can of course exist in relation to another as a class "in itself", but it can also become conscious of itself by developing a social and political ideology. In this case, it is transformed into a class "for itself". This ideology is not something external added on to the material conditions of existence of the class, but it is produced from and as a part of these very conditions. Ideology is the way a class has of conceptualizing the world and rendering it meaningful, and thus covers all processes of semiosis. (The preceding discussion is based on Marx & Engels 1975: 44-45, 50, 64, 67, 88, 94-95, 126; Marx 1976, I: 255-261; Godelier 1973: 24-26; Lefebvre 1971: 351, 355-356; and Gurvitch 1966: 37-38, 44, 88, 97).

These theoretical characteristics of social class led us to the hypothesis that the use of class as a crirterion should lead to significant results in respect to the issue of environmental conception. Next comes the definition of the operational factors, derived from the theoretical framework, which allow the specification of classes, and the adaptation of these factors to the data available for Greek conditions. We consider that a fair specification of classes is possible through the combination of the social division of labor with the degree of appropriation of the means of production and labor. Admittedly this static combination ignores the dynamic interconnections between the two factors, but it is not misleading.

The National Statistical Service of Greece uses seven broad socioprofessional categories, based both on the division into economic sectors and branches and on position within the economic sector. These categories are as follows: scientists, professionals, etc.; directors and higher managerial staff; clerical employees; merchants and salesmen; people employed in services; workers and craftsmen; and people employed in the primary sector (agriculture, husbandry, forestry, fishing, etc.). They are thus founded on the social division of labor, but include some classifications based on the degree of socioeconomic control over labor and the means of production. The Statistical Service also gives three other categories, which can be considered as a fair approximation to the degree of control over the means of production and labor, and which are: employers, self-employed, and salaried workers. We considered it more accurate to divide the first category in two, namely employers with eight employees or more and employers with less than eight employees; this distinction we believe is related to a significant distinction under Greek conditions in types of enterprises and to different class affiliations of the employers. In spite of some redundancy, the combination of the socioprofessional categories with the control variable is not far from the theoretical scheme outlined above.

The use of these categories leads to a matrix with 28 cells (7 x 4). For each cell its place in the class structure was determined on the basis of a combination of theoretical and empirical criteria (for a similar classification, see Kafkalas 1977). Thus, if we leave out the upper class which was for our purposes insignificant, we arrive at the classes and strata in Table 2 below.

Middle class
(a) Upper-middle stratum (UM). This consists almost exclusively of employers with eight employees or more, for all categories of the social division of labor.
(b) Middle-middle stratum (MM). This stratum covers all categories of the control factor with the exception of employers with more than eight employees. In the case of employers with less than eight employees, it includes all socioprofessional categories with the exception of the scientists and professionals (who belong to the upper-middle class by virtue of their education and status), and the workers and craftsmen. In the case of the self-employed and salaried workers, the middle-middle stratum includes only scientists and professionals, and directors and higher managerial staff.
(c) Lower-middle stratum (LM). This mainly consists of the self-employed; salaried workers in the socioprofessional categories of clerical employees, merchants and salesmen; and people employed in services; it also comprises craftsmen who employ less than eight salaried workers, and the self-employed in the primary sector.

Working class (W)
This class includes the workers and craftsmen who are self-employed or salaried workers, as well as the salaried workers of the primary sector and the small independent farmers.

In the present study the two first strata, upper-middle and middle-middle, were grouped together. Thus, our operational social divisions were this mixed category (which for the sake of simplicity we shall refer to as the middle class), the lower-middle stratum (which we shall call the lower middle class), and the working class. The great majority of the cases studied in the first category belong to the middle-middle stratum, since only ten out of 48 individuals (21%) are members of the upper-middle stratum and one individual, included for sampling reasons, belongs to the upper class.

It is evident that many problems remain to be solved after the matrix of social classes and strata has been established and during the allocation of concrete cases to its different cells; for example, what is the social class

Table 2. Statistical categories and class structure for modern Greece.

	Scientists & professionals	Directors & managerial	Clerical workers	Merchants & salesmen	Employed in services	Primary sector	Workers & craftsmen
Employers with 8 or more employees		UM		UM		UM	
Employers with less than 8 employees	UM	MM	MM	MM	MM	MM	LM
Self-employed	MM	MM	LM	LM	LM	LM	W
Salaried employees	MM LM*	MM	LM	LM	LM	W	W

* This category refers to professionals with diplomas from a technical or teachers' college but without university degrees who work as salaried employees.

UM: Upper-middle stratum   MM: Middle-middle stratum   LM: Lower-middle stratum   W: Working class affiliation of a working man or woman differing in social position from his/her spouse, the affiliation of a housewife, or that of a scientist individually involved in commerce (for example, a pharmacist)? As is clear from the above, ideology was not taken into account in the definition of social classes and strata, a fact due primarily to the practical difficulty in finding relevant data. While this is undoubtedly an omission, we feel that it does not have as serious incidences as some Marxist writers would lead us to believe, since primacy is given by Marxist theory to the objective position of classes and strata in the process of material production.

Applying our operational matrix with minor adjustments to the distribution of the active population of Macedonia in 1971 as given by the National Statistical Service of Greece (1977), we see that the proportion of the upper-middle and middle-middle strata amounts to 6.7% of the total active population; that of the lower-middle stratum to 65.5% of which 47.2% is the substratum occupied in the primary sector; and that of the working class to 27.8%. The social structure of Macedonia tends to be more traditional than that of Greek society as a whole, as can be seen from a comparison of the data for this area with those for Greece (8.2%, 61.4% [38.6% for the primary sector], 30.4% respectively). This tendency becomes extreme in the Macedonian rural areas (2.7%, 84.2% [78.9%], 13.1%), where the upper-middle and middle-middle strata are almost nonexistent, the presence of the working class is extremely low, and more than three-fourths of the active population is engaged in more or less traditional agricultural activities. On the other hand, the urban areas of Macedonia, due to the presence of Thessaloniki, present a totally different social composition compared to the rural areas (12.5%, 41.5% [6.1%] 46.0%), a composition comparable to that of the Athens metropolitan area. There is a far higher representation of the upper-middle and middle-middle strata and of the working class, a much lower representation of the lower middle class, and a very low presence of the rural stratum. Finally, the composition of the semi-urban areas (4.4%, 68.9% [54.5%], 26.7%) is much less traditional than that of the rural areas, though still very far from the composition of the urban areas.

Two other factors with a possible influence on environmental conception, which both seem to have a solid sociological foundation and are also prominently represented in the bibliography (as attested by the review in the preceding section) are gender and age. After the intricate theoretical discussion and empirical estimations needed to define social classes, it is something of a relief, in the case of gender, to deal with a social division of a dichotomous nature which can be determined with a high degree of accuracy, at least in current social situations, on the basis of a social experience even below average. As concerns age, we already observed in the previous section that our sociological orientation excludes subjects below twelve years of age in order to avoid the interference of ontogenetic development with the sociological categories. In fact, we limited our study to socially mature individuals and thus excluded subjects below the age of 19, the age corresponding to the end of secondary schooling in Greece (this incidentally allowed us to avoid the issue of the possible interference of maturation processes related to the cerebral hemispheres). A second demarcation divided the age continuum in two groups, the young (up to age 34), who were considered to be in a dynamic and developing phase of their life, and the mature (of 35 and over) who have passed to a more settled phase (for the same dichotomy, see Ledrut 1973: 35). Though this was our a priori categorization, the age groups which resulted a posteriori, and which were also used in the study of environmental conception, were the following: 19-27 (amounting to 22.9% of the sample); 28-34 (27.1%); 35-45 (35.4%); 46-52 (9.0%); and 53-70 (5.6%).

The three sociological factors discussed above, social classs, gender, and age, were considered as crucial for the constitution of the sample. Another, not major but important factor is familiarity, which was treated during the construction of the sample as a constraint, and only afterwards as a variable. We required a high degree of familiarity, and this was secured both directly and indirectly. The fact that an individual was born in Macedonia was considered as indirect familiarity with his settlement and area of residence. Concerning direct familiarity, we saw in the previous section that the type and degree of structuring of sketch maps seem to mature very quickly, in eleven weeks; the nucleus of the affective relation to the city seems to stabilize even quicker, and map accuracy seems to reach a final state within a one-year period. Given that, on the one hand, these conclusions seem to be tentative, and on the other, that we required a long exposure to the settlement of residence and directly or indirectly to its area and the characteristics and problems of the latter, we concluded that a lower threshold of four years of residence is in any case beyond any interference from the processes of maturation of the regional image. Of course it cannot be excluded that there are changes in environmental conception occurring after this maturation process as a function of the length of the period of residence in the area. To check this point, we also used the familiarity factor as a variable, by defining length of residence categories as they occurred a posteriori: 4 to 8 years of residence (8.3% of the sample); 10 to 15 years (11.1%); 16 to 33 years (57.0%); and 34 to 68 years (23.6%).

Several other secondary sociological factors were included in the questionnaire, but only five of these were systematically investigated. The first is the factor of control over labor and the means of production discussed above; according to degree of control, the following five categories were used: people not employed, including housewives; managers and merchants employing eight employees or more; people with income from real estate, together with university-trained professionals, managers, and merchants with less than eight employees; the self-employed of all types (university-trained professionals; office workers; merchants; people in services; farmers; workers and craftsmen); and employees (university and technically trained professionals working as employees; employees in services, offices, and commerce; lower-level managers; farm workers; industrial and construction workers and craftsmen). The representation of these categories in the sample, as it occurred after the fieldwork, is 12.7% for people not employed; 4.2% for higher-level employers; 4.9% for lower-level employers; 26.8% for the self-employed; and 51.4% for the employees.

The second of the secondary factors is the socioprofessional factor, which includes eight categories whose representation in the sample was also defined after the field work (as is the case for all the secondary sociological variables). These categories are people not employed (12.7% of the sample), professionals (16.9%), managers of all levels (11.3%), office workers (9.1%), merchants and salesmen (9.9%), people working in services (7.0%), farmers and farm workers (3.5%), and workers and craftsmen (29.6%).

The third factor is education, which was used according to two categorizations. We give below for each categorization the categories and their representation in the sample. The first is an analytical categorization recognizing five levels of education: completed primary school or less (30.5%); secondary school diploma (26.4%); diploma from a vocational or equivalent school (13.9%); degree from a technical college or teachers' college (5.6%); and university degree (23.6%). The second categorization is more general and includes the first of the above categories (30.5%) as the lowest level of education; the sum of the next two categories (40.3%) as the intermediate level; and the sum of the two last categories (29.2%) as the upper level of education.

Finally, two simple mobility factors were used. The first refers to regional mobility and is measured by the annual number of usual trips outside the settlement, by which we mean a frequency of more than three annual trips to the same place. This factor turned out to include four categories: low mobility of 0 to 24 annual trips (30.5% of the sample); medium low mobility of 27 to 76 trips (26.2%); medium high mobility of 84 to 162 trips (14.9%); and high mobility of 220 to 650 trips (28.4%). The second mobility factor refers to the individual's experience of different geographical settings during his/her lifetime and is measured by the number of places of residence for more than one year, excluding residence during military service in the case of men. This factor also turned out to include four categories, namely individuals who have lived in the same settlement all their lives (26.4% of the sample); individuals who have experienced living in two different settlements (45.1%); persons with an experience of three settlements (18.8%); and finally persons with a broader experience (up to six settlements, 9.7%).

Negatively, two factors which may be considered significant for environmental conception, ethnicity and political convictions, were not taken into account in our study. Ethnicity as a factor influencing environmental conception has preoccupied the relevant literature to some degree, which is not the case with the political factor. There are in Greece ethnic minorities living in relative isolation, but this is no longer the case today in Macedonia, as we saw in the previous chapter. Here, only the very elderly are bearers of lived ethnic memories, while the other generations were to a greater or lesser extent integrated into the general lifestyle - a fact which does not preclude ethnic pride, or more or less folkloric residues. Concerning political convictions, these are an ideological and not a material factor and thus fall outside our general perspective, since our primary concern was to study the influence of material social factors on ideological conceptions.

4. Corpus stratification, questionnaires, and methodology

The four settlements of the present study were selected, as we saw, according to the three regional criteria used: the city-country opposition, the settlement hierarchy, and their geographical position. The sociological criteria, on the other hand, helped us to define the social profiles of the individuals to be selected from each settlement. These profiles result from all possible combinations of the social categories included in the three a priori sociological factors, class, gender, and age; thus, they form the tree structure presented in Figure 4.

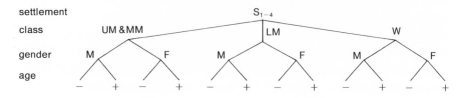

S_{1-4}. The four research settlements   UM & MM: Upper- and middle-middle stratum   LM: Lower-middle stratum   W: Working class   M: Male   F: Female $-$: Up to 34 $+$: 35 and over.

Figure 4. The twelve social profiles included in the corpus.

This tree structure delivers twelve social profiles (3 class categories x 2 gender categories x 2 age groups). In order to achieve a fair sample size for the different social groups composing the corpus, we chose three persons for each profile, a number giving a total of 36 (3 x 12) persons for each settlement and 144 (4 x 36) persons for the four settlements of the study.

The 144 persons were randomly selected in each settlement on the basis of the twelve social profiles, and interviewed there during the summer of 1986 by a group of six researchers including and led by the authors. From this random selection we excluded the professional specialists on spatial matters, in order to avoid as far as possible the intrusion of scientific metalanguages in the elicited spatial discourses. A structured questionnaire was used consisting of 39 questions, the answers to which were taped, transcribed, and then transformed into a total of 528 variables. If we exclude a few operational and sociological variables, the very great majority of these variables are of a semiotic nature and concern ways of apprehending the environment. The questionnaire contained a set of closed questions with multiple-choice answers, but the main emphasis was on the open-ended questions, in answering which the interviewees were continuously encouraged to elaborate further. The time for each interview varied, as can be seen from the length of the texts produced from the transcriptions. The texts were grouped in six categories: short texts, consisting of 513 to 1,320 words (1.5 to 4 typewritten pages) and amounting to 14.6% of all the interviews; limited texts, with 1,381 to 2,045 words (26.4% of the interviews); average texts, with 2,136 to 3,080 words (25%); extensive texts of 3,224 to 3,972 words (14.6%); lengthy texts of 4,054 to 5,277 words (14.6%); and long texts of 5,568 to 9,742 words (4.8%). The time period corresponding to the interview varied from approximately 30 to 90 minutes. Before answering the questionnaire, the interviewees were asked to produce a sketch map of their region on a white sheet of paper 24 by 34.5 cm., without any help from topographical maps.

Four parallel methods were used for the analysis of the material. The main method applied to the linguistic material is based on the structural semantics of A.-J. Greimas (1966); this was used for the textual analysis of the responses to most (eight) of the open-ended questions. For another set (six) of these questions thematic content analysis was used to define thematic categories, which were then integrated with the semantic categories resulting from the semantic analysis. A third method was applied to the pertinent spatial information provided by the regional discourse of the interviewees, which was mapped on topographical maps and then analysed by a combination of semiotic and geographical methods.

As noted above, to the linguistic material gathered were added the sketch maps, which are iconic in nature. Our interest in this material did not result simply from a desire to follow ritually the rules of current geographical research, and - contrary to common attitudes in behavioral geography - we considered the degree of accuracy of these maps in comparison to topographical maps a minor issue. What concerned us was the study of the conceptual structuring of space as revealed through a semiotic system other than language. Given that each system of communication imposes certain constraints on what can be expressed and how, it is reasonable to assume that the use of two different systems for the understanding of the same issue has the advantage of offering complementary data. This kind of approach to sketch maps has the additional advantage of rendering irrelevant the criticism of this mapping method that it cannot avoid the interference of graphic ability, since spatial structures are revealed even in the crudest sketch. The sketch maps were analysed in relation to the interests of behavioral geography and with its analytical instruments, but the goal of analysing the spatial structures they embodied obliged us to develop a semiotic approach for the syntactic and semantic analysis of sketch maps as well.[10]

On the whole, these four methods together represent a synthesis of semantic, geographical, and sociological approaches within the framework of a social semiotics. Their use resulted in both qualitative and quantitative data. These data were statistically analysed, with the help of a computer, for frequency counts and crosstabulations. Crosstabulations were performed on the basis of two major groups of programs, the sociosemiotic and the semiotic group.

The frequency counts refer to fourteen different programs: the whole sample; the cities; the countryside; each of the four settlements of the study; each of the three class groupings defined; men; women; the young; and the mature. The sociosemiotic group contains nineteen different programs which all share the characteristic that each time one sociological variable, whether regional or purely sociological, is crosstabulated with a wide standard set of selected semiotic variables. The sociological variables are, in the first instance, the main factors considered able to influence environmental conception, namely the city-country opposition (city: Thessaloniki and Veria / country: Axioupoli and Ormylia), the settlement hierarchy (Thessaloniki / Veria / Ormylia), social class (middle class / lower middle class / working class), gender (male / female), and age (both 34 or less / 35 or over and the five analytical age groups discussed above). A second group of sociological variables correspond to the combination of the city-country opposition and the settlement hierarchy with class, gender, and age; the first combination gives, for example, a variable with six categories: urban middle class, urban lower middle class, urban working class, rural middle class, rural lower middle class, and rural working class. A final group of sociological variables refers to the secondary sociological factors of familiarity (the four categories presented above); socioeconomic control (four categories); socioprofessional integration (eight categories); education (two different categorizations with three and five categories respectively); regional mobility (four categories); and regional experience (four categories).

The sociosemiotic programs allow us to study the relation of a semiotic attribute to the categories of one of the above sociological variables. In the case of a significant relation, it can be argued that the shaping of the attribute is a function of the differences between categories. On the other hand, the semiotic programs give data of a different, and complementary, nature. In these programs, only semiotic variables within a certain category of the sociological variables are crosstabulated with each other. The categories used are the whole sample (which may be considered as structurally representative of modern Greece); the cities; the countryside; the three social classes; men; women; the young; and the mature. Thus, the nineteen sociosemiotic programs show the determination of an *individual* semiotic variable by a sociological variable, while the ten semiotic programs show the *relation* of two semiotic variables in the context of one and the same category of a sociological variable.

Part III. The social construction and evaluation of space

Yet this experience of profane space still includes values that to some extent recall the nonhomogeneity peculiar to the religious experience of space. There are, for example, privileged places, qualitatively different from all others.... Even for the most frankly nonreligious man, all these places still retain an exceptional, a unique quality; they are the "holy places" of his private universe, as if it were in such spots that he had received the revelation of a reality *other* than that in which he participates through his ordinary daily life.

Mircea Eliade, *The sacred and the profane*

The image is always emotion, whether it impels us towards or away from an object, whether it terrorizes or charms.... Mythical or not, symbolic expressions imply the existential relations which support our relations with reality.... The city is a symbol and there is a symbolization of the city.... Like all "visions", the Image of the city is a "cultural product".... The situation of man confronting the city ... introduces ideology, and, more simply, the consciousness of things.

Raymond Ledrut, "The images of the city"

Chapter 6. The conceptual construction of regional space

1. Subjective settlement and involvement region

The foundation of our project is the concept of the *involvement region*, a concept which corresponds to what a social group or an individual considers to be the regional space intimately connected to the settlement of residence. The existence of such a meaningful unit was initially a working hypothesis, since there is no analytical bibliographical precedent for it in the sphere of subjectivist spatial studies. Environmental psychology has focused on simpler spatial units, empirically more manageable by the individual and thus apparently closer to the aims of psychology; that major part of geography preoccupied with environmental conception and experience, which is the natural candidate for the discovery of such a unit, is strongly oriented toward urban space; and spatial semiotics is oriented toward architecture and secondarily urban space, regional space being, with minimal exceptions, totally neglected (the only elaborated study of regional space is Pellegrino et al. 1983). The involvement region as a meaningful spatial unit is accompanied, as we shall see, by other equally subjective meaningful units, conceived of as larger or smaller than the involvement region.

A conscious attempt was made to minimize the interference of the researcher's views with the conceptual world of the research subjects. The fundamental research strategy was to impose no constraint on the interviewee other than that of expressing his/her views on a set of predefined issues and their modalities; thus, there was no attempt of any sort which aimed at orienting the interviewees as to the content of their responses. This is a fairly common goal in subjectivist spatial studies, though it is by no means the general practice. Indeed, there are many exceptions. The semantic differential studies use a predefined list of semantic scales, and this is also frequently the case with the constructs of the repertory grid test, in spite of Kelly's original emphasis on individual characteristics. This impoverishment, and probably in certain cases distortion, of the conceptual world may present a narrow advantage for technical operations, but it is hardly surprising that it delivers less significant results, in

spite of some optimistic views arguing for the efficiency of carefully selected constructs (cf. Adams-Webber 1979: 20-21, 23-27).

In addition to this imposition on a subject of a relatively foreign semantic universe, another practice is the relatively arbitrary (in respect to
the subject) use on the part of the researcher of a set of predefined signs,
a habit which seems to be related to experimental psychology and which
can also serve simplistic planning purposes. Two examples will illustrate
this practice. After criticizing the use of predefined semantic elements for
the study of spatial conception, Desbarats (1976: 453-456) adopts from
psycholinguistics the method of free word association. But while the author thus gets rid of one source of bias, she on the other hand provides
the subjects with the written names of the ten demographically largest
metropolitan areas in the U.S. and asks them to define the semantic similarities betweeen these areas and the dimensions underlying the similarities. In this way, the evaluations are made in function of signs which are
not due to the selection of the research subject him/herself. As a result, a
relatively significant semantic universe is located, but not *the* significant
one, given that the universe discovered is up to a point encyclopaedic for
the subject and bears an unknown relation to his/her really significant
universe, and - worse - the semantic elements that it includes, although
they may partly correspond to the subject's spontaneous selection, may
be distorted by the fact that they are taken out of context.

Our second example is borrowed from a study by Golledge (1978) on
Columbus, Ohio. In order to define in this study the "primary nodes" of
the city, the author used existing bibliography, personal experience, and
the responses of students, faculty, and others. After various simple technical operations, 24 places were located which are "most likely to be best
known in Columbus", the theoretical rationale behind this selection being
that "there are a limited number of places which have a high probability
of being defined as primary nodes by large subsets of the population"
(Golledge 1978: 81-86). We find here the behaviorist imposition of the
attributes of the physical environment on the subjective conception of
space and the neutralizing notion of the public image, both of which we
noted in Lynch, but also the additional problem of the use of a priori selected signs. Of course it could be argued that in this specific instance the
interest was oriented toward the conceptual distances between places and
the comparison of the spatial structures obtained with the topographical
map. But we should insist on the exact meaning of such an exercise, integrated with an experimental logic: while it provides us with some

technical information on the relations between conceptual and certain actual distances, it by no means delivers the corresponding relations for the unconstrained spatial conception.

Contrary to the cases discussed above, the involvement region, its attributes, and the other spatial units related to it were all selected in our study by the research subjects themselves. Thus, it was not considered that the researchers' own views, grounded to a greater or lesser degree in scientific data, as to which region should be considered as intimately connected to a research settlement, should provide any stable reference point. The consequent relativity of the involvement region drew with it the relativity of the conception of the settlement. In order, however, to secure that communication was established with the research subjects and that they were addressing themselves to our subject matter, we applied the constraint that the criterion of pertinence for the subjective definition of the region and the settlement should be that they could be logically considered as a region and a settlement, in spite of possible divergence from professional definitions. On the basis of this criterion we accepted that the subjective settlement could be considered as a settlement as long as it refers to a named spatial unit which was historically relatively autonomous, even if today it is integrated with other units, forming with them what is professionally defined as a single spatial unit.

The subjective settlement is generally a stable concept, but there were eight among the 144 subjects, seven from the Thessaloniki metropolitan area and one in the smaller city of Veria, who alternated between two or even three conceptualizations of the settlement. In the case of the *dual conceptualization* of the settlement, the subject alternates between conceiving as settlement his/her place of residence and the whole or the central part of the larger urban unit which has absorbed this once independent place; in the case of a *triple conceptualization*, the settlement is conceived of alternately as the place of residence, as the central part, and as the whole of the city. The triple conception of the settlement seems to provide us with the clue to the operations underlying the semiotic process of multiple conceptualization of the settlement. The relation between the place-of-residence-as-settlement and the city-as-settlement seems to be a syntagmatic relation of a part to the whole with which it is integrated, and which thus becomes its natural extension. On the other hand, the relation between the central-part-of-the-city-as-settlement and the city-as-settlement seems to be a relation following the principle of *pars pro toto*, the metonymic use of the part to signify the whole, the central city being considered as the city par excellence. While, then, we have here this *pars pro toto* operation, in the previous case there appears a kind of inverse *totum pro parti* metonymic operation. The two operations are not absolutely symmetrical, however, in that in the first case the two signs are alternative and interchangeable, while in the second only alternative. The instability of the conception of the settlement for 5.5% of our subjects should be attributed, not to some deterministic imprint of the external environment, but to their personal relations and choices in respect to a geographically, historically, and socially complex environment. Witness to this conclusion is the fact that for the remaining subjects the subjective settlement is fixed.

There was only one case in which the spatial unit provided by the interviewee as a settlement was considered as falling outside the reasonable and socially acceptable definition of the settlement. The subjective settlement in this case fluctuated between the house of the interviewee with the road in front of it and a small part of a neighborhood of Thessaloniki which was also considered as the involvement region. For eight subjects, only one of whom was a country dweller, the involvement region coincided exactly or approximately with the settlement, and this was considered as an acceptable extreme case of the involvement region. We should note that in all these extreme cases of regions, as well as in almost half of the extreme cases of settlements, the subjective region is scientifically only a settlement.

Certainly, the involvement region is not an everyday notion, and the interviewees did not dispose of any ready-made answers but had to fall back on a creative approach to their environment. The question is if this semiotic work delivers a fiction constructed by the interviewee and thought to satisfy the interviewer - which, again, would not be devoid of meaning - or if it is an elaborated exteriorization of an at least potentially preexisting notion. We believe that four reasons support the second view.

First, the five places the interviewees were asked to name on the limits of their involvement region were always places that they had visited. We can conclude from this fact that the involvement region is principally constructed on the basis of personal acquaintance and not of indirect information, being thus a part of personal experience. Second, the clarity of the conception of this region was assessed, on the basis of the interviewee's reaction to the first question concerning the drawing of the components of the region. Of the whole sample, 84% of the interviewees appeared to have a clear conception of their involvement region. But even in the cases of an initial hesitation, the interviewees showed no difficulty in elaborating on the region, nor did they present any special kind of inconsistencies. Next, the very great majority of the interviewees were personally involved in the discussion during the interview, because, as became apparent, they were interested in the issues discussed and eager to speak about their region. This atmosphere of most interviews convinced us that the interview did not represent for our subjects a neutral and boring exercise, but set in motion a regional discourse integrated into their regional ideology. Finally, during the analysis of the data collected in the field work we felt it necessary to recontact an important part (about 60%) of our subjects in order to confirm certain points and/or elucidate certain others. What struck us was their detailed memory of the first interview, their persistence on the same points, and the coherence of the new data in respect to the existing interview text.

These reactions, in our opinion, show not only that the involvement region is a genuine subjective notion, but also, and in relation to that, that it is built upon personal experiences, that it has a clear, substantial and coherent content, that it is an integral part of ideology, and that it is stable at least over a certain time period. We hope that the data presented in this book will be able to substantiate and elaborate our thesis.

The involvement region, as we shall see, is not necessarily an identity region, i.e., an experiential entity positively evaluated. There were a few cases when sentimental reactions extended the regions of our subjects into remote places of personal attachment which were unrelated to it geographically. This construction resulted from a misunderstanding through which the region of the settlement was replaced for the subject by a different region of association with the self. Since we had decided to concentrate on the involvement region, which is closer to a geographical logic, we in these cases reminded the interviewees of the form of the original question. Thus we did not intervene in the construction of the region, but simply clarified the question. The interviewees had no difficulty in acknowledging the issue and delimiting their region from the same perspective as that used spontaneously by the other interviewees.

2. Involvement region and social practices

The involvement regions corresponding to a settlement vary greatly in their spatial extension, i.e., the size the involvement regions would have if actualized in geographical reality, a size that can be estimated by the mapping of their signs onto a topographical map. The involvement regions of the four research settlements belong to an extremely broad field of sizes, ranging from 1 to 2,496 km^2. In Figures 5-8 the general signs of the involvement regions have been mapped onto topographical maps, and the frequency of mentions for each area of the involvement regions is shown for each of the research settlements.

For the city of Veria and the villages of Ormylia and Axioupoli there is a consensual nucleus for all the involvement regions (100% frequency of mentions) roughly corresponding to the settlements themselves. For Thessaloniki, this common nucleus appears with a somewhat lower frequency (94%) and refers to the part of the city closely connected to the central business district. For Thessaloniki, Veria, and Axioupoli, the most frequently mentioned roads are connected to the focal area which we named nucleus, while in Ormylia the settlement, to which the nucleus of the involvement regions corresponds, is at a distance from the highway, the main conceptual road. Around the focal areas, the frequency of mentions decreases outwards in a roughly concentric manner, a pattern indicating that the probability of an area being included in the involvement region bears some relation to its distance from the focal area of that region. This is, as we shall see, an overgeneralized observation, referring as it does to partial and relative phenomena and based on the superficial concept of distance, an observation which is not able to account as such for the formation of the general social involvement region and which should be modified. But even as it stands it leads us far away from Lynch's view that legibility is founded on the physical attributes of the environment.

Let us start with the example of Thessaloniki (Figure 5). The area immediately south of the central business district, about 4.5 km long, has a frequency of mentions (86%) belonging to the second highest category of frequencies, and the same is true for the following area (83%) of about 3.0 km, while the frequencies of the next two littoral areas (8% and 5% respectively) fall to the next to the last (8%-14%) and last (3%-6%) frequency categories. The category 8%-14% starts at a distance of about 7.5 km from the central business district, and the last category at about 13.5 km. To the west of the central business district, the neighboring area (length about 3 km) has a frequency (53%) belonging to the third frequency category, while its neighbor to the west (length about 1.5 km) has a frequency (45%) of the next category and the two following littoral

Figure 5. Frequency of mentions of the areas of the involvement regions in Thessaloniki.

areas have frequencies (17% and 14% respectively) of the sixth (17%-25%) and the next to the last (8%-14%) categories; the frequency of the area just beyond the last area (6%) falls in the last category. The distance from the central business district to the beginning of the last two areas is about 6 km. Finally, north of the central business district the categories follow the sequence 53%-72%, 42%-50%, 17%-25%, and 8%-14% (and the frequencies the sequence 72%, 50%, 25%, and 11%), the second category beginning at a distance of approximately 1 km from the central business district and the last at 4.5 km.

What we see from these data is that the succession of frequencies in different spatial directions is quite different, and the same holds for that of distances. In three different directions of the city the areas having about the same low probability of being selected (category 8%-14%) are 4.5, 6.0, and 7.5 km distant from the focal area to which corresponds the consensual nucleus of the involvement regions; to the west, the area corresponding to the frequency category 3%-6% is at a distance of 6.0 km, while the similar area to the south is 13.5 km distant from the focal area; the areas bordering on the focal area in the above three directions have different probabilities of being mentioned; the same is true for the areas of low frequency at the same distance of 6.0 km to the west of the focal area. We should note that the area to the west of the focal area is the port area, after which the city does not extend far, while the two areas to the south of it include the extension of the fashionable central residential area of the city, a fashionable residential suburb and the main peripheral recreation center. In addition there appears a small increase in the frequency of the easternmost area (category 28%-39%), which is at least 9.0 km distant from the central business district and is an important mountainous recreation center.

Thus, the involvement regions of Thessaloniki show us that the concentric pattern is combined with a sectoral one, since the frequencies of the areas surrounding the focal areas of the regions are different. We find the same phenomenon in Veria (Figure 6). There is a marked sectoral differentiation around the focal area, and this differentiation follows a specific logic: the two sectors "in front" of the city have the highest frequencies (61% and 59%). The expression "in front" tries to convey the feeling of the inhabitants - and of visitors - that the city, from its plateau in the foothills of Mount Vermion, overlooks the fields and orchards in the plains below, where most of the settlements surrounding the city are located. Veria's commercial center leads down to the focus-point of this facade of the city, the "balcony".

The frequencies of the five lateral sectors on both sides of the front sectors decrease (39%, 39%, 50%, 47%, and 44%), and finally there is a new and abrupt decrease in the frequencies of the four back sectors (14%, 14%, 17%, and 11%). The areas further to the west of these last sectors belong to Mount Vermion and all have frequencies in the last frequency category. Contrary to these low frequencies, the frequencies of the roads leading to the important town of Naoussa and to Seli, a ski resort of national attraction, are much higher (31%).

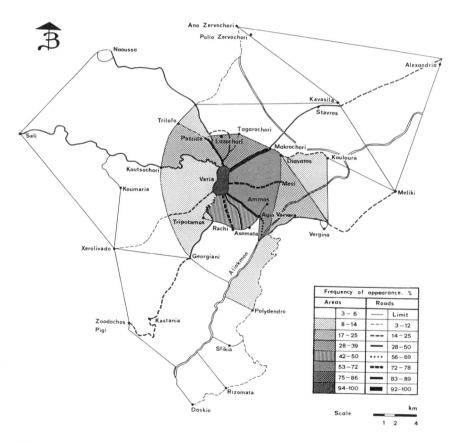

Figure 6. Frequency of mentions of the areas of the involvement regions in Veria.

In Axioupoli also (Figure 7), most of the westernmost areas on Mount Païkon form a region with frequencies in the last category. But this is not the case for the rest of the mountainous area, as witnessed by the areas to the north of Axioupoli which have frequencies of the category 17-25% in spite of the fact that their remotest villages are much more distant than the beginning of the western region. These northern areas belong to the commercial catch area of Axioupoli.

The major river of the region of Veria, the Aliakmon, does not play any particular role in delimiting areas with different frequencies. But in Ormylia (Figure 8), the stream between Ormylia and Vatopedi acts as a demarcation between two areas with quite different frequencies (83% and 67% respectively); at the same time, it separates the lands of two different social groups, "locals" and "refugees". We find a similar case in Axioupoli. All the areas on the west side of the river Axios, the side of the settlement, have much higher frequencies than the areas on the east side; only the frequencies of the two northernmost areas on the two sides of the river tend to coincide (17% and 14% respectively). All these areas fall within the catch area of Axioupoli, while the other side of the river is within the sphere of influence of Polykastro, the rival twin settlement of Axioupoli.

These observations give us some clues as to the factors underlying the formation of the involvement region, the roughly concentric pattern, and the sectoral pattern. Imposing features of the natural environment, such as rivers and mountains, are not semantized as such, but to the extent that they are related to social and individual practices; they acquire their meaning through these practices, which are equivalent to the "spatial activities" of the psychologists and geographers. Even if the physical presence of certain natural geographical features acted historically as constraints on these practices, what is significant for the individual semantization process is their integration into social practices, and for the general semantization process it is their degree of socialization. The observation that all places given as limits of the involvement regions are known from personal experience is in line with this conclusion. The double relativity in the concentric decrease of the frequencies of mentions of the different areas, relativity as to the gradation both of distances and of frequencies, also points in the same direction. Indeed, in Greece, the focal area is the common link of individual and group practices, which have a certain tendency to become less common the further we go from the focal area. It is this pattern of social practices which seems to underlie the roughly concentric pattern of frequencies. Geographical distance is a physical constraint whose apparent role depends on the social context, and which is thus socialized, like the physical environment, and relativized. This social context accounts for the spatial pattern of social practices, and its concentric and sectoral aspects. The semiotic consequences of the "friction of distance" is a misleading appearance.

It is not easy to reduce the pattern of practices simply to the pattern of the main regional trips made by the interviewees. After mapping the most frequented places (visited more than three times a year) inside and outside the involvement region, and the consequent axes of movement of the subjects, we compared the latter to the main axes of each involvement region as they emerged from the questionnaire. We used as a index of the degree of identity between these two kinds of axes the ratio of the "common" axes to the total number of axes (i.e., the sum of the number of the common axes and the rest of the axes). In half the cases, the degree of identity between the two patterns does not exceed 33% and in about two-thirds of the cases it does not exceed 50%; only in one-third of the cases is the identity 60% or higher, cases of evident identity (80% or more) accounting for 13% of the interviewees.

If we disaggregate the data and examine the separate social groups, we find that they show differing tendencies concerning this relationship between regional trips and the main axes of the involvement region. The sociosemiotic crosstabulation programs indicate that some of the groups show little tendency towards coincidence of the two patterns (60% or higher). Such is the case, for instance, with the urban lower middle and middle classes, city women, the inhabitants of Thessaloniki, and individuals with up to medium high regional mobility (up to 162 trips annually). Other groups, on the other hand, show an important tendency toward coincidence. The highest percentage of coincidence is found among Ormylia men and youth (more than 75% in the coincidence category); these two groups are followed by the rural working and lower middle classes and the Ormylia women (from 50% to 57%) and by individuals with high regional mobility (220-650 trips annually, 58%).

A general opposition between urban and rural groups emerges from these data. The axes of regional movement seem to be a major factor in explaining the geometry of the involvement region in the countryside, something that does not hold for the cities. It could be that the decrease in importance of this factor for the cities is due to the technical reason

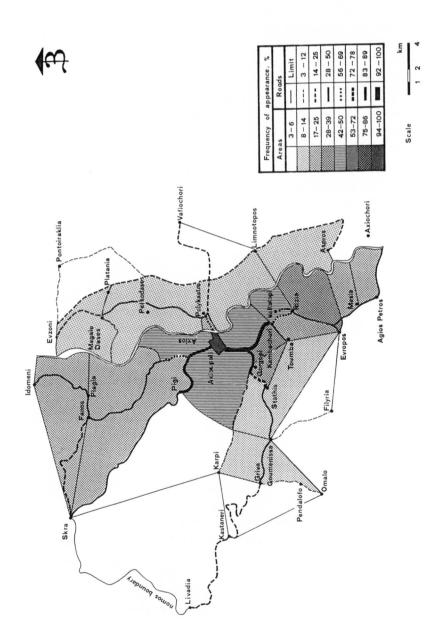

Figure 7. Frequency of mentions of the areas of the involvement regions in Axioupoli.

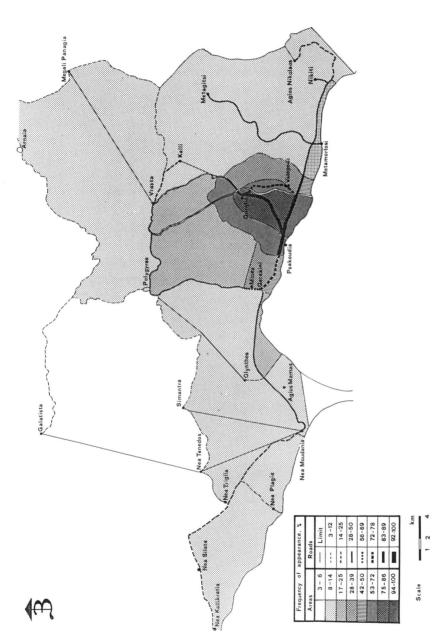

Figure 8. Frequency of mentions of the areas of the involvement regions in Ormylia.

that the subjects were asked to mention their regional trips, not their trips within the city. But the fact remains that, even for the rural groups, the formation of the involvement region for a substantial part of the subjects cannot be accounted for by the factor of regional trips alone. Thus, regional trips are an important factor in explaining the formation and the geometry of the involvement region, but other social practices need to be taken into account.

That practices underlie the semantization of an environmental unit should thus not be understood narrowly. In addition to regional trips, other kinds of practices seem to be crucial to the semantization process. Also, together with conceptualizing the environment in which some practice occurs, an individual may have the occasion to notice a wider environment through visual contact. Remote visual contact seems able to complete or delimit a part of the involvement region, or to articulate certain parts of it. It is manifestly absurd to consider that people have visited each and every place within their involvement region, and visual contact offers a possibility for enrichment of directly known places. We could also hypothesize on solid grounds that another source of enrichment is indirect information through social intercourse and the mass media. But a complete knowledge of the involvement region should be excluded. The regional environment is semantized as precise signs with a multitude of voids between them.

A look at Figures 5-8 gives the impression that the sizes of the involvement regions, while radically different within each settlement, are comparable between settlements, as is the distribution of sizes. We can further investigate this impression with Table 3. Veria and Axioupoli have the greater percentages of small regions belonging to the size category of from 1 to 13 km^2 (31% and 36% respectively), and Thessaloniki and Ormylia the lower percentages (8% and 14%), while in respect to the class of smaller regions in general, Veria and Ormylia have higher and almost equal percentages (75% and 78%), and Thessaloniki and Axioupoli lower and almost equal percentages (66% and 64%). All settlements are equal in respect to the category of very large regions (about 6%), but Thessaloniki and Axioupoli predominate in the class of larger regions in general (34% and 36%).

These data show that the impression from the maps is accurate. There is no differentiation of the size categories of the involvement region as a function of the size and importance of the settlement, nor is there any significant differentiation in the distribution of the size categories, for example, any positive relation between cities and larger regions, as might be anticipated. Maybe the smaller regions are rarer for the inhabitants of the Thessaloniki metropolitan area, but they are also very limited for the inhabitants of the village of Ormylia; and if they are well represented in the village of Axioupoli, the city of Veria is not far behind. On the other hand, if Veria and Ormylia are alike in respect to the smaller regions, the same is true for Thessaloniki and Axioupoli as to the larger regions. The independence of the distribution of sizes of the involvement regions from the ranks of the settlements in the settlement network is corroborated by the two sociosemiotic programs of the settlement hierarchy and the city-country opposition; neither the settlement hierarchy Thessaloniki/Veria/Ormylia nor the grouping Thessaloniki-and-Veria/Ormylia-and-Axioupoli correlate with the sizes of the involvement regions (x^2 test not significant at the 0.05 level of significance). Thus, there is generally a total separation of the involvement regions from the planner's concept of standard catch areas, a conclusion which shows the significance of our initial decision not to interfere with our subjects' judgments on how to define their region.

Table 3. Distribution of the size categories of the involvement regions for the four research settlements.

Size category/class	Surface of the involvement region, km²	Thessa-loniki %	Veria %	Ormylia %	Axioupoli %
Small regions	1 — 13	8	31	14	36
Medium regions	16 — 76	58	44	64	28
Smaller regions S_1		66	75	78	64
Large regions	78 — 352	28	19	17	30
Very large regions	428 — 2,496	6	6	5	6
Larger regions S_2		34	25	22	36

We can enrich these data with the maximum length of the involvement regions. The regions are of two types. They may have a continuous contour, or combine such a contour with projecting elements. In the second case, they were considered as having two maximum "diameters", one corresponding to the projecting elements and one to the contours, while in the first case we considered only the maximum diameter of the contour. Table 4 shows how the categories of the lengths of diameters are distributed for the four settlements. There are three groups of columns. The first group refers to the maximum crow-flight diameter of all the involvement regions, and the second to the maximum diameter of the contour, in both cases irrespective of the type of the involvement region. The third group reflects the actual (not conceptual) typical travel radii of the interviewees.

Concerning the diameter of the total region, the distributions for Thessaloniki and Axioupoli do not differ much; Ormylia shows a very high concentration (64%) in the category of 10-23 km, while in the category of 34-99 km Veria comes first (28%) and Thessaloniki last (14%). The city-country program shows no significant correlation between the settlement rank and this diameter. This is not the case with the settlement hierarchy program. Here, Thessaloniki is closely connected to the category of 24-33 km; the greatest share of Ormylia is in the category of 10-23 km; Veria is markedly represented in the categories of 34-99 km and especially 0-9 km, and its greatest share is in the category of 10-23 km (0.05 level of significance). The comparison between the two tables shows that the presence of Axioupoli in the city-country program, missing from the hierarchy program, causes a notable change in the relation between rural settlements and categories, and thus that the two rural settlements have very different characteristics. This comparison also corroborates the conclusion from the hierarchy program that the significant relations between settlements and categories are not strictly regulated by settlement rank.

For the diameter of the contour, Thessaloniki clearly comes first in the two higher categories taken together (67%) and in the category of 11-27 km (59%), but not in the highest category (8%), in which Axioupoli comes first (19%). Veria and Ormylia are comparable for the two higher categories, but we can see from the two lower categories that Ormylia has a clear tendency towards the category of 3-10 km. For this diameter too, while the city-country program delivers no significant results, the settlement hierarchy program does. As in the previous case, Thessaloniki is closely connected to the second highest category of diameters (11-27 km) and Ormylia to the third (3-10 km). Veria dominates in the lowest category, which also comes first for that city, but also in the highest, together with Ormylia (0.01 level of significance). Again, the comparison between the two tables shows the relative independence of the categories

Table 4. Distribution of the maximum diameters of the involvement regions of the settlements.

Max. diameter of total involvement region, %					Max. diameter of contour, %					Typical max. travel radius, %				
km	Thes.	Ver.	Orm.	Axi.	km	Thes.	Ver.	Orm.	Axi.	km	Thes.	Ver.	Orm.	Axi.
0– 9	6	19	3	17	0– 2	8	33	8	28	0– 9	19	30	25	31
10–23	36	36	64	25	3–10	25	25	58	22	12–48	22	18	28	19
24–33	44	17	14	41	11–27	59	28	20	31	52–76	45	52	44	50
34–99	14	28	19	17	30–99	8	14	14	19	80–99	14	0	3	0

from the settlement rank and their relation to idiosyncrasies, mainly of Veria. Further investigation in Section 4 of this chapter will complete this observation.

To conclude, the settlement rank and the geometric dimensions of the involvement region do not in general move in the same direction, even if some significant relations between them can be found. If finally we turn to the third group of columns and compare it for each settlement with the previous two groups, we find no systematic relation. The typical maximum travel radius is not able to account for the diameters of the involvement regions and replace the general pattern of practices, just as the main regional trips were unable to account for the semiotic axes of the involvement region.

3. Regional spaces, regional structures, and the city-country opposition

The involvement region generally surrounds the settlement, resulting in a kind of concentric construction of space. Does this form of construction proceed further and is the concentric pattern the only structure we impose upon regional space? In order to investigate this problem, we asked the interviewees if there is a region which is larger than the involvement region and to which the latter belongs, and, then, an even greater region to which their settlement belongs. In Table 5 we present the results in respect to these two questions for the sum of the four settlements, i.e., for the whole sample, which reflects Greek society in general. We combined these results with the distribution of the size categories of the involvement regions for reasons of comparison.

80% of the Greeks have the notion of a second, wider region surrounding the involvement region. There is some overlapping in size between these two types of regions. 94% of the involvement regions are of a size that does not exceed the category of the smallest second regions; only 8% of the second regions are in this smallest category, and only 5% of the involvement regions are above this category. More than 41% of the second regions (categories 1, 2, and 3) are of the same scale with the class of larger involvement regions, and 31% exceed this scale. On the other hand, only 63% of the Greeks have the notion of a third, widest region. Almost all of the third regions are larger than 94% of the involvement regions, while 14% are of the same scale. The size categories

Table 5. Size categories of the involvement, wider, and widest regions.

Surface of involvement region, km²	%	Size of wider (2nd) region	%	Size of widest (3rd) region	%
1. 1–13	21				3
2. 16–76	49			1. settlement & surroundings to scale of eparchia (38–488 km²)	
S₁₊₂	70				
3. 78–352	24	1. settlement to settlement & surroundings (116–488 km²)	8		
		2. scale of eparchia (350–2,400 km²)	13	S₁	3
		S₁₊₂	21	2. scale of nomos	11
4. 428–2,496	5	3. scale of nomos (1,100–4,400 km²)	28	S₁₊₂	14
S₃₊₄	29	S₁₊₂₊₃	49	3. scale of 2–6 nomoi	7
		4. scale of 2–7 nomoi	10	4. scale of Macedonia (9–13 nomoi)	16
		5. scale of Macedonia or Northern Greece (9–16 nomoi)	15	5. scale of Northern Greece (16 nomoi)	11
		S₅	15	S₄₊₅	27
		6. scale of Greece	6	6. scale of Greece	11
		S₆	6	7. scale of Europe	4
				S₆₊₇	15
none	1	none	10	none	23
		polarization	9	polarization	10
		don't know	1	don't know	4

of the second and third regions are quite similar, with the main difference that the third regions can reach the scale of Europe, even if very
rarely (4%). If we compare the second and the third regions, we observe
that, while up to the scale of the nomos the former show a far higher
concentration (49% vs. 14% for the third regions), the opposite is generally true beyond it. We can conclude from these data that though there
are no fixed limits between the three regions and their sizes can inter-
penetrate, there is a clear tendency of the involvement regions toward the
smaller spatial scales and of the third regions toward the larger, and that
the third regions tend toward larger scales than the second regions.

We saw that about half of the second regions are comparable in scale
with the involvement regions, not exceeding the scale of the nomos. This
percentage decreases, according to the city-country program, to 42% for
the cities and increases to 57% for the countryside. Another important
differentiation between city and countryside appears in the category of
Macedonia and Northern Greece, where the whole sample's percentage
of 15% levels out a striking difference between city (26%) and countryside (3%). The tendency of the city dwellers toward larger second regions is very strong (0.01 level of significance), and the same holds if we
abstract people who do not have the notion of a second region. This tendency is due primarily to the mature age group in the cities, as is evident
in the corresponding crosstabulation (0.01 level of significance) for the
city-country/age program, though both city age groups have larger second regions that their country equivalents. The distribution of frequencies for the four settlements shows that the two rural settlements are
somewhat comparable, and that there is a tendency for Thessalonikeans
to have larger regions. The hierarchy program (when some categories are
grouped together) corroborates this observation (0.05 level of significance), but also shows that Veria comes first in respect to the category of
the largest second region (Greece).

If we now compare the third regions of the cities and the countryside,
we see that the countryside comes first in respect to the regions comparable to the involvement regions (categories 1 and 2, 4% vs. 1% and
18% vs. 4%), while it is behind in all the other categories of the third
regions, mainly in the two categories of the larger regions (3% vs. 2)%
and 1% vs. 5%). The correlation between cities and larger third regions
is very strong (0.01) and remains strong if we do not take into account
individuals who do not conceive of a third region. The distribution of
frequencies for the four settlements shows a phenomenon parallel to the

previous one: the rural settlements are similar in the distribution of the sizes of the regions, and the tendency of the cities toward larger regions is mainly due to Thessaloniki. In this case also the tendency is significant, as revealed by the hierarchy program with grouped categories (0.05).

There is an important difference between the involvement regions and the wider and widest regions. The distribution of the main geometric dimensions of the involvement region (surface, diameters) is not generally influenced by the rank of the settlements; on the contrary, the distribution of the sizes of the two other regions is to a certain degree related to the settlement hierarchy, and very strongly to the city-country opposition. It seems that the involvement regions of individuals relate more to themselves, to their practices and thoughts, than to the size of their settlement, and this reference to the self corroborates the personal nature of the involvement region which we observed in the first section of this chapter. But then, the interference of the settlement class, and even precise settlement hierarchy, with the sizes of the other regions points to the influence on subjective judgments of the objective nature of the settlements.

We can get some insight into this influence by again inspecting the crosstabulations of the city-country program for the second and third regions. In the countryside, the great majority of second regions is, as we saw, of the scale of the nomos or smaller, the smaller regions representing about half of the cases; only a small percentage (14%) exceeds this scale. The distribution of sizes is quite different in the cities, where 42% of the regions correspond to the first case, with a restricted percentage among them referring to smaller regions (about 13%), but as many as 45% of the regions go beyond the scale of the nomos. We should remember here that the nomos is the fundamental administrative unit in Greece, since only in recent years has there been an attempt to reinforce the position of local authorities. Thessaloniki and Veria are the capitals of their respective nomoi and as such include all the central administrative services. The distribution of the sizes of the regions for the rural settlements usually shows a moderate estimation of sizes, corresponding to part or all of the nomos; only a limited percentage exceeds this scale. In general, the involvement region is related to a wider spatial unit enclosed within the nomos or to the spatial unit of the nomos itself. This is not at all the case in the cities, where the first pattern has a limited occurrence, and the two patterns together appear equally frequently with a pattern of an involvement region related to a unit much larger than the nomos. These different tendencies correspond rather well to the actual role of the rural and urban settlements, since the function of the rural settlement is limited within the boundaries of the nomos, while the urban settlement is also integrated into a larger region, with the nomos as the common link between the two cases. However, the fact that this tendency is very significant but not the absolute rule, and the variation in the selected size of the regions, show that different points of view on regional reality can be adopted by the interviewees.

If we now pass to the third regions, we observe that in the countryside an important part of the third regions is of the scale of the nomos or smaller (22%), important in comparison both to the rest of the regions (31%) and to the corresponding regions in the cities (5%). In the cities there is a strong predominance of regions larger than the nomos (68%), and a substantial part of these (25%) is of the scale of Greece or even Europe; the presence of these regions in the countryside is negligible (4%). The much more moderate estimations of the sizes of the third regions by the inhabitants of the rural settlements, and the important presence of (and thus enclosure within) the nomos show, as was the case for the second regions, a certain adaptation to regional reality.

The involvement regions, then, tend to be self-referential, *ego-centered*, but the wider and widest regions tend to be focused on the settlement as a depersonalized point of reference. While the involvement region tends to be a subjective creation, the two other regions are the result of the subjective evaluation of an external reality. In this respect, as well as by their size, these regions tend to be more abstract, and to rely on the official administrative organization of regional space. Indicative of this degree of abstraction is the response of one of our interviewees to the question about the widest region: "... That'd be the state. Let's say we don't locate it geographically? Yes, that's the state." These oppositions between the involvement region and the two other regions give us a clue as to the way the latter are constructed semiotically. As we saw earlier the involvement region is constructed mainly on personal practices and secondarily on indirect information. The opposite seems to hold for the second and third regions, which seem to rely heavily on indirect information and social stereotypes.

There is another series of data corroborating the abstract character of these regions, as well as the correlation between the city-country opposition and the sizes of the regions. Let us come back to Table 5. There are three categories at the bottom of the table, "none", "polarization" and "don't know". If the last category is self-explanatory, the other two deserve some explanation. 10% of the interviewees did not have any notion of a second region. A second region simply did not exist for them. This percentage is about the same for the city and the countryside. The lack of a third region is even more pronounced (23%); it is similar for Veria and the two rural settlements (about one-fourth of the interviewees) and shows the lowest values for Thessaloniki (14%). Polarization, on the other hand, means that the interviewee again does not have the notion of a region, but nevertheless conceptualizes an external space: this space does not bear a concentric relation to the previous one, but is the point (i.e., the urban center) by which the previous space is polarized. The frequency of this pattern is for the whole sample and the second region similar to that of no region at all (9%), but here there is an important divergence between city and countryside (4% vs. 14%); the by far greater frequencies appear in Axioupoli (22%). The frequency of this pattern does not differ for the third region (10%), and there is again a marked difference between city and countryside (4% vs. 17%). The sum of the three categories of non-conceptualization of a wider region shows that one-fifth of the interviewees do not conceive of a second region; this is the case for a more limited part of the city dwellers (13%) but for more than one-fourth of the country dwellers (29%). As for the third region, more than one-third of the interviewees (37%) do not recognize one; this number decreases to about one-fourth for the cities (27%) and increases to as much as almost half of the inhabitants of the countryside (47%).

We can conclude on the basis of these figures that the phenomenon of the lack of a larger region has a notable presence, and is clearly accentuated from city to countryside and from second to third region. We can explain these tendencies as the combined result of the class of the settlement and the abstract character of the second and third regions. They indicate that the construction of these regions presupposes a conceptual syntheses on an abstract level, which becomes all the more demanding when the settlement has a low profile and the region to be constructed is larger; the third region is more abstract than the second. Some people are not able to overcome these difficulties and either remain enclosed in a more immediate region, or have recourse to an external, concrete and limited spatial unit which is easier to conceptualize (polarization).

For the nonprofessional conceptualization of regional space, the settlement or residence with the involvement region surrounding it constitute a structure less complex than a concentric structure, a center with its periphery, which is also in current use among professional geographers and planners as well as in administration. Most frequently this structure is seen as a part of a wider concentric structure including also the second and third regions. We all know that the concentric pattern is the universal means used by geographers and planners for the construction of regional space according to the consecutive spheres of influence of settlements and regions. This construction, then, seems to follow the logic of regional influence. We shall consider the structure composed by at least two consecutive regions as a *concentric* conceptualization of regional space.

However, this is not the only structure used to conceive of regional space. The planner's construction allows for the polarization of a region by a spatial unit external to it, and this structure resembles the conceptual patterns falling into the category of polarization. There is of course a difference between the two constructions, since the professional view, more complete and sophisticated, integrates the region within a larger region created by the pole, thus semantizing the area between the region and the pole; the layman's view leaves this area largely blank. We shall say, in this case, that our interviewees have a *polarized* conception of regional space. It is interesting to note that this structure is almost nonexistent for the inhabitants of Thessaloniki, a fact relating to the way they conceive of the role of their settlement in regional space. We shall encounter a similar issue in Section 5 on settlement hierarchy. The final structure we located is not found in the professional literature. It is a structure beyond the limits of which, for an unspecified distance, there is nothing really meaningful, a structure corresponding to a feeling of isolation or autonomy. This is the *insular* conception of regional space.

These fundamental structures can be combined in all possible ways, as can be seen by the relation between the involvement region, the wider environment, and the widest environment. The relation between the involvement region and the wider environment leads, as we saw, to the three fundamental structures presented above. These structures in turn are related in such a way to the widest environment that they are recreated again on a larger scale. Thus, while the combination of the involvement region with the wider region follows the concentric structure, the new combination of this structure with the widest environment gives three possible structures. The first is the *multiple concentric structure,* in which the initial concentric structure is extended so as to cover all the area up to the limits of the widest region; in this case, regional space is uniformly constructed according to one and the same principle (59% of all the interviewees, Figure 9a). Next comes the *polarized structure with a concentric element,* which follows from the insertion of the initial structure into a larger polarized structure (6%, Figure 9b). The third structure is the *insular structure with a concentric element,* and here the initial structure floats within a kind of void of meaning (13%, Figure 9c). Thus, the relation of the concentric structure to its environment in this case can be seen, from the point of view of the researcher, as a logical opposition between an environment and the negation of an environment, between meaning and non-meaning; the subject, on the other hand, consciously focuses on meaningful space, separating it from meaningless space through an unconscious application of this opposition.

The second structure delivered by the relation between the involvement region and the wider region is the polarized structure. It is similar to the insular structure in that, with the exception of the pole, the area surrounding the involvement region is in the shadows of meaning. The relation of this structure to the widest region leads again to three possible structures. The first is the *concentric structure with a polarized element* (2%, Figure 9d), which represents a reversal of the second structure above. Then we have the *doubly polarized structure,* which represents a polarization in the second degree, since the involvement region is polarized by two consecutive poles; in this case, the two poles are hierarchically related (3%, Figure 9e). The third structure, the *insular structure with a polarized element,* is similar to the third structure above in that it is also composed of a structured interior and a meaningless external environment (4%, Figure 9f).

The combination between involvement region and wider environment can finally give the insular structure, this structure with the meaningless periphery. In spite of that fact, it may be integrated with meaningful entities. This is the case with the *concentric structure with an insular element,* in which meaning reemerges in relation to the spatial entity incorporating the insular structure, thus semantizing a posteriori and implicitly the blank area: what did not exist before is now part of the widest region (2%, Figure 9g). A similar semantization occurs with the *polarized structure with an insular element,* but here the environment exterior to the involvement region is only a pole (1%, Figure 9h). This structure resembles the insular structure with a polarized element, but while the two structures are comparable in their final state, they differ in the dynamics

of their construction, according to which the appearance of the meaningful pole depends on different spatial scales. Finally, there is one case in
which the insular structure remains accompanied by a meaningless periphery, the *fully insular structure* (6%, Figure 9i). Here, no matter how
far we go beyond the initial insula - within the limits set by the proposed
scales, of course - we do not find any real trace of meaning.

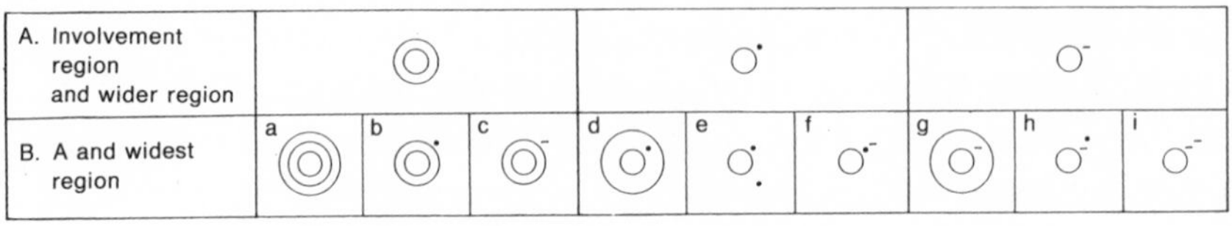

A. Involvement region and wider region	◎			Ȯ			Ō		
B. A and widest region	a ◎	b ◎̇	c ◎̄	d Ȯ	e Ọ	f Ō	g ◎	h Ȯ	i Ō

Figure 9. Conceptual structures of regional space.

Figure 9 shows the nine ways of conceptual structuring of the consecutive regional spaces. These structures are in reality more complex if we
take into account that the involvement region generally includes the settlement or the residence as a center. In addition, we can imagine that the
nine structures can be extended, as further scales are proposed to the
subjects, so as to cover all conceivable geographical space, and that this
extension will perhaps enrich the possible combinations of the fundamental structures by adding certain variants. However that may be, the nine
structures by no means exhaust the whole range of structures through
which we apprehend regional space, as we shall argue in Chapter 11
(Sections 3 and 5), where we study the structures of the involvement regions revealed by the sketch maps.

4. Social groups and the geometry of the regions

The ego-centered character of the involvement region was deduced from
the independence of its geometry in respect to settlement rank. But is this
subjectivity due to individual caprices or is it determined by any sociological factors? An answer to this question is possible through the examination of the sociosemiotic programs. Concerning the surface of the involvement region, no sociosemiotic program delivered any significant
sociological determination, at least for the analytical categories of Table
3. This is not the case for the two classes of size (smaller and larger re-

gions). There is a continuous increase in the presence of larger regions as we pass from the working class (17%) to the lower middle class (27%) to the middle class (44%), while in the class of larger regions the three social classes are represented in a similarly increasing order (19%, 31%, and 50% respectively; level of significance 0.05). An equally significant result (0.05) is given in connection to education. The least educated people, who attended at most primary school, present a greater tendency toward smaller regions, and the most educated, with higher education or a university degree, a tendency toward larger regions, while those who finished secondary school or a vocational or equivalent school hold an intermediate position. However, when these five categories of education are treated separately, the difference between those who attended at most primary school and secondary school almost vanishes, while people with higher education (but not a university degree) show a clear tendency toward smaller regions. In this case then, there is no one-to-one relation of the size of the involvement region with the degree of education, but only a kind of general tendency.

The sociosemiotic programs also deliver significant results for the diameter of the contour of the involvement region, but not for the total diameter. The only exceptions concerning total diameter relate to the hierarchy program, already discussed, and the analytical age groups. The latter show a general tendency toward increase of the diameter as a function of age, except for the age group 42-52 which is characterized by an emphasis on the smallest category of diameters. Most of the significant results, however, concern the diameter of the contour, not the total diameter. If we group the four categories of the diameters of the contour into two classes (0-10 km and 11-99 km), we observe a polarization between the urban working class, which tends toward larger diameters, and the rural working class, which is characterized by smaller diameters, a polarization which is repeated in reverse, though less intensely, for the rural middle class, with larger diameters as compared to the urban; the urban and rural lower middle classes use these categories of diameters almost equally. The hierarchy/class program, on the other hand, shows that the metropolitan working class and mainly the lower middle class, and provincial urban workers, tend toward larger diameters; the provincial lower middle and middle classes, the rural lower middle class, and mainly the rural working class, have smaller diamaters; and the middle class in both the metropolis and the countryside is divided equally between the two classes of diameters (0.05 level of significance). We can observe, if we compare the two programs, that urban (both metropolitan and provincial) workers show a significant tendency toward larger diameters, contrary to rural workers; the equal use of the two sizes of diameters by the urban lower middle classes conceals a very important divergence between Thessaloniki, with a very strong emphasis on larger diameters, and Veria; the emphasis in the hierarchy/class program of the rural lower middle class on smaller diameters is moderated in the city-country program, manifestly due to the presence of Axioupoli in the latter; and the increase of the participation of the larger diameters among the rural middle class if we compare the city-country/class with the hierarchy/class program is again due to Axioupoli.

These data are sufficient to demonstrate, even at this early stage of our discussion, that conceptions of the region are not mechanistically created by external realities, such as the incidences of the rank of the settlements, but are regulated by sociological factors. As we can see, even the different geometrical characteristics corresponding to one and the same notion, the involvement region, are not subject to the same sociological determinations, and are not influenced by then in comparable, or necessarily in expected, ways. We could hypothesize that the middle class is more mobile and has more opportunities to extend its direct spatial knowledge, and such an hypothesis would seem to be corroborated by the relation of the size of the involvement region with social classes. We could also think that the extension of spatial knowledge has some relation to education, and this seems to be the case, but there is the "irregularity" of people with higher education who tend to have smaller regions. Finally, every plausible a priori hypothesis is upset when the diameters of the contour of the involvement region are taken into account. Here, social classes in general are not able to explain the fluctuation of the diameter, and we must turn to the distribution of social classes in the different ranks of the settlement network. And this is not all, since the regularities found between surfaces and classes are radically transformed when we pass to classes in space and their diameters. If we combine these observations with those on the diameters of the involvement region in Section 2 of this chapter, we conclude that the geometric dimensions of the involvement region are subject to different types of determination. They follow determination by sets including either general sociological categories alone (as in the case of surfaces), or general and idiosyncratic sociological categories (total diameter, diameter of the contour). One and the same dimension can follow simultaneously different sociological paths and regularities.

The diameter of the contour of the involvement region is also influenced by other factors.[11] While gender as such does not influence the diameter, the regional distribution of genders does. City women show a tendency toward larger diameters (11-27 km), contrary to country women, who tend toward diameters not exceeding 10 km, and to city men who cover almost equally all the range from 0 to 27 km; this tendency of the city women is formed mainly in the metropolis. Also, the regional distribution of ages, but not age alone and only in respect to the hierarchy program, gives some significant results. Urban age groups differ markedly in the diameters they use. The metropolitan youth - where we mean by this term people up to the age of 34 - shows a close relation to the category of diameters from 11 to 27 km; the metropolitan adults - people over 35 - are mainly related to this category, but also to the immediately lower category (3-10 km); the provincial urban youth relate almost equally to these two categories and to the category of the smallest diameters (0-2 km); and the provincial urban adults are mainly related to the latter. In the countryside, youth tends toward the category of 3-10 km, and adults toward this category and also the largest diameters (30-99 km).

In conclusion, the diameter of the contour of the involvement region is determined by the combined influence of the *regional distribution* of classes, genders, and ages. The urban working class, the metropolitan lower middle class, metropolitan women and to some extent men, the urban youth and rural adults, and to some extent urban adults and provincial youth, all conceive of involvement regions whose real-world diameters tend to be large. The sociological determination of the diameter does not follow any simple regularity and is much more complex than any a priori working hypothesis.

This influence of the geographical distribution of the general social groups - classes, genders, ages - on the diameter of the contour of the involvement region leads to another interesting issue. Do these groups exert their influence as unified social groups but adjusted to the specificities of their spatial location, or are they fragmented into socially differentiated groups, sociogeographical groups, created on a territorial basis by the combined effect of social group and its location in a specific site? We can attempt an answer to this question by postulating what kind of reaction as to diameter size should be expected if the group adopted a unified perspective on this subject. We think that two possible attitudes can be attributed to a group. The one attitude would be a general ideological tendency to incline toward a certain kind of diameter; the other the tendency to adapt to actual local conditions and chose diameters in accordance to them, which is a realistic attitude. Any divergence, then, of a subgroup from these two attitudes should be considered as indicating the formation of an original sociogeographical grouping.

Turning now to our data, let us recall that we saw in Section 2 of this chapter that the diameter is influenced by the settlement hierarchy, not in the expected manner, but in a way pointing to the existence of some idiosyncratic elements. Our new data above suggest that within Thessaloniki, and to a somewhat lesser extent in Ormylia, the different social groups show similar tendencies which, in spite of their opposite directions, meet in the realistic recognition of the actual importance of the two settlements. The inhabitants of these two settlements have a common approach, of a more general character, and thus other autonomous sociogeographical subgroupings are not constituted. In Veria, we can locate as a cause of its idiosyncratic nature the existence of different groups with a certain social autonomy: men, adults, and probably the middle class, who all tend toward the category of the smallest diameters. Also, a specificity of country men should be attributed to the influence of the men in Axioupoli, given the non-specificity of men in Ormylia. We observe on the basis of these data the constitution of *autonomous social groupings,* in respect to the phenomenon studied, of a mixed social and geographical character; in this case, the general social groups are maybe not levelled out, but neither do they survive intact. Thus, the determination of a conceptual phenomenon by hybrid social groups can be due, either to their autonomous character, or to the geographical distribution of a general group that retains its character in spite of spatial fragmentation.

On the basis of the observation that the geometry of the involvement region is relatively independent from settlement rank, we concluded earlier that this region tends to be a subjective creation. We can now see that "subjective" does not mean in this case individual, but is to be understood as contrasted to the direct reflection of external reality. We have to do, in this case, not with the individual but with *collective subjectivities* interpreting space, although there are, of course, cases in which a semiotic attitude is not subject to any type of sociological determination and its variation can only be explained by individual idiosyncrasies.

In the previous section, we studied the regional influences on the size of the wider and widest regions. Other sociological influences are very poor in the first case, and nonexistent in the second. There is only one significant relation of the size of the wider region with a sociological factor, which in this case is the distribution of age groups according to the city-country opposition. The urban adults relate mainly to the class of sizes comprising regions at the scale of the nomos and 2-7 nomoi (categories 3 and 4, Table 5), and to the category of Macedonia and Northern Greece; the urban youth, while also related to the same categories, have a greater inclination toward the former class; rural adults and youth both tend toward this same class and that of smaller sizes below the nomos, but the young incline to the lowest class. These tendencies accord with the tendencies of the inhabitants of more important settlements to have larger regions and show that the size of these regions can be explained, in addition to settlement importance, as the combined effect of age groups with the city-country opposition.

We also used the semiotic programs to study the significant relations between geometric elements of the conceptual regions. The same relations between semiotic variables were tested for all ten semiotic programs, and the general (whole sample), city, and country programs proved to be the richest in significant relations. For the whole sample, the total diameter of the involvement region is very significantly related (0.01) to its surface, and the same holds for the other programs with the exception of the working and lower middle classes, and women; on the other hand, in no program is there any relation between the diameter of the contour and the total diameter or the surface. The significant relation is the expected tendency for smaller total diameters to be associated with smaller surfaces and larger diameters with larger surfaces. But although there is a kind of linear regularity uniting surface and total diameter of the involvement region, here as in all previous cases we can only speak of a systematic tendency, in the context of which overlappings between categories are the rule.

Also, for the whole sample, both the surface and the diameter relate to another semiotic variable, the richness of the signs of the sketch map. Richness measures the number of signs that appear on the sketch maps[12] (see Chapter 11, Section 1); it was thought to be a significant attribute of the way a subject conceives of space when he/she expresses him/herself through an iconic semiotic system. There are three classes of sketch maps in respect to richness: (a) very poor maps, comprising only 4-10 signs;

(b) maps of medium richness, with 12-16 signs; and (c) rich maps, 18-58 signs. The small-size involvement regions are markedly associated with classes (a) and (b), and mainly with (a); medium regions almost equally with the two classes, and less with class (c); large regions mainly with (c), but also (b); and very large regions mainly with (c) (0.01). The crosstabulation of the total diameter with richness gives comparable results.

The surface of the involvement region also relates to three other semiotic attributes, two accompanying the sketch maps and the third characterizing the interviewees' oral discourse on space. The first attribute is the typology of the maps as road, zonal, and mixed maps (see Chapter 11, Sections 1 and 2). We observe a systematic tendency for the surface of the involvement region to increase with the change in the manner of its iconic representation, from road to zonal to mixed maps. More specifically, four-fifths of the road maps correspond to small and medium-size regions; almost 90% of the zonal maps correspond to medium and large regions, and one-third to large regions; four-fifths of the mixed maps correspond to medium and large regions, and the rest to very large regions. Among the maps corresponding to small regions, 90% are road maps, and over half of the maps of medium regions are also road maps; road and zonal maps are used almost equally for large regions; and among the maps of very large regions, the proportions of road, zonal, and mixed maps are 1:2:4. It should be noted that this general and very significant tendency of the three map patterns to be associated with regions of different sizes does not exclude the possibility of a pattern being used with regions of any size - with the exception of the mixed maps that are never used for small regions.

The second attribute of the sketch maps which is significantly related to the surface of the involvement region is the degree of sophistication of the map, according to which maps were classified as elementary or simplistic; simple; and fairly sophisticated or sophisticated (see Chapter 11, Section 2). The relation between surface and iconic sophistication follows the previous regularity. Small regions tend to be related mainly to elementary/simplistic and to simple maps, and on the other extreme very large regions relate especially to fairly sophisticated/sophisticated maps; the tendencies of the two intermediate categories of size integrate into this general pattern.

The third semiotic attribute refers to another kind of richness, namely the total number of different codes used by the subjects in their regional discourse (on the concept of code, see Chapter 9 on regional discourse, Section 1). There are five categories of discursive richness: 1-11 codes, 12-14, 15-20, and 21-26 codes. Once more a similar tendency reappears, since larger regions are significantly associated with greater richness of discourse, although the category of 15-20 codes predominates by about two-thirds or more for all sizes of regions, with the exception of the very large regions.

These data reveal a tight nuclear structure composed of the relations between surfaces, total diameters, and iconic richness, but not including the diameter of the contour of the involvement region. The three variables of this structure show a tendency to move in the same direction when we examine the whole sample; the same structure is also apparent in the countryside and for adults. For example, the actual extension of regional space that is semantized by a subject tends to be linearly related to the number of places included therein that are also semantized when the subject is using an iconic system of expression. The increase, then, of the knowledge of extended spatial areas, such as the involvement region, is related, at least for the strategic view of the area, to an extensive, not intensive, phenomenon, in the sense that it is not limited to detailed in-depth elaborations, but associated with a broadening of spatial horizons.

We also found three other significant crosstabulations (for the whole sample) which evolve around this nuclear structure and relate to surfaces. These show a kind of linear relation between surfaces on the one hand, and discursive richness and map pattern and sophistication on the other. The use of a greater number of codes, the shift from road to zonal to mixed maps, and the greater sophistication of the sketch maps go together with an increase in the surface of the involvement region. On this basis we can extend our conclusion above. The increase in the surface of the involvement region is parallel to an increase in knowledge of the region, and is accompanied by an increase in the points of view (number of codes) adopted on it and in the sophistication of its graphic representation (not to be confused with accuracy), as well as by a change in map pattern.

In the first part of this section we analysed the sociological factors influencing surfaces and diameters. The semiotic study of the tendencies evident in the whole sample draws our attention to the fact that these geometrical dimensions correlate, not only with sociological factors, but also with each other and with other semiotic attributes. Two further conclusions may be drawn on the basis of the semiotic correlations. First, they indicate that graphic ability, as shown by the sophistication of the maps, is influenced by a factor independent of graphic skill, namely spatial extension (see for further discussion Chapter 11, Section 4). Second, there is since Lynch's *The image of the city* an ongoing discussion on the influence of familiarity with an environment on map pattern and the kind of elements used for spatial orientation. Lynch (1960: 49) suggests that increase in familiarity leads to a shift of emphasis from districts to roads to landmarks, and Appleyard's (1970: 112) conclusions point in a similar direction, but the opposite view has also been argued (see Evans 1980: 272-273). Our data here cannot address this issue directly, since they do not include the familiarity factor, but they nevertheless touch upon a comparable issue. They show that road maps relate to smaller regions and zonal maps to larger regions, while the combination of the two patterns tends to correspond to the largest regions. On the other hand, if we correlate the patterns of the maps with their richness (0.01) there is a partial reversal of the above sequence: increase in map richness is now followed by a shift from the zonal to the road to the mixed pattern. Of these two correlations, the second one is manifestly closer to the familiarity issue presented above; instead of familiarity, which implies a certain degree of spatial knowledge, we use the factor of spatial knowledge directly. So while the results from the more indirect variable, the surface of the involvement region, are partly aligned with Lynch's suggestion, those from map richness point in the opposite direction, though not of course in an absolute sense. What remains constant in both cases is that increased spatial horizons encourage the drawing of mixed maps.

The countryside program delivers almost the same relations with the whole sample and shows comparable regularities. But there is also one important divergence. The linear relation between surfaces and total diameter is partially upset, because, among smaller regions, the small regions tend to have larger diameters than the medium regions. More specifically, smaller regions have diameters mainly belonging to the categories of 10-23 km and 24-33 km, and show only a limited tendency toward smaller diameters, while the diameters of the medium regions are strongly associated with the category of 10-23 km and much less with the other categories, mainly those preceding and following this category (0.01). This difference points to the fact that the regularities ruling the relation between two variables of a semiotic program referring to one social group are not necessarily replicated for another program and another social group. Social groups can have their own specific character.

This can also be seen in the case of city inhabitants. For city inhabitants, the relation of the total diameter to the surface of the involvement region is the only significant relation (0.01) of the surface with the standard set of variables used. In this case, small regions are mainly associated with diameters from 0 to 9 km, but they also show tendencies to have diameters belonging to the categories of 10-23 km and even 34-99 km. Medium regions have diameters mainly in the category of 10-23 km, and then of 24-33 km. In the case of the cities, then, the break of strict linearity is due to a greater emphasis on the largest diameters. If we now compare the three programs, we observe that the relative break of the linear regularity in the countryside program in respect to small regions is counterbalanced in the general program by the greater emphasis by city inhabitants with medium regions on larger diameters, and especially by those with small regions on smaller diameters.

The general program is related to the city or the countryside program as whole to half. The association of the larger regions with the larger diameters is replicated in all three programs, a fact which points to the existence of a general characteristic, found as such in both the cities and the countryside; this is also the case with the association of the medium regions with the diameters from 10 to 33 km. Of course, there is no mirror reflection of the general program, a fact pointing to the existence of local variations on a national characteristic. The difference in the way small regions are related to the diameters is due to the specific characters of the cities and the countryside. In this case, the general program reflects only a mathematical mean, which is of course characteristic of it, but does not correspond to any phenomenon created specifically by the whole sample as representative of a sociological group.

In most of the other programs also there is a relation between surface and diameter. The middle class, men (0.01), and adults (0.01) give significant results and corroborate the national character of most of the partial aspects of the relation. It seems, then, that there are general characteristics, which are integrated into a kind of national regularity; but they have a weaker impact on the lower middle class and the working class and on women, where they do not lead to significant results. This regularity is thus supported by the different social groups, although they may create their own variations and even impose their own specific character.

The only two variables not presented so far, among the standard set used in studying the geometry of the involvement region and the scales of regional space, are the scales of the wider and the widest region. The scales of these two regions do not give any significant correlation with the variables of the standard set, but only with each other. The independence of these two regions from the size of the involvement region means that there is no systematic relation between the size of the latter and the scale of the former, that is, that the choice of the involvement region does not influence the selection of the second and third regions. The relative abstractness of these regions detaches them from a dependence on the immediacy of the involvement region.

On the other hand, the correlation between the two regions is very significant in general and runs throughout the semiotic programs, with the exception of the working and lower middle class and the countryside programs.[13] The significant regularities of the seven programs, including the general program, are very similar, and the same holds if we compare the remaining three programs with each other and with the other programs. Second regions smaller that the nomos are associated mainly with third regions from one to six nomoi; when the second regions have a scale of one to seven nomoi, the third regions tend to be of the scale of Macedonia or Northern Greece (9-16 nomoi); and second regions of this latter scale are accompanied mainly by third regions at least equalling Greece, while even larger second regions are exclusively associated with this kind of third regions.

Thus, the relation between regions seems to be another *national regularity,* expressed or reshaped by all the social groups. In this case, the different aspects of this regularity, i.e., the partial distributions which correspond to it, appear as different variants which tend to follow a kind of common pattern and can be considered as reflecting an established national characteristic. But as we saw, it may also happen that certain distributions diverge from this pattern to a greater or lesser degree. Under these circumstances we may speak of a *national tendency,* more or less pronounced according to the case.[14]

5. Settlement hierarchy and the nature of judgment

In the section on regional structures we analysed the geometrical nature of regional spaces and the conceptual relations between them. We shall now extend the study of these spaces, first by presenting a geometrical feature of the third region that we called "orientation of the wider region". This orientation was estimated without the explicit participation of the interviewees, and tries to catch the ways in which the extension of the third region is geometrically related to the home settlement and to the main pole of Northern Greece, Thessaloniki. On the other hand, among the fundamental structures of regional space figures the polarized structure, which appeared spontaneously, without any suggestion on the part of the interviewers. The semiotics of regional polarization was further examined with the help of two variables, which followed from two questions inviting the interviewees to pronounce themselves on matters of polarization. One question involved a general judgment concerning the centrality or periphericity of the home settlement, and the other an analytical description of its hierarchical position in the settlement network, through the enumeration of the settlements polarized by and polarizing the home settlement. The second question invited the subjects to think of a large region including Thessaloniki, and express their opinion as to for what places their settlement is a center, and on which cities and towns it is dependent.

In the case of orientation around the home settlement and Thessaloniki, the third region is oriented around Thessaloniki, that is, develops in a balanced manner around that city, for 55% of the inhabitants of Thessaloniki, while for the rest it develops without any general reference to the city. This percentage increases in Veria (strong orientation around the city, 71%; weak orientation toward the city, 4%) and attains its highest degree in the two rural settlements (more than 90%). The three social classes studied, and the two age groups and genders, are quite comparable as to strong orientation (around 75%). We should not confuse orientation in respect to the settlement with conceptual polarization, because many times this orientation follows automatically from the use of administrative units; also polarization is possible without orientation.

If we pass from orientation in respect to the settlement to orientation as to Thessaloniki, we observe that the third regions of an important part of the inhabitants of Veria (42%), Ormylia (50%), and Axioupoli (44%) are strongly oriented around Thessaloniki; on the contrary, the regions of more than one-third of the inhabitants of Veria, and about half of those of the two rural settlements, are constructed without any special reference to Thessaloniki, because they have either a local or a general character, or (rarely) appear to be haphazard.

It is possible to add a semantic content to these geometrical observations, on the basis of the crosstabulation (0.01) between orientation and position in the settlement hierarchy for the whole sample. Less than half

(44%) of the inhabitants of Thessaloniki with a third region strongly oriented around the city promote their city to the rank of main regional pole, the rest feeling a great dependence on Athens. The inhabitants of the other settlements which have regions strongly oriented around Thessaloniki almost unanimously consider the latter as a regional pole (93%); this is also the case for the inhabitants with regions weakly oriented toward Thessaloniki (100%). But the regions in these three settlements which are local and constituted independently of Thessaloniki are, nevertheless, felt to be strongly polarized by the latter when the subjects are asked directly (89%). As to the regions with a general character, 59% of them are felt to be polarized by Thessaloniki. Thus, the geometric feature of orientation of the third region and the sense or feeling of polarization on the part of the subjects do not generally correspond, though there may be cases of a close fit. The located pattern of the polarization of the third region by an external pole extends our typology of regional structures in the direction of polarized structures.

Thessaloniki, then, is considered by the inhabitants of Northern Greece as a dominant regional pole. We can follow the different aspects of this observation. Thessaloniki is considered as a pole by all its inhabitants and this fact is in line with what we observed in Section 3, namely that they do not have recourse to the polarized structure. The situation is not very different in the other settlements, since we find the same conception of Thessaloniki among more than 90% of the inhabitants of Veria and Axioupoli, and four-fifths of the inhabitants of Ormylia.

Thessaloniki, however, is not the only regional pole in Northern Greece, though it is the most important one, and other poles were also proposed, among which the rest of the research settlements have a prominent position. The description by the interviewees of the hierarchies in the settlement network and its main poles leads to certain conceptual patterns of regional organization, which are shown in Figure 10.

There are twelve types of settlement network, which can be grouped into four classes if the patterns of hierarchical structuring of the network are taken into account. From each class it is possible to deduce the rank attributed to the home settlement. Thus, in the first class the home settlement is considered as the *exclusive* pole of a large region (explicitly including Thessaloniki, according to the formulation of the question) and any dependence of the home settlement on other poles is ideologically excluded. In the second class, the home settlement does not cease to be considered as a strong pole, but there is a wider view of the functioning of the settlement network, in the context of which a *stronger external pole or poles* appear. In the case of one pole this can be Thessaloniki or some other settlement, and when more that one pole is involved these can be Thessaloniki or another settlement, alone or with one or more further settlements.[15] The integration of the home settlement into a wider settlement network also characterizes the two other classes, which however differ from the previous class in that the rank of the home settlement is consecutively lowered. Indeed, the home settlement in the third class is seen as a *weak* pole, polarizing no more than two settlements and depending on Thessaloniki, or Thessaloniki and another city. The lowest rank is presented by the home settlement of the last class, where it *no longer functions as a pole at all,* and is polarized by Thessaloniki and/or some other settlement, or by a small number of other settlements.

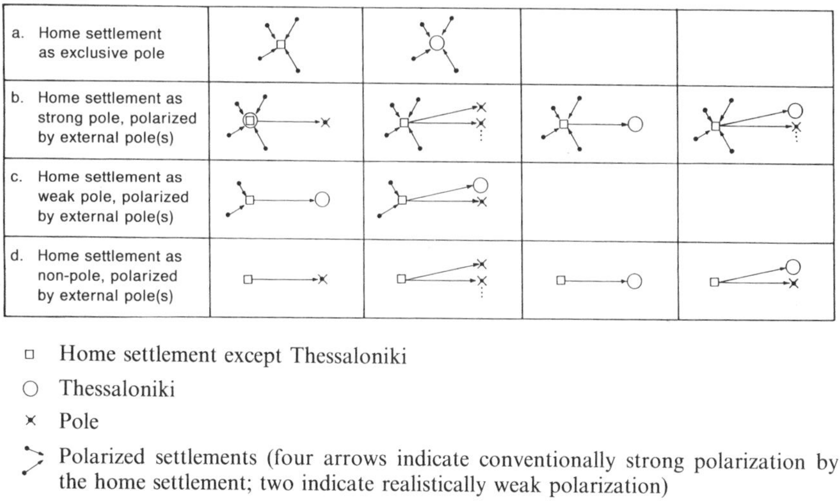

□   Home settlement except Thessaloniki

○   Thessaloniki

×   Pole

⤻   Polarized settlements (four arrows indicate conventionally strong polarization by the home settlement; two indicate realistically weak polarization)

Figure 10. Types of conceptual settlement networks.

The conception of the settlement as an exclusive pole is much more prevalent, as would be expected, in Thessaloniki than in the other research settlements (39% vs. 3%-8%); in Thessaloniki, the city is never seen as a weak pole or a non-pole. However, more than half the inhabitants consider the city as polarized by Athens, a view not accompanied by very friendly feelings toward that city, as we shall see in Chapter 7 (Section 2).

The inhabitants of Veria by 89% consider the city as a strong pole and do not in general situate their city in the two lower classes. But it is not only the inhabitants of cities who consider their settlement as an important regional center, since only 6% of the inhabitants of Axioupoli classify their settlement in one of the two lower classes. A partial exception to the rule is Ormylia, where 14% of the inhabitants consider it as a weak pole and 8 % as a non-pole. The sum of these percentages is high also when compared with data from social classes, genders, and age groups, where the equivalent sum in no case exceeds 11%. But even so Ormylia is generally promoted to an important regional pole on the discursive level. One of our interviewees gives a good example of the ideological discourse legitimating this promotion. While she believes that Ormylia is polarized by Thessaloniki and the capital of the nomos, she also states: "...But to buy the produce that Ormylia grows they come from all over Chalkidiki, they even come from Thessaloniki."

The regional "pride" of the inhabitants of Thessaloniki seems to be the major reason that lies behind the significant correlation between the four classes of settlement hierarchy and the hierarchy program, and the same seems to be the case for the very significant correlation of the classes of settlement hierarchy with the city-country program. Among the other sociosemiotic programs, only the city-country/gender program gives significant results in respect to this grouping of the position in the settlement hierarchy and leads us to some further insights. While the main weight for all four social types of this program is in the strong-pole class, there is a continuous increase of the participation of this class for each social type from city women (67%) to country women (75%) to city men (80%) and to country men (89%). On the other hand, city women are the most strongly represented in the exclusive-pole class (over half of the individuals in this class are city women, and 31% of city women fall in this class).

The judgments of the interviewees on the centrality or periphericity of their home settlement supplement the discussion above. These judgments proved to attribute to the settlements seven different ranks which we grouped in three classes: (a) clear centrality, or centrality with qualifications; (b) both centrality and periphericity (mainly centrality with some periphericity; equally centrality and periphericity; or mainly periphericity with some centrality); (c) periphericity with qualifications, or clear periphericity. The cases of centrality with qualifications; mainly centrality with some periphericity and vice versa; and periphericity with qualifications are rare, while the two extreme cases (centrality or periphericity) and the equal combination of both are much more pronounced. These three classes of settlement role are closely related to the previous four classes of settlement hierarchy, since class (a) logically corresponds to the settlement as an exclusive pole, class (b) almost entirely to the settlement as a strong pole, and class (c) to the settlement as a weak or non-pole. If we compare the distributions, on the basis of the frequency programs, of the three classes for the four research settlements, as well as the social classes, genders, and age groups[16] with the respective distribution of the settlement hierarchy classes, we observe marked differences which all follow the same general pattern: the concentrations in class (b) are many times lower than those in the strong-pole class, while the concentrations in classes (a) and (c) are many times higher than the concentrations in the exclusive-pole class, and the weak and non-pole classes respectively. In all cases, class (a) is dominant (from 40% to 64%), with the exception of Ormylia where this class is represented by only 22% and class (c) dominates by 61%.

Thus, the transition from the indirect estimate of the settlement rank based on the analytical description of its position in the settlement network to the direct judgments on centrality and periphericity made by the interviewees is accompanied by radical changes. The direct judgments are much less shaded and much more *polarized*. We can follow the pattern creating polarization during this transition, on the basis of the crosstabulation between the settlement hierarchy and the centrality-periphericity variable for the whole sample (0.01). People considering their settlement as an exclusive pole also in a great majority (85%) hold the view that it is central. But those conceiving of it as a strong pole remain by only one-fourth in the position of centrality-and-periphericity, while the rest split and move towards the two extremes, preferentially by almost one-half toward centrality and secondarily by one-fourth toward periphericity. Finally, people with the conception of weak pole or non-pole for their settlement behave like the first case in that the great majority persist in their views. The same trends are repeated in the three other sociosemiotic programs that deliver significant or very significant crosstabulations for the two variables under discussion (cities, women, adults). It is manifest that persons with initially extreme views remain extreme, while the majority of people with a mixed conception move toward extremities, as a rule toward the positive extremity.

The polarization shown by direct judgments is of a wider interest for social research because it shows the incidences of the nature of the questions asked on the responses obtained. But then, if questions are not innocent, how is it possible to locate the truth? Are we confronted with an endogenous, structural obstacle erected by the use of questionnaires? We do not think so, but we also believe that we are facing a real problem. One way of treating it is to abandon the notion of *the* truth and accept that people may hold more than one view simultaneously on the same phenomenon, views which may even be contradictory, and that all these views may be *equally true* for the subject. If we accept this position, we should further concede that an operational way of proceeding would be to define the extreme attitudes. We believe that our two variables are able to figure these extremes. The one follows from a question encouraging a relatively unemotional description of the settlement network (though this does not imply that all subjects were in a position to provide such a description), while the other results from a question calling for an involved judgment; the first corresponds to a *cool* description, and the second to a *warm* evaluation.

40% of the Thessalonikians, then, when they describe the role of their settlement consider their city as an exclusive pole, but from another perspective, if called upon for a more emotional judgment, 60% subscribe to the same view; 58% describe it as a strong pole, but only 25% feel this sentimentally; no one sees it as weaker than that, but some 10% judge it so sentimentally. In their descriptions 8%, but sentimentally as many as 64%, of the Verians promote their city to the highest rank, while 89% or 19%, respectively, hold a more moderate view. Descriptively 73%, but emotionally 17% of the Ormylians place their settlement in an intermediate position, and 22% describe it, but 61% feel it, as peripheral. Both contradictory judgments are equally "true" for the subject at the moment when he/she answers the question; the particular position chosen will depend on the perspective adopted, a perspective to some extent (but not entirely, as we saw) influenced by the type of question asked. We will encounter this issue again in Chapter 7, where we shall have the opportunity to study it in respect to regional feeling. For the moment, let us see how our warm semiotic variable behaves in respect to social groups.

Both the hierarchy and the city-country programs deliver very significant results for this variable. The inhabitants of Thessaloniki and Veria have a strong tendency to consider their city as a center, while the former are somewhat less inclined than the inhabitants of Veria to see the city as peripheral; on the contrary, the majority of the inhabitants of Ormylia, as we saw, evaluate their settlement as peripheral, while the rest are divided between centrality-with-periphericity and plain centrality. The presence of Axioupoli in the city-country program does not contradict the general predictions based on the hierarchy program, but attenuates the feeling of periphericity in the rural world (44%) and increases that of centrality (35%). It is possible to penetrate deeper into this situation. In Thessaloniki, mainly women and youth tend to centrality (approximately 70%), and the same is the case with the youth of Veria (72%), while periphericity is mainly felt by the youth of Ormylia (67%). The city-country/gender program, on the other hand, shows that country women and youth have the greatest tendency toward periphericity and away from centrality, while the tendencies of country men and adults are more equally distributed among the three classes of evaluations (0.01). But social classes also enter the game. Urban workers have a very strong tendency toward centrality (83%) and in general the urban classes support the notion of centrality, while the country working and middle classes tend toward periphericity (about 50%), the country lower middle class being split between centrality (46%) and periphericity (37%).

It is not without interest to evaluate the realism of the judgments made by the different social groups.[17] We may consider as an objective reading of reality on the part of our subjects the reading coinciding with a professional metalinguistic analysis. A professional analysis of the regional role of our research settlements shows that Thessaloniki can be considered as central in respect to Northern Greece, and as central and peripheral if Athens is taken into account; periphericity is a wrong judgment for Thessaloniki. Veria is an important city, but its closeness to Thessaloniki makes it impossible to ignore its dependence on the latter; Veria is neither a center nor a periphery but has elements of both. Ormylia is absolutely peripheral, and Axioupoli can be seen, depending on the point of view, as peripheral or peripheral with elements of centrality, in consideration of the extent of its catch area. In view of this situation, as much as 89% of the inhabitants of Thessaloniki, and 61% of those of Ormylia, have a realistic view of the role of their settlement, but only 19% of the inhabitants of Veria. Women and youth are somewhat more realistic than men and adults in Thessaloniki; in Veria and Ormylia the genders are quite similar, and the young are rather more realistic than adults in Ormylia.

If we now use the criteria of realism and homogeneity of views, presented in the previous section, in order to locate the possible autonomous sociogeographical groups, we find that the inhabitants of the metropolis and the provincial city are quite similar in their tendency toward centrality; this characterizes city dwellers in general, who thus constitute an autonomous group. The countryside, though it tends towards autonomy, is also internally differentiated, since the conception of centrality is formed there by the diverging tendencies of autonomous groups differing in extent and nature: different tendencies are shown by women in Ormylia and possibly in Axioupoli, and by the lower middle class, men, the young, and adults in the countryside. If we compare these autonomous groups with the groups behind the fluctuation of the diameter of the contour of the involvement region - which were Thessaloniki and Ormylia, as well as men, adults, probably the middle class in Veria, and probably men in Axioupoli - we now witness the emergence of quite different social groups throughout. We thus get the impression that the fluctuations of differing semiotic phenomena are due, though not necessarily exclusively, to the inclinations of autonomous sociogeographical groups entering into different combinations.

The opposite aspect of the degree of realism of the social groups is their degree of subjectivity. That women and youth in Thessaloniki are more realistic than their respective complementary groups means that they are less subjective, although 6% among them fall into subjectivity. But while the genders are very similar in their degree of objective reading of reality in Veria and Ormylia, they differ greatly if we compare the settlements. Almost two-thirds of each gender in Ormylia are realists, but this falls dramatically to around only one-fifth in Veria, while the other four-fifths have a subjective view of the geographical role of their city; the situation is quite similar in respect to the age groups. We thus observe once more that the conception of reality held by the different social groups is not a simple reflection of reality, but also a subjective interpretation of it. The social groups are characterized by their own combinations of these two modes of apprehending reality.

The distribution of realism in the research settlements helps in understanding the relation of and the true contents of cool and warm judgments. In Thessaloniki, the transition from cool to warm follows the observed pattern of polarization, in the context of which the major trend is the shifts occuring within the realistic view on reality (mainly the shift from centrality-and-periphericity to centrality, though there is also a limited shift to subjectivity which results in a total increase in subjectivity of about 10%). Things are totally different in Veria, because here this transition, which starts from a very high degree of realism (centrality-and-periphericity), results in a peak of subjective feeling of centrality for the city, while simultaneously there is as in Thessaloniki a limited pessimistic mood; the increase in subjectivity is 70%. The pattern in Ormylia diverges from both cities, since according to the data discussed so far, the dominant move is toward realism (periphericity) and the secondary is within subjectivism (centrality); the decrease in subjectivity amounts to approximately 40%.

The patterns of transition, then, of the three settlements all tend toward polarization, but diverge radically if the criterion of realism is applied. The transition for the Thessalonikeans implies a redistribution of the realistic views and the appearance of some subjectivity; it leads the Ormylians to a disillusioned recognition of their periphericity; it pushes the Verians to a subjective mode marked by a narcissistic enthusiasm. Thus, the settlements reveal differing global traits, synthesizing a multitude of different reactions on the part of the population subgroups, reactions of persistence in some point of view, or shifts from one point of view to another in various directions. As these shifts show, we should not simply equate the transition from cool to warm judgments with a rise in subjectivity, nor should we believe that the former are necessarily more realistic and the latter more subjective. Social reality is more complex than such simple correspondences, and also makes room for the transformation of cool forms of subjectivity to emotional forms of realism.

Chapter 7. Space and the fluctuation of sentiment

1. The experience of space: Beyond phenomenology

Together with the introduction, in the previous chapter, of the fundamental concept of the involvement region, we also presented and studied the characteristics of three subjective notions of a geographical nature, namely the settlement, the wider, and the widest region. One issue that concerned us in our study was the affective relationship of our subjects to regional space, as they conceived it through these notions and through certain other spatial entities which they themselves introduced spontaneously or which we suggested to them.

The notions of the involvement region and the settlement - to which correspond real-world referents of greatly varying size - are practically universal, though this is not the case with the wider and widest regions. The imbrication of the settlement within the involvement region creates the beginnings of a concentric structure. This pattern, as we saw, is not necessarily continued as the conception of space expands outwards. But each consecutive spatial entity, whether it is a region or a regional pole, is characterized by a greater distance, both subjective and actual, from the settlement. Expansion can also take place inwards. Four questions on our questionnaire concerned geographical differences internal to the involvement region and how our subjects evaluated these different locations. One of these questions asked for the general differences within the involvement region as the subject conceived them, without suggesting any particular point of view. In response to this question, a certain number of the interviewees (13%) spontaneously indicated a subregion around their residence smaller than the settlement. In these cases, there is an inward expansion of the concentric structure created by the settlement and the involvement region. All these spatial entities are at different distances from the self, and are organic in the sense that they were defined, or accepted and delimited, by the interviewees.

We shall begin this chapter by investigating (for the whole sample) the evaluation of and experiential relation to the above spatial entities, with the exception of the widest region (Section 1),[18] as well as the strategic attributes of the involvement and the wider regions (or the corresponding poles) in comparison to the settlement (Section 2). This analysis will also extend to include two spatial entities defined and suggested by the researchers: the first is the nomos, this fundamental administrative and functionally important unit, and the second is Northern Greece. Each of the spatial entities, from subregion through the settlement and the involvement region to the wider region (or the corresponding pole) is progressively more distant from the self; the same is true for the two predefined regions, but this pair of regions was intercalated in the series of the four organic spatial entities, and for this reason the continuous increase of distance which applies to the four organic entities does not hold for the whole series of the six spatial entities examined.[19]

For the evaluation of these spatial entities both direct and indirect approaches were used. The evaluation of the subregion was obtained through the micro-discourse elicited by the question concerning general differences within the involvement region and thus is derived from a question which was indirect in respect to the subregion (the interviewees were not asked to focus directly on the subregion). A similar, frequently composite, indirect evaluation was obtained for the settlement with a question concerning the similarities and differences between the involvement region and the settlement; another evaluation for the settlement is derived from the previously mentioned question on the differences within the involvement region, when the settlement appears as a significant unit in the responses. But evaluation for the settlement was also obtained through a direct question, where the interviewees were explicitly invited to express their affection or lack of affection for their settlement. The interviewees were also asked to express their degree of attachment to their involvement region. For this region, two other (composite) evaluations were elicited on the basis of a question investigating the associational chain related to the involvement region and another question inviting the interviewees to describe and evaluate the characteristics of the latter. In the first case, while the subjects are oriented towards the involvement region, they are not explicitly invited to evaluate. The associational nature of the question, however, encourages emotional reactions, and thus the question tends to function as a direct evaluation. In the second case, the request for evaluation is explicit, but there is no focusing on evaluation of the involvement region, which was deduced from the general configuration of the evaluations accompanying the descriptions of the various features of the involvement region. The wider region, finally, was evaluated indirectly in a manner similar to the settlement, from the responses to a question on its similarities and differences with the settlement.

Thus, with the exception of the holistic evaluations of the settlement and the involvement region elicited by the direct questions, all the other evaluations, which are frequently of a composite nature,[20] derive from micro-discourses of a more general content. On the other hand, the two predefined regions were evaluated in response to direct questions. Since an important number of our subjects define the wider region as the nomos, it was possible to compare in these cases this holistic evaluation of the nomos with the composite evaluation obtained for the wider region. The other predefined region, Northern Greece, was evaluated through the different grades of the affective relation of the interviewee to the terms of the pair "Northern Greek" vs. "Greek in general". We thought that these two terms might set in motion a censorship mechanism, and that the political sensitivity of the Macedonian issue, discussed in Chapter 4, Section 1, might weaken overt identification with Northern Greece. For this reason, we duplicated this evaluation with another one, deduced from an impersonally formulated question concerning differences between Northern Greeks and other Greeks.

The distribution of the different evaluations presented above are shown in Table 6 for the whole sample, the cities, and the countryside. In the case of questions which did not explicitly invite the subjects to pronounce value judgments, we felt the neutral position was probably overrepresented and consequently attempted to redress the corresponding statistical distributions. In this case, the Table gives both distributions: the actual percentages obtained, and the redressed distributions 2a, 6a, and 7a.[21]

On the basis of this table we constructed Diagram 1, where we retained only the positive evaluations of the different spatial entities and the marked tendency to identify with Northern Greece.

What is immediately apparent from Diagram 1 is that the percentage of positive evaluations elicited by the direct questions (inviting holistic evaluations) and the questions which function in a similar manner by tending to provoke sentimental reactions, is uniformly higher than in the other cases. We already encountered this phenomenon of the discrepancy between warm evaluations and cool descriptions when we discussed the judgments on the position of the settlements in the settlement hierarchy in Chapter 6, Section 5. In respect to the settlement, this discrepancy moves in the countryside from 9% to as much as 36%, and concerning the

Table 6. Evaluation of significant spatial entities in Greece, the cities, and the countryside.

Evaluations elicited by indirect questions	Positive orientation and tendency, %			Synthesis of opposites, %			Neutrality, %			Negative tendency and orientation, %		
	Greece	Cit.	Coun.	Greece	Cit.	Coun.	Greece	Cit.	Coun.	Greece	Cit.	Coun.
1. Subregion (differences)	*	57*	*	*	12*	*	*	6*	*	*	25*	*
2. Settlement (similarities/differences)	51	37	66	12	15	9	29	38	20	8	10	5
2a. Settlement: redressed distr.	69	57	78	16	23	11	4	4	5	11	16	6
3. Settlement (differences)	54◇	*	51	25◇	*	22	4◇	*	5	17◇	*	22
4. Involvement reg. (characteristics)	59	64	54	35	32	38	3	1	4	3	3	4
5. Involvement reg. (associations)	71	71	72	12	10	14	10	11	8	7	8	6
6. Wider region or pole (similarities/differences)	23	23	23	11	8	15	55	61	47	11	8	15
6a. Wider region: redressed distr.	30	32	30	15	11	19	40	46	32	15	11	19
7. Wider region (scale of nomos)	23	20	26	15	20	11	49	60	37	13	0	26
7a. Wider region: redressed distr.	30	27	32	19	28	14	34	45	22	17	0	32

Table 6 (continued).

Evaluations elicited by direct questions	Two positive grades, %			Moderate, %			Neutrality, %			Two negative grades, %		
8. Settlement	86	86	87	11	13	8	1	1	1	2	0	4
9. Involvement region	80	75	85	16	22	9	3	3	3	1	0	3
10. Nomos	59	60	58	13	19	7	8	6	10	20	15	25
11. Nomos (also a wider region)	71	62	80	12	19	5	5	5	5	12	14	10

Evaluations of Northern Greece	Inclination towards N. Greece (2 grades)			Equal inclination (N. Greece & Greece)						Inclination towards Greece (2 grades)		
12. Identification w. N. Greece	32	29	35	7	6	8				60	65	56

	Important differences N. Greek fr. Greek (min.)			Secondary differences						No differences N. Greek fr. Greek		
13. Identification w. N. Greek	50	55	47	23	21	23				27	24	30

* Sample size not satisfactory
◇ Cities not satisfactorily represented

involvement region it is 11% in the cities and 31% in the countryside; in the countryside, it is approximately 50% for the wider regions of the size of the nomos. The incidence of the nature of the questions asked on the evaluations elicited can also be seen in the fact that the question on the characteristics of the involvement region led to an important increase of the systhesis-of-opposites type of evaluation for all four settlements and all seven social groups of the frequency programs (social classes, genders, and ages).

The nature of warm evaluations is not deduced only from the fact that they are a spontaneous response to a direct request for a personal judgment. The sentimental reactions on which they rest become clear also from the themes connected with them. We asked our interviewees to provide us with the reasons why they evaluate their settlement and involvement region as they do. The prevailing thematic categories in both cases are quite comparable both in kind and frequency of appearance. Some significance is attached to aesthetic considerations: of the total number of reasons provided, the themes revolving around aesthetics - of the settlement in the case of the settlement and of the landscape in the case of the involvement region - have a frequency of 4% to 10% for most of the frequency-program groups. Somewhat more important are two other categories of themes. The first category includes themes referring to economy; this generally appears with a frequency of around 10% for the settlement and usually of more than 10% for the involvement region. The second category covers all themes connected to lifestyle and generally has a frequency of around 8% for the involvement region and from 6% to 19% for the settlement. But the overwhelmingly most frequent themes are those relating to the experiential world of the subjects, whether they focus explicitly on the speaker or are oriented toward his/her social micro-environment. The frequency of appearance of individual experiential themes, both for the settlement and the involvement region, is between 40% and 60% in all the frequency-program groups, and the frequency of the whole of the experiential category amounts to at least half of all the themes which occur and may be as high as three-fourths. We see, then, that the main foundation of warm evaluations is to be found in the experiential code.

If we attempt to correlate warm and cool evaluations for the settlement (cases 8 and 2, Table 6) and the involvement region, or different types of cooler evaluations for the latter, we find no significant correlation for any of the semiotic programs. The great divergence between warm and

Diagram 1. Geographical fluctuation of identity.

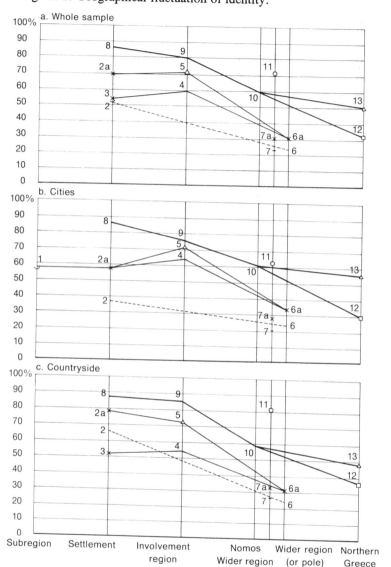

—,o Holistic evaluation after direct question

△ Evaluation from indirect question tending to function as a direct question

□ Censored evaluation

____ Evaluation from indirect question calling for evaluation, or according to redressed data

× Redressed evaluations

----- Evaluation from indirect question not calling for evaluation

⌣ Unstable data

The numbering from 1 to 13 follows Table 6

cool evaluations already reveals fluctuations, and thus instability, in the evaluative structures of our subjects. In addition, now we observe that the transformation from the one structure to the other does not seem to follow any regularity. Evidently the sentiment attached to one and the same spatial entity is far from monolithic and may fluctuate quite freely.

The warm curve falls continuously from the settlement to Northern Greece, but it is almost horizontal in the countryside between settlement and involvement region. The same image is given by the constellation of the valorizations elicited in the settlements and by the social groups we studied: the warm evaluations for the settlement move around 90%; the valorizations for the involvement region around 80% (with the exception of Thessaloniki, 66%); those for the nomos around 60% (with the exception of Ormylia, 86%, and Axioupoli, 31%), and those for Northern Greece (Northern Greeks) around 55% (with the exception of Ormylia, 42%, and the working class, 37%). The decrease of valorization when we reach the nomos scale is accompanied by an increase of negative evaluations (around 20% in most of the cases) which reaches its peak in Axioupoli (50%); negative evaluations are almost nonexistent for the settlement and the involvement region.

If we now consider the indirectly obtained cool evaluations, we observe that in the cities there is a small increase of valorization from the settlement to the involvement region, something found in both Thessaloniki and Veria. While in the countryside a similar phenomenon may occur, it seems here to be a special case, the current case being a decrease of valorization. We can draw two conclusions from these observations. First, there is in the cool evaluations a relative devalorization of the urban environment in the cities - also reflected in the valorization of the subregion - which remains hidden in the warm evaluations. The enthusiastic attitude towards the urban environment in the nineteen-fifties and sixties seems to be slowly giving way among urbanites to less rosy feelings. The second is the attachment to the involvement region, shown in the cities by the increase in valorization; the same attachment is observable in the countryside where the evaluation curve remains horizontal between settlement and involvement region. This attachment corroborates the subjective reality and importance of the involvement region, and brings out its character as the direct extension of the settlement. Finally, from the involvement to the wider region the cool curve falls drastically.

In order to study another aspect of the subjective relation to the settlement, we asked our interviewees if they would be willing to move to another settlement or would accept such a possibility for their children. Almost two-thirds of the city dwellers were negative for themselves, one-fourth declared that they would move under certain conditions, and only 15% had a positive attitude. This pattern changes somewhat for the children, in that the negative attitude to moving decreases to half of the cases, and moving under certain conditions increases to around one-third. The pattern for the parents in the countryside is similar to the one in the cities, but that for the children presents important divergences from the corresponding urban pattern, since the negative attitude falls to around one-third and the positive rises to the same level; 39% of the inhabitants of the countryside are not against moving themselves, which is similar to the percentage for the cities, but more than two-thirds adopt this attitude in respect to their children. The two urban patterns are similar to the corresponding patterns of the redressed cool evaluations of the settlement (2a), in the sense that there is a correspondence of the percentages between unwillingness to move and positive attachment to the settlement, inclination to move and negative attachment, and so on. But in the countryside, the attachment to the settlement falls when we compare evaluation and inclination to move, perceptibly in the case of parents and dramatically in the case of children. Thus, inclination to move and cool evaluations correspond rather closely, with the exception of the attitude in the countryside toward children moving. This does not reflect any contradictory behavior, but the aspirations of rural parents toward what they perceive as a better future for their children.

These general patterns, however, conceal important internal differences. If we consider the cities, half the inhabitants of Thessaloniki are not against moving themselves as against only about one-fourth in Veria. As to the countryside, while in both Ormylia and Axioupoli more than two-thirds of the interviewees are not against their children moving, the internal composition of their attitudes towards moving themselves is inverse: in Ormylia, the number of interviewees that would move under certain conditions (45%) is twice as high as the number of people who unconditionally want to move (22%), while in Axioupoli the second case is clearly more prominent (41% as compared to 31%). Among the other social groups, the least virtually mobile groups are the workers and the mature - 78% and 71% respectively are negative to moving; the workers are also characterized by a similar attitude towards their children (55%). On the other extreme there is the attitude of the middle class, more than half of which is not against moving and almost three-fourths of which adopt the same attitude for their children.

Discourse concerning the reasons for this willingness to move or desire to stay is very varied, but in the midst of this variability there are certain thematic categories that prevail. Two among them are dominant and present for all social groups: the reference to the experiential realm, which we already encountered on the occasion of warm evaluations and which is usually used as the rationale for staying, and the lifestyle category of themes. The frequency of the first category, which is again dominated by references to the self, oscillates between 18% and 33%, and that of the second is comparable, around 25%. Themes relating to economy, in contrast to the experiential themes, are usually given as reasons for moving and also have an important presence (14%-21%). Another important category is education for the children, especially prominent as a concern in the rural settlements and among the middle class.

What we note from these data is the widespread positive or, to be more precise, non-negative attitude toward mobility among our interviewees. People actually tending to be geographically mobile do not exceed one-fourth of the total for any social group. This tendency is stronger in respect to children and becomes extreme in Axioupoli. The strongest centrifugal tendency, if we include the cases of conditional moving, is expressed by the Thessalonikeans, and the strongest desire to stay by the Verians. When we come to virtual mobility, then, the disillusionment with urban, or at least metropolitan, life is clear in Thessaloniki, but it is not as prominent in Veria. The attitude of the Verians toward the mobility of their children is somewhat more moderate than that of the Thessalonikeans. But in the rural settlements personal attachments are put aside in the case of the coming generation and in the face of the objective difficulties of living in rural Greece.

But let us return to Diagram 1. In spite of certain variations, there is a general tendency for spatial valorization to fall with increase in distance from the settlement. We think that this inverse relationship between valorization and distance would be much more obvious were it not for the intervention of social stereotypes, such as the nomos and Northern Greece. We earlier had the occasion (see Chapter 6, Section 3) to point out the relative abstractness of the wider and widest regions, due to their focusing on the settlement as a depersonalized point of reference, which we opposed to the self-referential construction of the involvement region. Evaluation is related to an abstractness of another kind, having to do with subjective attachment to the spatial entities. The valorization of a spatial entity follows from an attachment to and identification with it, and from a feeling of belonging to it and the fellow persons it includes. Thus, valorization accompanies the feeling of a collective "we", which may appear at different spatial scales, and which may be precipitated at a relatively abstract spatial level by the associations of certain spatial units (the nomos, Northern Greece) with social stereotypes with sentimental connotations.

The synthesis-of-opposites, dualist type of evaluation generally shows a certain metalinguistic distancing from the spatial entity and a greater critical disposition towards it. The feeling related to this type seems to be a synthesis of identification with (or rejection of) and distancing from the entity, and, in respect to the collective "we", a synthesis of feelings of insideness and outsideness. The neutral type indicates indifference as to space and the community, and thus a feeling of non-integration with a social group. These two types of evaluation show a more abstract approach to the spatial entities and the "we" they represent, because they presuppose a lesser degree of identification with them. They are, however, not used only for the more remote entities, but also for the more familiar ones.

The interpretation of the negative evaluations is more complex. We think that, concerning the more familiar worlds, these evaluations express a feeling of hostility or more commonly of disappointment, and of opposition to the "we" or at least to the "here", and as such they are as emotionally involved as valorization; but in respect to the more remote worlds the dominant feeling in a negative evaluation is probably one of repulsion because of the inverted values they are invested with, frequently defined in opposition to the familiar or even to other valorized spaces.

It seems that there are two manners of experiencing space and the community, a concrete and an abstract, and different psychological modalities accompanying them. These manners and modalities offer us a critical tool for commenting on the phenomenological approach to geography. The cornerstone of the latter is the concept of place, that is, existentially recuperated space. It seems clear to us that valorized space is experienced as the (concrete) space par excellence, the *place,* and in this case the phenomenological approach can be considered as capturing the nature of the subjective experience of space. Humanistic geography also seems capable of analysing the negative experience of space. When this

Table 7. Manners and modalities of experiencing space.

Evaluation	Positive orientation and tendency	Negative tendency and orientation	Synthesis of opposites	Neutrality
Manner of experiencing space	concrete		concrete and abstract	abstract
Psychological modality of experiencing space	identification	detachment: disappointment, hostility, or repulsion	identification (or detachment) and distancing	indifference
Semiotic nature of space	place	anti-place or non-place	place and space	space

Competence of humanistic geography

Competence of the semiotics of space

with a social and spatial "we". This feeling of belonging is not limited to the areas closely related to everyday practices, but as is apparent may extend to relatively remote regions. We are dealing here with a continuously dilating "we" or, otherwise, with a series of "we" at different spatial scales; a series going from the most immediate to the more remote.

According to Pellegrino et al. (1983: 16-35, 55, 99-100, 108, 121-124, 131, 160), the most restricted "we" is the local community, which is distinguished from the "others"; "we" is in general inseparable from a place, "here", and differentiated from the "others", located "elsewhere". The feeling of identification is coherent only in this case, where we have an identification with "us" and a differentiation from the "others". The inseparability of "we" and "here" characterizes the autochtones, while the heterochtones locate their "we" "elsewhere" and differentiate themselves from the autochtones of "here" whom they consider as "others". This immediate "we", which can be positively, neutrally, or negatively evaluated, belongs to a wider "we", a point supported by our own findings as we saw above, and the immediate "here" may be included within a wider "here". The larger "we"-region integrates the relations between the local "we" and "elsewhere". We see, then, that the two notions "here" and "elsewhere" are not exclusive, since "here" can be extended on a wider scale to include "elsewhere"; also, as the authors note, "elsewhere" can be present in "here", as is the case with the transformations caused by tourism. The authors mention cases in which their subjects adopted an attitude excluding values conflicting with the identity of the community, but also point out the existence of contradictory evaluations which, as we saw in the previous section, can accompany any spatial scale.

Following Pellegrino et al., the identification of a local "we" is simultaneous with judgments founded on the conceived difference from the "others". They observe that there are two modalities of identification, exclusive and inclusive identification, connected to two different relations between the local and the regional. In the case of the exclusive identification, "we" is differentiated as a totality from other totalities, while in the case of inclusive identification, the "we" is differentiated as a part from other parts together with which it composes a totality. Thus, the identity of a community would be connected to the conception of its differences from other communities. The authors also observe that "we" and the "others" can also be considered as alike. We see that in this case the notion opposite to difference, resemblance, becomes explicit.

Finally, the authors study the relations between a given community and its surrounding communities. We can detect in their exposition four different kinds of relation in addition to regional polarization. The first kind is relations that follow from the actual flow of persons in the context of different activities; the second follows from references to affinities; then, the authors study the topological relations between two initial spatial entities (settlement and region) and other spatial entities named by their interviewees; the last kind of relations is the attitude of "we" in respect to the "others", which can be positive, neutral, or an attitude of aggressivity. These attitudes can be combined and the combinations related to the sentiment of identity.

We see, then, that the central concepts used by the authors are the dualist pairs "we" vs. "others" and "here" vs. "elsewhere". The first pair was derived from the study of the use of personal pronouns. Differences and resemblances, as well as evaluations, were attached to this pair. In our own study, the use of the first person pronoun was considered as indicating the existence of an experiential code, while we deduced the degree of identity, as we saw in the previous section, from the structure of evaluations, which we felt gives the actual coloration of the pronouns used. Following the same approach, we considered valorization as indicating the feeling of a collective "we". We consider the neutral evaluation as indicative of a feeling of non-integration with a group, which is thus experienced as an indifferent "other". Indifference becomes detachment from the "other" or at least from an "other" space in the case of negative evaluations. And the dualist (positive and negative) evaluation reveals a critical distancing from a "we" (or from a negative "other" or space) with which there is also a degree of identification.

Pellegrino et al. consider differentiation from the "others" as an essential component of identity. Our study employed different grades of resemblance and difference, including Pellegrino's et al. concept of relation through affinity; the involvement and the wider region are given attributes through these grades which were formulated by using the settlement as a point of reference. We also considered as an essential component of the relation to another space and other persons the concept of togetherness, which has affinities with certain of the topological relations of Pellegrino et al. We investigated this on the basis of the degree of conceived connectedness between the regions and the settlement. If evaluations reflect the degree of attachment to a region, the degrees of resemblance and togetherness are parallel modalities of relating to space, and it is to these modalities that we shall now turn.

Diagram 2 shows, for the whole sample, the cities, and the country-side, the curves for the different forms of judgments of resemblance and connection concerning the involvement and the wider regions (including the regional poles). The feeling of strong connection with the settlement is by far dominant for both the involvement and the wider region, although the percentage falls from the former to the latter, especially in the countryside, and inversely the feelings of weak and no connection generally increase. If we disaggregate strong connection into two different degrees of connection, close and fairly close connection, we observe that generally close connection is more strongly represented; this holds not only for the cases shown in Diagram 2, but also for each of the four settlements and the rest of the frequency-program groups. When there are exceptions to this rule, they only concern the wider region, and among them the most prominent case occurs in the countryside; this characteristic of the countryside is due to Ormylia, while in the other rural settlement, Axioupoli, a comparable phenomenon of decrease in the feeling of connection appears in that the category of no connection reaches the highest percentage for any group, 18%.

The general image from the curves for resemblance is quite different. The curve for strong resemblance connects much lower percentages and rises slightly from the involvement region to the next spatial entity, showing that these two entities are considered by an almost equal percentage of people (around 40%) as having a strong resemblance to the settlement. This is also generally the pattern for the other frequency-program groups. The share of the grade of close resemblance is exceptionally low (6%) for the involvement region in Ormylia, and the same is the case with Thessaloniki (3%) in respect to the next spatial entity. The curve of weak resemblance is close to that of close resemblance but has a falling tendency, and the percentages of no resemblance are much higher than those of no connection for both entities. The highest percentages in the resemblance-and-difference grade among all frequency-program groups for both the involvement region (17%) and the next entity (37%) appear in Ormylia, and the same is the case with no resemblance in Thessaloniki (35% and 44% respectively). There is thus a special emphasis in Thessaloniki on the difference of the two entities from the settlement, and the same happens in Ormylia in respect to the wider region.

Diagram 2. Resemblance and connection to the settlement of the involvement and wider regions.

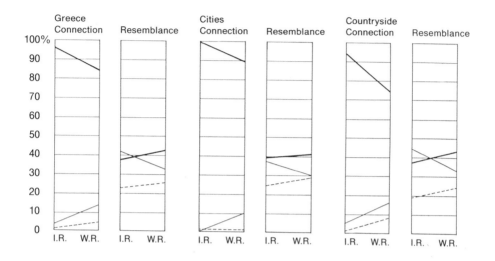

- — Strong (close and fairly close)
- — Weak (for resemblance; also resemblance and difference)
- ---- None (for resemblance; also opposite)
- I. R. Involvement region
- W. R. Wider region (or regional pole)

What we see then is that the percentages in the corresponding grades for resemblance and connection are very different for each of the two spatial entities studied. We might have supposed that there exists a systematic relation between resemblance and connectedness like the one shown in Figure 11, where strong connection and strong resemblance on the one hand, and no connection or resemblance on the other, are inextricably linked. We might further suppose that the evaluations of the two spatial entities to which the judgments of resemblance and connection apply are aligned with each other and with the nature of connection and resemblance. We might, for example, expect that strong connection goes together with strong resemblance, and when they apply to a valorized settlement they harmonize with a similar valorization of the next spatial entity. This would be a simple model relating judgments of connection and resemblance to evaluations.

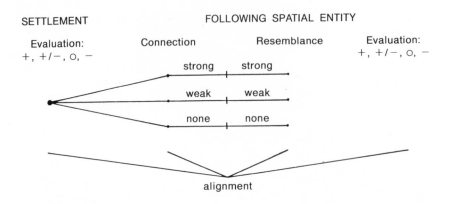

Figure 11. The simple model relating evaluation, connection, and resemblance.

However, the data for connection and resemblance seem to point in a different direction. This impression is corroborated by the crosstabulations between connection and resemblance for all semiotic programs, both for the involvement region and for the next spatial entity, which prove to be not significant. On the other hand, the warm evaluations of the settlement and the involvement region are for all semiotic programs correlated and in general very significantly, but this phenomenon is mainly due to the very important presence of positive evaluations. There also appears a correlation between the warm evaluations for the settlement and the nomos, but only for four among the ten semiotic programs, namely the whole sample (0.01), the cities (0.01), women, and adults. The situation seems different when we pass from warm to cool evaluations: the correlations between the non-redressed evaluations of the settlement (case 2, Table 6), the evaluations of the involvement region (case 4) and the non-redressed evaluations of the wider region (case 6) are not significant, and neither is the correlation between the involvement region and the wider region (cases 4 and 6). Thus, there does not seem to be any systematic relation between types of evaluation of the settlement and some following spatial entity, which means that the evaluation of the next spatial entity cannot be accounted for on the basis of settlement evaluation alone, presumably because of the integration of both into a wider, more general comprehension of space.

The lack of correlation between connection and resemblance contradicts the simple model of Figure 11: crosstabulation for the whole sample shows that all the combinations between grades of resemblance and grades of connection are possible, though not with the same frequency. For evaluations as well, crosstabulations between cool evaluations of the settlement and the involvement and wider regions respectively also show that, with very few exceptions, all combinations are actualized. What then becomes of special interest is to put together and extend these observations in the context of a complex model, allowing us to follow the whole path from one evaluation to the other through connection and resemblance. We present this complex model in Figure 12, where we also show the frequency of appearance for each path.

Many paths are the same for the involvement and wider regions, but many others differ; also, the paths of medium frequency (3.5%-6.5%) and higher are strikingly different for the two regions. A very high percentage (56%) of the paths of the complex model is not realized. The most inactive areas of the model are those corresponding to the following path groups: positive evaluation (of settlement) - no connection - all grades of resemblance and evaluation; synthesis of opposites evaluation - weak or no connection - all grades of resemblance and evaluation; neutral evaluation - no connection - all grades of resemblance and evaluation; and negative evaluation - weak or no connection - all grades of resemblance and evaluation. The most prominent path groups, on the other hand, are: positive evaluation - strong connection - all grades of resemblance and evaluation; and neutral evaluation - strong connection - all grades of resemblance and evaluation. The importance of the latter group is manifestly due to the presence of cool evaluations and we can guess that in the case of warm evaluations the incidence of the first group would be strengthened. Weak and especially no connection are quite underrepresented. The four high-frequency paths are, in order of importance: positive evaluation - strong connection - weak resemblance - positive evaluation; positive evaluation - strong connection - strong resemblance - positive evaluation; positive evaluation - strong connection - strong resemblance - neutral evaluation; and neutral evaluation - strong connection - strong resemblance - positive evaluation. Among these paths, only the second falls within the predictions of the simple model, and only one of the eleven paths of medium frequency can be related to the simple model. Our simple model is not only simple, it is simplistic.

Before drawing conclusions from our observations above, we shall turn to the correlation between comparable judgments for the involvement region and the wider region, specifically to judgments on connection and

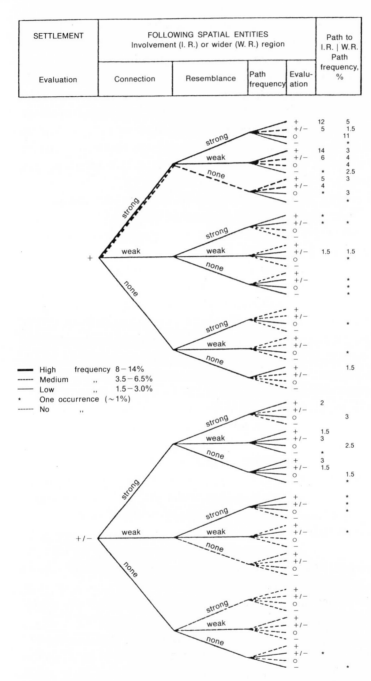

Figure 12. The complex model relating evaluation, connection, and resemblance.

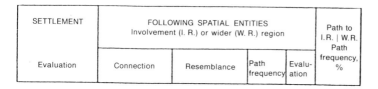

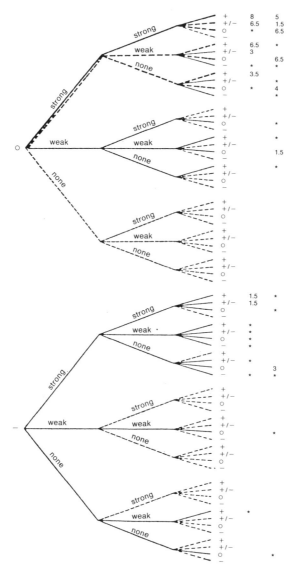

Figure 12 (continued).

resemblance. As in the case of evaluations, these correlations are not significant. There is only one exception, the correlation between judgments of resemblance in the case of the whole sample, where we observe a significant tendency for the same individuals to use the same grades of resemblance, though all combinations between grades are represented to a greater or lesser extent.

With the exception of this last case then, we do not observe any persistence on the part of our subjects in the use of similar evaluations, or similar judgments on connection or resemblance, for the consecutive spatial entities, nor do we find any significant relation between judgments on connection and resemblance for the same entity, nor were we able to discover any functioning of a priori logical patterns regulating the evaluation-connection-resemblance series. Of course, there are important statistical differences between path groups, but they do not point to the existence of a preferred a priori structure but in the direction of the regulation of this series in each case by a specific approach to a particular spatial entity. This conclusion is supported also by the form of the distribution of the realized paths, which are scattered all over the background of possible paths, giving the impression that all paths could become active; and the strong asymmetries between the paths for the involvement and the wider regions, showing the adaptation of spatial conception to the particular objects of contemplation. We could thus imagine a reversal of the statistical distribution in Figure 12 in dealing with inimical external spaces.

In comparison to the study by Pellegrino et al., then, our analysis brings to the foreground another factor relating to the pair "we" vs. "others" in addition to evaluation, namely resemblance. A larger spatial entity can be judged on the axis of resemblance as strongly similar to a valorized settlement, that is, as a wider "we", but it can at the same time be neutrally or even negatively evaluated, something that classifies it in the realm of otherness. This would seem to indicate an "other" which in some sense participates in the "we", an other ego. On the other hand, there may be no resemblance to the "we", but still a positive evaluation. We saw that for Pellegrino et al. identity, the integration with a "we", coexists with differentiation from the others. But in our first example above the feeling of identity may go together with an element of non-differentiation. As our model shows, the paths of spatial identity are many and intricate.

The modes of regional identity are generally attached to parts of the home settlement, then to the whole settlement, and then to consecutive regions (with the exception of the cases in which some wider region was replaced by a regional pole). We shall now examine the evaluation of two poles specified by the researchers and generally external to the home settlements of the subjects. The first pole is the focal settlement of the whole of Northern Greece, Thessaloniki, while the second is the national capital, Athens. Aside from a small number of interviewees who declared they were not in a position to answer, the great majority of our subjects are positively disposed toward Thessaloniki: as much as 86% of the inhabitants of Axioupoli consider Thessaloniki as playing a positive role for Northern Greece, and the same is the case for four-fifths of the lower middle class; the lowest percentage (58%) in the frequency-program groups appears among the Thessalonikeans themselves. Things are similar if we isolate the very positive evaluations among the positive ones, since the highest percentage (42%) derives from Axioupoli and the lowest (22%) from Thessaloniki; the last percentage also appears in Veria. Negative evaluations are limited for all groups (less than 15%) and the very negative among them never exceed 3%. With the exception of the Thessalonikeans, the other groups are by two-thirds to more than four-fifths positively inclined towards Thessaloniki. Among the city inhabitants the distribution of evaluations is comparable to that for the nomos, while in the countryside it is much more positive and is similar to that for the involvement region. We once more encounter in the cities the relative devalorization of the urban environment that we observed for the settlement, though this time it does not refer to the urban environment as such but to the regional function of the metropolis.

What is at stake with the evaluations of Athens, however, is surely not the urban environment. These evaluations represent a kind of reverse image of the evaluations of Thessaloniki. In the frequency programs the negative evaluations prevail over the positive to an important degree; they are generally the most frequent grade and in many instances account for over half the cases. The peak of inimical feeling towards Athens is reached in Thessaloniki, where as much as 70% of the inhabitants evaluate negatively (among them 20% very negatively) the role of Athens for Northern Greece. Without escaping from the general pattern, the working class is the least hostile and shows one of the highest frequencies of positive evaluations (25%).

Attachment to Thessaloniki and hostility towards Athens are the prevailing feelings in Northern Greece. As we discussed in Chapter 6, Section 5, another strong idea in Thessaloniki is that it is dependent on
Athens, but this is less accentuated than hostility. We indicated in Chapter 4, Section 1, the subordinate position compared to Athens in which
Thessaloniki found itself with the integration of Macedonia into Greece,
a position that has not changed over time. Thessalonikeans personify the
mechanisms of dependence, which they consider to be due to an Athenian
conspiracy. Hostility and the idea of dependence have become part of a
binary mythological conception, according to which Thessaloniki is the
innocent and promising victim while Athens is the blameworthy villain, a
conception which appears over and over again in economic, political, and
cultural life.[22]

3. The sociological logic of the semiotic universe

In this section we shall discuss the sociological determinations of warm
evaluations, and of the reasons for identification and willingness to
move, as revealed by the sociosemiotic programs. To begin with evaluations, the only factor that is significantly related to the warm evaluation
of the settlement is education. While in all three general levels of education (the lower, primary school education; the intermediary, secondary or
vocational and equivalent; the upper, higher education or university degree) more than half of the interviewees identify strongly with their settlement, there are nonetheless significant differences in the relationships
between levels of education and settlement evaluation. There is a close
relationship between the lower and the middle level of education and
strong identification with the settlement, but the middle level also shows
some tendency toward moderate identification. The higher educational
level, on the other hand, is less attached to the settlement, since it shows
a similar tendency toward moderate identification and another, more pronounced tendency away from strong identification toward fairly strong.
When we pass to identification with the involvement region there is again
only one social factor which gives a significant correlation, but this time
it is age. Adults have stronger feelings for their region than youth, and
this is particularly true for the oldest group (53 years old or more). As to
the young, the age group from 19 to 27 is closely related to strong and

then moderate identification, while the following group (from 28 to 34) is primarily related to the intermediate scale.

Attitudes toward the regional role of Thessaloniki are first shaped by the city-country opposition. As we might expect, the countryside is much more strongly connected than the cities to a positive attitude toward Thessaloniki. A new factor, however, is revealed to operate behind this opposition and this is the regional distribution of genders in these two domains. The positive attitude is mainly shaped by country men, and then by country and city women, who are closely comparable in their tendencies. In contrast, an emphasis away from this attitude is due to city men. On the other hand, in respect to the role of Athens for Northern Greece, education appears as one of the shaping factors. Indeed, the most negative attitude is found in the higher educational level, while the lower level appears as more tolerant and is almost equally divided between a negative attitude and a more moderate one (neutral or composite), even with a certain tendency toward a positive attitude; the middle level is comparably related to the negative and the positive attitude, but hostility to Athens is attenuated among people of this middle educational level. The same regional factor operating behind the approach to Thessaloniki, the city-country opposition, is also very significantly related to attitudes toward Athens: the cities are the primary source of the negative attitude, the countryside being more tolerant. Another factor also operates within the city-country opposition, namely the regional distribution of the age groups. It shows that the negative tendency is mainly shaped in the cities by adults, while young people also show an important positive tendency; the distributions of evaluations for the two countryside age groups are the same and show a comparable emphasis on negative and moderate evaluation.

These data help us to understand the nature of the social dynamics influencing evaluations. It is immediately apparent that we here encounter the same phenomenon as that discussed in Chapter 6, Section 4, which is that comparable semiotic dimensions cannot be mechanistically attributed to the same sociological determinants. Identification with the settlement is regulated by only one factor, education; more educated people are less attached to their settlement, while the opposite holds true for the less educated. Thus, higher education seems here to forge a less localistic consciousness, and the attitude of the less educated can be compared to the lesser virtual mobility of the working class (see Section 1); this result of more years of schooling could be attributed to the content of a more universalist education. But this openness created by higher education is definitely not oriented toward Athens, as the influence of education on the evaluation of Athens shows. This is possibly due to the fact that the professional activities of people with higher education make them more aware of the centralized control exercised by Athens on most aspects of economic, political, and administrative life. Identification with the involvement region, on the other hand, is influenced by age: adults are more attached to their region, an attitude which goes together with their lesser virtual mobility. Age is not a shadow factor camouflaging some real factor such as (in this case) years of residence, because the latter is not significantly related to evaluation of the involvement region. It is difficult to decide whether the sentimentality of the adults is original and thus up to a point explains their unwillingness to move, or whether it is a sentimental rationalization of their lacking the will or the ability to make a new start somewhere else.

So far, feelings and attitudes have been correlated to purely sociological factors. But as we have seen, attitudes can also be influenced by sociogeographical factors. In this second case the city-country opposition occupies a central position, significantly related to attitudes towards Athens and Thessaloniki. In both cases, the opposition is significant both in its pure form and in combination with another factor, age in the case of Athens and gender in the case of Thessaloniki. But the mutual relation between the pure and the combined form follows a different logic in each case. In respect to Athens, the significance of the combined effect of the city-country opposition and the age groups on evaluations is due to the two urban age groups, since the country groups have the same tendencies. This similarity goes beyond the age groups and the country appears as a homogeneous whole opposed to the heterogeneous city. Thus, the city-country opposition as such operates parallel to the combined form, city and country age groups. This is not the case concerning attitudes toward Thessaloniki, where the city and country women are comparable, but not the city and country men, to the opposed tendencies of whom the significant relation between the city-country opposition and evaluation of Thessaloniki should be attributed. Here, then, the significance of this opposition follows from the regional distribution of genders.

The autonomous sociospatial groups that emerge in respect to evaluations are thus the countryside, urban youth and urban adults, and urban and country men (women also constitute an autonomous group but without sociogeographical differentiation). Of these groups, we only encountered country men among the autonomous groups defined in Chapter 6; the rest are newcomers in the list of autonomous groups. It thus seems reasonable to hypothesize that any one of the sociospatial groups used in our study can achieve a status of autonomy, depending on the nature of the particular semiotic phenomenon under examination. On the other hand, not all semiotic dimensions are explained by social groupings, sociospatial or general. This is the case, for example, with the evaluations of the involvement region based on its conceived characteristics and on the associations connected to it; with identification with Northern Greece, and with resemblance and connection of the involvement and wider regions to the settlement, where no significant sociological regularities are observable for the data.

We shall now turn to the sociology of the reasons for identification (or not) and willingness to move (or not), starting with the sociological influences on the reasons for identification with the settlement. We identified 28 simple types of reasons, which appear alone or in combination and range from reasons referring to the economic activities and lifestyle of the settlement to reasons relating to the aesthetics of the settlement and personal factors linked to the family. If we classify these types in two categories, the one including at least one reason connected to economic issues and the other not including such a reference, we observe that these categories are significantly related to the settlement hierarchy; the most striking element of this relation is the total lack of economic references in Thessaloniki. Significant is also the relation of these two categories to the hierarchy/gender program. It shows that, while for all other combinations of Thessaloniki, Veria, and Ormylia with the male-female division, the non-economic reasons dominate, men in Ormylia show a special tendency to have recourse to economic reasons.

Very similar are the reasons for identification with the involvement region. On the basis of the two categories above, we observe that the lower middle class, the Ormylians, and people who have lived in three different settlements also tend significantly to use economic themes. For the classification of reasons for identification, again in two categories but this time according to whether or not they include a reference to spatial uses and services, class is revealed to be the significant factor, with the workers showing a significant tendency toward functional references while the lower middle class totally avoids them. If finally we classify reasons for identification according to whether they include reference to personal or experiential elements, we find that, while for all four categories of the city-country/age program experiential themes dominate, their presence is significantly attenuated for urban youth and rural adults.

Concerning the reasons for moving, the typology of which is very similar to that of the reasons for identification, no one among our sociosemiotic programs gave any significant results with a classification based on economic themes. This is not the case with the functional classification, which is related to a series of sociological influences. In the case of the reasons for identification, class was the only factor shaping the functional classification. With the reasons for moving, it is the city-country opposition that comes to the forefront, both in its simple form (0.01) and in combination with gender, age, and social class (0.01). The simple form of this opposition shows that city inhabitants do not generally use functional themes, but rural inhabitants use them much more (though almost two-thirds of the themes they use are not functional). Urban age groups and urban social classes are absolutely comparable in that none of them use functional themes, and the same holds for city men, while city women show a weak tendency towards these themes. Thus, functional themes are not of interest to city inhabitants, probably because the city offers a satisfactory range of services which are thus taken for granted, while the lack of services in the rural settlements causes complaints. On the other hand, the attitude toward functional themes in the countryside is generally not uniform: the workers and the lower middle class have a similar slight tendency to use functional reasons; country women as well as both rural age groups show an important tendency; this becomes stronger with country men, and reaches its peak with the rural middle class, more than half of whose members make reference to functional issues. While, then, in the case of identification it is the workers as such, independently of regional differentiations, who tend markedly to the use of functional themes, in the case of reasons for moving this characterizes the rural middle class. A significant use of functional themes is also observed among people with an important geographical mobility (84-162 regional trips per year).

Many sociological factors also correlate to the use of the moving themes when classified according to the experiential criterion, notably the combination of settlement hierarchy and age groups (0.01), the settlement hierarchy and the age groups alone, the city-country opposition, and geographical mobility. As many as approximately half of the adults in Thessaloniki and Veria, as well as half of the individuals with the lowest degree of geographical mobility (up to 24 and 24-76 trips per year) use experiential themes. Finally, if we classify moving themes on the basis of references to lifestyle, we see that approximately half or more of the individuals of the two highest educational levels together (higher education or university degree) who have lived in no more than two different settlements make references to lifestyle as a reason for moving or staying.

These data, interesting as they are per se, also allow us to establish with certainty certain major sociological conclusions, included implicitly or explicitly in some of our earlier observations made in the previous and the present chapter. A first conclusion is that it is not possible to establish a mechanistic rationale attributing specific semiotic dimensions to particular sociological factors. Comparable dimensions are influenced by different factors, and different dimensions by the same factors. Things become more complicated if we take into account that in many cases a semiotic dimension is shaped by more than one sociological factor. The sets of factors in these cases influencing similar or dissimilar semiotic dimensions can be independent or intersecting.

The second conclusion is that the social groupings derived from sociological factors of a regional nature can all acquire, ad hoc, the status of an autonomous sociospatial group with its own characteristic forms of spatial conception, comparable to conventional, not specifically spatial groups such as social classes. But then we must also note that there are semiotic dimensions which are not explained by any sociological factors used. It is possible that in this case some other social aspects of less importance constitute the explanatory factor; or that this function is assumed by endo-semiotic groupings; or, finally, that no factor is operating other than personal idiosyncrasies. As we see, then, there is a sociological logic behind the semiotic universe, but it certainly does not operate globally, or according to some simple and easily detectable mechanistic model.

Chapter 8. A multitude of spaces within the same space

1. Global, fragmented, and composite space

We encountered in Chapter 1, Section 2, the concept of mental map. As we saw, the rationale connected to this concept is that a multitude of psychological factors in our mind contribute to the formation of our image of the world, and within this context occur mental processes specifically oriented toward the environment and leading to the formation of mental maps; mental maps explain both the use of existing space by the intermediary of movement, and the change of spatial organization and form. The concept of environment, as used by psychologists and geographers (equivalent to what we in this book have called space), is wider than the concept of physical environment, i.e., built space; but we saw in Chapter 2, Section 1 that behavioral geography, the discipline which in practice has developed the study of mental maps, is mainly preoccupied with the mapping of the physical environment, and particularly with the legibility level of the representations of this environment and their accuracy. We also saw that preoccupation with legibility has led away from the study of deeper meaningful conceptual structures. In spite, however, of this narrowing in geographical practice, there is some provision in geographical theory for this deeper meaning. This is apparent, for example, in the view that a mental map includes three components. The first is the "designative" component, which is descriptive and corresponds to the locational ("whereness") and non-locational ("whatness") information included in the mental map. It also corresponds to the legibility level of the mental map, and to what is for semiotics the denotative level of spatial representations. The second is the "appraisive" component, which corresponds to values, preferences, and feelings; it can be compared to the connotative level of semiotics. Last comes the "prescriptive" component that relates to inferences and predictions. The definitions of the three components, on the other hand, are close to the concept of environment in that they do not apply to physical space only (cf. Pocock 1974: 1, 6-7). For geographers, physical space is but one aspect of the environment; as Pocock puts it (1972: 115), "Environmental perception is the cognitive structuring of the physical and social environments."

The multiplicity of conceptual spaces has not been theorized in geography beyond these initial statements. One manifest reason for that is geography's focusing on physical space, which we shall call physicalism. Physicalism is also omnipresent in spatial semiotics, which is not strange since most of the researchers in the field are architects. If behavioral geography deals principally with the conception of the relative location of objects and their general configuration, the conception of the precise geometric details of physical space is the local interest of spatial semiotics. We could say that environmental psychology is much less bounded by physicalism than these two fields, as witnessed by a review by Daniel Stokols concerning, among other things, research on environmental assessment. According to Stokols (1978: 266), this type of research can be grouped in three directions depending on the issue treated: physical assessments concerning the conceived quality of buildings; social assessments relating to the nature of interpersonal relations within organizations; and sociophysical assessments, which involve the evaluation of neighborhood and housing quality, as well as forecasts of the impact on the community of social interventions and changes in technology. These issues correspond to what the author considers as the physical, social, and sociophysical "dimensions" of the environment. As we can see from this example, environmental psychology, in spite of its broader scope, has advanced no further than behavioral geography in theorizing about the aspects of the environment; the sociocultural approach in human ecology is not very helpful on this matter either.

The issue of the aspects of space was approached in a more elaborated manner outside the subjectivist sphere. We can detect here three different tendencies. The one extreme tendency is represented by Lefebvre (1974: 15-19, 102-103, 324, 402-403), who argues for a theoretical construction of a global and unified social space - as opposed to neutral, empty space - considered by him as a "concrete abstraction", which would be an answer to the infinite analytical fragmentation of social space which he feels could be considered politically suspect; the study of the production of this global space would belong to what he calls the "political economy of space". This epistemological stance leads naturally to the identification of global space with actual empirical space. Of course, empirical space is not viewed empirically, since Lefebvre considers that social space is a part of the productive forces; influences the reproduction of the relations of production and is inherent in the relations of property; secures the hegemony of the state; and is an ideological superstructure. All these attributes of space are indicative of a theoretical approach, but they do not help us arrive at any analytical decomposition of empirical space.

The other extreme of Lefebvre's philosophical and political Marxist approach to space is formulated in a neo-positivist manner by Robert Sack. According to this author (see Sack 1980: 54-72, 87, 99-100 and 1972: 77), all non-logical concepts can be classified into three categories: spatial, i.e., physical geometric concepts, temporal concepts, and substance concepts, which refer to objects, powers, or facts of the empirical world. Empirical facts can be seen through two different points of view, the geometric or the substance point of view, and to these approaches relate two different kinds of laws, the laws of physical geometry and the non-geometric substance laws, which explain facts in a different manner. Facts in the first case correspond to spatial terms and are explained by the laws of physical geometry, which are static, unable to explain processes, and thus of remote interest to the social sciences. On the contrary, social sciences - including geography - as well as physics are concerned with space from a not purely geometric viewpoint. They use facts corresponding to substance concepts, in the context of substance laws. The latter include spatial information either implicitly or in the form of spatial concepts, and this connection of space and substance would correspond to the "relational concept of space", opposed to the absolute space of geometry. Thus, following Sack, social sciences by formulating substance laws simultaneously pose geometric laws. Since for Sack space is defined each time through substance, we can conclude that there are as many spaces as there are substances and thus an indefinite number of analytical spaces. The author extends his approach to subjectivist geography and emphasizes the relation between spatial concepts and their meanings, which correspond to real-world, geographically located substances. On the basis of our previous reasoning, then, we should conclude if we follow Sack that there is an indefinite number of subjective meanings of space and probably an indefinite number of analytical conceptual spaces.

From the unified actual space of Lefebvre we arrive with Sack at an infinity of material spaces and probably an infinity of semiotic spaces. But one could argue that the views of Sack, in spite of their interest, substantiate the fears of Lefebvre. While Sack defends the social sciences point of view, he does not seem to dispose of any sociological theory that would connect his utterly fragmented set of spaces. The answer to both these two extreme positions in respect to space, the philosophical-political globality of space which resists systematic analysis and which is thus potentially exposed to subjective judgments, and the logical, neutral, indefinite fragmentation of both actual and conceptual space, we feel should be looked for in the direction of the views of Castells, already touched upon in Chapter 1, Section 2.

We should clarify that we do not have in mind here the details of Castells' approach, an approach which he himself has criticized as overemphasizing the urban system and its elements and thus leading to exaggerated formalization at the expense of causative historical regularities. What we consider as the strong points of his proposal, including his self-critique, are first and foremost the adoption of a sociological and historical view on space; this is also the merit of Lefebvre. But Castells goes beyond Lefebvre (see Castells 1975: 166-67, 484-86), since he tries to decompose space into its main components and their elements, and that as a function of the social system. We do not have simple logical "substances" animating space, as is the case with Sack, but sociologically significant substances, theoretically, and frequently hierarchically, interrelated. Of course, Castells leaves aside the study of a very great number of spaces, and this for good reasons. It is obvious that it is not feasible to analyse all possible spaces when we want to explain actual space. The only realistic scientific strategy is to concentrate on the crucial factors operating in and on space - whence the need for a holistic sociological theory. Every other space we would like to investigate as further enlightening the dynamics of space should be articulated with these factors and this theory.

This brief review of the tendencies concerning the components of space outside subjectivism shows the possibility of considering the existence of a great number of analytical - as opposed to the unified empirical - material spaces; a possibility following from systematic theorizing about space. We saw that this kind of theorizing is not very elaborated in subjectivism, as here we operate at best with two aspects of (material and conceived) space, the physical aspect and an overgeneralized "social" aspect. Sack seems to indicate theoretically the existence of an indefinite number of conceptual spaces equalling the number of material spaces. There is an interesting parallel to this view within spatial semiotics. In their case study on regional conception in Switzerland, Pellegrino et al. (1983: 157) note that the regional discourse of their interviewees incorporates different "dimensions", i.e., points of view on space: a geographic, a climatic, a demographic, an economic, an administrative, an aesthetic, a social, etc. dimension. The study thus reveals a series of different kinds of meaning accompanying conceptual space. But do these dimensions, which we shall here call codes, always correspond to one and the same conceptual configuration (that is, in semiotic terms, set of signifiers), and thus compose with the latter a single set of polysemic signs, or can they be related to different signifiers, with as a result the creation of different sets of spatial signs and differing conceptual spaces? What are the characteristics of the sets of signifiers and signs (if there are several) derived from the individual codes and what are the characteristics of the set corresponding to co-occurrent codes? What is the degree of interpenetration of the analytical spaces defined by the individual codes, i.e., to what extent do these spaces overlap or diverge? We shall try to answer these questions in the rest of this chapter.

The signs elicited in discourse about space correspond to the designative component, that is, have a denotative meaning, but can also be the vehicles of an appraisive component, i.e., can also have a connotative meaning, belonging to the same or to a different code. In all the cases of conceptual spaces studied, it is the denotative signs that delimit these spaces. The appraisive component can never add new signs, since it is always supported by the designative; there is no connotation without denotation. In spite of the fact that we shall inevitably be operating through signs, our interest in this chapter will be oriented toward the signifiers, the conceived elements of actual space which are the vehicles of meaning for our interviewees. The codes animating them will be presented mainly in the next two chapters.

2. The semiotic reality of analytical spaces

In order to deal with the issue of conceptual spaces, spaces in ideology, we decided to investigate two types of regional space. We felt that we were moving on solid grounds in respect to the first type, in the sense that our research subjects should have no difficulty in conceptualizing it. This type is the spontaneous and global conception of regional space, about the existence of which there is no reason to have any doubts. The existence of spaces of the second type, however, is not given a priori. Our aim was to find out if our interviewees had a conception of, or at least in their conception could indicate the existence of, analytical spaces comparable to those suggested, for example, by Sack. One of these analytical conceptual spaces is physical space, the existence of which is corroborated by both psychology and geography. But what if we further disaggregate the concept of the (conceptual) "social environment"? We selected for study three different analytical spaces, all belonging to this "social" environment: economic space; social space, in the narrow sense of social groups; and functional space, corresponding to uses and services. We selected the first two spaces because of the importance of the corresponding material processes, and the last space due to its affinity to physical space, since physical space is closely connected to the uses taking place in it.

For all four spaces, i.e., the global and the three analytical spaces, the interviewees were asked to concentrate on the internal differences, if they judged that there were any, in their involvement region, but each time from a different perspective: through an unconstrained formulation of any differences in general for global space, and through the adoption of a specific code, or rather set of codes (economic, social, or functional) for the analytical spaces.[23]

We should clarify that with global space we do not mean the total global space known by the subject, which also includes his/her passive encyclopedic knowledge, but the active set of spatial signifiers elicited in unconstrained discourse, comparable to the equally active analytical spaces. Total regional space can be compared to the linguistic concept of competence, and our active spaces can be considered as following from the active performance of our subjects in pertinent contexts.

The study of each space is effected through the use of three variables. For global space the first variable, the *spatial richness variable,* shows the number of pratically all signifiers (or signs) used by the interviewees, while for the analytical spaces the richness variable shows only the number of signifiers that are absolutely pertinent for the perspective adopted; other signifiers that may have been elicited were omitted. In this way, our analytical spaces represent one among two possible choices; the other possible choice would have been to take into account also those signifiers which, although not literally pertinent, nevertheless appear in the discourse together with the pertinent codes as extensions or interpretations of them, but this would be to analyse the regional discourse rather than the conceived analytical spaces (something which we will return to in Section 4 of this chapter).

To arrive at the second variable, the *spatial sign ratio,* the above number was usually divided by the total number of signifiers (or signs) used by the interviewee for the four questions on spatial differences in the involvement region, a number which we considered as the potential pool of elements actively capable of semantization, i.e., immediately available for use by the subject in the construction of his or her regional spaces within the given context.[24] This ratio, then, gives the percentage of signifiers, in respect to the whole set of the active signifiers elecited, which were actually used to delimit each one of the four spaces.

The third variable is the *coverage ratio* and follows from the previous one. Each signifier corresponds to a real-world referent (location) with a surface calculable on the basis of a topographical map. The numerator and denominator of this variable are the sums of the surfaces corresponding to the signifiers in the numerator and denominator of the second variable, the spatial sign ratio. The third variable thus renders the degree of coverage of the active conceptual space (as defined by the interviewees in response to the questions on differences within the involvement region) that is achieved by their global or analytical spaces, when all these spaces are delimited through their real-world referents.

Conceptual spaces were classified in three categories according to the number of signs by which they are defined: poor spaces, including up to 6 signs; medium rich spaces with 7 to 8 signs; and rich spaces, with from 9 signs up to more than 20 (with a maximum of 28 signs in the case of economic space). The frequency programs show that for all social groups studied and all four spaces, poor spaces predominate, since they generally represent at least two-thirds of the cases. The average image is given by the data for the whole sample, according to which around three-fourths of the cases for each type of space belong to the low category of the spatial richness variable, around 10% of them belong to the medium category, and around 15% to the rich category; all four spaces are somewhat richer in the countryside (Table 8). The poorest spaces are functional space in Ormylia and in the lower middle class (94% and 90% respectively are poor cases), and social space in Veria (91%). On the other extreme we find Axioupoli, where poor spaces are under 60% for global, social, and functional space, and the corresponding rich spaces amount to around one-third of the cases.

Within each social group, differences in the richness of the four spaces are not generally acute. Two notable exceptions, however, are the divergence between functional space (94% poor cases) and economic space (69%) in Ormylia, and economic (86%) and social (64%) space in Thessaloniki. Global space does not hold any special position compared

Table 8. Spatial richness, spatial sign ratio, and coverage ratio for global and analytical spaces.

| Space | Spatial richness, % | | | | | | | | | Spatial sign ratio, % | | | | | | Coverage ratio, % | | | | | |
| | Greece | | | Cities | | | Country-side | | | Greece | | Cities | | Country-side | | Greece | | Cities | | Country-side | |
	up to 6	7+8	9–28	up to 6	7+8	9–28	up to 6	7+8	9–28	up to 50%	51–100%	up to 50%	51–100%	up to 50%	51–100%	up to 50%	51–100%	up to 50%	51–100%	up to 50%	51–100%
Global	76	11	13	80	13	7	71	10	19	61	39	74	26	48	52	65	35	64	36	66	34
Economic	77	8	15	85	7	8	69	8	23	59	41	75	25	44	56	65	35	69	31	61	39
Social	74	12	14	78	12	10	71	11	18	45	55	65	35	25	75	41	59	58	42	24	76
Functional	78	9	13	79	14	7	76	4	20	52	48	68	32	36	64	37	63	44	56	29	71

to analytical spaces, in the sense both that its distributions in the categories of the spatial richness variable are comparable to the distributions for the other spaces, and that its degree of richness relative to the analytical spaces varies with social groups.

Analytical spaces, then, behave in the same way as global space does. Since we consider the existence of global conceptual space as empirically given, this similarity would indicate that analytical spaces are or at least can be equally well conceptualized by the layman. Admittedly they are not especially rich, but neither is global space. On the other hand, analytical spaces, as global space, are conceived without ambiguities and with clarity, although some differences may occur in their degree of spontaneity: economic space, at least in the way we approached and defined it, appears to be somewhat less spontaneously conceived.

If the spatial richness variable refers to the absolute number of signs of a space, the spatial sign ratio variable relativizes this number and corresponds to relative spatial richness. If we group the ratios in two classes, up to 50% and from 51% up, then for the whole sample global and economic space are less represented in the high class (around 40%) than are social (55%) and functional (48%) space, and this is also the case with almost all the social groups; the greatest divergence between global and social space appears in Ormylia (37% and 80% respectively in the high class). Social and functional spaces also predominate for all groups in the category 76-100%. The predominance in the high class of these types of space holds equally for the cities and the countryside. There is, however, a profound difference between cities and countryside concerning all four spaces, because the majority of cases fall in opposite classes: in the cities, two-thirds to three-fourths of the cases (depending on the space involved) are in the low class, while in the countryside, from more than half to up to three-fourths of the cases are in the high class (Table 8). This opposition characterizes both Thessaloniki and Veria in respect to Ormylia and Axioupoli; the latter has the highest percentages (somewhat more than 40%) of all social groups in the category 76%-100% for all except economic space. The above observations are proved to be statistically very significant by the hierarchy and mainly the city-country program, not only when two classes are used, but also in the case of four categories.[25] The countryside thus appears to have consistently higher sign ratios than the cities.

The spatial sign ratio variable shows, as we saw, the proportion of signifiers which is activated on a specific occasion from a pool of elements which act as virtual signifiers in the context of this occasion. A higher ratio shows a more intensive semiotic work on this background, which parallels the work corresponding to greater spatial richness. The spatial richness variable revealed that the four types of spaces were equally elaborated by our subjects in an absolute sense, but the second variable shows that the same is not true from a relative point of view, since the degree of elaboration of global and economic space differs from that of social and functional space. It could be argued that this difference is due to technical reasons. We saw that the denominator for global space is the total number of signs of the involvement region, while the denominators of analytical spaces correspond to a subset of this whole. In the case of economic space this subset almost coincides with the whole, while for the two other analytical spaces the subsets are more restricted and comparable. It would then be possible to hypothesize that the difference between the two pairs of space comes from the difference in the denominators, since the numerators are of the same scale. But this viewpoint is not satisfactory, because it would be reasonable to expect our subjects to elaborate more on more complex subjects. What we find significant is that they do not do so. We are thus led to the conclusion that the global and economic spaces are less elaborated in the relative sense; social space, on the other hand, is generally somewhat more elaborated than functional space. The study of the spatial sign ratio variable reinforces our conclusion about the existence of analytical spaces, because it shows that the spontaneous conception of space, global space, is not a privileged area for the semiotic elaboration of regional space.

The results from the analysis of the coverage ratio converge with those of the spatial sign ratio variable in that they again show a predominance of social and functional space. As we can see from Table 8, these two spaces are generally much more represented in the high class of coverage (from 51% up), where around two-thirds of the cases concentrate, than global and economic space, the participation of which in that class makes up only about one-third of the cases. The distributions in the two classes for global space are quite comparable in the cities and the rural settlements (around one-third of the cases in the high class). Things are quite different with social space, for which the countryside and its settlements are much more represented in the high class (over 70%), while the presence of the low class is much stronger in the cities (over 55%). According to the city-country program, this inclination in the countryside toward high coverage for social space is very significant compared to the experience is attached to a more remote spatial entity, the latter becomes a *non-place,* but when negative evaluations are consistently attributed to familiar spaces they transform them into a rejection of place, an *anti-place.* But humanistic geography is insufficient when we turn to the more abstract experience of space and the related psychological modalities. The identification (or rejection)-and-distancing modality is an ambiguous relationship to space which is experientially transformed into *a* place, not presenting the uniqueness of *the* place, *our* place, and thus interchangeable with other places. The professional's metalinguistic relation to spatial entities is accompanied by a certain abstractness with which they are endowed, an abstractness considered by humanistic geographers as characterizing only non-experiential "space". But according to our data, "space" is an integral part of the non-professional, subjective experience of "place" and vice versa. The same experiential abstractness is evident when the connection to space is one of indifference, in which the spatial entity is felt as abstract and neutral, solely as "space". Pickles (1985: 154-155, 158, 163-167) attempts to connect space and place in the context of phenomenology by considering that the concepts of space, pure extension, and location are an abstraction from the place-character. But he does not avoid the same dichotomy as humanistic geographers between place as subjective experience and space as scientific abstraction, and does not face the mediating position of space as experience.

The different manners and modalities of experiencing space are presented in Table 7. As we can see from Diagram 1, humanistic geography is rather comfortable with the warm evaluations of the settlement and the involvement region, because they make the experience of space emerge as by far the dominant factor. But this experience becomes markedly partial when we are dealing with cool evaluations and larger spatial entities. It is at this point that semiotics enters the game. What we observe is that the inverse relation between valorization and distance translates a movement from placeness to non-placeness.

2. The paths of regional identity

In the previous section we studied the types and degrees of attachment to the different spatial entities from the subregion to Northern Greece. The degree of attachment is reflected in the global subjective evaluation of these entities, an evaluation which when positive indicates identification cities (we used the following four classes of ratios built upon the initial six categories: up to 5% was grouped with 6%-25%; 26%-50%; 51%-75%; and 75%-94% grouped with 95%-100%). The data for the two other types of space do not conform either to the city-country opposition or to the settlement hierarchy. On the other hand, economic space is significantly related to the age groups, even in the case of the six analytical categories: the young show a tendency toward higher ratios contrary to the mature. Veria and Ormylia have the highest percentages of all social groups in the high class for economic space (almost half of the cases), Axioupoli has a much lower percentage (31%), and Thessaloniki by far the lowest of all groups (14%). As to functional space, in the countryside the percentage of Ormylia in the high class is 58% compared to 80% for Axioupoli (which together with social space in Ormylia is the highest percentage for all spaces and groups in this class). We should note that the distributions, which are comparable when two classes of ratios are defined, turn out not to be comparable in detail when the six categories are used instead. On the other hand, the predominance of social and functional space remains even when we refer to the sum of the two higher categories (76%-100%). As to the top category (95%-100%), its highest percentage belongs to social space in Axioupoli (41%), followed by the percentages for functional space in Veria and the two rural settlements, the lower middle class, and women, as well as for economic space in Veria (all around one-third of the cases).

The coverage ratio presupposes the attribution of real-world spatial extension to semiotic elements. The spatial sign ratio, on the other hand, reflects a phenomenon taking shape exclusively within the semiotic domain. In spite of this difference, the results from the use of the coverage ratio duplicate in their general lines the situation revealed by the spatial sign ratio. They show that the semiotic predominance of social and functional space, due to the number of signs activated, is accompanied by a spatial predominance based on the referents of these signs.

3. Autonomous sociospatial groups and conceptual spaces: Towards an extension of Marxist theory

The material in the previous section indicates that country people have slightly richer spaces and a much better spatial sign ratio than urbanites. This means that the retrieval of conceptual space they effect is more systematic, which shows in turn that they have a better contact with spatial phenomena. We can now penetrate deeper into this situation for each type of space through the study of the relation of the spatial sign ratio to the different sociospatial groups. We first encountered these groups in our analysis of the geometry of the conceptual regions in Chapter 6, Section 4. Though constituted in the abstract through the simple regional distribution of the general, traditional social groups (classes, genders, ages), they emerge concretely through their statistically significant relation to the semiotic phenomena we studied. Marxist social theory would lead us to expect that either social classes as the most prominent general groups or the city-country opposition as the crucial regional differentiation are satisfactory for the explanation of the semiotic universe. But our initial decision to also take into account two other general groups (genders and age groups) and the settlement hierarchy (in addition to the city-country opposition), as well as the regional distribution (according to both the city-country division and the settlement hierarchy) of the general groups, was rewarded in Chapter 6. There we first witnessed the constitution of sociospatial groups, deriving from the regional distribution of the general groups, as relatively autonomous groups with explanatory power. In this section, we shall have the opportunity of some further discussion of these groups and of assessing their impact on Marxist theory.

Global space gives significant results with the dual classification of the spatial sign ratios (up to 50% and from 51% up) in respect to the combinations of the city-country opposition with class, gender, and age. The two groups included in gender and age present comparable distributions and thus cannot be considered autonomous sociospatial groups, something that would indicate that the tendency toward higher ratios in the countryside is formed among the social classes. Here, we find the tendency is strongest in the middle class, thouogh it is also present for the workers and the lower middle class. But the workers have the same characteristics with the city inhabitants in general, and thus do not show any autonomous characteristic which would allow us to speak of a conception specific to the working class as a group. The same lack of autonomy is shown by the rural lower middle class, the characteristics of which follow directly from those of the lower middle class in general. Thus, only the rural middle class presents a distribution different from all groups with which it could be immediately compared and must be considered as an autonomous sociospatial group in respect to this semiotic phenomenon.

We just observed that country people manipulate all types of space better than urbanites. Greater ease with space is not generally due, as one might think, to geographical mobility, because this factor does not give significant results in respect to the spatial sign ratio in general but only for global and economic space, and in the case of the former the cross-tabulation corroborates the independence of this ratio from increase in mobility. It is true that individuals with a medium high mobility (84-162 regional trips per year) have the greatest (in fact a very significant) tendency toward the high class of ratios (71% among them give ratios belonging to this class). But then follow individuals with the lowest (up to 24 trips) and the greatest (220-650 trips) mobility. Mobility is also very significantly related to the ratios of economic space, but again the greatest concentration in the high class of ratios (81%) is not shown by individuals with the greatest mobility but by those with only medium high mobility, and the second concentration (49%) is due to individuals with a medium low mobility (27-76 trips). In Chapter 6, Section 2, we saw that the geometric pattern of the most frequent regional trips is not by itself able to explain the formation of the involvement region. Now we see that the corresponding mobility index does not account for spatial abilities. In both cases, the decisive factor seems to be the details of spatial practices, which are in turn themselves almost exclusively related to sociospatial groups as far as spatial ability is concerned.

Economic space gives significant results mainly for the dual classification. We saw in the previous section that Verians incline toward the low class of ratios and Ormylians toward the high class. The hierarchy/class and the city-country/class programs allow us to penetrate deeper into this phenomenon. The lower middle and the middle class in Ormylia tend strongly toward the high class of ratios (75% and 83% of the cases respectively); this is the tendency which characterizes the countryside in general which thus acts as the autonomous sociospatial group forming the social basis of this semiotic characteristics, but the workers in Ormylia have the opposite tendency (64% in the low class), and follow the pattern characteristic of the working class in general. On the other hand in Veria, while the lower middle and the working class tend in markedly different degrees toward the lower class of ratios (58% and 83% respectively), the middle class inclines toward the high class (58%). The sociospatial groups emerge with clarity once more, and that at the expense of the traditional sociological category of social class. It is true that in respect to this particular semiotic phenomenon the working class more or less retains its unity, because it is comparable in Veria and Ormylia, although it is differentiated in Thessaloniki, where it tends more to the low class of ratios (82%) and is integrated into the relatively autonomous character of the city. But the lower middle class shows strongly opposed tendencies in Veria and Ormylia, and in Thessaloniki stands as an autonomous group somewhere in the middle; and the middle class appears as an autonomous sociospatial group only in Veria. Thus, the uniformity of social classes is broken, in this as in other instances we analysed, and is replaced as an explanatory factor by the regional distribution of classes, either in a form which allows us to still recognize them (i.e., the Verian middle class) or in a form integrating them into wider schemes which partially absorb them (i.e., the countryside).

Other sociospatial groups also emerge in respect to the spatial sign ratios of economic space, since this space is much less poor for men than for women in Thessaloniki, and the economic space of rural youth is richer than that of rural adults, while both are richer than the spaces of the corresponding urban groups (0.01 level of significance).

The regional distribution of social classes, genders, and age groups is also an important factor determining the distribution of the spatial sign ratios for social space. It influences both the binary classification of these ratios and their grouping into the four categories mentioned, and that both in the forms of the city-country opposition and of the settlement hierarchy. As much as almost a dozen different sociospatial groups emerge. Thus, the countryside, country men and women, rural workers, and Ormylia tend to have richer spaces than the city of Thessaloniki and the urban middle class, but the latter tend to have richer spaces than urban youth, Veria, and the urban lower middle class.

Almost the same sociosemiotic programs account for the distribution of the ratios of the last type of space, functional space. One more very significant relation is added, that of social classes with the spatial sign ratios, but the city-country/class program shows that it is a superficial result of the regional distribution of classes, as only the urban workers among the six groups included in this program do not constitute an autonomous group. The rural middle class has a very strong inclination to high ratios, followed by rural workers, while the rural lower middle class is mainly related to lower ratios. All three classes, however, have richer functional spaces than the urban middle and lower middle class. Sociospatial groups on a lesser scale are created by the Thessaloniki and Veria working class, of which the first has a very poor functional space, but the second a more elaborated one. Rural youth differs from rural adults as having richer spaces, but this relation is inversed in Thessaloniki, where adults have less poor spaces than youth; and finally the relation between city women and men to some extent resembles this last relation (0.01).

The social dynamics behind the elaboration of the different types of spaces does not show only that traditional social classes are transformed as a function of their regional distribution. A twin phenomenon is the comparable transformation of the general social gender and age groups into sociospatial groups. The four types of space are determined by different sets of sociospatial groups, and when these sets include the same group this latter can show similar and/or diverging tendencies. Thus, rural workers are quite comparable in their effects on social space (the distribution in its four categories of ratios is 25%, 8%, 29%, and 38%) and functional space (30%, 8%, 33%, and 29%), and the same is fairly true for the urban lower middle class (54%, 21%, 17%, 8% and 67%, 29%, 0%, 4% respectively); but this is not at all the case with the Thessaloniki adults in respect to the same spaces (6%, 22%, 56%, 16% as compared to 28%, 50%, 0%, 22%), or with Thessaloniki as a metropolis in respect to economic and social spaces (51%, 26%, 17%, 6% as compared to 23%, 23%, 46%, 8%). On the other hand, one and the same group can produce increasingly richer spaces as we pass from one type of space to the other, a case exemplified by the countryside and its influences on global, economic, and social space (12%, 36%, 28%, 24% as compared to 11%, 24%, 47%, 18% and 14%, 8%, 42%, 36%, respectively).

The new regional face of traditional social groups is equally noticeable in the strong appearance of the gender and age components together with class. At least concerning the spatial sign ratio, the class component does not hold any privileged position compared to the other two components. Such phenomena, though they may not invalidate Marxist theory, will evidently make it necessary to apply the theory with greater sophistication and maybe a new depth.

So far, our discussion of the sociosemiotic programs showed the existence of significant relations between the spatial sign ratios of individual spaces and sociospatial groups. But there are also regularities between these ratios for pairs of spaces within one and the same group, delivered by the semiotic programs. The majority of these relations is very significant, and all of them follow the same general model, according to which individuals who have a poorer space of type x also have a poorer space of type *y* and, inversely, those with a richer *x* have a richer *y*. Let us take one of the purest examples of this series of semiotic correlations, the relation between the categories of ratios for social and functional space in respect to the whole sample. The highest percentage of individuals (59%) in the category of low ratios of social space corresponds to the same category of low ratios for functional space; simultaneously, this percentage is equivalent to the highest percentage (42%) in the low category of functional space. The medium-low category of social space is strongly connected to the low and the medium-low categories of functional space: 47% of the individuals in this category correspond to the low category of functional space and 35% to its medium-low category. Individuals in the medium-high category of social space are mainly related to the medium-high category of functional space; the participation in the corresponding category of functional space amounts to as much as 73%. And the participation of the high category of functional space in the similar category of social space is 74%, while the percentage for the inverse relation is 61%.

Our data also lead to certain other interesting conclusions. What we just observed is that there is only one general model presiding over the significant relations between spaces. This means that the relations that do not obey this model are not significant and also that there is no relation following a different model, one, for example, in which individuals with a poor space *x* show a rich *y* and inversely. Of course cases of this kind may occur, but they do not lead to regularities. The general tendencies demonstrate that there are different degrees of semiotic work invested in the conceptualizations of space, but each individual is characterized by a specific range of performance in the accomplishment of this work that runs throughout all his/her elaborations on space. This range is generally more restricted for the low and especially the high category of ratios, while it is less limited for the other two categories: individuals who tend toward the extremities are more consistent in a specific degree of semiotic work, while those tending toward the medium categories appear as more flexible.

The significant crosstabulations for the whole sample are more numerous than those for the social groups, something which is generally true for our data; the only significant crosstabulations which are missing from the whole sample are the ones between global space and economic and functional space respectively, but these are also missing from all the other semiotic programs. If we now proceed to a discussion of the individual semiotic characteristics of the different social groups, we may begin with the observation that for the whole sample, and also for men and adults, global space is significantly associated with social space. The strict similarity between the distributions for all three social groups shows that the tendency in the whole sample springs from men and adults, and that most of the other groups do not contradict this tendency. Because this tendency is significant for only two specific groups, it cannot be considered as general, in spite of the fact that it appears in the whole sample.

Not only for the whole sample, but also for the lower middle class and the cities, economic space is also significantly related to social space. In the context of the general model presented above, in the lower middle class the low category of social space accounts for 71% of the same category of economic space, while the corresponding percentage for the whole sample is much lower (41%). This difference shows that in the lower middle class there is a tendency away from the specific regularity of the sample, a divergence mainly limited to the percentages in the low category of economic space. Like the lower middle class, the cities also show a certain divergence from the regularity of the sample. Contrary to the previous case, then, no group with a significant trend can here be considered as the origin of the specific regularity of the sample, which should thus be considered as reflecting a kind of neutral statistical average.

Continuing with the characteristics of social groups, there appears in the whole sample a very strong association between economic and functional space. While this association is limited to the whole sample, the association between the most elaborated (in terms of the spatial sign ratio) spaces, social and functional space, appears in all social groups with the exception of the working class. Thus in this case, within the context of the general model there are more or less important divergences between complementary groups - i.e., groups which when taken together reconstitute the whole sample - which show that the specific regularity of the sample is no more than a statistical average and does not reflect any regularity other than the general model. We can speak in this case of a broad tendency, which, however, is not adequately represented by the exact form show by the specific regularity of the whole sample. On the other hand, in the case of the relation between global and social space, men and adults follow the same specific regularity and may be considered as the origin of the comparable regularity of the sample.

These conclusions bring once more to the foreground the issue of the pertinent and autonomous social groups. For each specific case, the groups in the semiotic programs that are not characterized by some regularity are not pertinent; the appearance of a regularity within a social group endows it with explanatory power and consequently with a sociological value, provided it does not repeat a general national tendency which one would expect to find in all groups, pertinent or not. All our specific groups, with the exception of the working class, have proved their pertinence as far as the spatial sign ratio is concerned. In the sociosemiotic programs, a social group acquires its character from its difference in respect to the groups comparable to it, though it may at the same time show similarities to some other groups. This may also occur with the semiotic programs, where a group becomes pertinent when it acquires any significant character whatsoever which is not generalized and national, irrespective of its resemblance to another group; the only exception is when the group resembles its complementary group while no national regularity exists, something which shows that the resemblance springs from the similarity of two average situations.

The sociosemiotic programs gave extremely poor results in respect to the coverage ratio, but this is not the case with the semiotic programs. Concerning this ratio too, the significant crosstabulations for the whole sample are richer than for the other groups; they concern all combinations between the four spaces except the combination between global and social space. These crosstabulations are generally founded on a dual classification of the coverage ratios (up to 50% and from 51% up), and only the crosstabulations between social and functional space also give significant results with a fourfold classification (up to 25%; 26-50%; 51-75%; and from 76% up). All the crosstabulations for the dual classification, which are divided between significant and very significant, deliver, as was previously the case with the spatial sign ratio, variants of one and the same general model, according to which individuals with a poor coverage in space x tend to also show a poor coverage in space y and inversely. This is also the general model for the fourfold classification. There are for the latter a few divergences from this model that are so marked as to reverse it locally and the most pronounced among them refers to adults. Notably, one-third of the adults with a medium-low coverage (26%-50%) in social space show medium-high coverages (51%-75%) in functional space - and these individuals amount to almost half of the cases of this latter category of coverage - while almost half of the individuals with a medium-high coverage in social space show low coverages in functional space. A few divergences of this kind were also found in respect to the spatial sign ratio and again for the relation between social and functional space, though here the reversal was effected between the two lowest categories. Through the relation between the coverage ratios for the different spaces, we witness once more the emergence of autonomous social groups; at some point we find a significant pattern for a specific group, and this occurs with most of the groups used, this time including the working class.

We should point out that both the semiotic programs in the case of the coverage ratio and the sociosemiotic programs in the case of the spatial sign ratio, also corroborate the validity of the traditional, general social groups, which appear on equal terms with the sociospatial groups. All these groups are equally capable of appearing as autonomous, i.e., of providing the sociological basis explaining a particular semiotic regularity. The only two sociospatial groups in the semiotic programs correspond to the Marxist categories of the city and the countryside. If we add social classes, this set of social groups offers a solid Marxist foundation for the discussion of the two indices. But, on the one hand, our other set of programs, the sociosemiotic programs, displays emphatically a multitude of sociospatial groups which are not adequately accounted for in Marxist social theory; and, on the other, both types of programs show that the gender and age components are equally valid with the class component. In order for the interpretation of the indices to be complete, new original sociospatial groups, as well as gender and age, must be taken into account. In conclusion, our data indicate that, at least for the interpretation of semiotic phenomena, in other words social ideology, in spite of the penetrating concepts of Marxist theory, a further and deeper elaboration of it is needed which will allow it to grasp in its totality the complex social dynamics animating semiosis.

4. The thematic code structure of spatial micro-discourses

In the beginning of Section 2 we presented the criteria we used for the selection of analytical spaces: the criterion for the economic and social spaces was the importance of the material processes to which they correspond, and the criterion for functional space its connection to physical space, the favorite space of geographers and semioticians. The selection of the first two spaces was proven a posteriori to be sound also for another reason, to which we shall return immediately below. We will anticipate a little on our discussion of the structures of discourse on space in the next two chapters by presenting here the data on code structure relevant to the global and analytical spaces.

As we already had the occasion to explain, two of the micro-discourses we elicited from our interviewees were in response to questions asking them to describe and evaluate, on the one hand, the characteristics of the involvement region, and, on the other, the differences internal to it. For each question the codes used by each interviewee were noted; these individual codes were also grouped into larger sets of thematically and semantically connected codes.[26] This made it possible for us to study the thematic code structure of the micro-discourses elicited in response to each question.

In the responses of the whole sample to the question on the characteristics of the involvement region, the proportion of the social set of codes in the total number of codes used by all the subjects is the highest among all sets of codes and amounts to 27%, a proportion directly comparable both in rank and quantity to the share of the same set in the responses to the question on differences (22%). The second highest percentage is found for both questions in the economic set of codes (21% and 18% respectively; see Chapter 9, Table 10). Thus, when individuals hold a spontaneous discourse on space, social and economic considerations have a privileged position in their responses - which however is not the case with functional considerations.

The social set of codes holds the first rank in the answers to the question on differences for all the frequency-program groups with the exception of Veria - where it is lower than the economic set of codes by 3% - and the economic set generally holds the second position. Then follow the sets of topographical and built environment codes, whose share for all groups is between 12% and 18%, and then what we called the "personal" set which covers the experiential and aesthetic codes (5-13%, Table 10). These data give us some indication of the general semantic nature of the global space following from the question on differences (from which we have taken all data on global space so far), and the comparable space corresponding to the question on characteristics, as well as the related thematic structures of discourse.

In the rest of this section, we shall discuss the thematic code structures of the micro-discourses elicited in response to the three questions focusing on the three analytical spaces. For each type of space the code structures of all social groups of the frequency programs are strikingly similar, a fact which shows that we are here dealing with a national tendency. There are also some similarities bwtween the three series of data, and we shall start with a discussion of these similarities. First, given that each question aimed at orienting the subjects towards a different type of space, it is not surprising that the dominant code set corresponds each time to the type of space under discussion. Second, the topographical code set has a high rank (second or third) in the hierarchy of the sets (around 15%), something again to be expected due to the topographical orientation of the questions ("Are there within your involvement region any different *parts*...?"). Then, the social set of codes has a high rank in respect to all questions. And finally, beyond the three pertinent sets of codes and the topographical set, no other set of codes exceeds the level of 10% (they are frequently below 5%), with the exception of the built environment set in the responses to the question on functional space.

We shall now turn to the description of the thematic code structure of each type of space, based on the data from all our social groups. In discourse on social space, the participation of the social code set is markedly high (over half of the total number of codes); this set is followed by the topographical though at a great distance. No other set of any importance appears. For functional space, the participation of the functional set of codes is somewhat lower (around half of the codes), and here once more the topographical set follows, again at a great distance; immediately after this latter are the social and the built environment sets. Things are different for economic space. Not that the economic set of codes is not dominant, since it holds the first rank (around one-third of the total number of codes); but in this case the distance from the next set, the social codes, is far shorter, given that this set represents one-fourth of the codes. Third in order are the topographical codes, and the other code sets are underrepresented.

This is the total code structure of the micro-discourses on the specific spaces. What we can see from them is that the "purest" structure, i.e., the structure which in the highest degree concentrates on the subject under discussion and does not allow the preponderance of any other than the pertinent set of codes with the partial exception of the (largely inevitable) topographical codes, is the structure of discourse relating to social space. Relatively pure is also the discourse relating to functional spaces, which in addition to the topographical codes makes some room for the social and the built environment codes. Thus, when individuals focus on social space they do not need to have recourse to other sets of codes, which they tend to use in their spatial discourse only as *fillers*. But when they concentrate on functional space they use, besides these filler codes, the social and built environment codes as *supplementary* sets. Things are quite different with the structure of discourse referring to economic space. The pertinent code set and the social set are quite comparable in their importance, and the latter appears as a necessary *complement* to the former.

It thus appears that the most autonomous spatial discourse is the social: people are able to conceive of and speak of social space independently from the constraints of other codes. When they come to conceive of functional space, they are helped to a certain point by connecting it to the social and built environment codes. It is the discourse on economic space that is not really autonomous, because it cannot evolve without being integrated with the social codes.

5. Isomorphism and divergence between analytical spaces: A widening of the geographical and semiotic views

Geographers and semioticians alike approach conceptual space - the geographers even invented sophisticated mathematical techniques for its cartographic representation - with the implicit assumption that there is only one space of this kind, thus presupposing a simple structure for space in conception. However, the existence of analytical spaces places this issue in a new light. If all three of our spaces, and generally all analytical spaces, were (fully) isomorphic, in the sense that they included the same signifiers (and thus signs), then we should conclude that individuals conceive of a standard set of signifiers, which they couple for each type of analytical space with a corresponding set of signifieds all belonging to the set of codes defining each time the type of space they focus on. In this case, we could conclude that geographers and semioticians are in principle right and there is only one space, though we should extend this position by adding that it can be viewed from many different angles.

However, there is also another possibility. If we consider, for example, the three analytical spaces we located through our research, there may be a partial isomorphism between two of these spaces on the one hand and the third space on the other, in the sense that the sets of signifiers of the two spaces could each be a different subset of the signifiers of the third space; or even between all three spaces, in which case we would have consecutively larger sets of signifiers. This situation, that manifestly can be extrapolated to any number of spaces, complicates the issue. The most inclusive space would constitute the background against which the selection of the signifiers of the other spaces is effected, and the single conceptual space of the geographers could then be identified with this space. But now this conceptual space has been defined through a specific point of view, an issue which does not preoccupy geographical and semiotic thought, and the more restricted spaces are similar but not the same. The single space is not elicited automatically on all occasions and its standard use appears as an oversimplification.

The issue gets even more complicated if we face the possibility that analytical spaces may include sets of signifiers that overlap to a greater or lesser extent, in which case, for each pair of spaces some signifiers are common and some others diverge. No one among the analytical spaces can be identified with the single space as in the previous case, since no analytical space is composed by all the signifiers elicited. There is of course an active conceptual super-space composed of all the signifiers of all analytical spaces - which is a subset of what we have called the total global space in Section 2, and the signifiers of which, since it includes all possible analytical spaces, are more numerous than the sum of the signifiers of our three analytical spaces - but it seems to function as a potential pool of signifiers, a part of which is actualized as a response to the set of codes activated each time.

The first among the three cases referred to above, (absolute) isomorphism between analytical spaces, is an historical fact. Indeed, isomorphism is the current case in precapitalist societies. As one of the authors of this book has on many occasions pointed out (see, for example, Lagopoulos 1977: 58-67, 76-77 and 1983: 291-293), the regional organization of these societies follows a model, which is a general model governing all scales of spatial phenomena including architectural and urban organization. The geometry of this model copies a society's conception of the organization of the cosmos and thus the cosmic code is the prevalent code of the model. Precapitalist societies organize their thought and knowledge of the world in accordance with strict classification systems, composed of chains of notions. The chains are defined by the adoption of a specific point of view on reality, i.e., the adoption of a specific code, and each notion of one chain corresponds with strictness to equivalent notions in all the other chains. In this way, when a notion of one chain (for example, the notion of the "center of the world" in the cosmic code) becomes the signified of a geometric signifier of the spatial model (for example, the center of the model) the latter is also semantized by the equivalent notions of all the other codes (for example, the notion of the "navel" in an anthropomorphic code; that of the "beginning" in a temporal code; and so on). The spatial model is reinterpreted according to the different codes of the classification system, each one of which offers a space fully isomorphic to the spaces defined by all the other codes.

Is it possible to consider that isomorphism is also the current pattern in modern Western societies? In order to be able to answer to this question, we devised an index which we called the *divergence ratio*. This ratio gives for each pair of spaces of the same subject their degree of divergence, in the form of the number of signifiers that are not common to the two spaces divided by the total number of signifiers of both spaces whether divergent or coinciding, where each coinciding pair is calculated as one unit. As a general rule, the greater this ratio is, the greater the divergence of the two spaces, and vice versa. This interpretation of the index holds for all cases, provided we are not tempted to group divergent spaces that are partially isomorphic as convergent. A ratio of over 75% corresponds to a pair of spaces that tend to become autonomous in comparison with each other and a ratio belonging to the field 67-75% corresponds to spaces showing a strong divergence. A lower ratio (from 50% to 66%) refers to a noticeable divergence, while an even lower ratio to a pattern of convergence, the majority of cases of which tends toward isomorphism (up to 39%).

Keeping this in mind, let us turn to the data from the frequency programs, and start with the pair of social and functional space. The convergence category (divergence ratio up to 49%) represents for the whole sample more than 50% of the cases; 51% of the cases tend towards isomorphism (divergence ratio up to 39%) and among them 29% are fully isomorphic. These national averages conceal important differences between cities and countryside. In the cities the convergence category falls under 50%, while in the countryside it increases to cover almost two-thirds of the cases; simultaneously, the autonomy category (divergence ratio from 75% up), which in the cities covers more than one-fourth of the cases, in the countryside falls to under 10%. These differences are mainly due to the metropolitan city, Thessaloniki, where the convergence category is the lowest among all social groups (40%), as are also the cases of absolute isomorphism (9%) and of the tendency towards isomorphism (26%); conversely, the autonomy category is the highest for all groups (26%). In the countryside, the distribution for the two settlements is quite comparable. It is mainly Ormylia that presents the inverse image of the metropolis. Ormylia, together with Axioupoli and the middle class, has the highest share of all the groups in the convergence category (64%), and for Ormylia all cases in this category are cases tending to isomorphism. In addition, Ormylia has the highest share of the cases of absolute isomorphism (44%) and the lowest share in the autonomy category (5%), as can be seen from Table 9.

The divergence tendency is more pronounced on the national level when we pass to the pair of economic and functional space, because here the divergence class exceeds 50%. While the cities and the countryside present similar distributions, they are both internally dichotomized. Indeed, for all groups, the class of divergence is highest in Thessaloniki (69%) and Ormylia (65%), while it is lowest in Veria (45%) and Axioupoli (36%). The same happens with the autonomy category, which is over 35% in the former settlements and below 26% in the latter (this is also the case for the middle class and women). On the other hand, Thessaloniki and Ormylia present the fewest cases (together with men) of absolute isomorphism (11% and 6% respectively) and the fewest cases tending to isomorphism (20% and 29%), while Veria and Axioupoli have the highest percentage of cases of absolute isomorphism (25% and 22%; a similar percentage appears for women) and of tendency to isomorphism (55% and 64%).

The divergence tendency becomes stronger on the national level (almost two-thirds of the cases) with the last pair of spaces, economic and social space. The cities are more or less comparable, and the same holds for Thessaloniki and Ormylia, but there are very acute differences between the two rural settlements. For all groups, the class of divergence is highest in Thessaloniki (71%) and Ormylia (74%), and lowest in Axioupoli (44%). The autonomy category reaches its peak in Thessaloniki (43%) and is lowest in Axioupoli (19%). Absolute isomorphism is not found in Ormylia, is limited in Thessaloniki (11%), and is highest in Axioupoli (19%) and Veria, as well as for the working class and women. The tendency to isomorphism is lowest in Thessaloniki (20%) and Ormylia (17%), and highest in Axioupoli (50%).

Thus, the sharpest differences between complementary social groups are found between settlements, which also manifest the most extreme

Table 9. Distribution of the divergence ratio for the paired analytical spaces.

Paired spaces	a 0%	b up to 39%	1 up to 49%	2 50–66%	3 67–75%	4 76–100%	2+3+4 50–100%
Thessaloniki, %							
Social-functional	9	26	40	20	14	26	60
Economic-functional	11	20	31	9	17	43	69
Economic-social	11	20	29	14	14	43	71
Ormylia, %							
Social-functional	44	64	64	14	17	5	36
Economic-functional	6	29	35	14	14	37	65
Economic-social	0	17	26	23	17	34	74
Greece, %							
Social-functional	29	51	55	15	13	17	45
Economic-functional	16	42	46	13	11	30	54
Economic-social	13	31	37	18	12	33	63
Veria, %							
Social-functional	28	53	53	14	5	28	47
Economic-functional	25	55	55	17	3	25	45
Economic-social	19	36	36	17	11	36	64
Axioupoli, %							
Social-functional	36	61	64	11	14	11	36
Economic-functional	22	64	64	11	8	17	36
Economic-social	19	50	56	19	6	19	44

a. Absolute isomorphism b. Tendency towards isomorphism 1. Convergence category 2. Noticeable divergence category 3. Strong divergence category 4. Autonomy category 2+3+4. Divergence class tendencies. The settlements are not systematically opposed on the basis either of the city-country opposition or of the settlement hierarchy. Neither is their relation to convergence-divergence necessarily systematic, though Thessaloniki always tends to divergence and Axioupoli has the opposite tendency. For all three pairs of spaces and all social groups, the highest share (almost two-thirds of the cases) in the convergence category appears between social and functional space in Axioupoli and Ormylia and in the middle class, and between economic and functional space in Axioupoli. On the other hand, the lowest share in this category and consequently the highest in the divergence class is found between economic and social space in Ormylia, where this class covers three-fourths of the cases. For the whole sample, we can observe that, of the two opposite tendencies convergence is just barely stronger for the pair of social and functional space, while the reverse is true for the pair of economic and functional space; this latter tendency toward divergence intensifies noticeably with the last pair of economic and social space.[27]

We are now in a position to answer the question of the extent of isomorphism of conceptual spaces in modern Western societies. The tendency towards isomorphism, and convergence in general, is a widespread pattern, but by no means the dominant one as in precapitalist societies; partial isomorphism also appears. On the whole, the configurations of the analytical spaces diverge rather than converge, and non-isomorphism between these spaces is the most current pattern. In this context, all three models of the relation between spaces, and all the three constructions of space to which they correspond, which we presented in the beginning of this section, are actualized in Western societies. These constructions are not exclusive for the same individual and may coexist. It is clear that when the divergence construction is combined with the isomorphism construction, the former acts as the general framework within which the latter appears as a special case.

The semioticians of space, as we saw, envisage their subject matter very much as the geographers face their own subject: they presuppose a unified conceptual space that is directly comparable to the single space of the geographers. The epistemological consequence of this hypothesis is the assumption of the existence of a single and manifestly oversimplified scientific field, leading directly to the concept of a single semiotics of space. In fact, our analysis demonstrates that there are more than one semiotic spaces, and points to the existence, at least theoretically, of a number of semiotic spaces as high as the number of possible codes, an observation verifying the insight of Sack. We thus arrive at a series of analytical semiotic spaces, often differing in their signifiers (and their signs), but united by the common characteristic of evolving around space. Whether diverging or converging, the existence of analytical spaces demands the extension of the semiotics of space in a manner allowing for the development of a semiotics of *spaces*. This important epistemological issue is accompanied by a second one. Since the definition of a scientific field presupposes the adoption of a specific point of view, and since each analytical space comes into existence by the adoption of a determined code - i.e., a determined point of view on space - and thus the scientific study of an analytical space is bound to move within the limits of a unique viewpoint, we could at the extreme create as many different semiotics of space as there are spatial codes.

Between the single and innocent semiotics of space and the extreme fragmentation of an indefinite number of different semiotics for different spaces, there are many other possible solutions which we shall not discuss here. Any solution to the issue must be both theoretical and empirical. It should involve a coherent theory of the production, dynamics, structuring, and hierarchy of spatial representations - a theory for spatial representations comparable to Castells' theory for urban space - as well as the simultaneous elaboration of a systematic metalanguage on the classification and hierarchical imbrication of the semiotic codes. Whichever this solution will be, such a theory will offer a general context integrating all the partial approaches to conceptual space.

These conclusions were based on the study of the conceptual relations between analytical spaces for each subject. In the previous section, on the other hand, we presented the general code structure referring to the analytic spaces and drew certain conclusions concerning the discourse on each space. The same data also allow certain observations concerning the relations between pairs of code sets revealed by the comparison of the corresponding code structures. The economic and social codes are on the whole the most closely related: although the structure for social space does not seem to require the economic codes, the social codes are intermingled with the economic codes in the structure for economic space. The social and functional codes have some relation: the discourse on functional space is supplemented by a social discourse. The codes which are practically independent from each other are the economic and the functional.

The above relations are not replicated when we come to the geometric relations between analytical spaces analysed above. The spaces for which the corresponding codes are the most related, the economic and the social, present the greatest divergence; the ones having codes with a partial relation, the social and the functional, show the least divergence; and the spaces with independent codes, the economic and the functional, show an intermediate degree of divergence. Thus, for example, it seems that when people hold an economic discourse on space they use social codes in order to clarify, explain, and interpret it, but the spatial referents of these codes have a relative independence from those of the economic discourse. The relations between spaces do not mirror the relations between the codes corresponding to them.

This observation brings us back to our criticism of behavioral geography (Chapter 2, Section 1), notably to the point referring to the exclusive focusing on legibility and its isolation from the wider ideological framework. The discrepancies between codes in the spatial discourse and the geometric relations between spaces can of course not be used to explain the use of the specific signifiers selected each time, but they nevertheless give some clues to this wider ideological framework. They show first of all that such a framework exists, since spatial relations prove not to be the only level of spatial conception. They thus show that spatial conception is not exhausted with legibility. Simultaneously, it becomes clear that the dynamics of spaces cannot be extrapolated to the wider framework, on which the current approach in behavioral geography remains silent. The geography of spaces evolves within a wider spatial discourse which should not be ignored.

Part IV. Talking about space

... les hommes *parlent* de la ville.... A travers ce discours nous voyons apparaître une certaine "image" de la ville et, selon les discours ... des images diverses voire opposées du monde urbain.... L'image apparaît ainsi comme une "unité symbolique". Le mode d'existence de l'Image de la ville est celui d'un ensemble significatif complexe et particulier.... L'Image de la ville est semblable au "mythe" ou à "l'oeuvre littéraire".... L'Image de la ville est une "figure": évocation et manifestation.

[... people *talk* about the city.... Through this discourse we perceive the appearance of a certain "image" of the city, and, depending on the discourse ... different, even opposed images of the urban world.... The image thus appears as a "symbolic unit". The mode of existence of the Image of the city is that of a complex and specific meaningful whole.... The Image of the city is like a "myth" or a "literary work".... The Image of the city is a "figure": both evocation and manifestation.]

Raymond Ledrut, *Les images de la ville*

Chapter 9. Discourse analysis and the region

1. The 32 modes of apprehending the region

The interviews which form the basis of our research on the conception of the region included several open questions, in response to which the subjects were encouraged to speak rather extensively. Our choice of the interview format, and our desire to focus on the spontaneous structure of the discourse, tended to exclude the techniques of analysis commonly used in behavioral geography (personal construct theory and semantic differential; see Chapter 2, Section 2). We did not wish to present our subjects with a predefined range of responses but rather to enable them to define for themselves the issues they wanted to talk about, something which they were usually eager to do. The interviews thus produced not so much a set of isolated answers as a body of *discourses* on regional space, a corpus which we wished to analyse not only for the specific pieces of information about the region that it contained, but also - and chiefly - for the whole manner of talking about space that it embodied.

The method we chose for this analysis was a modified form of structural semantics as elaborated by Algirdas-Julien Greimas (1966). A more usual choice would perhaps have been content analysis, and indeed modern content analysis does not in practice differ very much from the first steps of a structural semantic analysis, except in its orientation towards the use of computer scanning of texts and quantitative techniques. The use of the computer for the preliminary analysis of the texts, however, presupposes the existence of a word list covering all the lexical forms of the semantic concepts which the researcher has decided are relevant to his/her purpose. There is no such list for the analysis of geographical space, and we could not construct one on a priori grounds since we did not know what concepts would turn out to be relevant to our subjects' conception of the region. We thus preferred to rely on manual analysis of the texts, the more so since our use of a semiotic methodology allowed us to introduce the concept of the semantic competence of the researcher-analyst. In the case of our own project, the researchers-analysts come from roughly the same culture as the subjects-speakers and can thus be presumed to share approximately the same semantic system. The analyst thus has a more or less native-speaker's knowledge of the semantic structures he/she is analysing, and can be trusted, on the whole, to perceive which are the significant distinctions made by the speaker.

The notion of a semantic competence shared by speaker and analyst does not in itself resolve all problems of subjectivity of judgment in the analysis of the corpus; it does, however, provide an assurance that such subjectivity will move within reasonable limits. We also made use of some practical aids toward a higher degree of objectivity which are commonly applied in content analysis. Two analysts worked independently on all texts. Both were trained semioticians with considerable experience in textual analysis. In addition, the establishment of the basic list of codes for talking about space required a preliminary analysis of about 20% of the corpus, something which effectively acted as a pilot study allowing us to refine the technique which was finally applied to the whole corpus.

Structural semantics as developed by Greimas is a method for the analysis not only of natural language but of any semiotic system. It rests on the hypothesis that the basic semantic elements and structures of a culture underlie all the semiotic systems of that culture. Our conception of the world around us is filtered through and finally shaped by a cultural grid. This grid is composed of a set of semantic components, each one of which is a specific manner of approaching and apprehending the world - in this case, geographical space. With the use of these components we are able to think and speak about, literally to make sense of, the world by applying to it these various perspectives. Greimas and Courtés use the term *isotopy* for a simple set of unitary semantic units related by belonging to the same semantic perspective. This relation is the result of their sharing a set of recurring semantic markers or *semes* - i.e., elementary semantic units - each seme being part of a binary *semic category* (Greimas & Courtés 1979: 37, 197-198).[28]

The concept of isotopy was developed by Greimas primarily as part of a method for linguistic analysis and is designed to define semantic units on the level of lexemes or below. It can, however, be extended to larger units - Greimas himself has successfully introduced the method for the study of narrative, where the semantic units analysed correspond to whole episodes in the plot. Since we were interested in the semantic analysis of the micro-discourses on space elicited by our interviews, we adapted the method to a certain level of generality. Thus, we defined "umbrella" isotopies by having recourse to semantic units that generally correspond to the level of the phrase. We did not project preselected isotopies but defined them on the basis of the analysis of our material. An umbrella isotopy, with the subordinate isotopies that it includes, defines a semantic field, and such a field is delineated in its general outlines by each of our isotopies. The structured form of this field, and thus of the semantic components of the grid used to apprehend geographical space, constitutes what we have called a semantic *code*.[29]

The constitution of the isotopies and codes, and the consequent classification of semantic units during the stage of analysis, is a fundamental and extremely delicate operation. It is fundamental in the sense that all the results depend radically on the accuracy of this procedure. And it is delicate because it should satisfy two very different conditions: to catch as far as possible the actual conceptual structuring of the "native thinker" and simultaneously to be suitable to the aims of the specific study. Other aims would lead to a different set of isotopies, but any possible set should be so constructed that it will not betray the conceptual grid of the native thinker. It should be obvious that this approach makes no claims to objectivity in the positivist sense, since it involves a constant, delicate dialectic between the researcher and his/her subjects.

Our central concern was space, and the set of codes we defined for space is more elaborated that the codes corresponding to other phenomena. Thus, for example, we distinguish not only between economic and social spatial codes, but between four different economic codes. On the other hand, codes like the historical code are not further subdivided. Codes which belong to the same general semantic field consitute what we called a *code set*. We located in our corpus 32 codes, which we grouped into eight sets. They represent 32 ways of conceiving of and speaking about regional space in Northern Greece. These codes that structure our conception of regional space, grouped into sets, are as follows (three dots in the examples indicate a hesitation pause).

a. Economic codes

i. Code of economic activities. This code underlies references to economic activities and descriptions: "Most people live off of tourism"; "Krini had a lot of sheep and cattle raising"; "A lot of people work in the mines in Gerakini"; "In Triglia they live mostly by farming."

ii. Code of economic development. This is used in reference to the level of economic development of a region: "Yes, there's a lot of money in Ormylia, it's a very rich place."

iii. Code of natural resources. Covers references to the fertility of the soil ("badlands, like, they're not productive") and to other natural resources ("We're in a good spot, we've got water"; "There's quite a lot of metals there").

iv. Code of cost of living. With this code we have comments on the level of the cost of living: "In Moudania it's easier to find a place to rent, but it's awfully expensive."

b. Social codes

v. General social code. We considered that this code was used when there were observations of a social nature without further specifications: "The people around here, they're okay, I'm happy."

vi. Code of social groups. Corresponds to statements concerning any kind of social group, i.e., social class, profession, gender, age group, and so on: "In Ormylia there are farmers and a lot of workers"; "The old people still speak the dialect"; "They have no young people at all there"; "You gotta be tough, like, strong [to make a living burning charcoal], not everybody can do it, like"; "Foreigners have bought land, built houses - lawyers, that kind."[30]

vii. Code of social origins. This is also a code related to social groups, but the accent here is on the origins of the people referred to. In our case, the great majority of there references are to ethnic groups: "Here we're locals. Over there they're refugees"; "They have their own traditions." But there are also references to migration groups: "Because of the mines, they come fron all over Chalkidiki."

viii. Code of wealth. This code is also related to social groups, but concerns specifically the income or wealth of people (as opposed to the wealth of a region as a whole, which is covered by the code of economic development): "People generally are pretty well off."

ix. Code of lifestyle. Concerns statements touching upon any aspect of lifestyle: "There isn't so much movement there, they're more quiet areas; in the city there's much more pressure"; "People here, they believe in hospitality"; "And they're really hardworking, too."

x. Code of mentality. This code refers to the mentality and character of people: "More educated people, who raise the level with cultural activities"; "The other guy is friendly with you because there's something in it for him"; "They're good people, polite."

xi. Political code. Related to statements on the political beliefs of people, political parties, and the political situation: "In Chalkidiki we consider Ormylia the most progressive [i.e., left-wing] village"; "But unfortunately we're divided by the parties"; "When the Conservatives were in power it was the same, and now it's just the same."

xii. Code of property. In another study, this code might have been grouped with an independent set of legal codes. But for our needs, and given its very low frequency, it was grouped with the social codes. It refers to ownership: "That [stretch of land] belongs to the community, or maybe ... it belongs to some ministry and that's why it can't be divided up like they say."

c. Functional codes

xiii. General functional code. Like the general social code, this code is used for observations of a functional nature in general: "Within Ormylia, things are equally convenient for everybody. But in all of Chalkidiki, things aren't as convenient for everybody as they are for us in Ormylia."

xiv. Code of shopping. Used for statements concerning shopping as a consumer activity, a service, not commerce as an economic activity (in which case the code of economic activities is used): "In Ormylia you can find most anything you need"; "They've got lots of stores, it's really convenient in Moudania."

xv. Code of leisure. Statements using this code are related to entertainment, recreation, and cultural activities: "We'd go swimming there in the afternoons"; "That's the only place where there's a disco"; "The last two years we've even had a film club, but the trouble is, the club won't work unless the movies are a bit more ... people want them really easy."

xvi. Code of administration. Refers to public administration from the point of view of the services provided: "Everything's in Polygyros. Everybody goes to Polygyros. Law courts ... of course it's a problem ... courts, government agencies, eveything's at Polygyros."

xvii. Code of education. References to the educational system, again as a service provided: "It used to be we were really badly off for schools ... but now the secondary school's finished"; "There's a technical school there."

xviii. Code of health. References to the system of health care, once again as a service: "And then, we haven't got a hospital here, just the agricultural health service."

xix. Code of transport. The references here are to public transport: "Then there's Vatopedi, a little village here really isolated, hardly even the bus goes by there."

xx. Code of housing. This code underlies statements on the availability and the quality of housing: "In Ormylia, if you're looking for a place to live, you won't find a house to rent."

d. Ecological code

xxi. Ecological code. This code is used for observations concerning the natural environment or environmental pollution: "We have about the same climate with Gerakini but not with Vrasta, it's much colder there, it's more mountainous"; "The first thing I think of is the sea, the ocean here"; "In Chalkidona you can find fresh air, on the other side there's the smog, the exhaust that the cars bring with them. Like in Diavata, because the industrial zone's over there. Those people really have a hard time."

e. Topographical codes

xxii. Topological code. This includes topological notions such as here vs. there, inside vs. outside, up vs. down, center vs. periphery: "Down by the beach"; "Up there"; "All around there's mountains."

xxiii. Toponymic code. In the context of this code, references to locations are made by using place names: "Ormylia, Vatopedi, Nikiti, Vrastama, all these villages, I know them inside and out."[31]

f. Codes of the built environment

xxiv. Code of building morphology. While the code of housing considers buildings from an instrumental viewpoint, the code of building morphology concentrates on architectural form: "Look, the villages by the seashore, like Nikiti, like Metamorphosi, even the houses they've built, they're all a different style from Ormylia"; "It's got apartment houses and that sort of thing, which I don't like much."

xxv. Code of historical monuments. This code is related to the previous code, but it concentrates on archaeological sites and on what the subjects consider as monuments, old or recent: "Olynthos has other attractions, they've got the archaeological site that reminds them of their history"; "Down there, I don't know if they told you, is the ancient city of Sermyli"; "The village hasn't got any sights for the tourists to see."

xxvi. Code of technical networks. This code covers the references to infrastructural networks (roads, water, sewage, electricity, etc.): "There's just a dirt road between Vrasta and Polygyros."

xxvii. Urban code. This code underlies all references to the settlement as build environment: "Vatopedi ... is a new village, it was built with regular roads, with a plan ... but Ormylia is old, and you'll find very narrow roads, very densely, one house on top of another"; "They've done a lot of construction there"; "They can't build because they aren't included in the [city] plan."

xxviii. Regional code. Related to this code are all statements concerning regional organization and the relations between settlements, administrative relations included: "Chalkidiki, the place where we live ... there's no city. It's all villages"; "It's the most central place in all of Sithonia ... Ormylia is a crossroads"; "The village is a bit isolated"; "Gerakini belongs to the City of Polygyros."

xxix. Demographic code. Covers the population characteristics of settlements and regions, and population movements when seen from a demographic point of view: "It has to do with the population in that area. Vatopedi is too small"; "There's a lot of foreigners, they rent houses, it doubles the population"; "There are no young people there at all, just 5-6 kids in the elementary school and about that many in secondary school. After that, above 20 years old, there aren't any, especially not educated people. They go to Thessaloniki. Just lately there's been some people returning, because they're getting some tourism in the summer."[32]

g. Code of history

xxx. Code of history. In this code we have references to the past, whether social or geographical (which may be in the form of a personal memory): "Of course things were different then"; "Ormylia used to belong to the monks [of Mt. Athos] ... that's why there was very little Turkish influence here"; "Pretty soon now ... the difference that used to exist, refugee villages and local villages, it won't exist anymore."

h. Personal codes

xxxi. Aesthetic code. Covers references to the aesthetics of the natural or built environment: "As far as I'm concerned it's the most beautiful place"; "The houses are nicer-looking there."

xxxii. Experiential code. Here, ther references explicitly concern the subject. The code functions as a catch-all for any reference to the individual or to the individual in his/her relation to persons and space, and covers anything from personal feelings and memories to personal attachments: "I was born here, my memories are here, I married here, I had my children here - it's our whole life, this place"; "My sister-in-law is from Chanioti"; "We have a good time there"; "The people I know, my relatives, the neighbors, all that sort of thing"; "I've never been there."

These regional codes were located initially in the discourses elicited in response to the eight open questions inviting the subject to comment on the involvement region and on the similarity of the latter and the wider region with the settlement. As we already mentioned, for the other six open questions (the results for some of which were presented in Chapter 7, Section 1) thematic categories were defined. It is interesting to note that all the thematic categories that concern geographical matters can be integrated into the 32 regional codes of the semantic analysis. Of course, all codes are not found in response to all questions, neither do they all have the same importance for the same question, nor does a specific code necessarily have the same importance when questions are compared. But in the corpus of the eight open questions - which include the very specialized questions of the analytical regional spaces - no set of codes is missing in the whole sample, and the highest percentage of codes missing from the responses to any particular question amounts to only 16%. The number of missing codes is higher in the case of the questions analysed thematically; it can be as high as almost half the number of codes, since thematic analysis is less detailed than structural semantic analysis, and not all codes can easily be represented among the themes elicited in response to a particular question. Certain sets of codes can be entirely absent: the topographical codes do not correspond to any theme, themes corresponding the the historical code are rare, and once even the personal codes fail to appear.

This absence of certain codes is what one would expect when microdiscourses are elicited from the subjects on matters as diverse as different views on the involvement region; similarities of external spaces to the settlement; reasons for moving ot staying, and for identification with the settlement and the involvement region; the ideal future of the involvement region, and the kinds of changes needed for it to progress. In fact, what is striking is that the basic, general questions concerning the associations attached to the involvement region, its characteristics, and its overall internal differences, elicited the *complete* grid of regional codes.

This cannot be accidental. We feel it shows that the grid elicited reveals the fundamental semantic components structuring the apprehension of the regional environment; though there may be other codes which also participate in this apprehension (we found one use of a sexual code), their presence is weak and spurious. These observations do not concern isolated individuals but the whole sample, and the grid located is thus of a *cultural* nature. This grid constitutes the stable cultural background against which social groups and individuals make their discursive choices, choices which may vary according to the context of their regional discourse.

It can be convincingly argued that the grid of the 32 regional codes is not restricted to the inhabitants of Northern Greece only, but is much more far-reaching. One first reason is the composition of the sample, that makes it representative of Greece in general. The second reason is the semantic nature of the codes found, that seems to reflect a very general manner of apprehending regional space. Finally, there are indications that this manner goes beyond Greek culture and is applicable to modern Western culture in general. We are referring to the findings of Raymond Ledrut (1973) in his study on urban conception in France. Ledrut locates in his material some 20 codes, which are on the whole quite comparable to our own, though there are certain technical differences between his analysis and ours. Some of his codes we do not consider as separate codes (for example, "big" for Ledrut belongs to a separate code of spatiality, while for us it is only a qualification classified with the code of the element qualified: "a big city" indicates the presence of the urban code). Other codes that Ledrut sees as separate are by us grouped together (instead of his codes of naturality and hygiene we use the ecological code) and some are further subdivided by us (for example, his economic or functional codes). But only one of Ledrut's codes is missing from our study (the moral code), and almost half of his codes are directly comparable to ours.

The resemblance between the semantic grid actualized in France for the apprehension of the urban environment and the Greek grid for regional space both reinforces and generalizes the partial findings of the two studies. This generalization is of a double nature. Given that the resemblance is one between urban codes and regional codes, we can consider that there is a general *spatial language* regulating the conception of macro-environments. Then, the striking convergence between two Western cultures as different as the French and the Greek culture allows us to formulate the hypothesis that this language approximates to a universal spatial language of contemporary Western culture.

2. The two aggregate models of regional space

In the previous section we presented the nature of the general grid of regional codes. Here we will discuss certain aspects of the structuring of these codes and its transformations according to the discursive context. A first aspect of contextual structuring concerns the relative predominance of certain sets of codes in the responses to different questions. We saw in the previous chapter (Section 4) that for the whole sample, in response to the questions on characteristics and differences the social codes prevail, followed by the economic codes; this holds true for most of the frequency-program groups in respect to the question on differences, and the same observation can be extended to all the groups for the question on characteristics. The situation is comparable for the two questions on similarity: the social codes again prevail, but this time followed by the codes of the built environment. For most of the social groups then follow the economic codes, which for certain social groups may acquire a higher rank, but rarely a lower one. As we mentioned already, the built environment codes occupy the third rank for the question on differences, together with the topographical codes. Thus, for all four questions the social codes are prevalent, covering for the whole sample around one-fourth of the codes used. The economic codes are ranked second in the basic questions (around one-fifth of the codes used for the whole sample) and third in the questions on similarity (19% and 15% for the whole sample). For the question on differences the built environment set follows the economic set (around 14% for all social groups), while for the other basic question its importance falls to the level of the remaining sets of codes; on the other hand, for the questions on similarity it rises to occupy the first or second rank (one-fourth of the cases of code use for the whole sample) - Table 10.

This hierarchical structuring of the sets of regional codes based on their relative prevalence, i.e., the number of uses of the codes compared to the total number of codes used, reflects the importance of certain perspectives on regional space. The most important, as they emerge from spontaneous regional discourse, are the social, the economic, and the physical perspective (in that order). In the previous chapter we had the occasion to point out, on the basis of the analysis of the questions on characteristics and differences, that the prevalence of the social and economic codes justified our selection for analysis of the social and economic spaces among the set of analytical spaces. The present discussion of our data leads to the same conclusion. In addition, the strong presence of the codes of the built environment shows that geographers and semioticians of space also deal with an important analytical space.

We can get some further insights into the hierarchical structuring of codes by disaggregating the sets of codes. Table 10 presents all the codes which were used with a frequency of over 15% (i.e., by more than 15% of the subjects) and indicates the relative prevalence of each of them. While in terms of sets of codes, for the four questions discussed above (the first four questions of Table 10) it is the social codes that prevail, followed by the economic codes, this situation is reversed on the level of individual codes: here, it is the code of economic activities that prevails throughout (with a frequency that varies from 8% to 73% for the social groups and from 25% to 56% for the whole sample), followed by the ecological code (11%-59% for the groups and 21%-48% for the sample) and the code of lifestyle (11%-56% and 16%-47%).

So far our emphasis has been on the similarities of code structuring between the regional micro-discourses elicited by the four first questions of Table 10. However, in addition to these similarities, Table 10 also reveals an important difference. On the basis of the number of important codes, regional discourses can be divided into two groups. The first group includes the discourses elicited by the questions on characteristics and differences, and the second those corresponding to the questions on similarities. Discourses of the first group show a high number of important codes, approximately 15 codes (almost half of the grid), while the number of important codes of the second group falls to about one-third of this number (around 15% of the grid). Thus, while for all questions all codes of the grid are activated to some extent, the relation between important and complementary codes is dramatically altered as we pass from the first group to the second. This alteration demonstrates once more the context sensitivity of the discourses elicited. The focused context (similarity of *a* to *b*) produces a *focused* discourse, which revolves around a few important codes with a low frequency supplemented by many codes of secondary importance, and is thus *oligo-codal,* while the loose context leads to a *diffused* discourse, involving a great number of important codes covering a wide range of frequencies and an equal number of secondary codes, a type which we might call *multi-codal.* This opposition is parallelled by the difference in the number of codes per person used in the two contexts: around 2.0 for the oligo-codal discourse and 5.5 for the multi-codal discourse.

This is not the only opposition following from the discursive context, as we can see if in Table 10 we turn to the data for the associational question. So far, we have left the data from this question out of our discussion. They present some continuity with those from the other questions, as attested by the fact that the social and the economic codes are still highly ranked. But they now occupy the second and third rank instead of the first and second respectively, and their relative prevalence is 13% and 12% as opposed to that which they held in the other questions (around 25% and 18%). Instead we find a strong prevalence - by 32% - of the personal codes, in which the experiential code has a particularly

Table 10. Rank, frequency, and relative prevalence of codes in aggregate micro-discourses.

Code/Code set	Question on characteristics					Question on differences				
	Rank	Frequency, %		Relative prevalence, %		Rank	Frequency, %		Relative prevalence, %	
		Whole sample	All groups	Whole sample	All groups		Whole sample	All groups	Whole sample	All groups
1. Economic activities	A	56	40–73	10	~10	A	54	47–67	10	~10
2. Economic development	C	38	17–46	7	3–9	D	25	3–42	5	~5
3. Economic (set)	**B**			21	13–24	**B**			18	~18
4. Social groups	E	19	9–34	4	1–6	E	17	11–25	3	1–5
5. Wealth	D	29	21–36	5	~5	E	21	15–26	4	~4
6. Lifestyle	B	47	40–56	9	~9	C	38	33–50	7	~7
7. Mentality	D	27	~27	5	~5	E	18	9–29	3	1–5
8. Political	E	16	11–23	3	~3					
9. Social (set)	**A**			27	~27	**A**			22	~22
10. Leisure	D	27	14–42	5	~5	E	20	13–31	4	2–6
11. Functional (set)										
12. Ecological	B	45	31–59	8	5–11	B	48	31–64	9	~9
13. Ecological (set)										
14. Topological	D	25	19–34	5	~5	C	37	17–61	7	3–10
15. Toponymic	D	22	17–29	4	~4	B	44	31–59	8	5–10
16. Topographical (set)						C			15	12–18
17. Architectural form										
18. Urban						D	27	14–48	5	3–8
19. Regional						E	18	3–28	3	1–6
20. Built environment (set)						C			14	~14
21. History (set)	D	28	18–39	5	~5	E	20	6–29	4	1–6
22. Aesthetic	C	34	25–50	6	~6	D	24	6–39	5	1–7
23. Experiential	C	37	25–55	7	5–10	D	28	~28	5	~5
24. Personal (set)	C	13		13	~13	**D**			10	5–13

Table 10 (continued).

	Question on similarities involvement region-settlement					Question on similarities wider region-settlement					Associational question				
	Rank	Frequency, %		Relative prevalence, %		Rank	Frequency, %		Relative prevalence, %		Rank	Frequency, %		Relative prevalence, %	
		Whole sample	All groups	Whole sample	All groups		Whole sample	All groups	Whole sample	All groups		Whole sample	All groups	Whole sample	All groups
1. A	A	30	19–44	12	8–19	A	25	8–38	14	5–18	C	21	9–34	7	3–11
2.															
3. C	C			15	10–31	B			19	6–27	C			12	4–22
4.															
5.															
6. B	B	25	~25	10	~10	B	16	11–25	9	6–14	D	17	9–25	6	3–10
7.															
8.															
9. A	A			28	23–35	A			25	14–39	B			13	10–21
10.											C	25	17–39	9	6–13
11.											D			11	7–15
12. B	B	21	14–39	8	5–17	A	22	11–40	12	6–20	B	29	22–42	11	8–15
13.						C			12	6–20	D			11	8–15
14.															
15.															
16.															
17. C	C	17	3–25	6	1–10										
18. A	A	29	14–55	11	5–19	B			11	6–20					
19.						A	19	12–36	25	16–39					
20. B	B			24	13–32						D			10	5–14
21.															
22.											C	22	10–39	8	3–13
23.											A	68	57–80	24	~24
24.											A			32	~32

strong presence (24%). This presence is also shown by the very high frequency of the code, which is used in all groups by more than half of the subjects and can be used by as many as four-fifths. The personal codes, and especially the experiential code, have in the responses to the associational question a position radically different from that which they hold in respect to the other questions. The personal codes are third in importance for the question on characteristics (relative prevalence 13%), fourth for the question on differences (prevalence 10%), and come next to last in rank for the questions on similarities. For the first two questions, the aesthetic and the experiential code participate on equal terms in the set; the experiential code has a relatively low prevalence (of 7% and 5% respectively) and a frequency for the whole sample of 37% and 28%.

The discourse elicited by the associational question thus to some degree shares the characteristics of the oligo-codal focused discourse that we found in the responses to the questions on similarities. But its radical difference from both this discourse and the discourses on characteristics and differences lies in the importance of the experiential code. For all four of these questions, the relative prevalence of the social and the economic codes together moves between 40% and 50%, while the experiential code does not exceed 7%. For the associational question, these two sets of codes together account for just one-fourth of total code use, a proportion equal to that of the experiential code alone. Thus, in the context of the associational question, there is almost a complete reversal of code structuring: the dominant code sets no longer dominate over the experiential code. The importance of this code is also attested by two further data: its distance from the second code is much greater than the corresponding distances in the other questions, and its share in the total prevalence of all the important codes is also much greater than the corresponding share of the first code in the other questions. This importance puts a distance between the experiential code and the other important codes which appear in the context of the associational question - in order of importance: the ecological code, the code of leisure, the aesthetic code, and the code of economic activities - and thus splits the set of important codes. The code structuring produced by this question is in fact a triple layering of codes, including one dominant code, a limited set of important codes, and a large set of supplementary codes. The oligo-codal discourse of the associational question is not unrelated to a *mono-codal* discourse.

Regional discourse is not value-free. Of course, in the responses to the three basic questions and the questions on analytical spaces, it is possible to locate in the whole sample codes which as a general rule are used without any value judgments attached; these are the topological code and the toponymic code. There are three more codes among the codes of Table 10 which are usually used in a neutral sense: the code of social groups, the regional code, and the code of history. People also to a large extent tend to use the code of social origins in the same neutral way and, though this code is not among the codes of Table 10 but appears most frequently in the context of the question on analytical social space, this phenomenon deserves some comment. It appears in its clearest form in the context of the question on social space, the aim of which was to invite the interviewees to comment on social differences within the involvement region. In response, a great majority among the interviewees (78%) referred to ethnic groups, an issue which may be politically or socially sensitive, depending on the group referred to. A very large proportion (54%) of these references are without any value judgment, and it can be suspected that most of the speakers handled the sensitivity of the issue by talking freely about ethnic differences but simultaneously neutralizing their value judgments by imposing, consciously or unconsciously, an internal censorship.

Most of the codes, however, are accompanied by value judgments which, though they cover all the range of positive, negative, neutral and synthesis-of-opposites, color the use of the codes with tendencies diverging from neutrality. Thus, the code of economic activities and the ecological code, although they show some neutral use, are marked mainly by a tendency toward positive evaluations. Positive evaluations, together with the synthesis-of-opposites type, are also the tendency for the three social codes of wealth, lifestyle, and mentality; the value judgments accompanying the political and the urban code, and the code of building morphology, are dispersed among all the evaluational types.

We shall finally comment on value judgments in the experiential code. If we leave aside the responses to the associational question, this code is mainly found with positive and neutral judgments, though it may also carry other types of evaluations. However, the distribution of evaluations in the context of the associational question is quite different. Here, individuals who use this code with exclusively positive evaluations amount to more than two-thirds of the total number of users of the code. As for the remaining one-third, 15% use the code neutrally and the rest divide almost equally between exclusively negative value judgments and the use of both negative and positive evaluations (synthesis-of-opposites type).

We see, then, that for the associational question use of the experiential code is strongly linked to positive evaluations.

We already had the opportunity (in Chapters 6 and 7) to discuss the marked differences between cool and warm evaluations, as well as the relationship of cool evaluations to more or less unemotional descriptions, and of warm evaluations to involved judgments and emotional reactions. We also pointed out, on the basis of thematic analysis, that warm evaluations are mainly founded on the experiential code. The present analysis of regional discourse completes these observations. The associational question leads to a discourse radically different from the discourses elicited by the other questions, with radically different, almost inverted code structuring; this opposition is mainly due to the function, rank, and evaluation of the experiential code. In the same manner in which this code underlies warm evaluations of regional space, it dominates the discourse on the associational question and is linked to positive evaluations. On the other hand, it is underrepresented in the other questions and its value orientation is much more dispersed. We have not only cool and warm evaluations, but also *cool* and *warm discourses*. The cool discourse is descriptive and, given its orientation towards outer reality, "objectivist", while the warm discourse is expressive, emotional, and "subjectivist", since it mainly revolves around subjective experiences.

All these observations converge in the conclusion that there are two contrasting general modes of apprehending regional space, modes which can be distinguished by the hierarchical structuring of the codes of the regional grid and the importance and orientation of the experiential code. To these modes correspond two different *models* through which the region is conceived. They are not related to different social groups, but to the metamorphosis of the mood of one and the same group in response to the alteration of the discursive context. They are both equally representative of the group. The two models are not derived from analysis of the structure of any particular individual discourse, but from the general configuration in the use of codes by the social groups as totalities; thus, since they are related to the code structuring of the group's discourse in general, we shall call them *aggregate* models.

Society, economy, and the built environment generally form the substance of the "objectivist" conception of the region as we can see from the code sets, and the nucleus of this conception consists, according to the structuring of the individual codes, of a preoccupation with economic activities, and then with the natural environment (ecological code) and lifestyle. In function of the context it may include references to economic development, personal experiences, and aesthetics (question on characteristics); place names and topological notions (question on differences); urban matters (question on similarities involvement region-settlement); or regional matters (question on similarities wider region-settlement). On the other hand, the substance of the "subjectivist" discourse is composed mainly of personal reactions, with some references to society and economy; its nucleus revolves predominantly around personal experiences and extends to ecology, leisure, aesthetics, economic activities and lifestyle. The two models tend in opposite directions, but they are not polarized: the "objectivist" model makes some room for the subject, and the "subjectivist" model for a contact with the external world.

It is important to note that every social group makes use of both models. Some differences of emphasis may occur, but we cannot say that some groups conceive of the region in objectivist terms and others in subjectivist. The models are context-determined, not sociologically determined. They represent two faces of the same coin, two modes of approach to regional space that apparently form part of the general semiotic competence of all groups.

3. The discursive regularities of regional discourse and the fundamental modes of conceiving the region

The aggregate models indicate clearly that regional discourse is not flat. The selection of the regional codes is not neutral and indifferent to the social groups: some of the codes or code sets may dominate certain regional micro-discourses, others may be stressed to a lesser degree, while others may be quite underrepresented or missing. This pyramidal structure of codes represents the essence of the semantic structure of regional - or any other - discourse.

But it is also possible to study the internal structuring of codes in the discourse of the individual interviewees. In order to approach this issue, we may make use of two criteria: the frequency with which a particular code is used by the speaker, and the order of appearance of codes in his/her discourse. Both criteria indicate the relative importance of a code. Frequency alone might seem a sufficient indicator, but it is also possible to argue that the sooner a code appears, the greater its importance. For each interviewee, we noted the three most frequently used codes, and the three codes which first appeared, in response to each question. The frequency counts and the crosstabulations between them show that the two criteria are closely related, and allow us to define a fundamental regularity in individual code use; they also lead us to the definition of models for the internal structuring of individual discourses.

Several different types of crosstabulations were attempted. First, we used as a background all the social groups of the sociosemiotic programs. Secondly, we selected a wide set of differing micro-discourses (responses to different questions). Then, we operated both with individual codes and sets of codes. Finally, we checked crosstabulations not only for the first rank of codes, but also for the second and third ranks. Due to technical constraints, a part of our checks dealt not with individual codes but with groupings according to sets of codes. When groupings of codes are used, the meaning of a correlation is that there is a tendency for the nth in order of appearance code and the code holding the nth rank in the hierarchy of frequencies to belong to the same set.[33]

The results are very striking. In half of the cases studied, frequency and order of appearance are correlated, almost always very significantly (as a rule at the .0000 level of significance). In the case of the responses to the three questions on analytical spaces, the correlations between frequency and order of appearance for the individual codes are as strong as those for the code sets, but are more common. We should also add that the results for the whole sample are always positive and very significant.

The correlations between code sets, in combination with those between individual codes, indicate that the relations revealed by the code sets are due to the more or less systematic correspondence between order and frequency of appearance of the individual codes. The extent of this correspondence shows that often our two criteria, frequency and order, are interchangeable. Of course, there are cases where this equivalence does not hold. But this discursive regularity is so insistent and multifaceted that it presents itself as a national - we dare say universal - rule. The issues that a speaker first addresses are also the issues to which he or she tends to return nost often in the course of developing his/her micro-discourse, and vice versa. A similar conclusion for a semiotic system other than natural language is mentioned by Evans (1980: 264), referring to a study by Milgram and Jodelet: they found that the elements first drawn on a sketch map and those most frequently recognized in a picture-recognition test were closely related.

The regularity defined above points to a hierarchical structuring of the codes of individual discourse, a structuring internal to these discourses. Thus, by examining the results on frequency and order for the social groups we can arrive at internal code structures characteristic of a particular group. We can follow this structuring for the questions on characteristics and differences, and the associational question, and compare it to the aggregate models discussed in the previous section. We shall use as an example the data for the whole sample, which figure in Table 11.

This Table shows, for the three questions, the codes most frequently occupying (see "position") the first three ranks of frequency and appearance; thus the percentage in each box of the Table corresponds to the number of persons using the code. Since a code used by a person in one rank cannot by definition be used simultaneously by the same person in another rank, when the same code appears in more than one rank it is used by different persons. If we then add the percentages of the same code for the different ranks, we obtain a percentage corresponding to the total participation of this code in the first three ranks and the total number of users of the code. On the basis of this sum, as well as the distribution of each code among the three ranks, we classified the individual codes that appear in the nine boxes of each Table in order of importance. This cumulative rank index for the codes appears in Table 11 at the bottom of each table.[34] Under this line figures the hierarchical structuring of the codes presented in Table 10, on the basis of which the aggregate models of regional discourse were defined. Let us now attempt an interpretation of this material.

We first observe the expected close fit for each question between the code ranking following from the frequency table and the ranking from the order-of-appearance table. But in addition, there is a very close fit between the first four codes in all four rankings for the two questions on characteristics and differences. In these questions, three codes dominate the internal structure of regional discourse: in order of importance, the code of economic activities, the ecological code, and the code of lifestyle. But, as we can see from a comparison of Tables 10 and 11, this is exactly the same set of codes as the nuclear codes of the "objectivist" aggregate model of regional discourse, and the ranking of the codes in the two cases is very similar. In addition, the contextual variations due to the two questions introduce into the structure of individual discourse further codes that are almost identical with those attached to the aggregate model. On the other hand, the regional conception related to the

Table 11. Frequency and order of appearance of codes in internal regional micro-discourses for the whole sample.

Question on characteristics							
Rank according to frequency							
Posi- tion	1st	%	2nd	%	3rd	%	Sum, %
Rank							
1st	econ. activities	17	lifestyle	17	econ. development	12	46
2nd	ecological	13	lifestyle	12	econ. activities	10	35
3rd	econ. activities	10	ecological	8	aesthetic	8	26

Cumulative percentage of a code:

1. econ. activities, 37%   2. lifestyle, 29%   3. ecological, 21%
4. econ. development, 12%   5. aesthetic, 8%

Ranking in aggregate model:

A1. econ. activities   B2. lifestyle   B3. ecological
C4. econ. development   C5. experiential   C6. aesthetic

Question on characteristics							
Rank according to order of appearance							
Posi- tion	1st	%	2nd	%	3rd	%	Sum, %
Rank							
1st	econ. activities	14	econ. de- velopment	13	lifestyle	12	39
2nd	econ. activities	14	experiential	10	ecological	9	33
3rd	ecological	10	aesthetic	9	econ. activities	8	27

Cumulative percentage of a code:

1. econ. activities, 32%   2. ecological, 19% & econ. development, 13% &
   lifestyle, 12%   5. experiential, 10%   6. aesthetic, 9%

Ranking in aggregate model:

A1. econ. activities   B2. lifestyle   B3. ecological
C4. econ. development   C5. experiential   C6. aesthetic

Table 11 (continued).

	Question on differences						
	Rank according to frequency						
Posi-tion	1st	%	2nd	%	3rd	%	Sum, %
Rank							
1st	ecological	15	econ. activities	13	lifestyle	8	36
2nd	ecological	13	econ.	12	lifestyle	8	33
3rd	econ. activities	9	activities		lifestyle	8	25
			topological	8			

Cumulative percentage of a code:

1. econ. activities, 34% 2. ecological, 28% 3. lifestyle, 24%
4. topological, 8%

Ranking in aggregate model:

A1. econ. activities B2. ecological B3. toponymic
C4. lifestyle C5. topological

	Question on differences						
	Rank according to order of appearance						
Posi-tion	1st	%	2nd	%	3rd	%	Sum, %
Rank							
1st	ecological	19	topological	13	econ. activities	11	43
2nd	ecological	11	econ.	10	lifestyle	9	30
3rd	econ. activities	11	activities		topological	7	25
			ecological	7			

Cumulative percentage of a code:

1. ecological, 37% 2. econ. activities, 32% 3. topological, 20%
4. lifestyle, 9%

Ranking in aggregate model:

A1. econ. activities B2. ecological B3. toponymic
C4. lifestyle C5. topological

Table 11 (continued).

	Associational question						
	Rank according to frequency						
Position	1st	%	2nd	%	3rd	%	Sum, %
Rank							
1st	experiential	50	ecological	13	aesthetic	6	69
2nd	experiential	10	aesthetic	9	leisure	9	28
3rd	leisure	7	econ. activities	5	lifestyle	4	16

Cumulative percentage of a code:

1. experiential, 60% ecological, 13%

2. leisure, 16% & aesthetic, 15% & 5. econ. activities, 5% 6. lifestyle, 4%

Ranking in aggregate model:

A1. experiential B2. ecological C3. leisure
C4. aesthetic C5. econ. activities D6. lifestyle

	Associational question						
	Rank according to order of appearance						
Position	1st	%	2nd	%	3rd	%	Sum, %
Rank							
1st	experiential	43	ecological	15	aesthetic	8	66
2nd	experiential	15	leisure	10	aesthetic	8	33
3rd	leisure	6	econ. activities	5	ecological	5	16

Cumulative percentage of a code:

1. experiential, 58% 2. ecological, 20% 3. aesthetic, 16%
4. leisure, 16% 5. econ. activities, 5%

Ranking in aggregate model:

A1. experiential B2. ecological C3. leisure
C4. aesthetic C5. econ. activities

associational question is dominated to a large extent by the experiential code, and then by the ecological and the aesthetic codes, the code of leisure, and the code of economic activities. The ranking of these codes in both frequency and order of appearance is absolutely identical and is almost an exact replica of that of the nuclear codes of the "subjectivist" aggregate model of regional discourse. Once again the contrasting nuclei of the two models emerge, this time on the basis of the internal structuring of regional discourse. They now reappear as *internal* models of this discourse.

Our decision to stop at the three first codes was relatively arbitrary. The gradation of the percentages of the three codes in the first rank may be either abrupt or very smooth; the sum of the percentages of the three codes may be very high or relatively low; but the percentage of the third code tends to be around 10% or less, something which indicates that the following codes are not very important. Generally, the gradation is smoother for the second and especially for the third rank, and the sum of the percentages of each consecutive rank decreases, with the result that the sum of the third rank is not over 30%. Thus, in the third rank, the percentages of each code are rather low, the differences in the importance of the codes are not generally acute, and the three codes together account for a rather limited part of the codes used in this rank. In this case, then, some rather important codes may not appear.

However, although the data of Table 11 perhaps theoretically do not exhaust all the important codes, they are unlikely in practice to be a distortion of the actual code structure. In addition, their close resemblance to the nuclear codes of the aggregate models and the correspondence of the rankings of these two sets of codes legitimates the way they were selected, while also revealing a crucial aspect of regional conception. Not all social groups show the same close fit. This is true mainly for the ranking of the codes, where the correspondences may be looser. But the codes of the two sets are always very similar. Thus, the nuclei of the aggregate and the internal models correspond, at least as to the set of the dominant codes and usually also as to the tendencies of the specific hierarchical structuring of their codes.

This is a crucial point for the study of regional conception. The aggregate models derive from regularities in an abstract collective text, abstract in the sense that it does not exist as a concrete text but is a composite of the discourses of all the members of the collectivity and is constructed only analytically. On the contrary, the internal models derive from collective regularities in the internal aspects of concrete individual texts. The coincidence of the nuclei of these two kinds of models allows us to go beyond the partial aspects of regional discourse to the very roots of the conception of the region. It shows that the "objectivist" and the "subjectivist" models of the previous section render for all social groups two deep and fundamental modes of experiencing the region, two modes which are contrasted but not polarized, and which are connected through the umbilical cord of preoccupation with the natural environment.

4. Richness of regional discourse

Another aspect of the internal organization of regional discourse concerns the number of codes used in response to a question by each interviewee, i.e., richness of code use, and the number of codes used with value judgment; in both cases we made a distinction between the total number of codes used and the spatial codes pertinent to the particular question (see Chapter 8, Section 2).

Richness of code use shows clear context sensitivity, as shown by the average number of codes per person. For both the total number of codes and the total number of evaluated codes, the richness of the questions on characteristics, general differences, and functional differences is approximately the same, with a certain prevalence of the first question. In both cases, the poorest responses are those to the associational question, followed by the responses concerning social and economic space. Responses on the latter spaces also rate low for spatial codes, for which the question on differences elicits the greatest number. The question on differences also elicits the richest responses in terms of the maximum number of codes used (up to 14 codes), although the percentage of subjects with very high code use is low.

The total number of codes used and the total number of evaluated codes are closely interrelated, as indeed is shown by the crosstabulation of the data: the more codes a subject uses, the more codes are likely to be used to express value judgments. This tendency is context-free and apparently universal: it holds for both objectivist and subjectivist discourse and appears in all social groups as well as in the sample as a whole, usually independently of what categories are used to group the data.

A subject who uses a high number of codes to respond to one question often tends to use a high number of codes in response to other questions.

This tendency is most marked in the whole sample, where it is often very significant, but it also produces occasional crosstabulations within various social groups (most regularly among women). The same is apparently not true for evaluated code use: frequent value judgments in response to one question do not necessarily imply frequent value judgments in response to other questions. But, as might be expected, high code use in response to one question is generally related to high code use in the whole interview, though here again the tendency appears in the sample as a whole rather than in the separate social groups. Here, however, a certain context sensitivity is noticeable: systematically, for practically all social groups and for the sample as a whole, high code use in response to the question on services implies high total richness of codes, and the relation is often very significant. It seems that discourse on functional space is particularly indicative of the relative richness of codes used by a speaker, a rather intriguing observation that indicates, we would speculate, the importance of functional aspects in the regional conception of our interviewees.

The frequency tables occasionally show differences in richness of code use among the social groups, but they are not systematic with reference to any particular group. Thus, in some cases, women and workers show poorer code use, while men and the lower middle class richer. Sometimes the inhabitants of Veria are poor in code use, while in Thessaloniki and Ormylia richer and poorer code use vary from case to case. There are some significant differences, as the sociosemiotic programs show, and there are some tendencies which become clearer when we examine the sociospatial distribution of the results.

There are a few instances where richness of code use correlates with social class, though generally this does not seem to be the case. When there is a correlation, the working class shows lower code use than the other two classes. The lower middle class shows particularly high use of evaluated codes in response to the question on services (31% of the class are in the high category of 4 to 6 codes as compared to 21% of the middle class and only 8% of the workers). Total richness of codes, however, is not significantly related to social class.

Social classes grouped according to the city-country division are significantly correlated with richness of code use in response to the question on social differences within the region. Workers tend toward use of fewer codes both in the city and in the countryside, and the lower middle class in the cities is predominantly (63%) poor in code use, but in the countryside the lower middle class is by over 80% in the middle and highest categories of code use (42% each in the 3 and the 4-6 codes categories); the city middle class is evenly distributed, and the country middle class is heavily (by 50%) in the top category.

Age as such also does not seem to be a particularly significant factor in determining richness of code use, though for a few questions the results indicate that the young use significantly fewer codes that the mature (and color less with value judgments the codes they use when speaking about social differences within the region). On the other hand, age gives more significant results when the age groups are further disaggregated in accordance with the city-country division and the settlement hierarchy, a fact indicating that there is often no unified pattern for an age group but the group is spatially differentiated. In the question on social differences, country youth are richer in code use that country adults, but poorer in their use of evaluated codes. The conclusions concerning evaluated codes can be extended with the help of the distribution of the age groups in the settlement hierarchy. In both the cities, the mature tend to use more codes than the young, but Thessaloniki clearly shows richer code use than Veria for both age groups (in fact, Veria has the poorest code use values of all three settlements).

We have already remarked (Section 2 of this chapter) that discourse on social differences within the region tends to avoid value judgments, and indeed the use of codes with evaluation in response to this question is generally poor for all groups, though the mature in all settlements show somewhat higher values; the only exception are the mature in Thessaloniki, who by close to 40% fall in the highest category of richness of evaluated codes (5-8 code). This should probably not be taken as an indication of more overt social prejudice among them, but rather reflects the nature of the social differences which form the object of this discourse in the metropolis: the social distinctions which the inhabitants of Thessaloniki are concerned with, in addition to those of ethnic origin (a subject on which the discourse of all our subjects tended to be carefully neutral) are those connected with the relatively recent population movements of urbanization.

The social factor which produces the most significant results in richness of code use, however, is neither age nor class but gender, and here the relationship is systematic: men regularly use more codes than women. The relationship is almost context-free, since it appears in response to both general and specific questions, but there are a few cases where the opposite tendency asserts itself. In subjectivist discourse, women tend to make somewhat more use of evaluated codes than men. And when speaking about services, women also tend to use more evaluated codes than men, in spite of the fact that they do not show significantly higher code use for the question in general. In all other cases, men systematically tend to use more codes than women.

The systematic tendency of men to use more codes than women is evident also when the grouping by gender is seen in relation to the city-country division and the settlement hierarchy, though here both men and women are further differentiated into smaller groups. Most of the significant results concern discourse on social differences within the region, though there are correlations also for discourse on economic differences. Women tend to use fewer economic codes than men, but in this respect code use for both sexes in the countryside is slightly higher than in the cities. Women in Thessaloniki generally tend to use more codes than women in Veria and Ormylia, and the same is true for men; at the same time, within each settlement the male discourse is richer than the female discourse (the difference is most pronounced in the metropolis). Both men and women in the three settlements tend to avoid evaluated codes in discourse on social differences, with the exception of men in the metropolis.

Richness of code use also occasionally gives significant correlations with secondary social factors, though the results are not systematic and not easy to interpret. Richness of code use is related to education, but not in a linear fashion: college graduates show a relatively high code use in discussing differences within the region, but speakers with only primary school education or less show a code use quite comparable with that of speakers who have completed secondary or vocational school. It seems an intermediate level of schooling (at least in the traditional Greek school system) does nothing to enrich spatial conception, and may perhaps even act as an inhibiting influence on discourse.

Geographical mobility (annual number of trips outside the settlement) also correlates with richness of code use, though the relationship is not linear and no clear trend emerges. Low mobility is connected to low code use and high mobility to high code use, but in the intermediary categories the relationship is reversed. Low mobility is connected to a rather marked increase in the use of evaluated codes in subjectivist or associational discourse (low movers account for 80% of the cases in the highest category of evaluated codes used), but all other categories of mobility show more or less equally low use of evaluated codes, so it cannot be said that value judgment decreases as mobility increases; possibly one might venture the hypothesis that there is a threshold of geographical mobility beyond which value judgments about one's region become markedly less frequent in general.

Length of residence in a settlement correlates very significantly to code richness in discourse on social differences, but the relation is not very clear. As a general trend, few years of residence seems to imply fewer codes while longer residence increases code use. But the percentage of the most stable residents (34-68 years in the settlement) showing the poorest category of code use increases sharply in comparison to the preceding group (residents for 16-33 years) - 47% of the most stable residents use only up to 2 codes - while at the same time a rather large proportion of them (38%) is in the richest category (4-6 codes). These tendencies are so different as to create the impression of some rather marked internal divisions within this group of long-term residents.

Many changes of settlement also affect code use; in this case the correlation is with total richness of codes rather than with any particular discursive context, and again seems to involve a kind of threshold effect. People who have lived in two different settlements show somewhat higher code use than those who have never lived anywhere but in their home town, and people who have lived in three places show even higher code use, which would indicate that there is some relation between the experience of a greater number of life settings and total code richness. But those who have moved often (4-6 different settlements of residence) show markedly lower code use (50% of the group are in the low category of total code richness, up to 14 codes) in their regional discourse as a whole, which is a curious inversion of the expected trend. No other social groups show significant tendencies in connection to total richness of codes, which means that the groups are more or less equally rich in this respect.[35]

5. Complexity of regional discourse

Most of our analysis concerned the quantitative data on code use that we have presented above: hierarchy of code use and aggregate models of regional discourse; internal structuring of discourse through frequency and order of appearance of codes; internal models of discourse; and richness of code use. But we also attempted to extend our analysis of the structure of regional discourse to the level of relationships between codes in the discourse of each individual speaker, i.e., to the relative semantic *complexity* of discourse.

Complexity was estimated qualitatively for each interviewee on the basis of the responses to all eight open questions, and indicates how and to what degree the semantic codes are related in the discourse of the speaker. Let us look, for example, at the beginning of a response by a woman in Veria (three dots indicate a hesitation pause):

> I mean ... about Veria, it's a very wealthy place, all the villages around here are ... rich, because they have rich fields, they have ... fruit trees that ... you know, that set them very high, like, on the level of ... money.

The discourse begins, after a slight hesitation, with a reference to the toponymic code (*Veria*) which is immediately articulated with the code of economic development (*a very wealthy place*). It continues with a regional and a topological reference (*the villages around here*) and then returns to the code of development (*rich*); thus, the second phrase repeats the structure of the first with some slight variation (instead of the city of Veria the reference is to the villages around it). The next set of phrases relates very closely the code of economic activities (*they have fields, they have fruit trees*) and the code of natural resources (*rich fields*). Then the speaker returns to the topic of wealth, but now she refers not to what a wealthy place this is but to the income of the inhabitants (*very high on the level of money*). The articulations of the codes in the discourse are clearly expressed through explicit logical relationships (*because* they have, *that* sets them very high). If we leave out the toponymic and topological codes, we might describe the code sequence of this discourse as:

(a) development - (b) economic activities - (c) natural resources - (d) wealth

If we consider the logical argument of the segment, we could diagram the semantic structure as:

c / b / d / a

where / stands for an articulation, in this case an explicit logical relation of cause and effect: the fields are fertile, the inhabitants are fruit farmers, hence their income is high, therefore the place is wealthy.

This passage is an example of discourse with what could be considered as rather high complexity. The speaker uses many codes which she relates in a carefully structured whole with explicit logical articulations. This is not the only possible structure of discourse. People talk differently. Some give laconic responses of a few words. Others talk a lot, but use few codes which they repeat constantly:

> Well, like ... like intellectually you know the people in the villages you might say still haven't reached the degree where, like the intellectual level, you know, of the people in the cities. Mostly it's lower than what you'd expect.

Here the speaker (a man from Veria) starts out with the code of mentality (*intellectually*), articulates with the regional code (*villages*), and then repeats the same sequence in reference to the city. The next sentence repeats exactly what he said before, using the same code of mentality. The code sequence can be described as:

(a) mentality - (b) regional code - (a) mentality - (b) regional code - (a) mentality

and the semantic structure corresponds to the repetition of a simple statement:

$$a \,/\, b, \ a \,/\, b$$

The discourse shows a certain looseness of structure, adding words and phrases without new information, and is almost mono-codal.

Other speakers string together codes without systematic articulation, in a series of isolated phrases:

> Like it used to be, mulberry trees, bicycles, flowers, the ocean - and like it is now, noisy, smelling of souvlaki, pizza, all the cars ... like that.

The speaker (a young woman from Veria) changes codes with practically every word. The articulation which structures the sentence is the founding antithesis of the historical code (*used to be* vs. *now*); the other codes - ecological (*mulberry trees, the ocean* vs. *noisy, smelling*); urban (*bicycles* vs. *cars*); morphological and aesthetic (*flowers*) - are articulated with this opposition but are not further connected to each other. The speaker makes no attempt to relate the various things she mentions beyond grouping them chronologically in two different historical moments.

But it is also possible to find articulated discourse which is not based on logical relationships. The previous example already makes us suspect that behind the lists of words there is an implied reference to a code of lifestyle. There are other cases where this implied reference to another, silent code is even clearer:

And the roof tiles, the brick roof tiles had - have an important role to play in the city. When I say roof tiles ... the neighborhood and the area ... the apartment houses I mean ... there's a huge difference ....

To analyse this fragment of discourse (by a woman in Veria) one really has to draw on the context of all the responses of her interview, since many of the speaker's value judgments become evident only in the course of the whole interview. The above passage comes at the end of a lengthy nostalgic description of the city where the speaker has lived all her life and the changes it has undergone. Here she first makes reference to an element of building morphology (*roof tiles*) which she personifies (*has a role to play*) and to which she ascribes great significance (*an important role in the city*). This significance she attempts to explain in the next phrase, which is a metalinguistic reference to her own discourse (*when I say*), by the opposition between the old *neighborhood,* with its low houses and red tile roofs, and the new, impersonal *area* with its high-rise apartment buildings. But this *important role* is not a matter only of building morphology: the *huge difference* lies in the new way of life which has come with the apartment buildings. The semantic structure of this discourse is based on a series of metaphors: the brick roof tiles for the traditional low houses, the houses for the old neighborhood, and that in turn for the traditional lifestyle (perhaps for the people) which is now lost. The codes are explicitly articulated, but not logically so; the high complexity of the discourse results from a structure which is fundamentally metaphorical.

There is a certain relation between our criteria of semantic complexity of discourse and Basil Bernstein's concepts of restricted and elaborated sociolinguistic "codes".[36] Bernstein defines his codes primarily in syntactic terms, and considers that their different syntactic characteristics give rise to a different range and type of meanings which can be expressed within each code (Bernstein 1971: 125): "In the case of an elaborated code, the speaker will select from a relatively extensive range of alternatives and the probability of predicting the organizing elements is considerably reduced. In the case of a restricted code the number of these alternatives is often severely limited and the probability of predicting the elements is greatly increased."

Bernstein does not define his codes in terms of vocabulary, but recognizes a relation between more complex vocabulary and more elaborated code. Thus (Bernstein 1971: 145), "it is likely that the lexical differentiation of certain semantic fields will be greater in the case of an elaborated code" and (Bernstein 1971: 128) the verbal planning involved in the use of an elaborated code "promotes a higher level of syntactic organization and lexical selection.... This does not mean that these meanings are necessarily abstract, but abstraction inheres in the possibilities." Our own criteria of discourse complexity ignore vocabulary as an indication of complexity, and our findings thus do not reflect this aspect of discourse at all. In addition, we define complexity of discourse in terms of the degree of articulation between semantic codes, not in terms of complexity of syntax. For both these reasons, our results are not directly comparable to Bernstein's.

However, as Bernstein's definition of code demonstrates, and as indeed his argument explicitly recognizes, semantic complexity is not unrelated to syntactic complexity. Syntax is one major means of creating explicit logical relations between semantic codes. In addition, many of the elements that Bernstein points to as indicative of an elaborated code are not syntactic in the strict sense of the word but are aspects of discourse coherence, resulting from the desire for explicitness implied in the use of an elaborated code, where "meanings will have to be expanded and raised to the level of *verbal* explicitness" (Bernstein 1971: 128). Thus, many of the characteristics of Bernstein's elaborated code are directly related to what we have called articulations between semantic codes. And indeed, many of Bernstein's observations about restricted and elaborated codes show striking parallels to what we have defined above as degrees of semantic complexity.

Thus, a user limited to a restricted code (Bernstein 1971: 134) will show speech "epitomized by a low-level and limiting syntactic organization.... The rigid range of syntactic possibilities leads to difficulty in conveying linguistically logical sequence and stress. The verbal planning function is shortened, and this often creates in sustained speech sequences a large measure of dislocation or disjunction. The thoughts are often strung together like beads on a frame." This is closely reminiscent of the enumerative discourse of the young woman from Veria in our third example above.

Again, in a restricted code (Bernstein 1971: 134), "a restriction in planning often creates a high degree of redundancy. This means that there may well be a great deal of repetition of information, through sequences which add little to what has already been given." This is a very exact description of the almost mono-codal discourse of our second example above. The close relationship between an elaborated code (verbal explicitness, higher level of syntactic organization and lexical selection) and our criteria for high complexity of discourse has already been pointed out; many of them are well exemplified in the logically explicit discourse of the woman from Veria in our first example.

There is, however, one aspect of semantic complexity which is not at all related to the explicitness and syntactic organization of Bernstein's elaborated code. This is what we have identified as metaphorical speech, exemplified in the last discourse fragment we discussed above. A characteristic of metaphorical speech is precisely the fact that it achieves its semantic complexity without explicit logical relationships between codes, through juxtaposition; not the juxtaposition of items "strung together like beads on a string", but a patterned, intentional juxtaposition that creates articulations without specifying logical relationships. A definition of discourse complexity based on complexity of syntax cannot classify such a form of discourse as elaborated - the speaker in our last example can scarcely even be said to finish her last sentence. In fact, metaphorical language is one of the characteristics which Bernstein consistently refers to in order to point out that the classification of a code as restricted does not necessarily imply that it is a qualitatively poorer speech form (Bernstein 1971: 136): "It is important to realize that a restricted code carries its own aesthetic. It will tend to develop a metaphoric range of considerable power, a simplicity and directness, a vitality and a rhythm; it should not be disvalued." It is thus particularly interesting to note that according to the criteria of our own research, this form of discourse is considered semantically highly complex (Bernstein himself, 1971: 5-6, points out its similarities to poetry). The relationship between semantic complexity and syntactic fragmentation, due in these cases to a condensation of meaning and not to a simplification, is clearly a fruitful area for further investigation.

In our own research, we made an estimate of the total degree of semantic complexity of discourse shown by each subject on the basis of the kind of analysis indicated by the examples discussed above. The simplest form of code arrangement in response to a question we considered to correspond to the one-word response. Somewhat more complex is the almost mono-codal, oligo-codal type of discourse; the next level of complexity refers to enumerative discourse marked by a lack of articulations between codes; and the two forms of articulated discourse (logical and metaphorical) were considered the most complex. Of course, a speaker may well show various levels of complexity for the different questions of the interview; one question may draw a very brief response while another may result in a highly structured piece of argumentation or a rich personal narrative. The estimate is based on the discourse as a whole (i.e., on the responses to the eight open questions which were analysed using structural semantics); if anything, it is probably weighted a bit in favour of higher values, since sections of discourse with somewhat higher complexity tend also to be longer and therefore take up a proportionally larger part of the interview than sections of low complexity.

More than half our subjects show a relatively high degree of complexity of discourse: 29% of the whole sample were rated as showing high complexity, 25% as fairly high, and 26% as average, while only 10% were rated as rather poor and 10% as poor. The distribution is not significantly different for most social groups, though marginal differences exist, and this is a point which requires some discussion. Bernstein's studies (Bernstein 1971: 135) indicate that middle-class speakers have more ready access to an elaborated code than working-class speakers: "It is considered that the normative systems associated with the middle-class and associated strata are likely to give rise to the modes of an elaborated code whilst those associated with some sections ofthe working class are likely to create individuals limited to a restricted code." To the degree that our criteria of complexity of discourse are comparable to Bernstein's criteria for restricted and elaborated codes (and we remind the reader that the two sets of criteria are not fully compatible), one would expect middle-class speakers to show higher complexity of discourse than working-class speakers.

We already noted (in the previous section of this chapter) that something like this differentiation appears to be true for richness of code use: the working class for some questions shows significantly lower code use than the other two classes, though total richness of codes is not significantly related to social class. We also noted, however, that there seem to be some differences between social classes in the cities and in the countryside. In the case of complexity of discourse, no significant correlation to social class exists. Although the distributions of the frequency tables show that indeed working-class speakers on the whole have a somewhat lower degree of complexity than the other two classes, this difference is not statistically significant. It seems that the possibility of articulating a semantically complex discourse is not, in present-day Northern Greece, dependent on one's social position.

There are of course many reasons why such a discrepancy between Bernstein's findings and our own might appear. There may be differences in the composition of social classes in Greece and in England, or the discursive patterns of the Greek working class may differ from those of Bernstein's subjects. Bernstein relates discursive behavior not directly to social class but to patterns of socialization, primarily in the family and secondarily in the school, and considers these socialization patterns class-related; it may be that socialization patterns in Greece differ, or are differently related to class membership. Finally, as we have already remarked, semantic complexity is not directly comparable to Bernstein's codes; there may well be differences in syntax and vocabulary between our subjects which were outside the scope of our present study. The fact remains, however, that semantic complexity of discourse for our subjects does not seem to vary significantly in relation to social class. It also does not appear to be significantly affected by age, or by sociospatial distribution: people in the countryside do not use significantly less complex discourse than people in the cities. There is, however, one striking correlation of discourse complexity and social group: men show very significantly higher complexity of discourse than women. 66% of the men are in the high and fairly high class, as compared to 42% of the women; 49% of the women are in the average and rather poor class as compared to 25% of the men.

Complexity of discourse is almost linearly related, often very strongly, to total richness of code use, both for the sample as a whole and for several social groups. High complexity of discourse implies a high number of codes used, and vice versa. More unexpected is perhaps the fact that complexity of discourse seems to be related to richness of code use in the responses to one particular question, the question on differences within the involvement region. Richness of code use in this question is frequently very strongly related to complexity of discourse, again in an almost linear manner, both for the whole sample and for most of the separate social groups. This is particularly interesting since significant relations between complexity and code richness in the question on the characteristics of the involvement region are very limited, and there are no correlations at all with code richness for the associational question.

In addition, the use of certain specific codes and code sets in responses to the question on differences is correlated to complexity of discourse. Thus, complexity of discourse is correlated, sometimes very strongly, with use of the code of economic activities (for the whole sample, cities, youth, and women); the code of lifestyle (whole sample, cities, workers, and youth); the urban code (whole sample and women); and the experiential code (countryside and men). It is also correlated with the use of certain sets of codes: the economic codes, the social codes, and above all the topographical codes (for the whole sample and several social groups); the functional codes (for the whole sample, the cities, and the middle class); and the personal codes (in the countryside).

The general pattern of all these crosstabulations is the same: the use of a particular code is mainly related to high or fairly high complexity of discourse, in such a manner that almost always, more than 50% of the individuals with this degree of complexity of discourse use this code in response to this particular question, and more than 60% of the subjects using the code show this degree of complexity; for all codes, the percentage of users of the code decreases as complexity decreases. The only exception to this latter observation is the topographical code set, for which this decrease is not usually linear. In the case of the sets of economic (for the whole sample, cities, and youth) and social codes (for the whole sample), higher complexity is mainly related to the use of codes with negative evaluations or evaluations of the synthesis-of-opposites type. It seems that sometimes negative value judgments or balanced discourse is significantly connected to more sophisticated discursive forms.

The code richness of the micro-discourse on differences within the region is thus for many social groups a rather satisfactory index of the total degree of complexity of their regional discourse. But what comes as a surprise is that not only code richness but the use of individual codes and sets of codes can also function as such indices. Among sets of codes, the use of the social and the topographical codes is a quite generalized index of discourse complexity. Apparently, preoccupation with social differences and more detailed descriptions of geographical space are connected to a semantically more articulated and structured regional discourse.

6. Relevance of regional discourse

Both richness and complexity of discourse are correlated to the index of discursive relevance. While richness and complexity concern (quantitatively and qualitatively) the internal structure of discourse, relevance concerns the relationship of a particular discourse to a context, linguistic or situational, and is thus to some extent an indication of communicational competence (as defined by Dell Hymes, 1974: 75).

For the purposes of our study we defined relevant use of a code as use with reference to the space which a particular question explicitly asked about, i.e., economic, social, or functional space respectively. The distinction between codes used with pertinent spatial reference ("spatial" codes) and those used without reference to the pertinent space ("nonspatial" codes) proved to be generally unimportant, since the overwhelming majority of codes were used with spatial reference in all pertinent cases. It proved interesting, however, for the study of the structure of individual discourses through the use of an index of relevancy, which was constructed as the general ratio of "spatial" codes to the total number of codes used in the three questions on specific differences within the region.

We should note that under this definition of relevance, a perfectly "relevant" answer is not a very "good" answer. If in response to the question concerning social differences within the involvement region we receive the reply "Yes", this answer is 100% "relevant", but not very interesting. Let us say that instead we receive a more elaborate reply:

Oh, and there are a lot of gypsies in Veria, minorities, like we said. A real problem, that, with the gypsies. The city government is concerned about it, too, and they don't know how to handle it. And we are, too, a lot of times. We had a case ... when the kids were singing Christmas carols this year, here in my neighborhood ... two gypsy kids came up to them ... they grabbed the older one by the throat and

said "give us your money or we'll kill you" or something like that,
like I said, it's a real problem.

This answer is less "relevant" in that only about half of it refers directly to spatially located social differences, but it is much more interesting and informative. A relevance of 42%-58% spatial references in relation to the whole of the discourse (average relevance) is indicative of a
pretty effective answer, and high relevance (60%-83%) also usually indicates an adequate answer; above 83% relevance the answer tends to become "too relevant", too monotonous and undeveloped. But when the ratio falls below 42% the discourse tends to include a lot of nonspatial references, and below 35% it usually indicates that the response does not
really address the question.

For the whole sample, 16% of the subjects show low relevance, 35%
average relevance, 43% high relevance, and 6% too high relevance.
Thus, the great majority of our subjects were able to hold a relevant discourse. City inhabitants have lower relevancy ratios that inhabitants of
the countryside. Though in both groups the majority of subjects divide
bwteen the average and high class of relevance (very few fall in the category of too high relevance), the countryside predominates in the high
class (it accounts for 60% of the cases in that class), and over 25% of the
city inhabitants fall in the low relevancy class (accounting for 83% of the
cases there). Between other social groups, differences in relevance are
not significant.

There is some correlation, often very significant, between the relevancy
index and richness of discourse, both for the whole sample and for several social groups. These correlations generally concern code richness in
the responses to the individual questions for which relevance was calculated. For any particular question, relevance decreases as code richness
increases: low relevance is definitely connected to the use of many codes;
average relevance to high or average code use; high relevance to average
or low code use; and too high relevance usually to the use of few codes.
Thus, the two problematic categories of relevance (low and too high relevance) are related to the extreme categories of code richness, while the
pattern of effective discourse is more complex. If we examine total richness of code use (which correlates with relevance for the whole sample,
cities, and the mature), the pattern is similar, but simpler and less linear.
Too high relevance is definitely connected to lower code use, while the
three other classes of relevance all tend toward richer code use. But the

discourse of speakers with richer code use clearly tends to show average or high relevance: around 70% of these speakers fall in the average or high relevance classes and the rest drop to the low class.

There is also not unfrequently a correlation between relevance and complexity of discourse. Poorer complexity is clearly related to too high relevance, while average complexity tends to imply high or average relevance. But higher complexity does not necessarily imply low relevance: though the great majority of discourses with low relevance fall in this class, around 70% of speakers with high complexity of discourse show average or high levels of relevance.

Thus, it is clear that indeed the extremely "relevant" discourse is over-simplified, makes few articulations between codes, and tends to use few codes. But in the case of very irrelevant discourse, which tends to use many codes and show high complexity, complexity is a result of simple loquacity, of a tendency to chatter. Complexity as such, richness as such, is no guarantee of effective language use. If our definition of relevance is taken as an indication of ability to respond to an invitation to think and talk about a particular topic, as an indication of conversational competence, then we might venture to say that the most substantial responses would be the ones that combine complex code structure and rather rich code use with average relevance, roughly half the discourse being specific references, in the narrow sense, to the topic proposed by the interviewer, and the other half explanatory, contextual, or peripheral. This is, in fact, where a large part of the cases of highly complex discourse are to be found.

Chapter 10. Ideological models of the region

1. Discursive habits of the social groups

Our analysis in the previous chapter showed the existence for all our groups of two models of conceiving the regional environment: the cool objectivist and the warm subjectivist model. These two contrasting models emerged by suggesting to our interviewees two semantic contexts tending to appeal to opposite attitudes towards their region. Since all groups are similar in that they all have both models, we may ask if this coincidence of spatial ideology is the only conclusion we can draw on the conception of space by different social groups, or if these models coexist with other patterns marking the groups' exclusive character. More specifically: are there any codes whose presence or absence is characteristic for a specific social group? is there any code structure corresponding to a particular group that allows us to differentiate it from other groups?

We shall approach the first issue with the help of the sociosemiotic programs. As we saw in Chapter 5, Section 4, our study defined primary social groups on the basis of both sociological and sociogeographical criteria: social classes, genders, and age groups, on the one hand, and the cities, the countryside, and the three settlement ranks on the other, as well as the groups resulting from the combinations between these two sets. This gives us a total of 47 primary groups, in addition to the whole sample that is an indication of the tendencies of the country as a whole. Our secondary social groups are the educational groups, the groups defined by different degrees of familiarity with the settlement, the groups with a differentiated degree of socioeconomic control and those with a different socioprofessional integration, the different groups of regional mobility, and the groups defined by different degrees of regional experience. The number of these secondary groups is 28. We examined the possible correlation of each of these groups to the use of specific codes in response to the questions on the characteristics of the involvement region and the general differences within it.

Of the 76 social groups, 55 (72%) show at least one significant (occasionally very significant) positive or negative correlation to some code in their responses to the question on characteristics. Only six of the

48 primary groups show no such relation. Code use is thus another aspects which confirms the analysis in the previous chapters: any of the sociospatial groups can acquire the status of relative autonomy, since almost every group can be significantly related to some specific code use. The number of individual codes characterizing a group runs from one to four, or if we include code sets, five. Not all 32 regional codes are significantly connected to some group, but almost half of them are; so are five of the eight sets of codes. The individual codes most frequently correlated with the groups are the code of economic activities and the code of economic development, the code of leisure, the urban code, the code of history, and the experiential code.

As expected, the significant case of a group totally lacking a code or using it throughout is extremely rare. The usual cases are more shaded and the groups show a whole range of mixed tendencies in respect to a code, starting from a definite tendency to use the code (positive correlation); through a tendency to use accompanied by a weaker tendency to avoid use of the code (dominant or important positive); a tendency to non-use with a weaker positive tendency; a balance of use and non-use; and ending with different degrees of avoidance (negative correlation). We shall not give a scholastic account of the tendencies of all the social groups toward specific codes, but will try, in giving an account of this complex situation, to discern certain general patterns.

The only significant attributes of women as a group in their responses to the question on characteristics of the region are the total lack of the code of social origins and the almost total lack of the political code. These codes are no more significant if we divide women into city women and country women. These two groups have in common a significant relation to the toponymic code and the code of history, but their tendencies in respect to these common codes are different. City women tend equally to use and avoid the toponymic code, while country women avoid it to an important degree. City women are more negative in respect to the historical code, and country women definitely avoid it. They also diverge in that city women show a positive tendency toward the experiential code, while country women markedly avoid the code of leisure. Thus, women as a whole do not consider political issues characteristic of their region, and country women show a pronounced lack of historical discourse of any kind in this context, while city women seem to like to elaborate on their personal experiences.

The nature of women's regional discourse is further qualified when we pass to more restricted groups. Women as a group are significantly related to the code of leisure, but while country women tend to avoid it, metropolitan women balance avoidance with a certain focusing on the code, a tendency which is reinforced among provincial city (i.e., Veria) women. Metropolitan women are also characterized by a pronounced avoidance of the code of economic development. Here they differ from provincial women and the women of Ormylia (i.e., of a rural settlement), since in Ormylia the women are divided in their preference for or avoidance of this code, and women in Veria show a clear preference for it. The code of economic activities is not significantly related to metropolitan women, but it is significantly related to the two other groups: the main tendency of Ormylia women is toward use of this code, and this tendency becomes stronger with the provincial city women. On the whole, metropolitan women have a certain tendency to see their region in terms of leisure, but clearly avoid matters of economic development; provincial women are preoccupied with leisure to a greater degree, but are also involved with developmental and other economic matters, and are almost totally uninterested in ecological issues; and Ormylia women also show an interest in economy, but less pronounced.

City men are not much inclined to describe their involvement region in terms of politics or leisure, and unlike city women they show little desire to recount their own experiences, but they have a much greater interest than both city and country women in historical references of all kinds (balanced use and non-use of the historical code). Country men, on the other hand, operate with these codes in a totally different manner. They definitely avoid matters of leisure (as country women do) and are less interested in history than city men, but they are much more inclined towards politics than the latter, being characterized by balanced use and non-use of the political code.

Men, like women, show no significant tendencies toward the economic codes when they are studied according to the city-country division. But, as with women, this is not the case when we further disaggregate them. Provincial men are significantly related to the codes of economic development and economic activities, but are less involved with these matters than provincial women, being quite comparable to the women of Ormylia. Contrary to provincial women who show no interest in ecology, provincial men tend to use this code rather more than they avoid it. Among the six sociospatial gender groups deriving from the settlement hierarchy, the men of Ormylia on the whole show the greatest involvement with economic matters.

There are fewer significant tendencies toward code use among the age groups. Rural youth has a certain orientation toward the code of natural resources, and a much stronger one toward the functional set of codes, while adults in the cities tend to some degree to make references to urban issues. Provincial adults, like provincial women, show a strong inclination toward the code of economic development, and while this tendency is not exclusively positive, it is much stronger than that of provincial youth; the case is similar with the code of leisure. In the metropolis it is youth that shows this tendency toward the code of leisure in talking of the characteristics of the region, while the mature definitely avoid these issues. If the preoccupation with development characterizes provincial (Veria) adults as compared to provincial youth, the situation is reversed in the rural settlement of Ormylia.

As with the age groups, significant correlations with social classes are rather limited. All three urban classes have some inclination toward the code of history, but to different degrees. The urban lower middle class shows the strongest orientation toward this code (though the tendency is not exclusively positive), while avoidance is stronger with the middle class and becomes marked with the workers. The urban lower middle class is much more positively predisposed to the functional and built environment sets of codes. It shows a similar preoccupation with references to personal experiences, a preoccupation that decreases (as is the case with the code of history) as we pass to the middle and then the working class. It seems members of the urban lower middle class like to speak about the built environment, the provision of services, and their personal experiences, and to a lesser degree about events of the past, when they describe their region. It is interesting to note that the habits of the rural lower middle class are quite different from that of their urban counterparts. The disaggregation of classes to smaller local groups shows a pronounced if unequal interest among the Veria and the Ormylia classes in matters concerning economic activities; the only exception is the lower middle class in Veria.

Among the secondary social groups, individuals with a lower educational level show a certain equilibrium between use and avoidance of the code of wealth, but this is a much more positive tendency toward the code than the tendencies of the two higher educational levels. A similar balance is shown by the highest level of education in respect to the code of history, while the lower group is very reluctant to use this code. A greater preoccupation with history is shown by minor employers and the self-employed. The group with the highest degree of socioeconomic control, the major employers, has a much more negative relation to this code, and the relation of the employees is even more extreme, resembling that of the lower educational group; thus, employees and individuals with little formal education seem to be uninterested in historical references, as are country men.

From this complex social dynamics some general patterns can be discerned. When a general social group, such as the middle class or women, has a significant tendency in respect to certain codes, it does not follow that the sociospatial groups derived from it will be characterized by the same tendency; quite the opposite. On the other hand, the fact that some general groups show no such significant tendencies at all does not prevent their derivative sociospatial groups from doing so. The directly comparable, i.e., *complementary* groups, such as city and country men or the Thessaloniki, Veria, and Ormylia lower middle class, which together constitute a general social group, may be significantly related to the same or different codes, the usual case being a mixture of both. When they are related to the same codes, the patterns of use of the common code rarely coincide; occasionally they are comparable, but usually they differ to a greater or lesser degree. The *parallel* groups, i.e., groups which belong to the same geographical unit, such as young and mature in the countryside or the social classes in Veria, usually show a relation to a common core of codes (though they will probably also be related to other codes which are not common to all of them), but their tendencies in respect to the same code usually diverge.

The emergence of the sociospatial groups has already focused our attention emphatically on the importance of the spatial dimension of social life. This same dimension now surfaces again with the greater homogeneity of the geographical units in comparison to the general social groupings; homogeneity here is to be understood, not in the sense of holding the same specific discourse, but in the sense of speaking or keeping silent about particular topics. The complexity of the discursive tendencies of the social groups also brings out a second issue, one that we first encountered in the discussion of the sociology of evaluations and the reasons for identification and moving; this discussion led us to the general conclusion that, though there is a sociological logic in the semiotic universe, this logic is not simple or mechanistic (Chapter 7, Section

3). It is clear that the discursive tendencies of the social groups are one more instance of this general aspect of the sociology of semiosis.

There is a last issue raised by the discursive preferences of the social groups. The results presented above are based on the question on the characteristics of the involvement region. But if we turn to the results from the question on the general internal differences within that region, the picture is quite different. Not that there are not certain common points. Thus, the results from the question on differences, as those from the question on characteristics, show that a small number of the socio-spatial groups (less than one-fourth) have no significant relation to any code; that the number of codes characterizing any one group varies from one to six; that the gender groups show more significant tendencies than the age groups and classes; and that the total number of codes significantly related to some social group again represents almost half of the total number of regional codes. But this last similarity hides an important difference: the significant codes emerging from the two questions do not coincide throughout, but only by 60%. The codes most frequently showing significant use are, once more, the codes of economic activities and history and the urban code, but in the responses to the question on differences we also find correlations with the regional code, the aesthetic code, and the code of social origins.

The most important differences, however, between the results from the two questions lie elsewhere. The question on characteristics shows that both the sociospatial groups connected to the city-country division and those connected to the settlement hierarchy tend in their code use towards a comparable number of codes. But in respect to the question on differences the codes used significantly by the groups connected to hierarchy are much more extensive than those used by the other groups. To the same general image belongs the observation that it is unusual for the same code to be significantly related to the same group in the context of both questions, and when this occurs, the tendencies of the group are far from identical for the two questions.

The sociospatial differentiation of the ideological tendencies is the result of the significant relations of particular codes to specific social groups. The positive correlation to a code or set of codes in fact is related to the thematic preoccupations of a specific group, emerging from its particular way of experiencing space and the particularities of its life context. Thematic preoccupations when seen in their own context have a detectable logic, but the themes selected seem to be determined by an extremely wide range of factors: social position and roles of the group, productive and generally social activites, local issues and problems, even geographical or ecological features of a locality, to name only some of the more obvious ones. The logic of thematic regularities is micro-sociological or anthropo-logical, and to render it explicit would require a more detailed analysis than we could undertake within the scope of the present study.

However, the assumption of a social logic underlying thematic preoccupations seems to be challenged by the context sensitivity of the discourses produced by the interviewees. This issue does not come as a surprise. We first encountered context sensitivity with the estimate of the position of the settlements in the hierarchical settlement network (Chapter 6, Section 5) and it acquired a central position with the objectivist and the subjectivist modes of experiencing the region. We feel that context sensitivity, in the present case as in the previous ones, should not lead us to the agnostic conclusion that the social groups present no stable set of basic code selections and have no patterns of discourse specific to each one. It is clear, however, that the concept of a specific regional discourse for a particular group has to be approached with caution.

An easy way out of agnosticism would seem to be to analyse all possible regional discourse instead of using answers to isolated questions. But this solution has two drawbacks. First, since each different context offered to the interviewee seems to attract its own pattern of semiotic responses, the concept of a unified regional discourse for any group becomes elusive, given that it would be next to impossible to foresee all possible pertinent questions. And then, an enterprise of this kind would tend to become a reconstruction of what could be considered as the subject's competence rather than an analysis of performance. Instead, we chose to select one type of performance, the responses to the question on characteristics, as a privileged indication of regional discourse. Our experience during field work strengthens the hypothesis that this question tends to deliver the spontaneous, nuclear, but also *stereotypical* discursive habits of our subjects on matters of regional space.[37]

However, context sensitivity is not the only trait of the spatial codes used by the subjects. Code use may also show the opposite phenomenon of *impermeability* to context. This is the case when we find the use of the same codes in the discourses elicited by the two different questions on characteristics and differences. In other words, we observe on the intertextual level a phenomenon of code persistence. The persistence in the

use or non-use of certain codes, a trait parallel to the significant relation
to specific codes, can be considered as another group characteristic, in
this case a characteristic that is related to the traditional social groups
(for whom we often have very significant correlations).[38]

Men persist in the use (or avoidance) of the codes of economic activities and wealth, the urban code and the code of lifestyle and history, as
well as in the two personal codes, the aesthetic and the experiential.
Women also consistently use the personal codes, as well as the economic
set of codes and the toponymic code. Persistence in certain patterns of
use, especially of the personal codes, but also in reference to economic
issues (i.e., in the use of these sets of codes, not necessarily the same
individual code) is so repounded in all groups that it can be considered as
a national trait (something also corroborated by the results for the whole
sample). It seems that the Greeks can be classified as "personophile" versus "personophobe" and as "economophile" versus "economophobe".
What then comes to differentiate men from women is the consistent pattern of men in respect to use of the codes of wealth, history, lifestyle,
and the urban code, and the insistence on the toponymic code among
women.

The mature, like men, are consistent in the use of the codes of wealth
and history and the urban code; their insistence on the urban code is
further extended to the whole set of the codes of the built environment.
On the other hand, the mature, like women, insist on place names. Both
the young and the mature show a persistent use of the code of history,
but the young are differentiated by their consistent preoccupation with
social groups.

Workers are consistently preoccupied with wealth, while it is urban
matters that preoccupy the middle class; the lower middle class is very
poor in respect to consistency and persists only in use of the code of
history. City inhabitants persist in two codes, the urban code and the
code of history. They thus differ from country people, who persist in
using the codes of wealth, lifestyle, and social groups, as well as one that
we do not encounter in any other group, the code of leisure.

The persistent codes are not as a rule identical to the codes revealed to
be significantly related to each group in the discourses on characteristics
and differences. Thus, it is not the codes which are significantly used by
a group in a particular context that are most consistently used by that
group. On the other hand, the frequency of appearance of the persistent
codes in each group covers all the range from low to high, and we can

conclude that both high-frequency and low-frequency codes bridge the various fragments of regional discourse.

2. Regional models

In the previous section we considered the patterns of the social groups in respect to the use or avoidance of a particular code or set of codes, whether context sensitive or persistent across discursive fragments. But it is also possible to consider how particular codes are correlated within the responses of one and the same group, that is, if the group can be said to show a significant structure of code use. This is the second issue we would like to discuss, through use of the semiotic programs and with reference to the discourses produced in response to the question on characteristics, which as we saw above delivers the most spontaneous responses. Such code use structures correspond to specific articulations between codes, which are indicative of the particular thematic preoccupations of a groups, its concerns and problems, as well as its recurrent ways of conceiving and assimilating regional space; in other words, of its regional discursive *tropes*. The complex of the articulated semantic tendencies of a group constitutes the ideological attitude of the group as a whole towards its region and can be considered as the group's ideological regional model.

The patterns of the articulations between codes may vary. A significant correlation between two codes does not necessarily mean that all individuals, or even a great majority of individuals, in a group use both codes. By far the most frequent pattern of articulation is the dualist pattern, in the context of which the group is mainly divided into people using both codes and people using neither. There may also be a threefold pattern of mainly users, non-users, and individuals who use code a but tend to avoid code b and whose importance varies. In very few cases the center of gravity of the articulation lies with this third category of individuals. However, what is generally significant in the above cases are not the specific patterns of articulation but the systematic and polarized nature of the relation: the tendency of individuals to adopt or to avoid a pair of codes. We shall thus concentrate on the dualist aspect of code articulation and largely ignore its specific characteristics.

For each social group studied, we crosstabulated pairs of codes, representing all possible combinations between thirteen selected codes (since the combinations of all 32 codes would lead to too high a number of operations). The criterion for the selection of the codes was their importance, judged by their frequency of appearance on the group level.[39] The discussion below on the semantic tendencies of our social groups will revolve around sets of complementary groups (social classes, genders, age groups, city/country), since the nature of each group can be better understood by comparing it to the complementary group(s) of the same kind.

2.1. Social classes

The first set of complementary groups we shall discuss are the social classes, starting with the working class. There is a consistent tendency in part of the working class to associate the code of economic development with the code of ecology; in fact, the working class either avoids reference to these codes altogether, or, if it uses one of them, then it also uses the other. The same duality appears with the codes of wealth and of lifestyle: the working class brings together these codes by either avoiding them altogether or adopting them both. But the code of wealth is also correlated with a code of a very different nature, the topological code, according to a threefold pattern: users of this pair of codes, non-users, and workers who use the code of wealth but avoid the topological code. The topological code is also correlated with the toponymic code, i.e., working-class subjects using topological notions also tend to an important degree to use place names and vice versa. Finally, the codes of lifestyle and history also appear together, again following the threefold pattern which in this case takes an extreme form, given that the workers who use the code of lifestyle without also using the code of history have on the whole an equal weight with those using both codes.

How are these correlations to be interpreted? We have already suggested that they are the statistical representation of thematic preoccupations, something like the characteristic regional discourse tropes of a particular social group, marking its ideological model of the region. Thus, we see that the working class seems to adopt a certain geographical determinism: it associates development with ecological features. It brings into the same context statements touching upon lifestyle and references to the past, but it also associates lifestyle with comments on wealth. It shows an interesting tendency to have recourse simultaneously to these comments and topological notions of location in space, and has the geographical aptitude of harmonizing topological notions with the use of specific place names. It is also significant, however, for members of the working class that many of them avoid these pairings in their regional discourse. Any other use or non-use of a pair of codes among the codes selected for study is devoid of statistical significance for this group.

Most of the above codes are also found in the regional model of the lower middle class, but their pairings are different throughout. Ecological issues are associated for this class with topological notions, and with the code of economic activities, not the code of economic development as is the case with the working class. The codes of economic activities and development are manifestly akin, though they represent different ways of conceiving of economic life: the one describes the economic activities of the inhabitants of a region in static terms, while the other sees the economy of the region as such, in terms of its achievements and potential (evidently considering that the opportunities for the inhabitants to find work depend on the general level of economic life in the area). The preference of the lower middle class for the code of economic activities in association with the ecological code may thus indicate a tendency to see economic life in more neutral and individualistic terms. It is also this code of economic activities, instead of the topological code, that is significantly used together with the toponymic code. Another new code also appears in addition to the code of economic activities, namely the code referring to the mentality and character of people, which is used together with the code of wealth.

While there is an important resemblance between the codes used by the working class and the lower middle class, the codes of the middle class are strikingly different from both of the above sets. As is the case with the lower middle class, the codes of economic activities and wealth occur, but here they are interrelated. The code of lifestyle, that also occurs in the working class, here coexists with the aesthetic code, and the issues referring to leisure, i.e., entertainment, recreation, and cultural activities, are related to the urban environment.

The regional models of the social classes thus differ radically. Even when they include the same codes, no one pairing of codes is the same for all classes. Both the working and the lower middle class relate ecological and economic issues, but for the working class these issues are kept separate from topographical concerns. The individual topographical codes are related to each other, as are the social codes of wealth and lifestyle, and a bridge is created between these two sets of codes. Ecological, economic, and topographical issues are related for the lower middle class, but contrary to the working class, this class does not connect the two topographical codes; two among the social codes are related, as is the case with the working class, but this micro-structure does not coincide with the corresponding micro-structure of the working class, since the lower middle class seems to prefer to see wealth as connected to mentality rather than to lifestyle. The middle class does not relate economic issues either to ecology or to topography, but to social issues. Social codes are not related to each other, but to personal judgments of an aesthetic nature. Finally, for the middle class, functional issues are paired with matters concerning the built environment.

2.2. Genders

There is a partial overlapping between the regional model of men and the model of the lower middle class: in both cases we have associations between the code of economic activities and the toponymic code, and between the ecological and the topological codes. The same economic code is also associated with the topological code, and ecological references co-exist with issues of leisure: we can hypothesize that the natural environment is seen in terms of recreation. If we pass from the individual codes to the sets of codes, we observe associations comparable to the above: the set of topographical codes is related to both the ecological code and the set of economic codes. Thus, the topographical codes appear as the nucleus of the semantic articulations of the model of men, in which their separate economic and ecological interests meet.

The model of women, like that of men, includes the two topographical codes, one of which, the toponymic, plays the same role as nucleus for the semantic articulations as the topographical set of codes does in the male model. But in the female model the two topographical codes are related to each other. Women give a rather privileged position to place names, since they also relate this code to personal experiences and to urban matters, which is not the case with men.

The male and female models are similar in that their nucleus belongs to the topographical set of codes. But this is their only similarity, because this set of codes articulates two radically different perspectives on regional space. The male perspective concerns the relation of ecology or economy to types of spatial locations and of the former to leisure, while the female perspective concerns the relation of personal experiences and urban matters to specific places indicated by name.

2.3. Age groups

In the models of the age groups very significant crosstabulations (0.01) between codes are rather strongly represented, while as a rule crosstabulations in the other models discussed are on a somewhat lower level of significance (0.05). An important part of the model of youth coincides with the male model; it consists of the two correlations of the code of economic activities with topology and place names respectively. This model also includes the code of leisure, as was the case with the middle class and men, but here this code is associated with personal experiences. We also observe two other codes already located, the urban code (used by the middle class and women) and the code of history (found in the working class), but it is only in the model of the young that these codes are related. When we pass to the aggregated level of sets of codes, a new and unexpected relation appears between economic codes and the personal codes (the aesthetic and the experiential).

The model of adults partially coincides with the male model in that they have in common the two correlations between the ecological and the topological code, and the ecological code and the code of leisure; the latter is also associated with the aesthetic code. The two topographical codes are once more related in this model, as we observed in the cases of the working class and women. What is interesting with the model of adults is that on the aggregated level totally new relations emerge. The set of personal codes, to which the aesthetic code belongs, is correlated on this level with the topographical set of codes, the topographical set with the codes of the built environment, and the latter with the code of history; finally, the social set is related to the functional.

The adult model is thus very different from the model of the young; they share many of the same codes, but the codes are quite differently related. In the model of the young economic considerations are related to topographical concepts and the personal codes respectively, and among the personal codes the experiential code is associated with leisure. In the model of the mature it is the other personal code, the aesthetic, that is associated with leisure, and the set of personal codes is not related to economy but to the set of topographical codes. Instead of the relation between economy and spatial location, the model of the mature shows a relation between ecology and spatial location. A last characteristic of this model is the relation established between general social and functional issues.

2.4. Cities and countryside

The urban model of the region partially overlaps with the model of the adults, the common part of the two models being the two correlations of the ecological with the topological code, and the topological with the toponymic code. This model includes the association between the code of economic activities and the toponymic code, as well as the relation between this economic code and the experiential code, a relation between individual codes comparable to that between the corresponding sets of codes in the model of the young. It is also characterized by the unique association of the code of lifestyle with the urban code; it seems that city inhabitants tend to see lifestyle as closely connected to the urban environment as such.

All the pairs of individual codes of the rural model are already known from the other models, but their coexistence within the framework of one and the same model is quite original. Developmental and ecological issues are associated, and the same happens with the code of economic activities and the topological code. The code of leisure is related to the aesthetic code (a relation valid also for the mature) and to the urban code (a relation we found among the middle class). The rural model is characterized by the unique association of personal experiences to lifestyle issues; however, though this association is characteristic for the countryside, it should be noted that the individuals using both codes are a small minority, because there is a tendency in the countryside to avoid references to personal experiences altogether. This is even more true for the relation between the code of leisure and the urban code, which is used only marginally, though a similar relation appears on the aggregate level between the functional set of codes (which includes the code of leisure) and the codes of the built environment (which include the urban code). For the people of the countryside, the urban environment is apparently seen primarily in terms of the entertainment and services it provides, and which country inhabitants often feel are lacking in their own rural settlements.

Once more the regional models of complementary groups are different. The only similarity between the urban and the rural model is the association between economy and topographical concepts, but even in this case the topographical codes included in the two models do not coincide. In the rural model, economy is also associated with ecology, while in the urban model ecological issues are associated to topographical concepts of location in space. In the urban model economy is related to the experiential code, but in the rural model the experiential code is associated with lifestyle; in the rural model, lifestyle is not connected with urban issues as in the urban model, but the urban environment is related to leisure, a code that does not appear at all in the urban model.

2.5. Regional models and social groups

This discussion of the regional models of our social groups allows us to conclude that the models of the complementary groups differ radically. Generally, each one of the models found is unique compared to the others, with as a result that each group presents an original character of its own. These models spring from the association between pairs of codes within a group, in contrast to the group tendencies studied in the previous section that follow from the significant association of a group with individual codes. As we saw in Section 1 of this chapter, the individual code tendencies of the traditional groups (including the cities and the countryside) are extremely poor; this is also the case with some of the sociospatial groups, while other sociospatial groups present a richer image. From this point of view, the regional models of the traditional groups studied in the present section are much richer than their tendencies towards particular codes.

If we now compare the regional models that emerge from the responses to the question on characteristics with the models following from the question on differences, we observe a phenomenon similar to the one we encountered in the case of tendencies towards individual codes, namely that the two sets of paired codes are quite different for one and the same group. Both the code structures and the thematic concerns of a group appear to be context sensitive. It is likely that in the case of the questions on characteristics and differences context sensitivity leads to a differentiation between stereotypical and ad hoc discourse; the question on characteristics tends to elicit an immediate, standardized discourse, while the question whether there are differences within the region tends to provoke a more thoughtful and specific response, almost as though the issue of differences within the region implied a more critical perspective.

We should also note that the same factor of context sensitivity is the factor operating at the very root of the differentiation between the objectivist and the subjectivist model of the region. The regional models of the social groups that we have discussed in this section are derived from a context similar to that of the objectivist model. It is true that the opposition between the objectivist and the subjectivist model is founded on two equally spontaneous modes of experiencing the region which are fundamental for all social groups, at least all of the traditional groups. But while the social groups are identical in respect to the appearance of these models, this fact does not prevent each group from displaying its originality through its own regional model. The regional models may thus be considered as significant variations of the objectivist mode of experiencing the region.

Contrary to this multiplicity of regional models, Ledrut in his study on urban conception in two French cities finds only two urban models. He calls the first model "functionalist" and "abstract", and recognizes as its foundation judgments concerning the utilitarian qualities of urban space and life. This model shows for Ledrut a distancing of the conceiving subject from the city itself. Such a model could not appear at all among our regional models, for the simple reason that we did not define any separate code grouping such judgments. Ledrut's second model is the "hedonistic" and "concrete", which revolves mainly around the experiential and the moral codes, but also the ludic code. Again, we do not have any code comparable to the moral code (defined by the pair of concepts "freedom" vs. "constraint"), but Ledrut's ludic code is closely related to our code of leisure. Subjects using this model retain affective ties to their city.

Ledrut (1973: 356-386, and in general 157-386) observes that the two models correspond to two different dimensions of the experience of urban life, the realistic dimension and the pleasure dimension, and are actually opposed. He does not consider them logically exclusive, but proposes that in the present conditions of urban life social groups are not in a position to reconcile these dimensions of experience; thus, reality is reduced to instrumentality, and pleasure to passivity. He also observes that in spite of the overlappings between social groups, there are clear-cut distinctions in the use of the models, especially between social classes;

thus, the workers tend towards the functionalist model, and employees and managers towards the hedonistic model. The tendencies of the classes towards isolated aspects of the urban totality is, for Ledrut, an indication of their alienation.

Our regional models give a much more complex image of the experience of space than the one given by Ledrut. Our findings also lead to a different conclusion, considerably more optimistic, in respect to alienation. In fact, our objectivist and subjectivist models may be said to represent two different approaches to space, a descriptive and less involved, i.e., realistic, approach, and an involved, affective and ego-centered approach. Though the structure of our two models may not be comparable to that of Ledrut's, their quality is, because manifestly the objectivist model has a close affinity to his functionalist model and the subjectivist to his hedonistic model. Now, what we found in respect to our models is that they are not generally exclusive, but on the contrary coexist for all social groups and emerge in function of the discursive context. These models are of a statistical nature and do not exclude the existence of cases of spatial alienation, but nevertheless we can conclude on the basis of their relative universality that geographical alienation is not the general rule among our subjects.

Ledrut's study reinforces our conclusions from the present study that the semantic level of spatial representations is not incoherent, but is subject to certain ordering principles. We can also find a corroboration of this conclusion in the research done by David Lowenthal in collaboration with Marquita Riel, published in 1972 in eight small volumes. The authors try to define the semantic models of different micro-groups as a response to exposure to four sets of urban routes through an equivalent number of U.S. cities. They invited their subjects to express their impressions and judgments on these routes in written form, and they used as a central device a list of 50 fixed concepts, organized in pairs of opposed attributes, the semantic space between which was divided into five grades (i.e., a direct borrowing from the semantic scales of Osgood which, contrary to Ledrut and to the present study, predefines the codes of spatial apprehension).

Lowenthal and Riel (1972, 1: 2-5; 5: 59-62; 6: 1, 9-13; 7: 1, 30, 37; 8: 2-4, 43) observe that the experience from the urban environment is not amorphous, but has a definite structure which revolves around clusters of attributes. Some clusters vary with the social group and some others with the specificities of the environment, and the impact of the environment is more important than the social integration of the subject. The authors also address an issue of special attraction to geographers, the subject of the universals of environmental experience, and conclude that indeed there is a universal cluster of attributes. Thus, in spite of its sociological and technical differences, the study by Lowenthal and Riel also finds consistencies in the manner of conceiving space.

It is now possible to summarize the types of spatial code dynamics studied so far and the main theoretical conclusions that can be drawn from our analysis. The first type we studied (Chapter 9, Sections 2 and 3) is the hierarchical structuring of the codes, seen from two different aspects: an aggregate aspect connected to the code structuring external to individual discourse, and an internal aspect based on the structuring of individual discourses. Both these aspects showed the existence of an objectivist and a subjectivist model, which correspond to two semiotic approaches to the region used simultaneously by all social groups. The two models are different, but they are also similar in that they both characterize all social groups. But if from this point of view differences between groups are levelled out, this is not the case with the last type of code dynamics studied, the models derived from the significant association of pairs of codes. Here, as we found, the regional models of the groups are different throughout. The objectivist and the subjectivist models are not *group sensitive*, but regional models are. On the other hand, both kinds of models are *context sensitive*, and this context sensitivity in the case of regional models led us to the distinction between stereotypical and ad hoc models.

The second type of code dynamics studied (in the previous section of this chapter) refers to patterns of code use, i.e., to the codes the presence or absence of which marks a social group. Group sensitivity and context sensitivity is the general rule for these sets of codes. The third type finally (also previous section of this chapter) refers to the codes which persist through different contexts. While the sets of these codes are also group sensitive, their very existence points to the issue of *context insensitivity*. These sets also show a certain *group insensitivity*, since they include certain codes common to all groups.

The study of the types of spatial code dynamics emphasizes in a particularly forceful way two fundamental factors underlying the processes of semiosis: social group, i.e., a sociological factor, and context, a semiotic factor. When the two factors act together the semiotic factor is secondary, in the sense that it leads to variants within the specificity of social groups. But the same study also shows that group and context sensitivity are only partial aspects of semiosis. Semiosis is also subject to the opposite factors of group and context insensitivity, i.e., it can be independent from the specificity of the groups or the context. The specific forms of context insensitivity should be explained by the specificity of the groups. The explanation of group insensitivity, on the other hand, should be sought for in the characteristics of society as a whole, or perhaps even in human nature.

3. Envisaging the future

Individuals do not only have a structured conception of their present regional environment, but they also hold views on the future of their region. We studied these views with the help of two different questions. The first question invited our subjects to describe what they would consider as the ideal future of their involvement region, and thus encouraged them to adopt a long-term and rather utopian perspective on their region. The second question on the other hand concerned a short-term perspective, since it invited them to discuss the changes needed in order for the involvement region to "progress". Some 30 different themes were catalogued in response to each question, all of which were found to be compatible with the grid of regional codes already elicited. The relative prevalence of each theme or group of themes (calculated on the total number of themes) can give us a fair image of the regional interests of our interviewees.

In the objectivist aggregate model of regional apprehension, the most frequent set of codes was the social set, followed by the economic set or the built environment set. The situation is different with the ideal regional model. Here, in the frequency-program groups, it is the themes of the built environment that generally predominate (for the whole sample, 33% of the total number of themes are themes referring to the built environment, and for the groups the percentage varies between 30% and 43%), with the exception of Ormylia (16%), the countryside in general (29%), and the working class (24%), where the economic set is dominant. In all the other cases, the economic set occupies the second rank or is very near to it (24% for the sample, between 13% and 35% for the groups). This importance of the built environment and the economic themes, as well as the hierarchical ranking of these sets, is also confirmed by the frequency of dominant themes, i.e., the themes which are the main concern of the interviewee and which frequently structure and integrate his/her ideal model. The third rank (occasionally the second) is occupied by the functional themes (19% for the sample, between 12% and 30% for the groups). The social set of codes, dominant in the aggregate model, is here limited to the fourth rank and is clearly underrepresented (9%, 5-12% respectively). There follows concern for the ecological improvement of the environment, a theme which acquires some importance only in the metropolis (11%).

Thus, the ideal future is dominated by preoccupations concerning the improvement of the built environment, the economy, and services. The only radical proposal is the reshaping of the urban environment into something like a garden city (9% in Thessaloniki). The preservation of the historical character of buildings preoccupies only a small minority of people, and the same is the case with urban aesthetics. The proportions of "optimists" who believe that no changes are needed and "pessimists" who claim that it is too late to do anything are both quite limited.

The short-term priorities of people, however, do not coincide with their long-term aspirations. While the individual themes are quite comparable in the two cases, the ranking of the sets of themes is very different. The participation of the economic set of codes is of the same order with that in the ideal model (27% for the sample, between 17% and 34% for the groups), but now the set generally comes first in frequency, with the exception of Thessaloniki (17%) and by extension the cities (21%), the young (24%), and the middle class, where the first rank is occupied by the functional and/or the built environment set. The functional set (23%, 18%-25%) frequently holds the second or lower rank and is very close to the social set (20%, 8%-31%). As was also the case with the ideal model, the ecological improvement of the environment is of some importance only in the metropolis (12%).

So far we have been interested in the quality of the changes needed in the involvement region, but our subjects were also asked to estimate the extent of the necessary changes. The general reaction of the social groups is accurately rendered by the data for the whole sample, where one-fourth of the subjects stated that radical changes were necessary and around one-third that important changes are needed; thus, a little less than two-thirds of the subjects incline towards great extent of changes. Only one-third of the subjects are more optimistic and incline towards limited extent of changes, divided between the positions of some changes (one-fifth) and few changes (14%). Certain groups, however, present their own peculiarity. The working and the middle class depart from the above distribution in two different directions: only half of the workers incline to great extent of changes, while this is the case for as much as three-fourths of the members of the middle class; the same divergence is observed between the inhabitants of Ormylia and Axioupoli. We might hypothesize from these data that the working class appears to be more reconciled to present reality and less revolutionary - or perhaps more realistic in its aspirations.

As we saw, in the short-term priorities economic preoccupations generally prevail, while the built environment decreases in importance in comparison to the ideal model. On the other hand, preoccupation with changes in social life increases drastically. An important part of this preoccupation is political in nature (12%, 9%-21%) and includes the themes of political and administrative changes, changes in political mentality, and changes in the social structures; the second and third of these are much in evidence in Ormylia (10% and 11% respectively). The comparison between short-term proposals and ideal model shows that the groupings of themes present much greater differences in emphasis in the case of the ideal model, a fact reflecting the greater concentration on the built environment. The importance of economy and services is the point of convergence between the needed and the ideal, but then the two start to diverge in that immediate needs are conceptualized in conjuction with changes in social life and politics, while the ideal future is heavily preoccupied with physical space. Another point of convergence between the needed and the ideal is their realism: the ideal model is far from being utopian.

Discourse on the ideal region is not very elaborated. The average number of themes used by the interviewees is less than three; the themes in any one interview vary from one to eight. About half of the subjects of all groups use two to three themes and around one-fourth of them four to five themes. A somewhat richer number of themes appears among the inhabitants of Axioupoli, while the opposite is true for Ormylia. As we already noted, all the themes of the ideal regional model can be integrated with the regional codes already defined. The semiotic programs show that for all social groups there is a very significant correlation between the number of themes and the number of the corresponding codes. This means that there is a generalized tendency to avoid themes that are closely related - in the sense that they are expressed in the same code - and to shift from one code to another with the multiplication of themes. From this point of view, the discourse on the ideal region can be considered as scattered and perhaps rather superficial, but also varied and inventive.

It is possible to classify the groups according to whether or not they make reference to a particular theme. On this basis, we can see from the sociosemiotic programs that countryside inhabitants have a significant tendency to refer to economic themes. If again we focus on the built environment themes, it is the inhabitants of the metropolis who tend very significantly to use them. If we further isolate the urban themes among those of the built environment, we find that city people, and mainly the inhabitants of the metropolis, are intensely preoccupied with these issues.

It is also possible to relate the groups of interviewees to the dominant theme of their ideal region. We selected seven classes of dominant themes: economic, social, functional, and ecological themes, themes of the built environment - with the exception of the planning themes that were classified separately - and aesthetic themes. The only significant relation found is that between social classes and sets of dominant themes. Social classes present quite distinct tendencies: the workers privilege economic themes; the lower middle class social and functional themes; and the middle class the built environment themes. When we group the dominant themes according to whether or not they refer to economic issues, the workers again tend significantly to economic concerns, but so do the lower educational level and the countryside (which as we saw also inclines to economic themes in general). The classification of the dominant themes as to their reference to the built environment again shows the interest of the middle class in these themes, a tendency that is here very significant; they also give significant results for education, in that the heterogeneous groups of individuals with a secondary school diploma and those with a university degree both incline very strongly to built environment themes.

Similar results are obtained when the same kind of grouping is attempted for the themes that appear in the short-term perspective of our interviewees. The countryside and individuals with a lower level of education tend again significantly to refer to economic themes, something which also tends to be of concern for women. We observe that once more people of the metropolis show a very strong tendency to the built environment themes; they show a similar tendency for the whole class of environmental themes (ecology and built environment), a tendency that is also found among the youth of Veria. It is also youth, but this time urban youth in general, that inclines to ecological themes and, among the built environment themes, to urban issues.

The comparison of all the data on the desired future of the involvement region reveals a main opposition between social groups. Different urban groups (cities in general; Thessaloniki; urban youth; and the youth of Veria) are marked by their preoccupation with environmental matters of all kinds, and the most systematic interest in these matters is found in the metropolis. On the other hand, the countryside (as a whole and in Ormylia) aspires to a better economic future. The same divergence between an interest in environmental, and specifically built environment, issues and an interest in economic issues differentiates the middle class and the more educated from the working class and the less educated. Economy is the target of the underprivileged, while the quality of life catches the attention of the wealthy.

People do not reflect passively on the future of their region. Quite the opposite, they are willing to participate in order to achieve the desired changes, and feel that they can have an impact on the course of things. There are of course individuals who feel that they have nothing to contribute, or that their participation makes no difference. This feeling of having no share in the shaping of the future is not widespread (it is found among only 13% for the whole sample), though it may vary between social groups: it is most repounded among the middle class, in the metropolis, and among women, who in this respect differ significantly from men. The feeling is at its lowest (7%-8%) among the working class and men, and in Ormylia. The individuals who feel that they already participate and help in one way or another, and are willing to continue their participation, make up more than half of the whole sample, and approach two-thirds of the total in the lower middle class, men - who are significantly correlated to this category - and Ormylia. The lowest proportion of these individuals (47%-48%) occurs among the workers, women, and the Verians, who thus appear to think of themselves as currently less politically active. The individuals who have no previous participation, but who nevertheless believe that they can make a greater or lesser contribution in the immediate future, amount to almost one-third for the whole sample and are highly represented among the working class (42%), which thus seems to contain a pool of people willing to become more active if given the opportunity.

Half of our interviewees estimate the degree of what they consider as their actual contribution or of their willingness to contribute as very high or rather high; the first category is more heavily represented. This share falls to around 40% for the middle class and the Thessalonikeans, two groups with the highest share of individuals feeling that they cannot contribute. The only social factor that gives significant results for the degree of participation is age: a very high willingness to contribute is characteristic of the age group of 46-52 years old; a division between the next two categories of rather high and average willingness to contribute marks mainly the 35-45 group but also the 28-34 group; the younger people (19-27) tend to the average degree of willingness to contribute, while older people (53-70) tend to feel that they cannot help at all.

The manner in which our subjects conceive their participation in the future of their region helped us in systematizing the conceived modes of involvement. The two major classes of participation that emerge are social participation, i.e., involvement through participation in wider social organizations and schemes; and individual participation, in isolation from any wider context. Forms of social participation can be divided into two main groups, the one including the categories referring to more active forms of participation, such as participation in official organizations (for example, political parties), through the social benefits felt to derive to the region from one's professional practice, or through financial contributions; and the other constituted by more passive forms of participation, such as voting in elections and exemplary behavior in defined social settings. Individual participation can also be divided into two groups: exemplary participation, where the individual sees him/herself as providing a personal - professional or civic - model of behavior; and isolated participation, such as the raising of one's own political consciousness. We can superimpose on this grid of the form of participation another grid deriving from the nature of the conceived participation: political, economic, professional, cultural, civic, or any kind. The tendency to want to make a contribution through professional practice is characteristic of the two higher educational levels.

Social participation is by far the dominant form of participation, since it is envisaged by more than three-fourths of the members of all social groups, with the only exception being the Thessalonikeans (65%); the Ormylians occupy the other extreme (90%). It does not, then, come as a surprise that, while the share of individual participation is usually less than 10%, in Thessaloniki it reaches a peak of 16%. Almost all social participation is conceived as active participation. Political participation and participation of any kind are best represented (25% each for the whole sample), followed by professional (18%) and civic (12%) forms. Once more the inhabitants of Thessaloniki and Ormylia move in opposite directions: the share of the forms of political and any kind of participation falls to 14% in Thessaloniki, and that of civic participation increases to 23%, while inversely the shares of the former in Ormylia increase to 39% and 34% respectively, and that of the latter falls to 3%. These data fit well with those on the extent of participation. The main opposition in matters of participation is between the political orientation of the Ormylians, both in the wide sense of involvement and in the strict sense of organized party politics, and the low profile of the Thessalonikeans.

Part V. Imagining space

We may arrive at a provisional and general characteristic of the mythical intuition of space by starting from the observation that it occupies a kind of middle position between the space of sense perception and the space of pure cognition, that is, geometry. It is self-evident that the space of perception, the space of vision and touch, does not coincide with the space of pure mathematics.... Perception does not know the concept of infinity; from the very outset it is confined within certain spatial limits imposed by our faculty of perception. And in connection with perceptual space we can no more speak of homogeneity than of infinity.... Here ... each place has its own mode and its own value. Visual space and tactile space are both anisotropic and unhomogeneous in contrast to the metric space of Euclidean geometry...

Ernst Cassirer, *The philosophy of symbolic forms,*
Vol. 2: Mythical thought

Chapter 11. Mental maps revisited

1. Surface and deep structures of the sketch maps

So far, we have discussed the data which our study elicited through the use of verbal questionnaires. But this is not the only method through which one can acquire information on the manner in which space is conceived. Additional information can be obtained with the help of sketch maps drawn by the subjects. These sketch maps are for behavioral geographers also an expression of the mental maps of the subjects, accurate to a greater or lesser degree depending on their graphic ability. As we saw, the sketch map, according to D.C.D. Pocock (1975: 7, 11, 53), does not correspond to the whole depth of the mental map but only to its "designative" component, i.e., the information on the location and nature of spatial elements. For the same writer, this component is the "skeletal framework" of the global mental map, which in addition has an affective and symbolic component.

Geographers are mainly interested in the content and accuracy of the sketch maps. The interest in the content concerns the specific spatial elements depicted and the interest in accuracy revolves around the comparison of the sketch map to real space as rendered by a topographical map. Both these orientations bear witness to the vivid preoccupation of geographers with the connection between the mental maps and actual spatial organization. Quite apart from the theoretical objections one might have against the current approach to this issue (see Chapter 2, Section 1), there is no doubt that the study of these questions is doubly useful, since it both gives us knowledge of the manner in which space is represented and, with the help of this knowledge, offers insights for physical intervention through the design process. The orientation of the present study, however, is not primarily towards this level of analysis. What is at issue for us are the conceptual structures through which space is apprehended; as a result we are concerned not with the specific content of the sketch maps, but with their general arrangement.

The issue of the arrangement of the sketch maps is not absent from the geographical literature, and some first systematic insights can be found in the work of Kevin Lynch. Lynch (1960: 88-89) differentiates the sketch maps and the corresponding spatial representation "according to their structural quality: the manner in which their parts were arranged and interrelated", and distinguishes "four stages along a continuum of increasing structural precision." The representations belonging to the first stage include dispersed spatial elements that are not related to each other. The representations of the second stage show a positional structure, where the elements remain disconnected but are roughly and indirectly related by means of their general orientation or relative distance. The structures of the third stage present parts that are loosely and flexibly connected, and the structures tend to become rigid in the last stage. Parallel to these stages, Lynch also discerns in the sketch maps two structures of another kind. The first is *static*, and synchronically and hierarchically organized as a series of wholes and parts. The second structure is more *dynamic* and its parts are interconnected by means of their sequence over time in accordance with the actual experience of moving through the city.

These concepts underlie Appleyard's typology of sketch maps, which is widely used in some form or another. Appleyard uses two criteria for the classification of sketch maps: the type of the predominant element, and the degree of accuracy, which for him is directly related to the degree of complexity of the sketch map. On the basis of the first criterion, he distinguishes between *sequential* maps, where connections (roads) predominate, and *spatial* maps, mainly composed of individual elements and/or zones (cf. Lynch's dynamic and static maps); he also observes that the most accomplished maps effected a synthesis of these two classes of maps. This division of the sketch maps follows directly from the definition and classification of the unitary elements. The impact of Lynch's (1960: 46-48) classification of these elements into paths, edges, districts, nodes, and landmarks has dominated throughout geographical literature. In semiotic terms, Lynch defined five paradigmatic categories according to which the semantic elements of the maps can be classified (a paradigm is a set of elements that can occupy the same position in a syntagmatic chain; the latter is an actual combination of elements simultaneously present). Since it is clear from Lynch's definitions that nodes accompany paths, edges are the interface between districts, and landmarks, as they are the extreme case of districts, are comparable to districts - as points are to planes - we may conclude that the predominant semantic elements of the maps are either roads or zones.

Appleyard (1970: 103-109, 115) distinguishes four types of maps within each class. The first type in the sequential class is the *fragmented* type, which includes fragments of the road network; this is the most primitive type of the sequential class. The second type is the *chain*, composed by a main axis that is laterally undeveloped. The lateral development of branches and loops leads to the *branch-and-loop* type. The last type is the *network,* exhibiting a more or less complete road system; according to Appleyard, this type is often an accurate representation of reality.

Of the spatial maps, the most primitive are those in the *scatter-and-cluster* type, which are characterized by unconnected individual elements; these maps are not necessarily inaccurate. The second type is the *mosaic,* composed of zones delimited by schematic boundaries and internally subdivided into smaller zones; these maps depict the general relationships between zones and are less specific or accurate than the preceding maps. When individual elements and districts are connected with schematic linkages that occasionally represent parts of the road system, we have the *linked* type. Finally, the most complete and accurate spatial maps are the *patterned* maps. Appleyard calls the two first types of each class *topological*, because they are limited to giving some general idea of spatial relations, and the last two types *positional*, given that they try to render topographical reality.

Lynch's and Appleyard's typology has been the starting point for several others. David Canter (1977: 60-62) suggests separating the two criteria of predominant element and complexity, and proposes a typology based solely on the latter. He believes that each sequential type is a less complex version of the corresponding spatial type, and he thus arrives at what he considers as eight successive stages in the development of sketch maps. But this proposal does not take into account either the difference between corresponding sequential and spatial maps, which cannot be composed because of their different formulation, or the similarity between corresponding types, which do not differ in their degree of complexity.

Pocock on the other hand (1975: 53-57) finds that the sketch maps of his subjects for the city of Durham are not accounted for by Appleyard's typology, and expresses doubts on the implied invariance of that typology in respect to culture, scale, and instructional set (on this last point, see also Canter 1977: 59). However, the author doesn't question Appleyard's criteria but simply proposes a modification of his categories, namely one omission in the sequential class (fragmented type); two additions in the same class (branch-spinal and branch-focal types); a twofold division in the superior type of each class (he divides the network type into a net-spinal and a net-patterned type, and the patterned zonal type into a pattern-sketch and a pattern-map type); and one inversion, that between scattered and mosaic type, which does not go against Appleyard's view from a certain standpoint, since he also considers the mosaic type as the most primitive and inaccurate.

New complaints appeared in the bibliography in response to Pocock's typology, this time on the part of Murray and Spencer (1979: 387). The authors write that the three judges they used for the classification of the sketch maps generally had no disagreements as to the classification of the maps into sequential and spatial, but disagreements occured with Pocock's subtypes. They instead propose the same threefold division for each class of sketch maps, low, medium, and high degree of organization; the low degree corresponds to Pocock's line (equivalent to Appleyard's chain) and branch-focal types of sequential maps and to the mosaic type of spatial maps, while the high degree relates to the two superior types in each of Pocock's classes.

The views and debates over the typology of the sketch maps is a very useful background for a theoretical discussion of the issue. Ever since Lynch, inherent in the typology of sketch maps is the comparison to reality with the help of a topographical map, in other words the degree of accuracy of the sketch maps. But this way of operating goes counter to a fundamental thesis in semiotics, namely that the referent, in our case real space, must remain outside semiotic analysis (see, for example, on this matter Eco 1972: 59-64). As Eco rightly observes, the referent may be useful to logicians, who are interested in the truth value of signs, but it is damaging to semiotics. It is thus indispensable to geographers when they are interested in the truth value, i.e., accuracy, of the signs they operate with, in our case those of the sketch maps. But no typology of the sketch maps as semiotic texts should have recourse to something external to them, just as no literary scholar would attempt a typology of the novel on the basis of how many real-life characters or actual places and events are included in the plot. Sketch maps are the manifestation of a particular semiotic system, and their inherent meaningful structures should not be judged against any external reality.

A semiotic approach to the typology of sketch maps would thus, from its theoretical premises alone, lead us to the position that the accuracy of the sketch maps should be separated from their internal structure. We shall investigate this matter further in Chapter 13 (Section 4). For the moment, we would like to point out that we can find an empirical corroboration of this position in the ranking of the scattered and mosaic types made by Appleyard. He ranks the scattered type lowest on the basis of its internal semiotic characteristic of being more simplistically elaborated, but in this manner he violates the ranking according to accuracy, since he acknowledges that the mosaic type is less accurate. On the other hand, Pocock considers the mosaic type as the most primitive, which manifestly it is not on semiotic grounds, probably because he as Appleyard considers it less accurate than the scattered type. Thus, Appleyard in this case gives priority to the internal, semiotic criterion of degree of elaboration, Pocock to the comparative criterion of accuracy.

However, the resemblance of the approaches presented above conceals a very important difference. Appleyard and Pocock define an important part of their sequential types on the basis of their precise geometric form. Murray and Spencer make a step toward greater abstraction because they subsume Pocock's geometric forms under general categories that they also use for the spatial types. This approach brings them closer to Lynch, whose typology is based solely on the combination of different degrees of arrangement and accuracy and is devoid of any specific geometric form. Lynch's typology has the obvious advantage of offering umbrella categories able to accomodate any geometric form. That insistence on the criterion of form narrows the scope of the typology can be seen from Pocock's addition to the typology of Appleyard of the branch-focal, i.e., the radial, type, that does not figure among the types given by Appleyard. This narrowing is also testified to by the difficulty Murray and Spencer had in adapting Pocock's typology in their study, something that pushed them to look for their own general categories.

The discussion of the typology of the sketch maps concentrates on their accuracy and arrangement. Aside from accuracy, what are the researchers looking for? The two major classes of maps are distinguished according to the type of the predominant elements, which is defined following the semantic opposition *movement* (vs. stasis) vs. *place* (vs. non-place). This criterion relates to the manner in which the maps are formulated, which is a surface realization comparable in semiotic terms to the use of dialectical features in a language.

We would like to point out that this classification of sketch maps according to the semantic opposition *movement* vs. *place* is manifestly not the only possible one. This classification concerns the syntactic level of the maps and refers to two classes into which their signifiers can be grouped. These (paradigmatic) classes were defined on the basis of the above asymmetrical opposition between the distinctive features (*phemes*) of "movement" and "place". Due to the nature of urban and regional space, this opposition is of crucial importance. But other semantic oppositions may also present some interest for the surface analysis of the maps.

As an example, we might take the opposition *culture* vs. *nature*, which leads to a differentiation of the maps according to the inclusion of signifiers belonging to the class of culture only (built, artificial space) or belonging to both this class and the class of nature (mountains, fields, rivers, etc.). The study of this opposition delivers some interesting results. Just less than two-thirds of the maps incorporate both terms of the opposition. This opposition as a whole is significantly connected to certain structural characteristics of the maps. Thus, it is very strongly connected, for the whole sample, to the map patterns: it accompanies pratically all the mixed patterns and two-thirds of the spatial patterns, but just over half of the sequential patterns. It is also very strongly connected to the biaxial deep static structure, and the pendulum deep dynamic model (in the case of the latter there are also significant relations with half of the social groups of the sociosemiotic programs), while it is not an important characteristic of the radial structure and model when they are compared to the whole of the maps (on these structures and models, see Section 3). The same opposition is significantly used mainly by the middle class, the country lower middle class, men, and adults; and by individuals with a higher education or university degree.

The classification according to the opposition *movement* vs. *place* is thus not the only way of classifying sketch maps, but it is the most current in geographical literature. This classification according to predominant element is combined with a another crucial classification based on the manner in which the parts of the maps are interrelated (Lynch), the complexity and style of the maps (Appleyard), their sophistication (Pocock), or their degree of organization (Murray and Spencer). The concept of "style" renders nicely the object of interest for the researchers and emphasizes its semiotic nature, but it is rather general - because, as we shall see, the same concept may also be applied to another aspect of the maps - while the other concepts are more specific and, what is more interesting, remarkably similar. What is at stake is the *coherency* of the maps and its different degrees of complexity, which go together with the degree of *elaboration* of the maps. Both these concepts relate to the syntactic structure of the maps, and the corresponding phenomena have direct incidences on their appearance, their "look". Of course, coherency may be given by the imposition of an arbitrary simple geometric pattern, i.e., a "good figure" (Figure 13; see also Pocock 1975: 67), but most currently it is achieved by the realistic "look" of the map. We can speak about different degrees of *realism,* provided this concept is not taken to denote the exact reflection of reality (accuracy in the case of the sketch maps) but the cultural conventions creating the impression or connotation that a text is a representation of reality; it is in this sense in which the concept is used in literary criticism.

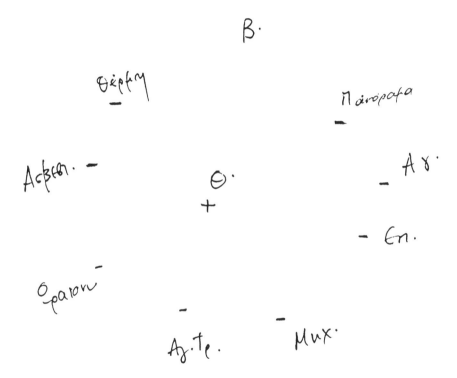

Figure 13. Sketch map tending to a "good figure".

The typology which we ourselves arrived at consists of four degrees of coherency equally applicable to sequential maps, which we prefer to call *road* maps, and spatial maps, for which we would suggest the term *zonal.* These degrees are of a general nature and do not correspond to specific geometric forms. The most primitive degree corresponds to the *discontinuous* maps, which are *fragmented* (Figure 14, 1a) in the case of the road class (cf. the fragmented type of Appleyard and the two first stages of Lynch) or *scattered* (Figure 14, 1b) in the case of zonal maps (Appleyard's scattered type). Of a more complex coherency, but *schematic,* are the maps in the second degree, which are *skeletal* (Figure 14, 2a) when they belong to the road maps (this type is wider than Pocock's three first types and corresponds to the third stage of Lynch) or *diagrammatic* (Figure 14, 2b) when they are zonal (Appleyard's mosaic type). *Realistic* maps are either *pictorial* (Figure 14, 3a) if they are road maps (this type is wider than Appleyard's branch-and-loop type and also corresponds to the third stage of Lynch) or *loose* (Figure 14, 3b) when they are zonal (Appleyard's linked type). The most complex maps from the point of view of coherency are the *elaborated* maps that divide into *network* maps (Figure 14, 4a - see Appleyard's network and Lynch's last stage) and *coherent* maps (Figure 14, 4b - see Appleyard's patterned maps).

Thus, the sequence of road maps from the least to the most coherent is fragmented-skeletal-pictorial-network map, and the sequence of zonal maps is scattered-diagrammatic-loose-coherent map. The first two types in each class are less coherent and elaborated, and only give a general idea of the spatial organization they depict, relating to the general topological organization; this is why we would agree with Appleyard who calls them *topological.* The two most coherent and elaborated types are more cautious in respect to geometric forms and locational details, being closer stylistically to a topographical map, and we shall call them *topographical* (positional for Appleyard).

The typology of the degree of coherency or elaboration of the sketch maps and the major map patterns (road and zonal maps) are the only structural aspects of the maps that have provoked some substantial discussion among geographers. There are, however, also other structural aspects, to which we shall now turn. The first, which attracted some interest on the part of Lynch, is the dynamics of the development of the sketch map during drawing. Lynch (1960: 86-87) defines five modes of development. According to the first mode, the map first develops lengthwise along familiar lines of movement, and then outwards. The second mode is characterized by the opposite movement, since first an enclosing outline is drawn and then there is an inward movement towards the center of the enclosed area, filling in various spots in the interior. For the third mode, a general background is set (Lynch mentions the

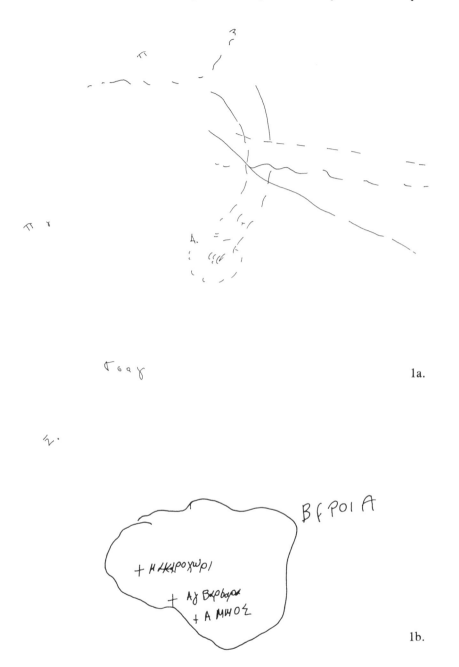

Figure 14. Sketch map patterns: 1a. Road map, fragmented. 1b. Zonal map, scattered.

gridiron system), on which then details are added. Another mode of drawing maps is to start with adjacent regions and then add details on their connection and internal characteristics. Finally, some people start from a central nucleus and all consequent additions revolve around it, a movement outwards comparable to that of the first mode. Lynch ventures the hypothesis that the development of the map is connected to the actual development of spatial knowledge with increasing familiarity, a point in respect to which he is followed by Canter (1977: 62).

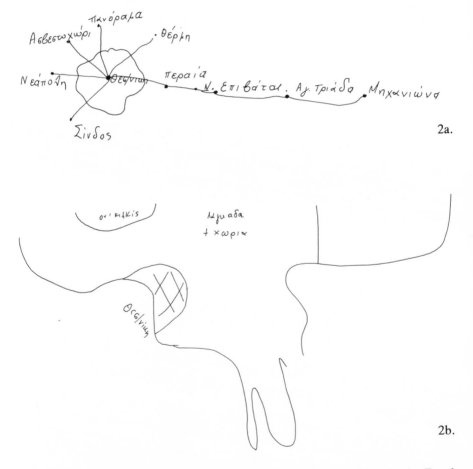

Figure 14 (continued). Sketch map patterns: 2a. Road map, skeletal. 2b. Zonal map, diagrammatic.

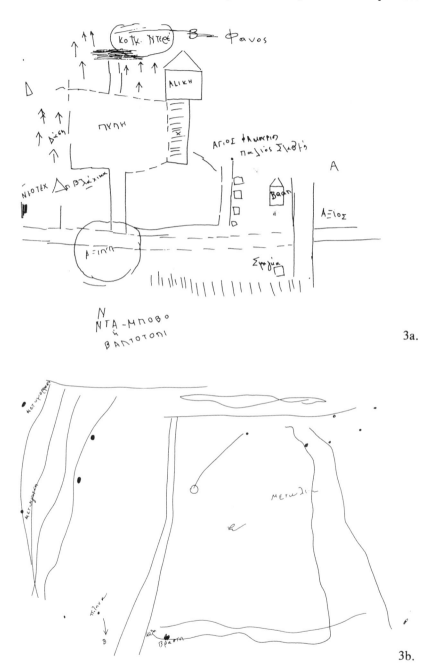

Figure 14 (continued). Sketch map patterns: 3a. Road map, pictorial. 3b. Zonal map, loose.

The mode of development of the sketch map is definitely another syntactic and stylistic aspect of the map and corresponds to one of its structural characteristics. It is the manner in which space is dynamically rendered, and we may compare it to what is known in literary theory as the techniques of narration, such as point of view. Beyond this, however, there are additional structural characteristics, situated at a deeper level of

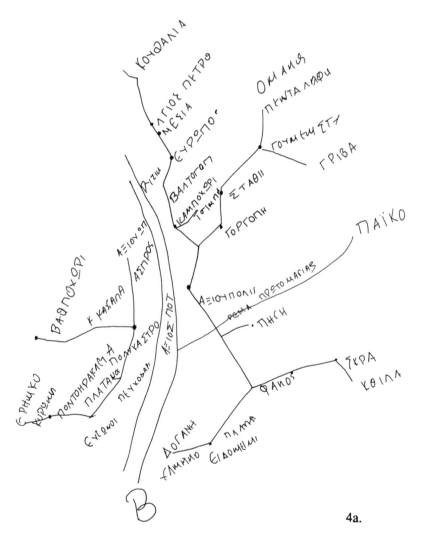

4a.

Figure 14 (continued). Sketch map patterns: 4a. Road map, network.

analysis. This level was systematically explored by psychology (see Section 5), but the same did not occur in geography. We may, however, approach it, not only through the psychological perspective, but also by using linguistic and semiotic sources. In his *Aspects of the theory of syntax,* Noam Chomsky (1965: 134-135, 141) puts forward a comprehensive model of his transformational grammar, according to which the syntax and the meaning of a sentence can be traced back to a common system of generative rules generating the *deep* structures of sentences. In this way, the empirically observable linear structure of a sentence can be derived as a *surface* structure from a corresponding deep structure.

The concepts of deep and surface structure in the generative grammar of Chomsky are essentially limited to the level of the linguistic sentence. But the semiotics of Greimas goes beyond this point and extends to whole texts, where as text should be understood not only a linguistic text

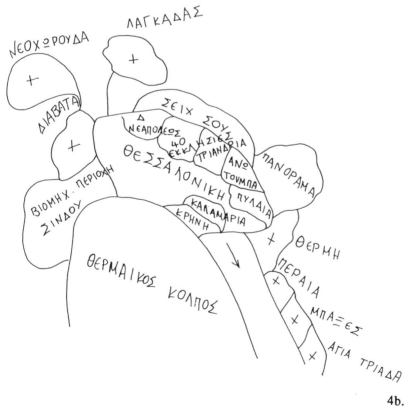

4b.

Figure 14 (continued). Sketch map patterns: 4b. Zonal map, coherent.

such as a novel, but any kind of semiotic text, whether a painting, the composition of a meal, or a conceived region. Greimas (Greimas & Courtés 1979) also distinguishes between two levels of syntax, a deep level and a surface level, which however do not correspond closely to Chomsky's levels. The deep level includes the "semio-narrative" structures, while the surface level is composed of a series of interlocking superimposed levels, to which correspond different kinds of syntax.

The coherency and the major patterns of the sketch maps, as well as their mode of development, can be considered as complementary structures belonging to the same level of analysis, because the former structures describe a static, finished text and the latter structure the dynamic mode of its development. This level of analysis is not much distanced from the actual look of the maps, their empirical reality, and should thus be considered as a surface level. But behind and below these surface structures we can locate two deeper syntactic structures. The first structure lies below the *surface static structure* and is the general organizing scheme underlying the map, which should follow from the manner space is semantically structured as to its fundamental characteristics; this structure can be compared to a *deep static structure*. The second structure underlies the *surface dynamic structure* and embodies the dynamic principles which the development of the map follows, which should correspond to the logic used to reconstitute space as a whole when it is grasped step by step; we can speak in this case of a *deep dynamic structure*.[40] The typology of the dynamic structures and the deep static structure will be discussed in the next two sections.

We shall close the present section with a brief mention of a couple of semiotic characteristics of the sketch maps complementary to the structures presented which will also be discussed in more detail below. The first characteristic is the degree of *sophistication* of the maps, a criterion parallel to their degree of elaboration; however, two maps of an equal degree of elaboration may differ in their degree of sophistication and inversely two maps of a different degree of elaboration may show the same sophistication. The second characteristic is the *richness* of the maps from a quantitative point of view. Richness relates to the number of signifiers included in each map (a similar variable is also used by, for example, Murray & Spencer 1979: 388, and Evans et al. 1981: 88). We considered as a distinct signifier each pictorial vehicle of a sign such as "settlement x", "road y", or "mountain z"; repeated similar signifiers corresponding as a whole to a sign were considered as one signifier (i.e., a set of buildings denoting a built area, a series of mountain-tops denoting a specific mountain, a series of trees denoting a plain). It is to richness that Canter (1977: 60, 63-70) oddly reduces all the surface structures presented above, with as a result the isolation of the elements at the expense of their relations and consequently the loss of the concept of structure.

2. Sketch map styles

Each one of our subjects was asked to draw a sketch map of his/her involvement region including everything he or she considered as characteristic of it. The sheet of white paper provided was 24 x 34.5 cm. and there were no limits to drawing time. Only in exceptional cases was the drawing strategy so weak as to oblige the subject to use a device (change of scale, discountinuous drawing by using an accidental empty part of the sheet) in order to complete the drawing.

The technique devised for the study of the dynamic structures of the maps is quite simple. The subjects were given, in fixed order, pencils in different colors which were changed after four signifiers.[41] It was thus very easy during the elaboration of the data from the field work to reconstitute the development of the maps over time. Some practical inconveniences during the drawing of the maps made it difficult for the researchers to absolutely maintain the four-signifier rule; this is why occasional minor corrections were made later on redrawn maps. Sketch maps of regional space are not at all central in geographical literature, which focuses on urban space, but may appear sporadically (see, for example, Murray & Spencer 1979: 387). We elicited them in a manner encouraging the subjects to actualize their spatial knowledge in performance, and thus the regional space figured by them is an active global space (cf. Chapter 8, Section 2).

The data from our field work fit quite nicely the patterns defined above of the surface static structures. All eight patterns were located, but they differ greatly in their frequency of appearance. Thus, for the whole sample, the most frequent pattern is the skeletal road pattern (27%), followed by the pictorial road pattern (20%) and the diagrammatic zonal pattern (15%). The frequency of the loose zonal and the network patterns is around 10% each, while the presence of the three other pure patterns is negligible (around 1% each). We also observed certain mixed patterns, where by mixed we should understand not only the combination of the highest degrees of coherency of the road and the zonal class, as Appleyard seems to suggest, but also various other types of combinations. In fact, there are combinations of the same degree of coherency - not only the highest - for the two classes, as there are combinations between two different degrees of the two classes or two different degrees within one and the same class. The ratio of the road to the zonal to the mixed maps was found to be 4:2:1.

We should remind the reader that the road and the zonal maps are not exclusively composed of roads or individual elements and/or zones respectively, but take their character from the predominant elements. It is thus not surprising that more than 40% of the zonal maps include at least one road and more than 55% of the road maps at least one zone. As for landmarks, they appear on around 85% of the mixed maps and on three-fourths of the zonal maps. On the total number of maps, landmarks and roads appear with a frequency of more than 80%, while zones appear somewhat less frequently (70%). The presence of the simple topological maps and of the more complex topographical is equal, and they are equally present among road and mixed maps, the only exception being the zonal maps where the topographical maps are overrepresented by 50%.

The skeletal road pattern is underrepresented mainly among the middle class and men (the lowest share is that of the middle class, 18%), while the opposite is true for the working class and women (max. 38%). The pictorial road pattern has a lower-than-average frequency mainly among the middle class, women, and the inhabitants of Thessaloniki (min. 6%), and a high frequency for the working class, men, and the inhabitants of Axioupoli (max. 27%). The working class and the inhabitants of Veria show a low frequency (9%) for the diagrammatic zonal pattern, and in this respect they differ markedly from the middle class (25%). The presence of the loose zonal pattern is negligible for the working class, the inhabitants of Veria and Axioupoli, but reaches a peak in Thessaloniki (23%), and the same is true in respect to the network pattern for the inhabitants of Thessaloniki and Ormylia in comparison to Veria and Axioupoli (max. 15%). Thus, concerning the pure static surface structures, we observe opposed tendencies between working and middle class, men and women, the metropolis and the provincial city, as well as the metropolis and Axioupoli.

In contrast to the mixed patterns, which are more or less evenly represented among the freguency-program groups, the 2:1 ratio between road and zonal patterns in the whole sample greatly varies for some of these groups. The distance between the two patterns is maximized for the working class, Veria, and Axioupoli (max. ratio 6:1), the two patterns are equally weighted for the middle class, and finally their relation is reversed in Thessaloniki (1:1.4). The sociosemiotic programs show that this contrast between Veria and the metropolis is significant, and the same contrast between the tendencies to draw road and zonal maps is observed between individuals of a lower or intermediate education and individuals with a higher education or a university degree. In this respect also, then, the working class is differentiated from the middle class, and the metropolis from the province and the rural settlement. Finally, there are variations in the ratio of 1:1 between simple and complex maps. The most extreme divergence from this ratio appears between men and women, and in two opposite directions: men have a tendency toward complex maps (1:1.8), but women tend toward simple maps (2:1); this opposition is shown to be very significant by the sociosemiotic programs. One possible explanation of this divergence could be that women have a poorer conceptualization of regional space. On the other hand, given that the surface static structures are the only ones among our four different kinds of structures that are influenced by the factor of graphic ability, we could interpret this divergence as the result of a socially defined difference in this ability between the two sexes. We shall return to this point below.

As we already saw, the degree of sophistication of the sketch maps is another criterion for the classification of the look of these maps. From this point of view, the discontinuous patterns are always elementary, i.e., they correspond to the lowest degree of sophistication. This includes the elementary map forms, but some schematic patterns are also elementary. At the other extreme, the sophisticated maps, the skillfully executed maps, are always elaborated, and vice versa. The next-to-the-lowest degree of sophistication, that including the simplistic, diagram-like maps, is always alimented by the schematic patterns, although a certain part of the latter may be simple maps, which represent the medium degree of sophistication and begin to look realistic. The fairly sophisticated maps, that look more like a conventional map, are always realistic, but the realistic maps are in their great majority simple maps as far as their sophistication is connected. Simple maps are thus, according to the case, either schematic or realistic, but the majority are realistic.

The frequency distribution for the whole sample shows that 40% of our subjects drew maps of a simple kind and an equal part maps of rather low sophistication. When we pass to the social groups, we find again, as was the case with map elaboration, certain interesting oppositions. Veria and Ormylia are comparable in their production of less sophisticated maps, which is somewhat above average, but they differ markedly in respect to the simple maps, which in Ormylia constitute a maximum of 52% and in Veria a minimum of 24% of the whole; as a result, in Ormylia the more sophisticated maps are almost absent, while in Veria they show above-average representation (30%). The sociosemiotic programs show that indeed the Verians tend significantly to higher sophistication and that the results for Ormylia are mainly due to the mature. Thessaloniki shows the lowest share in both the extreme degrees of sophistication, for which the corresponding maps are practically absent; it has the greatest share of fairly sophisticated maps (21%), and it is below average in the case of less sophisticated maps.

Once more the working and the middle class differ (though not significantly): though both have a share of simple maps almost equal to that of the whole sample, the maps with a lower degree of sophistication in the working class approximate half of the total, while in the middle class they are less than one-third. A similar relation is observed between women and men: it is true that men are more represented in the simple-map category, but their share in lower sophistication is less than 30%, while the women's share is half of the total; the sociosemiotic programs show that the differences between men and women are significant. An emphasis on higher-sophistication maps is also found among individuals with a higher education or a university degree. The degree of sophistication of the maps is an even better index of graphic ability than the degree of complexity of their coherency, and we should probably conclude that men are culturally superior to women in graphic ability. Thus, the inferiority of women in map complexity could be attributed, at least partially, to drawing difficulties.

The development of the maps is effected according to different modes. In our case we distinguished approximately 40 modes and we can speculate that there are many more. But these modes, which describe the development of the maps closely, can be grouped into eight wider classes of map development. The description of the modes of development and their groupings necessitated the definition of a set of abstract concepts, able both to account for the development of any individual map in our corpus and to offer a theoretical framework for the description of all possible modes of map development. The main concepts defined are: *focal* element, *peripheral* element, and their *connection*.

The focal element may be of a punctual and zonal, or axial nature; explicit or implicit; geometrically central or not. We considered as an implicit focal element an element which tends to acquire a focal position in the sketch map, but which is not overtly shown as such; usually this element corresponds to the place of residence of the subject. The peripheral element is peripheral to an explicit or implicit focus, or even to an empty focus, and may cover a greater or lesser extent. The focus of this element may be internal to it or located on it. The connection between focus and periphery may be abstract, as is the case with a geometric center and periphery: a center is by its geometric definition connected to its periphery. Otherwise, the connection between focus and periphery is achieved in four different ways: through the periphery itself; with the help of punctual (or zonal) elements; by using simple linear elements ("radii"), corresponding to channels of traffic; or by the use of "radii" with ramifications. The dynamic pattern created by the iconic elements corresponding to the main concepts discussed may appear once on an individual map, or may be recurrent.

Thus, a movement from a focal to a peripheral element may originate from an axial element (cf. Lynch's first mode of development, previous section) or take place through non-linear elements (cf. Lynch's fifth mode of development). The focal and the peripheral elements are defined by their relative position and by the semantics of the center, not necessarily by their geometry, this is why the movement from focus to periphery may be a movement between adjacent or even parallel figures (cf. Lynch's fourth mode of development). The movement between adjacent elements when a focus does not exist is a movement along a periphery.

On the basis of these concepts, the eight classes of the surface dynamic structures of the maps and the five groups into which they can be classified are the following:

Group A. *Development from focus to periphery* (63% of the sample).
Class 1. From focus to periphery in a simple manner (36%).
Class 2. From focus to periphery with the use of at least one radius with ramifications (27%).
Group B. *Movement along the periphery* (6%).

Class 3. The development of the map is restricted to a peripheral zone with no focus.

Group C. *Development from periphery to focus* (cf. Lynch's second mode of development; 12%).

Class 4. Movement from the periphery to the focus by simple means (10%).

Class 5. Same movement but with the use of at least one radius with ramifications (2%).

Group D. *Creation of a general framework and development toward the periphery* (17%). In this case, the subject sets a general framework for his/her sketch map and then adds details in the interior of it and probably extensions around it. This case corresponds to Lynch's third mode of development, with the difference that the frameworks we found are not of the gridiron type mentioned by Lynch, but are composed of a focus and a periphery.

Class 6. Movement to the periphery by simple means (13%).

Class 7. Movement to the periphery through at least one radius with ramifications (4%).

Group E. *General framework, development toward the periphery, plus return to the focus* (2%).

Class 8. Same pattern with group D with the addition of a return movement to the focus.

Together with the typology of the surface dynamic structures, we also gave above the share of each mode of development in the whole sample. We see that by far the dominant group of these structures is group A, development from focus to periphery, and that the simple form of this development is the most current mode of development, followed by the complex form of the same group. Next to this group is group D, according to which the whole framework of the map, composed of a focus and a periphery, is set in advance and then follows a movement toward the periphery; after this comes group C, of the development from periphery to focus. The two other groups are underrepresented and this is also the case with classes 5 and 7 including ramifications.

Group A is clearly underrepresented in Thessaloniki (40%), due to the poor presence of both the classes it includes (20% each), while the opposite is true for the two rural settlements (around 75%). The share of this group in Veria, as well as for the working class and women, is very close to the average, but in these cases the frequency of the simple form is more than double that of the complex form; on the other hand, the complex form overtakes it and is strongly represented (around 40%) in the case of Axioupoli, the lower middle class, and men. Group D is overrepresented in Thessaloniki and among the middle class (24%) while its share is low for the middle class and women (12%). There is a strong opposition between men and women in respect to group C, which is ranked second for women (21%) but is just barely felt among men (5%). A last characteristic of Thessaloniki is the strong presence (17%) of group B including the maps without focal elements.

Contrary to the preceding typologies, which are qualitative, map richness is a quantitative aspect of sketch maps. We already encountered a similar variable, which we named spatial richness, in the discussion of the different kinds of superimposed regional spaces (Chapter 8, Section 2), though there richness was calculated on the basis of the answers to the oral questionnaire. We defined six categories of map richness: the very poor maps, including 4-6 signifiers; the poor maps, having 8-10 signifiers; the medium rich maps, with 12-16 signifiers; the rather rich maps, with 18-20 signifiers; the rich maps, with 22-32 signifiers; and the exceptionally rich maps, with 36, 38, or 58 signifiers. The two lower categories can be grouped into a class of poor maps, and the three higher give the class of rich maps.

For the whole sample, the class of poor maps represents almost one-third of the total, in which the majority are in the category of poor maps (19%). The class of rich maps, on the other hand, covers another one-third of the total, in which the rather rich and rich maps have an equal share (15%) and the exceptional maps are clearly underrepresented. When we compare this distribution with the data from the spatial richness variable, we can conclude that the sketch maps are much richer that the spaces following from the questionnaire, something that does not come as a surprise, among others things because of the strong presence of the roads in the sketch maps, which tend to disappear from the answers to the questionnaire.

Among the frequency-program groups, there is a certain tendency among the young to produce poorer maps, while the opposite is the tendency of the adults, and the same difference is repeated in a more acute form between women and men. Indeed, the class of rich maps by men shows an above-average frequency (42%), which is the highest for all groups and is mainly due to the rather rich maps; while the opposite is true for women, who show the lowest frequency (23%) in the rich-map class; women do not present any exceptionally rich maps, while 7% of the men's maps belong to this category. Also, the second highest percentage of poor maps appears among women (39%; the first is in Ormylia, 47%), while the share of these maps among men is the lowest (20%); this difference is mainly due to the very poor maps, which are pratically absent among men, but represent almost one-fifth of the total for women. The sociosemiotic programs show that the divergence between the genders is significant, and that even among women there is a significant difference, the country women drawing the poorest maps. The workers are comparable to the young and women in the production of poorer maps, and the maps of the inhabitants of Ormylia are the poorest for all groups; the opposite tendency appears among the middle class and the inhabitants of Axioupoli.

3. Deep spatial structures

It is now time to pass to the study of the deep structures of space, which underlie the stylistic aspects presented in the last section. These structures lead us to the definition of the fundamental manners according to which our subjects grasp regional space, both statically and dynamically. We shall begin with the deep static structures. Their number is limited to seven and they are the following:

a. *Central* structure (19% of the total number of structures located/used by 32% of the subjects in the whole sample). In the context of this structure, the subject focuses the construction of regional space on a marked central point, which thus condenses the whole regional experience; there is a periphery which may be a marked or an unmarked element of the structure.

b. *Peripheral* structure (5%/8%). This represents the inverse of the previous structure, in that the subject constructs space along a periphery with an empty geometric center; however, a peripheral focus is not excluded.

c. *Concentric* structure (11%/19%). This is an extension of the combination of the two previous structures and consists of a center and a series of concentric peripheries; regional experience revolves within this setting. In exceptional cases, the center may not be a marked element.

d. *Radial* structure (25%/42%). This is a development of the central structure, since a set of elements that can be described as linear converge on a center. For this structure, regional space is held together by its center, which represents its quintessence.

e. *Axial* structure (16%/26%). The previous structures are constructed on the basis of the affirmation or the negation of a center. This center is not at issue with the axial structure, because here space is constructed on the two sides of an axial element. The latter is either notional or actual; in the second case, the axis may be linear and thus explicitly drawn, or it may be implicit and deduced from the arrangement of non-linear elements.

f. *Biaxial* structure (20%/34%). This represents a development of the previous structure, since now a new full or half axis is added perpendicularly intersecting the axis of the axial structure. The intersection of the two axes need not necessarily be a marked point of regional space. When it is, we have the combination of the biaxial with the central structure, a combination akin to the radial structure. The nature of the axes of the biaxial structure is the same as that of those of the axial structure, explicit or implicit.

g. *Serial* structure (4%/6%). Space is seen according to this structure as a series of adjacent zones, but these zones do not compose a curve, something that would result in a transition to the peripheral structure. This structure was not found alone in our corpus, but only in combination with some other structure or structures.

As we saw, the first percentage given above represents the share of each structure in the total number of structures for the whole sample. This number exceeds the total number of maps drawn, since in many cases there were more than one structures underlying a map. The maximum number of structures per map for the whole sample was found to be three, and the average is 1.5. According to this series of percentages, the radial, the biaxial, and the central structure are the most common, followed by the axial and then the concentric structure; the appearance of the peripheral and the serial structure is rather rare (this ranking is exactly replicated by the second series of percentages based on the total number of subjects). The share of the radial structure is maximized (around 35%) in Veria and Axioupoli and for the working class, for which it is the by far dominant structure, while it drops drastically in Thessaloniki, Ormylia, and for the middle class (around 15%); for this structure, then, there is no consistent difference between city and country. In the context of the sociosemiotic programs, on the other hand, we grouped all the subjects using a particular structure together and contrasted them to the subjects not using it. These programs show that the use of the radial structure in Veria is very significant; they also show that the Ormylia workers and the Thessaloniki lower middle class have a tendency to use this structure.

Of the total number of structures, the biaxial structure reaches a peak in Ormylia and for the middle class (around 30%), where it is ranked high, while its frequency is minimized in the two cities, for the lower middle class, and women (around 15%); in this case, the city and the country differ. According to the sociosemiotic programs, the tendency to use this structure characterizes various social groups in the countryside, such as the country middle class and men, as well as the mature in Ormylia and individuals with a higher education or a university degree. It is again in Ormylia that the central structure reaches its peak (33%), while it is underrepresented in the two cities (around 12%). The sociosemiotic programs show that many groups in Ormylia contribute to the frequent appearance of the central structure: mainly the lower middle and the middle class, men and youth. The low shares of the radial, biaxial, and central structures in the total number of structures in Thessaloniki are compensated for by the doubling of the shares of the concentric and peripheral structures in comparison to the whole sample; in fact in the metropolis the concentric pattern is the most frequent.

The deep dynamic structures are closely comparable to the static structures, both as to their nature and their limited number. They represent the dynamic models according to which the structural parts of space are assembled over time in order to reconstitute the whole. These models amount to eight and are as follows:

a. *Central* model (17%/29%). In the context of this model, the subject uses as a permanent point of reference as he or she reconstructs space a stable central point; the periphery of space may be marked or unmarked.

b. *Peripheral* model (17%/31%). According to this model, space is structured through a circular trajectory, in such a manner that the point of arrival and the point of departure are close to each other. The direction of movement is either clockwise or counter-clockwise. It is a model without a center and as such the inverse of the central model, but it may include a peripheral focus.

c. *Concentric* model (7%/12%). When this model is used, space is constructed as a series of consecutive concentric zones revolving around an actual or notional center.

d. *Radial* model (24%/43%). The model leads to the reccurent use of radial elements all radiating from a marked center. It is one of the forms of the outwards expansion of the central model.

e. *Axial* model (14%/24%). When a subject uses this model, he or she first completes the reconstruction of a first part of space situated on one side of an axis and then passes to the other side of the same axis; the axis may be actual or notional.

f. *Biaxial* model (4%/8%). The model embodies the reconstruction of space according to a pattern of three parts or four quarters, i.e., around two perpendicular axes. Thus this reconstruction of space always revolves around a center, which either corresponds to the abstract intersection of the two axes, or to a marked element of the sketch map which coincides with the intersection.

g. *Serial* model (3%/5%). In the case of this model, space is structured by a series of consecutive areas that develop linearly in the same or opposed directions; in this way, the point of departure and the point of arrival may or may not compose the two extremes of the model. If a circular trajectory is followed, we get the peripheral model.

h. *Pendulum* model (14%/25%). According to this model, the subject structures space by starting from one part of it and consequently moving to an opposite part, then moving to a part opposite to the latter that does not necessarily coincide with the first part, and so on in a pendular or zigzag movement.

Among the dynamic models, as in the case of the deep static structures, the radial pattern prevails. There is again a similarity with the static structures in that the central dynamic model occupies a high rank, but then models and structures diverge because the peripheral model is among the most important models, while the peripheral structure is ranked very low. The axial model, like the corresponding structure, occupies the fourth rank and is equally frequent with the pendulum model, which is the only model that does not have any equivalent among the static structures. The appearance of the rest of the models is infrequent. They include the biaxial model, the importance of which decreases dramatically in comparison to the biaxial static structure. As was the case with the static structures, the study of the participation of each model and model ranking was based on the total number of models (first percentage; the second percentage refers to the subjects using the models, but the ranking of the models according to the second percentage is practically identical to the first). The maximum number of dynamic models per map amounts to four, and the average number per map is 1.6.

The maximum percentages of the radial model (around 32%) appear in Veria and Axioupoli and among the workers (for whom it is the dominant model), while in Ormylia and among the middle class we observe the lowest percentages (around 15%). The sociosemiotic programs show that a multiplicity of social groups in Veria incline to the radial model, for example, the genders and age groups, the working class and the lower middle class. Thus, both the radial model and the radial structure are characteristic of Veria. The Ormylians are not very fond of this model, but the workers in Ormylia have a definite tendency to use it, while in the metropolis it is used by the lower middle class, trends that we already observed in respect to the static radial structure.

The frequency distributions show that the central model reaches a peak in Ormylia (38%), where it is by far dominant, and the opposite happens in the other three settlements. According to the sociosemiotic programs the tendency of the Ormylians towards this model is very significant, and this tendency parallels the use of the corresponding static structure. Among the other social groups, only the middle-class Verians have a certain inclination to the central model. Only the urban lower middle class has a significant tendency to use the concentric model. As for the biaxial model, individuals with a university degree and those with a degree from a technical college have a certain tendency towards it, parallel to their tendency towards the corresponding static structure. The frequencies show that for the peripheral model, as for the central model, there is no distinction between city and country, since its frequency is maximized in Veria and Axioupoli (around 25%), and minimized in Thessaloniki and Ormylia (around 10%); the use of the model by the Verians is very significant. On the other hand, Thessaloniki shows the highest frequency for the pendulum model (21%), which is there prevalent together with the radial model.

Now that we have seen the nature of the static and dynamic deep structures it is easy to understand why they are independent from graphic ability, and the same holds for the surface dynamic structures. All these structures can be incorporated without distortions even into the simplest forms of the sketch maps. We can see that if we use as an example the sketch map 1a of Figure 14, a map of elementary sophistication and very poor in richness, drawn by a woman belonging to the lower middle class (north is to the left). The central zonal signifier corresponds to Axioupoli, from which a road leads to the Polykastro area, shown as a point encircled by a boundary; the road crosses the Axios river, and parallel to the river runs another road. Two other settlements appear on the map, in connection with Axioupoli. In spite of the fact that these settlements are not shown as related by roads to Axioupoli, the map should be considered as a road map, given that its basic organizing principle consists of two settlements united by a road; the map represents the most primitive degree of coherency of the road maps, the fragmented pattern.

The development of the map started from its geometric center, Axioupoli, and then moved through a simple radius to the rest of the signifiers of the map, considered as elements to a greater or lesser extent peripheral (group A, class 1, of the surface dynamic structures). The deep static structure of the map is central, because all the construction of space revolves around its center, while the periphery around this center does not become a marked element. This is no longer true for the deep dynamic model, because the reconstruction of space is effected through a continuous and integrating circular counter-clockwise movement originating from the center: we have here a combination of the central and the peripheral model.

There are of course also maps incorporating a more complex conception of regional space. An example is given by the map in Figure 15 (map 4a of Figure 14), a sophisticated map of exceptional richness, drawn by a man of the lower middle class (north is down). The center of the map is constituted by two poles, Axioupoli to the right and Polykastro to the left, situated on the two sides of the Axios river. From these poles the map develops outwards in different directions according to radii with ramifications passing from and uniting all the settlements depicted on the map. The result is a network map, a map of the most complex coherency. The map belongs to group A, class 2, of the surface dynamic structures, since it develops from a focus outwards through radii with ramifications, a pattern that is recurrent. The deep static structure of the map consists of three structures. The first is the radial structure just described. There is a second, biaxial structure, the two axes of which are the river and an axis perpendicular to the river suggested by the division of the map into an upper and a lower part; this division corresponds to the semantic opposition "mountain" (up - the lower part of the map) vs. "plain" (down - the upper part of the map). There is also a third structure consisting of a (double) center and a peripheral area. The series of ramifications of the road network suggests the possibility of more than one

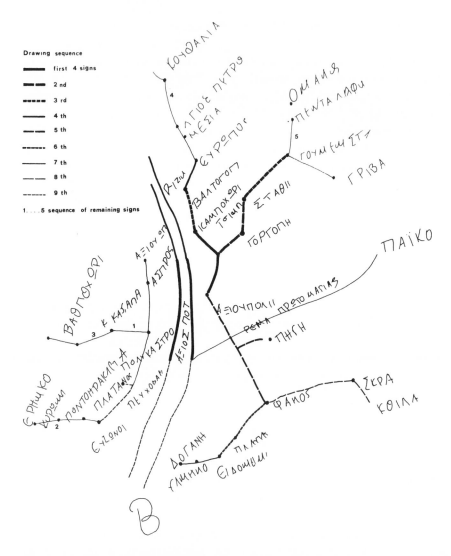

Figure 15. Dynamic development of a sophisticated road map. In the original sketch map, the drawing sequence is recognizable through the use of nine different colored pencils. In the reproduction above these colors are represented by lines of different thickness and continuity. This is an unusually rich sketch map, drawn by a subject who exhausted the full range of colors and continued drawing an important number of signifiers with the last colored pencil. The sequence of this last set of signifiers is shown in the figure through the use of numerals.

peripheral zones, and since this is in fact the case, as we shall see, the third structure is a concentric structure.

The first dynamic model of this map is once more radial, since the logic of all the movements from focus to periphery is radial. Even the river was drawn according to the same radial logic, since the part of it in the upper part of the map was drawn much earlier than that in the lower part, as can be seen from Figure 15. The signifiers last drawn were the leftmost and the uppermost signifiers, which define a zone encircling the previously drawn internal zone, whence the appearance of the concentric model and the corroboration of the concentric structure. From the focus of the map the subject passed to the right upper part of the map, came down to the right lower part, passed to the left part and ended with the uppermost part. He thus reconstructed space, as in the previous example, through a continuous circular movement, with the difference that this time the movement is clockwise and spiral. At the same time this movement involves the drawing of a first quarter of the map, then a second, and finally the left half of the map. This succession shows, first, that the river is still conceived as an axis in spite of its fragmentation into radii, and second, that the axis perpendicular to it is still present in the form of a half-axis. It should be noted that the existence of, for example, a biaxial deep static structure does not necessarily imply a corresponding deep dynamic model. In one case, for instance, the deep static level consisted of two structures, one biaxial and one serial, but both these patterns are lost on the dynamic level due to the use of the pendulum model.

But let us come back to the issue of the deep static structures. We already encountered it in Chapter 6, Section 3, when analyzing the structuring of the consecutive regional spaces on the basis of the questionnaire. There, the conceptualization of space was constrained by the request for an outward scanning effected in successive stages and the focus was on the relation between consecutive spaces. The structuring of the consecutive regions was dominated by the concentric structures. Here, on the other hand, the subjects are channelled towards the interior of their involvement region and the connection between neighboring spaces. It seems reasonable to assume that if they were directed toward the interior of a larger region, for example, the wider region, they would conceptualize space according to the same structures which emerged for the involvement region. Now that we have defined the nature of these deep structures, we can envisage the possibility that even in the case of the relation between consecutive spaces these structures could be activated, beyond the use of the concentric structure alone. We can imagine, for example, that in the place of the pole of a polarized structure there is an adjacent region, with as a result the appearance of the serial structure; or that, beyond this transformation, a conceptual axis could be added - corresponding for instance to a river, a mountain, or the national boundaries - leading thus to the appearance of the axial structure, and so on. We should probably attribute the limitation of our subjects to the concentric structure to the limits set by the questions posed.

The structures elicited through the questionnaire present two elements that do not explicitly figure in the structures from the sketch maps, namely the poles and the voids of meaning. However, the voids of meaning are far from absent from the map structures; they are in a certain manner embedded in them, since as a rule these structures emerge from the relation between elements that can be constituted as separate entities by their relations to the empty, meaningless spaces intercalated between them. But the map structures were elicited from the familiar, the involvement region, where the voids recede to the background, while the structures from the questionnaire emerged from a focusing on the less familiar, resulting not infrequently in a strong affirmation of the voids.

Though the questions of the questionnaire may have acted as a constraint on the production of the deep static structures, a production which was liberated by the sketch maps, this disadvantage was compensated for by the fact that they brought to light the polarized structure. Of course, the central, the concentric, and the radial structure are also polarized, but by an element internal to them. The pole of the polarized structure, on the other hand, is external to the involvement region, and this structure could not easily be located through the sketch maps, since they are oriented toward the interior of the involvement region. All the deep structures found and their combinations can coexist with an external pole. But this is not the only possible way in which to affect the reconcilation of such a pole with the map structures. An external pole could belong to a partial view of space which, when completed, would reveal that what seemed to be an external pole is in reality an internal center; it is reasonable to expect in this case that the completed structure could figure among the deep structures located.

The resemblance between the structures revealed by the oral questionnaire and the mapping method points not only to the complementarity of the data from two different semiotic systems, but also to the importance of these structures. This last observation is strengthened by their close similarity with the deep dynamic models. Instantaneous structuring of space and structuring through a trajectory over time converge in a striking manner. The convergence is not only typological, but some deeper bonds unite the similar static and dynamic structures, and it is these bonds that we shall examine in the last section of this chapter. This analysis will be based on the correlations between deep static structures and deep dynamic models. But there are also certain other connections between map structures, which we shall first discuss.

4. The connections between map structures

Deep and surface structures present certain connections. The road maps are very strongly linked, for all the groups of the semiotic programs, with the radial static structure. There are exceptions to this connection, as we can see from the whole sample, where more than one-fourth of the individuals with road maps do not use the radial structure. The exceptions are very rare for the inverse case: only 5% of the users of this structure do not show road maps. The zonal maps, on the other hand, are connected to the central structure.

Concerning the dynamic structures, there are generally no relations between surface and deep structures. The only exception is the correlation between the map development groups and the radial model (valid for the whole sample, the cities, and the young). We observe that more than 80% of the users of the radial model develop their maps from focus to periphery. Thus, there is a definite connection of this mode to the radial model, which does not exist either for the opposite mode from periphery to focus or for any other mode; among the subjects developing their maps from periphery to focus, less than 13% also show the radial model. We conclude on these grounds that the radial construction of space encourages a reconstruction starting from its marked center, and that the opposite reconstruction towards the center is independent of the radial model.

There is a very significant connection between surface static and surface dynamic structures (for the sample and the cities), which is due to a series of associations. The road maps are associated to the mode of development from focus to periphery, something that does not come as a surprise, since as we saw the road maps are related to the radial structure, the development from focus to periphery is related to the radial model, and the two radial patterns are intimately connected. The peripheral mode of development is almost exclusively associated with the zonal maps, but the opposite is not necessarily true, since more than half of the subjects with zonal maps draw their maps from focus to periphery. A last association is that of the mixed maps with the mode of development from periphery to focus, but also with the mode of the setting of a focus and a periphery followed by a movement toward the periphery.

The sophistication of the sketch maps presents some significant relationships only with the deep structures. In the case of the deep static structures, these relationships do not characterize all the structures and mainly concern the whole sample. They show that the maps with a biaxial structure have a strong tendency, and those with a concentric structure a very strong tendency, toward a degree of sophistication of simple or higher, while the rest of the maps as a whole tend to be of a simple or lower sophistication. More than one-third of the concentric maps are of higher sophistication (this is also the case for these maps among city dwellers) and the same is true for biaxial maps. There is a difference, however, between the two structures in that the maps with a concentric structure represent one-third of the maps of higher sophistication, while those with a biaxial structure more than half. On the other hand, the maps with a central structure are obviously less sophisticated, since their sophistication rarely exceeds simple (only 7% of them are of higher sophistication).

These results are almost duplicated for the dynamic models. While the biaxial model is not now correlated with sophistication, the concentric model is, not only for the whole sample, but again also for the cities, and further for the lower middle class. Not a single map with a concentric model shows lower sophistication, in strong opposition to the maps with the central model, almost half of which exhibit lower sophistication. The crosstabulations for the dynamic models also reveal another notable phenomenon. For all social groups of the semiotic programs - with the sole exception of the working class - more than half of the maps that have been executed with the pendulum movement show higher degree of sophistication (significance level 0.01); also, almost three-fourths of the maps in the whole sample with this degree of sophistication have been drawn through the pendulum movement.

Sophistication is also correlated to map richness, very strongly and for all semiotic programs. The pattern of the correlation is in all cases the same, and we shall use as an example the whole sample. About 60% of the maps with lower sophistication are poor in sign richness and the rest of these maps show medium richness. Around 80% of the maps with simple sophistication are almost equally divided into rich and medium rich maps, and almost 80% of the maps with higher sophistication are rich. On the other hand, the maps of lower sophistication constitute the great majority of poor maps (80%); the medium richness maps are almost equally divided between lower and simple sophistication and are occasionally (12%) of higher sophistication; and the rich maps are also divided, but this time between simple and higher sophistication, never being of lower sophistication. The general picture from these data is that there is a strong tendency for poor maps to show lower sophistication; the maps of a medium richness are usually of lower or simple sophistication and occasionally of high sophistication; and the rich maps can show simple sophistication but usually show higher sophistication. We have here a strong and persistent regularity, according to which richness and sophistication go hand in hand.

In Chapter 6, Section 4, we discussed the relationship between the size of the involvement region and map sophistication, from which we concluded that graphic ability seems to be influenced by a factor other than graphic skill, namely spatial extension. We also discussed the relationship between surface and map richness, the comparison of which to the previous relationship implies the possibility of a new relationship between map sophistication and richness. The data just discussed not only corroborate this possibility, but also give its real meaning to the influence of the size of the involvement region on graphic ability: the latter is not literally influenced by spatial extension, but by the richness of spatial knowledge which in turn covaries with spatial extension.

Map richness is also correlated with map structures. While there is no correlation with the surface dynamic structures and only one correlation with the major surface static structures (examined in Chapter 6, Section 4), richness presents a certain network of relationships with both the static and the dynamic deep structures. The maps in the whole sample with a biaxial static structure show a significant tendency to be rich when compared to the rest of the maps (even if just over half of them show a lesser degree of richness) and this is also the case with the maps of the middle class and those of the countryside. A comparable association is observed for the whole sample in respect to the concentric structure (0.01) as well as in respect to the concentric model, but only in the lower middle class. But richness of the pendulum maps is a fact characterizing -

frequently very significantly - all the social groups of the semiotic programs, with the sole exception of the working class. We find here a persistent regularity, strengthened by the fact that there is a correlation between the use of the pendulum movement and total richness of codes in the interview: among the individuals with the highest code use (21-26 codes), more than 60% in the whole sample use the pendulum movement in drawing their maps, and the individuals using this movement never show the lowest code use (up to 11 codes).[42]

The opposite association characterizes the central structure, since maps with this structure show a tendency to be poor, a tendency that is very significant for the whole sample and for youth, and significant for the middle class, the countryside, and women. The radial structure seems to hold an intermediary position, in comparison to the biaxial and the concentric structures on the one hand and the central structure on the other, as it is mainly related to medium richness, but this observation is not strong since it does not appear in the whole sample but only in one social group, women.

5. Spatial logics and spatial universals

We shall now examine the bonds between deep static structures and dynamic models. In order to study these bonds, we prepared a series of crosstabulations showing the individuals using similar static and dynamic map patterns (though they may show other patterns at the same time). This was done by isolating each time the individuals with comparable structures and grouping the rest of the subjects together. The correlations for the radial pattern are very significant (0.0000) for all ten social groups of the semiotic programs. For the whole sample, more than 95% of individuals using the radial static structure also use the radial dynamic model, and only 5% do not use it; simultaneously, more than 90% of those using the radial dynamic model also have the radial static structure, and less than 10% do not have it.

Things are comparable, if not so clearly delimited, with the central, axial, and serial patterns. We saw that the frequency of the biaxial pattern is very different for the static and dynamic patterns (20% and 4%), something that excludes any biunivocal correspondence between them. Indeed, for the whole sample, 80% of the individuals with a biaxial static structure do not use the corresponding dynamic model. There is, nevertheless, a correlation between the two patterns - for half of the semiotic programs, and generally very significant - given that at least 86% of the individuals with the biaxial dynamic model also use the biaxial static structure. In the case of the concentric pattern, again part of the individuals with the static structure do not show the same dynamic model (from 17% to 64% for nine groups), but the very significant correlations are mainly due to the fact that no person using the concentric model uses any other static structure than the concentric. We also observe from the crosstabulations that individuals who have a conception of space including, exclusively or not, the static concentric or biaxial structure frequently tend to construct space dynamically by using the pendulum model (these correlations refer to seven and to all the groups respectively, and are generally very significant); the analytical data allow us to conclude that both these structures have a close relation with the pendulum model.

We thus see that the comparable static and dynamic patterns are systematically and very strongly correlated to each other, and these correlations reveal a tendency of comparable patterns to coexist. The only exception is the peripheral pattern, for which there is no correlation between the static and the dynamic structure, something which seems to indicate that the peripheral dynamic model is only a manner of conceptually moving in space and does not constitute an integrated whole together with the corresponding static structure. From this viewpoint then, the peripheral dynamic model is comparable to the pendulum model, for which there is no static equivalent. This tendency is not an absolute rule, since there is not always a biunivocal correspondence between comparable patterns: a given structure can be associated with one or more models different from the model comparable to this structure, while the comparable model can be associated with one or more different structures. The general picture, however, is that the tendency of a model to be associated with the comparable structure is much more persistent than the opposite tendency. This association of comparable patterns points to the existence of a limited set of *fundamental integrated spatial logics* that constitute the backbone of spatial structuring. These logics harmonize with and surpass the comparable static and dynamic patterns, in the sense that they prove them to be partial aspects of integrated elementary manners of structuring space. The relative predominance of the tendency from the dynamic model to the static structure gives the impression that these logics are activated by the dynamic element. In spite of their unity, however, their constituent parts can be found separately and may enter into different wholes, which thus integrate other combinations between structures and models.

The fundamental spatial logics (Figure 16) are not only elementary in the sense that they cannot generally be further broken down into subordinate structures, but also because they can be described through elementary semantic relations, usually applied to elements that can be described with elementary geometric concepts. The semantic relations are: *here* vs. *there,* in isolation or in connection with *here* vs. *around here,* or *here* vs. *there* vs. *further away* and so on, in isolation or in connection with *here* vs. *around here* vs. *around there* and so on; *adjacent to* and *next to;* and *on the one side* vs. *on the other side,* in isolation (axial pattern) or reduplicated (biaxial pattern). Another basic topological relation is *up* vs. *down,* which is not systematically connected to specific geometric elements. All these relations are set against the background, implied by the very delineation of the involvement region, of the relation *inside* vs. *outside.* The geometric concepts which describe the elements of the spatial logics are: *center, periphery, radius, axis,* and *plane.*

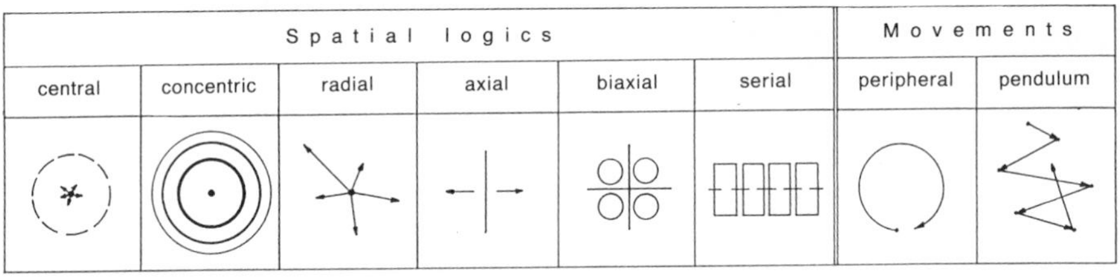

Spatial logics						Movements	
central	concentric	radial	axial	biaxial	serial	peripheral	pendulum

Figure 16. Fundamental spatial logics.

The nature of the semantic relations, of the geometric concepts and the figures corresponding to the latter, and of the combinations of these figures, are such that we get the impression that the set of possible fundamental spatial logics cannot be much wider than the logics located. If this impression is correct, the caliber of the logics found would be greater than Northern Greece or even Greece. Of course this impression could be checked by means of a comparison with similar studies effected in different contemporary contexts, but the bibliography is rather silent on this matter. There are, however, certain archaeological, anthropological, and psychological data that may offer us a clue as to the generality of our spatial logics.

A first part of these data is due to the genetic psychology of Jean Piaget and its use by other psychologists, as well as by Rik Pinxten in anthropological studies. Piaget (1972: 11-58) distinguishes four periods in the cognitive development of the child. The first period is that of the sensori-motor actions of the infant, which closes with the appearance of the semiotic function (occuring in the stage from 18 to 24 months) and the acquisition of language. In this period, the infant is initially conscious neither of itself as a subject not of the objects (including other subjects) surrounding it; its only relation to objects is action. The non-coordination of actions, the non-differentiation between subject and objects, and the centering on the body, a center not conscious of itself, mark this state. It is followed by a de-centering of actions in respect to the body, as well as by a first awareness of the body as an object, and of the self as a subject and the source of movement. During the sensori-motor period, there is a gradual increase in coordination of actions.

A similar transition from centering to de-centering is observed, for Piaget, between the first (age 2 to 4) and the second (5-6) stage of the pre-operational thought period. The schemes of sensori-motor intelligence are not based on concepts and the infant is not conscious of their existence due to the lack of the semiotic function. From the first stage of the new period, a new type of action is superimposed on the simple action securing the direct interdependence between subject and objects; simple action is now reconstructed on a higher level, since it becomes internalized, represented, and conceptualized with the use of preconcepts. It is on this new level that centering reemerges, followed by de-centering in respect not only to actions, but also conceptualized actions. During the stage of de-centering, a pre-logic is in operation.

This stage is followed by the period of concrete cognitive operations, also comprising two stages. In the first stage (7-8) internalized actions, due to the progress of coordination, from regulations become operations, where by the term operation is meant the anticipatory correction of mistakes as opposed to correction after the fact; operations are constituted as integral systems. At this stage, abstraction and reversibility of operations first appear. The general equilibrium of concrete operations is attained at the following stage (9-10), which is in turn (starting with the stage from 11 to 12) followed by the period of formal operations, i.e., operations on operations, reasoning on the basis of hypotheses and not objects.

These periods are closely related, according to Piaget, to major types of spatial representation, and these types are topological, projective, and Euclidean (a case of metric) space (see Pinxten 1976: 129-132). Following the sensori-motor or perceptual space of the first period, topological space is gradually constituted in the second period, while in the third period the projective and Euclidean spaces are elaborated, on general lines simultaneously, though projective space appears slightly earlier. Empirical research (Evans 1980: 266) indicates that, in spite of the de-centering of the second stage of the preoperational period, the representation of space remains egocentric, i.e., space is seen from the point of view of the subject. The fundamental relations (operations) of the topological space system of the second period are the following: neighboring of elements, the most elementary spatial relation; distinctness of elements; order of succession in a set of elements, which represents a synthesis of the two previous relations and implies a primitive notion of betweenness; enclosure, that is, the distinction between an inside and an outside presupposing the existence of a boundary; continuity and discontinuity, always referring to concrete elements.

At this point, we should like to open a brief parenthesis in order to point out a certain similarity between Piaget's diachronic view on the succesion of spatial representations and Leonard Talmy's synchronic view on the semantics of two different levels of language. Talmy (1983: 225-229, 234, 258-262) studies English prepositions as an instance of one level of language, the "fine structural" level, which for him includes the closed-class elements of language; these elements compose a fixed and limited set. Talmy argues that his conclusions on the English prepositions are also valid for the corresponding elements of other languages and further for the rest of the closed-class elements referring to space, and that his interest is oriented toward the universal properties of language. The closed-class elements ascribe to physical objects certain geometric properties which are in general not metric and especially not Euclidean. These properties are generally more qualitative, topological, and also include type of geometric configuration, degree of subdivision and distinctness of parts, and boundary conditions.

Following Talmy, this topological function of the closed-class elements is one among three functions they fulfill. The first function is the idealization of the spatial referent, i.e., the application to it of an abstract "schema" composed of a set of elementary geometric components, a process comparable to the processes in Gestalt psychology. The second function is abstraction, which is complementary to idealization and involves the abstraction of those properties of the referent not retained by the idealization process. Then comes the topological function, which specifies the character of idealization as a process that operates with topological notions. The linguistic elements which, contrary to the topological function of the closed-class elements, assume the function of reference to metric spaces are usually not these closed-class "grammatical" elements but the full lexical elements, numerals included, which found the other level of language, the "macroscopic expository" level. The similarity between Piaget's psychology and Talmy's linguistics thus lies in the fact that for Piaget the psychological topological structures are temporally prior to projective and Euclidean spaces, a difference connected to the periods of cognitive development, and for Talmy topological space is expressed on a linguistic level different from that which is used to formulate metric spaces, something which distinguishes the linguistic vehicle of these spaces.

Piaget (1972: 46) further observes that in the first stage of concrete operations we witness the appearance of operations relating to different perspectives, i.e., points of view, on the same object. He adds that only later - at the second stage of concrete operations - is the child able to coordinate perspectives in respect to a set of objects; the objects are related in a whole by means of one, two, or three natural (i.e., non-metric) coordinates. In this way, there first appears a coordination of perspectives which is independent from the egocentric viewpoint. The abandoning of spatial egocentrism appears with the relativization of the personal point of view, as well as the possibility of conceptualizing both the point of view of other subjects (virtual or actual) and the perspectives between objects, in other words the differences between points of view.

It is the consciousness of his own point of view that initially allows the child to construct the projective line and perspective, which later can be objectified. The elementary projective space is founded on the fundamental topological relations, now incorporated into a point of view. Thus, the incorporation of the relation of betweenness into a series of three different points of view leads to the relations right/left, in front/behind, and up/down respectively. The coordination of perspectives in the context of projective space allows the segmentation of space into geometric sections (according to Pinxten 1976: 132-135).

Like projective space, Euclidean space is founded on the topological relations. On the other hand, it also follows from projective space and is of a metric nature. Within the context of Euclidean space, the construction of a system of abstract coordinates becomes possible, which represents an evolution of the natural coordinate system. Thus, each following spatial system integrates the previous system on a higher and more complex level. Though the spatial systems are successive, this fact does not prevent emphasis on previous systems, even after the completion of the structuring of the highest system and without abandoning it, since the previous systems are incorporated into it. Thus, studies have found that the degree of familiarity with a new environment has a direct impact on the representational system used, as well as the accuracy of the representation. Researchers argue that the first contact with an environment causes an egocentric construction of space, a greater familiarity with the environment brings the projective construction of a set of fixed elements, and finally the Euclidean representation appears, based on a system of abstract coordinates (see Evans 1980: 266-272). Egocentric representations of space can then appear at any age. An example is given by a study by Whittaker and Whittaker (1972) who analysed the sketch maps of the world drawn by university students of different countries. The authors observed that the home countries and broader regions are drawn larger, a phenomenon they consider as geocentrism, and are frequently depicted in the central part of the world map.

On the other hand, the spatial systems and their stages are closely related to the basic modes of orientation in space. Preoperational children orient themselves mainly through egocentric relations. In the first stage of concrete operations appears place learning, according to which orientation refers to a fixed proximate element. Later, orientation is based on the spatial relations among proximate elements, and finally it refers to a broader area and is achieved with the use of an abstract coordinate system, such as the cardinal points, independent of the position and the viewpoint of the observer (see Evans 1980: 273).

Since the three major types of spatial representation are related to the periods of the ontogenetic development of the child, they are for Piaget universal. This last point was examined by Pinxten in his study mentioned above (Pinxten 1976: 164-166). In order to define what he considers as the universals of the representation of space - what he calls "epistemic" space - he analysed the spatial conceptions of ancient Chinese, Egyptian, and Greek culture, two Pre-Columbian cultures and the Columbian Indians of South-America, and some African cultures. The author concludes that all the topological relations presented above, plus the adoption of a perspective and the coordination of perspectives - but only these operations of projective space - constitute epistemic universals; thus, for example, and unlike Piaget, he generally excludes the Euclidean operations from the domain of universals and considers them as culture and/or language dependent. He also clarifies that what is universal is the presence of the elementary form of these structures, without taking into account the cultural investment of these structures with further meaning.

On the basis of this rather long parenthesis, we can see the fundamental spatial logics found in our own study in a new light. *Here* vs. *there* first emerges from the very early consciousness of the position of other elements in respect to the subject. The extension of this relation to a series of *theres* presupposes the establishment of a point of view relative to which the elements on a line appear in succession. The relation *here* vs. *around here* is directly connected both to the relation *here* vs. *there*, and the relation *inside* vs. *outside,* since what is around here is also outside. As we saw, the distinction between inside and outside is one of the fundamental structures of topological space. The neighboring relation (*adjacent to*) and the ordering relation (*next to*) are two other fundamental structures of that space. The directional relations (*on the one side* vs. *on the other side, up* vs. *down*) follow from the imposition of a point of view on the topological relation of betweenness. Finally, the segmentation of space found in some of our spatial logics follows from the ability of coordinating different perspectives.

In conclusion, *all* the semantic relations and spatial segmentation underlying the general spatial logics we found are among the elementary structures of spatial representations that both Piaget and Pinxten consider as spatial universals. It goes without saying that the fundamental topological relations not mentioned above (distinctness and continuity/discontinuity) are integral parts of all the spatial logics. These logics are situated on an abstract level, but their manifested forms are composed of a number of concrete elements. The structures describes above do not only apply to the general lines of the spatial logics, but also to partial aspects of them.

We can conclude on the basis of the above data that, since our spatial logics are founded on widespread semantic structures, these logics are likely to be found outside Greece as well. There are also, however, certain other data that allow a most definite answer as to the generality of the spatial logics. According to previous studies by one of the present authors (summarized in Lagopoulos 1983), there is in all precapitalist societies a model of spatial organization operating on different spatial scales - from architecture to the settlement to the region - that coincides with the organization of the world as conceived by this society. The geometric forms of the models of precapitalist societies can be grouped into two classes. The first is the "centric" class, which includes radial or concentric models having a circular contour. The second is the "orthogonal" class, which comprises spatial models frequently organized according to a cross made of two perpendicular axes and having a square, rectangular, or free polygonal contour. Both classes are dominated by a central element. A third, heterogeneous class of models is also found, including the "diametric" models (showing two parts on both sides of a central axis), the models combining the cross with the circular contour, and the models combining the two latter models with the models of the centric class.

The author observes that the analogy between the settlement and the world is achieved through orientation and concentric repetition. More specifically, in the case of the centric class, we have a multiple orientation inwards, towards the center of the settlement - that connotes the center of the world - and an undifferentiated orientation outwards, towards external space as a whole - the world - materialized in cosmic radii and related to a circular contour or a series of concentric contours. In the case of the orthogonal class, there is an outwards orientation toward selected points of the compass, the cardinal points, originating from a central point, the center of the settlement and the world.

If we compare the conclusions of Lagopoulos with the views of Pinxten (1976: 156, 161, 163-165) on the non-universality of the Euclidean representation of space, there seems at first sight to be a disagreement between the two authors, since Lagopoulos implies a certain universality of the notion of geometric figure. But this is not actually the case. In fact, while Pinxten is inclined to consider the geometric figure as culturally determined and thus not universal, he indicates that this position may be due to a lack of empirical evidence. On the other hand, he does not mean that he did not find some geometric figures in the ambiguous cases - actually he did - but he seems to require a rather extended set of these figures in order to consider them as integral to the culture in question.

The three classes of spatial models defined by Lagopoulos (1983: 291-293) are not for him contemporaneous, but first appeared in specific historical succession. The most archaic class is the centric, which seems to have preceded the practice of agriculture, while the appearance of the centric class with a cross and the orthogonal class are linked to the appearance of agriculture. The reason for this connection is that the cross is a cosmic one derived from the cardinal directions, the consciousness of the latter presupposes the observation of seasonal cycles and hence the movement of the sun, and the experience of these cycles is an integral part of agricultural practices. In this perspective, the diametric models represent the historical transition from centric to orthogonal models.

What is manifest in this succession is the close parallels to Piaget's ontogenetic development of spatial representation. In fact, the centric class is founded on spatial egocentrism, the diametric presupposes the establishment of a perspective, and the orthogonal integrates egocentrism into a coordinated system of perspectives. This succession can also be compared to the impact of familiarity on spatial representation. In the succession of the types of conceptual structuring of space, ontogenetic development, micro-historical increase in familiarity, and macro-historical processes show close similarities.

The ontogenetic development posits the universality of a series of successive spatial representations and structures. The historical succession of spatial models does not necessarily contradict such a universality, because we may consider that, in spite of the fact that all the models were created by peoples capable of applying the whole set of these structures, specific social and cultural conditions oriented them each time to emphasize in their models some kinds of structures at the expense of others. This would be a sociological explanation compatible with the existence of psychological spatial universals and parallel to the psychological interpretation of the impact of familiarity on spatial representation.

It is also manifest that close similarities exist between the spatial models of precapitalist societies and the spatial logics operating in contemporary Greece. These similarities demonstrate that indeed the logics are not specifically Greek but have actually appeared in very different cultures, historical periods, and geographical settings. The initial intuition that the logics operating in Greece seem to more or less cover the set of possible spatial logics is thus proved to be sound. Two differences, however, between precapitalist models and contemporary spatial logics should be noted. Precapitalist models of space are explicitly stated, while modern spatial logics constitute an implicit social knowledge. Also, the precapitalist models have a specific (and simple) geometric form, which is not the case with contemporary spatial logics that show loose forms, although directly comparable to the geometry of the models. But these differences do not invalidate the structural coincidence of models and logics.

The appearance in contemporary Greece of the spatial logics found both in other historical societies and in the "primitive" societies confronts us with the issue of spatial universals. It may be accounted for in two different manners. Either we should accept the existence of spatial universals, as posited by the Piagetean school (without excluding the intervention of sociological and psychological factors in the relative prominence given to them). Or we should dismiss the hypothesis of universals, while simultaneously accepting that the number of ways in which we can conceptually structure the physical environment are indeed very limited, a fact that would explain the close similarities between spatial representations of radically different cultures. In either case, we should not forget the dynamics of intra-cultural transmission in the form of tradition and inter-cultural influences. Further research on this issue would certainly be welcome.

Chapter 12. Regional images

1. The psychological nature of mental images

As we remarked in the last chapter, we elicited data concerning spatial information both through linguistic means and through the use of sketch mapping. The aim in both cases was the same, i.e., the reconstruction of the social representation of regional space. Our reconstruction is a metalinguistic construct, which attempts to render the subjective structuring of space. But what is the nature of this subjective space itself? Linguistic information is not presented spatially, but in the sketch maps spatial information is spatially rendered. Is there any close relation between this second form of information, which is of an iconic nature, and the mental representation of space? in other words, do we find map-like structures in the cognitive domain?

The geographical terminology points in this direction, and indeed many geographers would contend that such is the case. We already referred to the mental maps as outputs of the cognitive mapping processes (Chapter 1, Section 2). The term "mental map", a borrowing from cognitive psychology, if taken literally indicates the existence of maps, i.e., picture-like representations, in our heads; these maps would be surveyed by our "mind's eye", the means by which they are "read" or interpreted (Kosslyn & Pomerantz 1977: 60). In this case, the sketch maps would be more or less a projection in the external world of the mental maps generated in our minds. On the other hand, some geographers, also inspired by cognitive psychology, express doubts as to the reliability of the concept of the mental map and believe it can be used only in a metaphorical sense. Since the debate in geography on the nature of spatial representations is a second-hand debate originating in cognitive psychology, we shall turn directly to the latter in order to throw some light on the issue.

There are certain attributes of space for which it is hardly conceivable that they are iconically processed in cognition; one of these attributes is the feelings we have for space and the values with which we invest it, discussed earlier in this book. We can assume that an important part of the appraisive, i.e., connotative, component of spatial representation (see Chapter 8, Section 1) is in any case non-iconic. Thus, at least one of the dimensions of the "mental map" is generally non-iconic. But then we also have the designative, i.e., denotative, component, providing information on the direct properties of space and spatial location.

Now, to reason from the map-image to images in general, no psychologist would deny that the introspective observation that some kind of mental images do exist is reliable; and this in spite of the fact that some people report that they do not experience images (Anderson 1978: 249, 251, 259; Pylysshyn 1973: 2; Kosslyn & Pomerantz 1977: 56, 64). Our study also encountered the phenomenon of the lack, maybe not of images in general, but of a specific kind of images, those attached to the involvement region, since 18% of our subjects reported not having such images. "Non-imagers" are not equally represented among our various social groups: metropolitan people and youth are much more inclined toward spatial imaging (less than 10% non-imagers) than the Ormylians and the adults (approximately 30% non-imagers). This occasionally observed non-occurrence of images, however, is not considered by psychologists as disproving the reality of internal imagery. The issue, then, is not the existence of images, but their cognitive nature. To the extent that people use such conceptual images when thinking about space, we should conclude that they use some kind of pictorial iconic signs and thus some kind of pictorial signifier.

Given the above, what is the image debate all about? In order to better understand the main issues involved in this debate and the different views on them, notably on the nature of mental images, a wider discussion of the principal theorerical positions seems to be indispensable. One extreme position, which no longer finds much support among cognitive psychologists, is that of British empiricist philosophy, for which all thoughts are mental images. On the other hand, a frequent position, which is also the most direct and empirical, is that there exist two types of internal representation of knowledge, a verbal system and a set of perceptual iconic codes;[43] the latter cover all kinds of iconic phenomena, such as visual and acoustical representations (Kosslyn & Pomerantz 1977: 55; see also Pylyshyn 1973: 3; Shepard & Chipman 1970: 15). In the context of this "dual-code" model, it follows from Allan Paivio (1965) that the verbal system undertakes the processing of words with abstract meaning, while the processing of concrete nouns is assumed both by that system and a visual iconic system.[44]

Zenon W. Pylyshyn (1973: 4-7) formulated in 1973 a more abstract view on the nature of mental representations on the grounds that, in order to translate visual mental images to mental words or the other way around, the postulation of a quite different mediating system, an interlingua, is necessary. This third system is for him a system of propositional knowledge, i.e., a system of knowledge based on propositions by which sentences and images are necessarily interpreted. In this manner, the propositional system corresponds to the linguistic deep structure. Pylyshyn defines propositions as the logicians do, differentiates them from actual utterances in a natural language, and considers them as composed of abstract concepts and relations which are judged against the criterion of true or false. It is not necessary that the propositional concepts should always be expressed in words of natural language, since there are concepts that have a perceptual origin, i.e., are abstracted from sense data, for which there are no equivalent words (which does not mean, however, that it would not be possible to create a vocabulary for them).

Stephen M. Kosslyn and James R. Pomerantz (1977: 55-56, 62-63), on the other hand, counterargue that the mapping of the one system onto the other is not a matter of world knowledge, but of transformational rules including information on the two systems under translation. On this basis, they consider as superfluous a third intermediary medium and form of representation. They also add that a "three-code theory" is less economical than the dual-code model, and that, even if it is assumed that a third system is needed, it remains to be shown how the translation is effected from images to propositions and from the latter to the verbal system. Translation problems are already present for the dual-code model, but they increase with Pylyshyn's proposal if its two translational steps do not coincide.

The current concept of mental image implies for Pylyshyn a picture metaphor, which is misleading in that it suggests that, like pictures, mental images are preformed entities offered to subsequent interpretation by the "mind's eye". But, he argues, this is not the case with mental images, since any image consists of already meaningful parts, as shown by the fact that it is possible to focus even on very fine details, or abstract qualities such as anger. A vague image is not an image where some geometrically definable parts are missing, but one in which what is missing are meaningful attributes or qualities. Thus, the memory image cannot be compared to the direct perceptual image, which is a pattern only partly if at all interpreted and perceived simultaneously more or less as a whole. On these grounds, Pylyshyn argues that the concept of image cannot be considered as a primitive explanatory concept, but is to be equated with a dependent variable (Pylyshyn 1973: 2-3, 8-10).

It is of special interest for to us to understand what is the nature of the mental image in the context of Pylyshyn's viewpoint. To start negatively, the author states, as expected (Pylyshyn 1973: 10-12; see also Pylyshyn 1981: 21), that it is not a high- or even a limited-resolution pictorial image resembling a finite two-dimensional grid, the elements of which would contain a set of attributes. He asserts that the mental image "differs from *any conceivable* picture-like entity" and that a representation meeting his theoretical requirements "is much closer to being a description of the scene than a picture of it." This description is of a propositional form, it includes finite information, and, as is the case for Fodor (see below), it contains both abstract and iconic elements.

Around 1980, Pylyshyn (1981: 16-25, 30, 31-32, 34, 41) emphasized the distinction between what he calls the "functional architecture" of the mind, that is the intrinsic properties and primitive functions of the representational media, and tacit knowledge, which consists of conventionally encoded representations. Tacit knowledge involves the encoded knowledge of reality, and the encoding of rules for transforming representations and drawing inferences, as well as beliefs and goals. An important part of this knowledge cannot be introspected or verbally expressed, as is the case with the knowledge of grammatical and logical rules, most social conventions, and many physical regularities. Thus, tacit knowledge is used by the author as another term for propositional knowledge.

The above distinction is used by Pylyshyn in his argumetation against the imagery (imagistic, iconic, pictorial, or analogical) position, in conjunction with the concept of "cognitive penetrability". He considers a representational function as cognitively penetrable if it follows from operations effected on conventionally encoded representations, i.e., with the help of tacit knowledge. One instance of the use of this form of knowledge is the interpretation and the beliefs of subjects concerning the "task demands" during imagery experiments, which has the result that they further use tacit knowledge attempting to simulate the real situation.

As we shall see below, the representation of images is assumed, for supporters of the imagery position, by a specific representational medium with its own functional properties, one of which is to operate according to Euclidean principles. Such a medium would belong to Pylyshyn's functional architecture. The fundamental issue, then, of the image debate is for him whether there is a special type of cognitive processing operating in connection with a specific medium where reality is iconically represented in spatially arranged images, i.e., whether the imagery level is functional and cognitively impenetrable, or whether the processing of images is cognitively penetrable, in which case it is undertaken by tacit knowledge and need not have its own properties. In the latter case, images would not be functional and constitute a special and thus explanatory form of cognition, but would be both epiphenomenal and integrated into the unique form marking all cognitive processes: images would not depict as pictures do, but refer like descriptions.

This debate is not only epistemological and theoretical, but it is also grounded in accumulated experimental results and their possible interpretations. In his 1973 article, Pylyshyn attacked the imagery position in favor of his cognitivist propositional approach, promoting rule-governed (formalist, informational, or computational) processes. But in 1981 (Pylyshyn 1981: 16, 24-25, 30-31, 44; see also Kosslyn et al. 1979: 546) he seems to have modified his initial view, which we shall call "stronger propositional", since he emphasizes the possibility that the tacit knowledge account may not cover all the area of image processing and that there are some analogue functional properties embodied in the functional architecture.

There are close similarities between Pylyshyn's line of argumentation and the approach used by Jerry A. Fodor. For the latter (see Fodor 1975: 152, 157, 172-195), human beings use various systems of internal representation, something which allows them a greater adaptation during the performance of different tasks. One of these systems is the iconic system, which supports images resembling the images from visual perception and seems to play an important role for cognitive processes. But, Fodor argues, having a thought cannot be equated with having such an image. If we imagine a language or any other representational system in which there are images instead of words, the sentences of this language could no longer be images, because sentences are true or false and thus cannot resemble that which verifies them. Fodor concludes that, since thoughts in a representational system using images are like sentences in that they are true or false, they cannot be iconic, but are discursive; it follows that images integrate with a discursive system.

It is because of this position that he disagrees with the adherents of the developmental views, among whom he cites Piaget. We saw (Chapter 11, Section 5) that for Piaget the acquisition of the semiotic function and language characterize the last stage of the first period of the child's cognitive development. Following the acquisition of the semiotic function, the child becomes able to use pre-concepts; before that, the child only uses the schemes of sensori-motor intelligence. Fodor does not deny that children may use images to a greater degree than adults or that their concepts may be more concrete; what he denies is that there is a period in their development in which all cognitive processes, including thoughts, are connected to some non-discursive medium.

For Fodor, thinking, as the vehicle of truth judgments, must be discursive and abstract, and images are not sufficiently abstract to assume that role. Only the assignment of some property to some object can acquire truth value and this cannot be done with the use of an image alone. Thus, the reference to objects through images presupposes the description of how the images should be understood: the reference is not effected by an image, but by an image-under-descriptions. The construction of such an image would be effected by a computational system that functions with descriptions as inputs and the corresponding images as outputs, i.e., that maps descriptions onto images. The image-under-descriptions mode of reference must be the same during all periods of human life. In fact, there would be an innate language of thought closely comparable to natural language, which would include formulae resembling the corresponding sentences of a natural language.

This understanding of mental images leads Fodor to conceive of their nature in a specific manner, which we also encountered with Pylyshyn. The nature of thought varies, following Fodor, along a continuum going from the most abstract and discursive thoughts to thoughts that are to the greatest possible degree concrete and iconic. We observe here that the two extremes of Fodor's continuum correpond to the digital-discrete and the analogue-continuous modes of representation respectively. Excluding the abstract extreme, all other thoughts are, for Fodor, unstable images-under-descriptions, which resemble their referents only as to the properties that happen to be pictured; thus, images-under-descriptions are not very similar to their referents. A mental image covers all the range from a full-scale portrait to a stick figure in the case of poor imaging. In the latter case, what makes the stick figure stand for something is the meaning attributed to it by the subject.

Thus, both Pylyshyn (around 1980) and Fodor leave room for an analogical medium, though within rather different contexts: the former plays down the importance of such a medium for cognitive processes, while the latter fully acknowledges its functional role. Both, however, subordinate images to computational processes. In any case, Pylyshyn is moving towards a camouflaged bridging position, which we shall label "weaker propositional". But there is also another bridging position, originating in the imagery camp, which we shall now examine.

This last bridging position, which is also probably the most systematic imagery position, is that formulated by Kosslyn and his collaborators. Kosslyn (Kosslyn & Pomerantz 1977: 57, 61, 65, 74) differentiates the dual-code model, which he considers as the stronger imagery view, from a weaker view that allows for the conjunction of images, which are considered to have original properties and fullfil specific functions, with propositional representations; he states that according to this latter view there are at least two representational systems, the one processing images and the other propositions. He himself finally inclines towards the weaker imagery view. The working hypothesis of this view is that visual mental images may be compared to displays produced on a cathode-ray tube by means of a computer program using stored data. The simulation of mental images is attempted by using a model including a "surface matrix", corresponding to a surface display medium and short-term memory, where the image is represented as a set of points, and "long-term memory files". Mental images would be temporary spatial configurations in active, short-term visual memory, generated from representations in long-term memory.

For the weaker imagery view, the generation of mental images is due to two different froms of long-term memory deep representations. The first form corresponds to the perceptual, "literal" memory of the appearance of an object, on which we would suggest the weaker-imagery theoreticians hold contradictory views: on the one hand, they state that the pictorial information stored "is not raw and uninterpreted" and the pictorial elements are labeled, but, on the other, that this same information is not connected to propositional representations and semantic interpretations. It is not strange that these authors cannot define, not even approximately, the exact nature of the labeling of the pictorial elements in "literal" memory and are limited to the negative definition that it "is not simply 'symbolic'". From a semiotic point of view, there is no third possibility and no such thing as quasi-signification: either an element is significant or it is not. And the very recognition of an element, i.e., labeling, already belongs in the realm of signification.

However that may be, in the weaker-imagery model, this perceptual memory dictates the arrangement of the points of the surface matrix in view of the depiction of some object. The image files are composed of both central and secondary iconic elements hierarchically organized. The second form of long-term memory representations is discursive information, i.e., statements about the imaged object in a propositional form (Kosslyn et al. 1979: 536, 539-541, 576, 577; Kosslyn & Pomerantz 1977: 59).

Thus, images would depict information, without containing any knowledge, in an innate special spatial medium, which would be a neural tissue having its own physiological properties, probably coinciding with the cortical medium used for the representations originating from visual perception. Once a display has been formed, an interpretive mechanism would intervene - what is metaphorically called the "mind's eye" - and work over - metaphorically "look at" - the display, a process resulting in the classification of the display in terms of semantic categories. We saw that for Pylyshyn this is not correct, because images are already meaningful at the time of their appearance. This should logically also be the conclusion of Kosslyn and his collaborators, since their model presupposes the semantic classification of objects in "literal" memory, with the result that, when the display appears, it is already the signifier of a specific signified. Instead, the authors state that the "Gestalt wholes" composing the image are subject to "some" visual pattern recognition and interpreted "in a perceptual sense" (sic), but are "not yet labeled or identified with semantic categories" (see Kosslyn et al. 1979: 536, 541, 546, 547, 576; Kosslyn & Pomerantz 1977: 60, 65, 66). This argument may be in accordance with the argument on the nature of the elements of "literal" memory, but it again presupposes the existence of some invisible third between signification and non-signification. In fact, having a mental image presupposes the *knowledge* of having it, and this knowledge is not the knowledge of having some image in general, but of having *that* image specifically. Configuration and interpretation go hand in hand and constitute the two aspects of one and the same semiotic process. An image without meaning does not have any essential existence.

Kosslyn and his collaborators (Kosslyn et al. 1979: 536-539, 541, 547, 572, 575-577; Kosslyn & Pomerantz 1977: 57-58, 65-66, 73, 74) accept the cognitive penetrability argument of Pylyshyn, but disagree as to the extent of this phenomenon. They posit the existence of two types of imagery structures: the spatial medium and the long-term memory files, and three types of processes: the image construction process, the image interpretation process, and the image transformation process. They also argue that, given the resemblance (but not identity) between imagery and perception (which is denied by Pylyshyn), if a particular perceptual element, shared by imagery, is cognitively impenetrable, that element should have the same property also in respect to imagery. The authors understandably predict that the spatial medium, which they consider as common to perception and imagery, is not congitively penetrable. The image files, the authors hypothesize, should not be completely distinct from the stored representations at the service of the visual pattern recognition process, but they are inconclusive as to the penetrability of these files. The process detecting and interpreting spatial configurations should be the same for imagery and the visual system, and it may be assumed, on the basis of visual pattern recognition, that a part of it is penetrable. The two other processes, image construction and transformation, are not common with visual perception and should be at least partially penetrable.[45]

For the weaker imagery view, images are not the epiphenomenal product of a non-pictorial process, but are an integral part of cognitive processes and have functions of their own. During their construction, images are not retrieved as wholes, but elaborated by integrating coherent parts stored separately in long-term memory. As to their nature, images show Euclidean spatial relationships and are thus able to provide topographical information, but they do not necessarily have a determinate relation to their referent, i.e., images as representations are not necessarily concretely isomorphic to their referent; nevertheless, certain of their elements are iconically related to the latter. They are not strictly pictorial, but quasi-pictorial, and have spatial extent, the maximum size of which is constrained by the extent of the medium which supports them. Having spatial extent, they both represent the relative metric distances between real-world objects, and have spatial boundaries. As we move from their focus towards their periphery, images gradually fade off.

We do not think that the weaker imagery theoreticians give us an unambiguous account of the pictorial nature of the mental image. To our understanding, however, the mental image as conceptualized by them is to a considerable extent anchored in the configuration of its referent, and is, or at least can be, more or less isomorphic and pictorially more or less similar to it. If this is so, a more abstract view of the pictorial nature of the mental image is held by Roger N. Shepard. Shepard (1978: 127-136; Shepard & Chipman 1970: 1-3, 15) accepts the existence of both logical and analogical thought processes. He believes that the latter make use of an innate and largely unconscious visual perceptual knowledge of the aspect and transformations in three-dimensional space of moveable objects, a knowledge due to a long period of prelinguistic evolution. He thus posits the equivalence between imagery and perception, but also between both of these and the corresponding objects.

Shepard clarifies his understanding of the nature of the equivalence between these internal representations, and between them and the external objects. He states that there is no concrete, "first-order" structural isomorphism between the internal representation of an object and the object itself, implying that there is no visual similarity. The perception of an object causes the creation of an internal event, perhaps the activation of a specific group of neurons in the cortical medium, which has no spatial configuration resembling the object. The perceptual or mental image of an object is more abstract than a picture of it, but it is nevertheless iconic and may retain a systematic biunivocal relationship with it, in which case we have an abstract isomorphism (thus, the neural representation of a square probably consists of a four-fold structure). However, while the neural constitution of the mental image is not photographic in respect to the object, it contains the information needed to construct a highly accurate picture of the object.

As we just saw, the neural image is produced, for Shepard, by a corresponding function in the brain, which is the same for both the perceptual and the mental image, whether this latter emerges from imagining or remembering the object. When two objects are similar, the corresponding functions are closer and interact; we can say in this case that the representations of the objects are functionally related. This quality of functional relation establishes a "second-order" isomorphism between representations and their external objects, according to which the functional relations between representations reflect at least those relations between the objects which are most important for the organism, a behavior that facilitates the adaptation of the organism to its environment. Similarly, the equivalence of imagination and perception implies the same kind of isomorphism, since the functional relations between imagined objects coincide more or less with the functional relations between the same objects when actually perceived. In spite of their proximity, perceptual images differ from the images of imagination and memory in that they are more vivid and rich in detail and color. Nevertheless, as is apparent from the above, the perceptual and the mental image resemble each other more than either of them resembles a concrete picture.[46]

We hope that by now the main issues of the image debate have become reasonably clear. The debate emerges from a main polarization, images versus propositions, and a secondary one, verbal versus propositional meaning. As we saw, from each extreme of the first polarization there has been a movement of goodwill towards the other pole, a dynamics creating the preconditions for some degree of convergence (see also Shepard 1978: 135). Nevertheless, if we believe Anderson we should be sceptical as to the scientific benefits from such a convergence. Indeed, Anderson - who is sympathetic to the dual-code model, while also pointing out that its visual part is pictorial and its verbal part non-representational - thinks that it is not possible to define the nature of internal representations on the basis of behavioral data alone, in other words simply on the basis of the input to and output from a process, without any actual knowledge of what is taking place between these two extremeties. He argues that in such a model, the position for a particular form of representation refers back to an assumption about the underlying processes, and that these processes are posited each time ad hoc in order to account for the observed results. Thus, if a model is built including a set of assumptions on the nature of representation and a corresponding set of processes, it is possible to simulate its behavior with several different models having their own sets of assumptions on representation and processes. The only way to get out of this indeterminacy is to have recourse to firm physiological data, as yet not available (Anderson 1978: 249, 252, 262-270, 271). Of course - since the members of our scientific community of passionately debating cognitive psychologists demonstrate the unusual quality of paying attention to the views of their opponents and thus maintaining a continuously open line of communication - Pylyshyn (1981: 29) counterargues that the explanatory power of a model is a satisfactory criterion.

What answer can we then give to our initial question on the nature of subjective space? We should be careful to distinguish between the unconscious *neural* mental image, and the conscious and "phenomenological", *introspective* "mental" (or rather conceptual) image. It is manifest by now that no unequivocal answer can be given in respect to the neural mental image. We would judge, however, that a contact with the image debate undoubtedly enriches our knowledge on this point. Our first conclusion is of a negative nature, namely that the neural mental image does not seem to be picture-like, meaning that it is not like a picture; at the most it is quasi-pictorial, a kind of phantom picture. The above discussion delivered four main views on the nature of mental images. From the most concrete to the most abstract, a neural mental image would be: a. a quasi-pictorial *image* (Kosslyn and collaborators), b. an *image-under-descriptions* (Fodor), or c. an *abstract image* (Shepard); or d. (mainly) a *description*-with-images (Pylyshyn).

The different views on the nature of the neural mental image lead to diverging conceptualizations of the relation of the introspective image, which is the meaningful image (being thus of a semiotic nature), to the neural image. When the scientific interest is focused on meaningful phenomena, as is the case with semiotics and subjectivist geography, the crucial starting point of analysis cannot but be this introspective image. But the interests of semioticians also extend beyond this point, as is the case with psychologists. For semiotics, the non-significant material supporting the signifier, or form of the expression, is the substance of the expression. The relation of the introspective to the neural image allows us to better understand the nature of this substance in the context of the above views.

For Shepard, the signifier of the introspective image closely resembles the external object, but not its corresponding neural image, to which it owes its existence. For this view, then, the support of the introspective signifier and sign, which is itself external to this support, is the neural image, which thus functions as the substance of the expression. The relation between the signifier of the introspective image and the substance of the expression is at best one of abstract isomorphism.

For the weaker imagery view, the neural image is a quasi-pictorial set of elements depicting without also describing. If this were the case - which, as we saw, it cannot possibly be - these elements could not be signifiers, since they would not be attached to any meaningful entity, and, as with Shepard, would constitute the substance of the expression. The difference with Shepard, however, is that this view considers that the signifiers of the introspective image are identical to the elements of the quasi-pictorial neural image. The constitution of the signs of the introspective image starts from these elements, which are incorporated into the signs, and is completed with the signifiers attached to them after the intervention of the interpretive mechanism, the "mind's eye". Because of this identity of the signifier of the introspective sign with the neural image, we can conclude that in the case of the weaker imagery theory the introspective image is closer to the neural image than in Shepard's view.

Finally, for Pylyshyn and Fodor the neural image is an amalgam of forms and meanings, of signifiers and their signifieds. Under these circumstances, the neural image already consists of signs, both iconic and non-iconic. The introspective image is constituted by these signs, and thus coincides with the neural image. In this manner, the two authors avoid the unnecessary split between a meaningless and a meaningful image. Both images no longer consist of iconic elements and their iconic relations, as in the previous cases, but of a series of individual iconic elements semantically related. The substance of the expression is in this case deeper than the neural image and should be sought in the processes underlying the formation of this image. Each process takes place within the context of some medium and according to Fodor two such media are needed for the processing of mental images, one iconic and one discursive. In spite of their differences, all the authors cited above converge in this conclusion.

Lloyd (1982: 533) points out that the construction and use of spatial representations is an integral part of behavioral geography, and that a difference in the assumed nature of mental maps results in alternative sets of scientific concepts. The imagistic view leaves room for the cognitive construction of map-like structures. According to Shepard, the form of the introspective, but not the neural, image is almost like a picture, whence we conclude that the form of the sketch map is almost the projection of the introspective image. If we follow the weaker imagery view, the quasi-pictorial form of the introspective and the neural image coincide, and the conclusion is that the sketch map, being fully pictorial, may be similar to these images but is not the same, and is something like a projection of them through the use of graphic conventions (see Eco 1972: 178) which has the quality of rendering them more concrete. For the imagistic views, then, the projection view holds to a greater or lesser degree. But it no longer holds for the propositional views, which lead us to see only the separate elements of the sketch maps as iconically corresponding to the individual elements of the neural and introspective image; the graphic, topological and geometrical relations in the sketch maps would find no equivalent in the mental images, since they would correspond to discursively stated relations.

It is manifest that the psychological and geographical description of the conceptual map changes in accordance with the perspective - imagistic or propositional - adopted, a fact that converges with Lloyd's second observation. Observations of this kind also justify his first observation on the

issues concerning conceptual maps as constituting an integral part of behavioral geography. The nature of these maps has a direct impact on
spatial semiotic and subjectivist geographical conceptualizations, something that we hope justifies our rather lengthy exposition of the image
controversy. We also hope that the rest of this chapter, which mainly
concentrates on the nature of the geographical introspective signifier, will
be able to show the interest which the study of conceptual maps and
other geographical images present for the semiotician and the
geographer.

2. Introspective signifier: Gestalt or Euclidean?

Speaking about architectural and urban semiotics, Greimas observes that
the level of the distinctive features of architectural form consists of oppositions of a geometric nature, such as *straight line* vs. *curve* or *right
angle* vs. *non-right angle;* the terms of this oppositions are the "elementary spatial categories". From these categories are generated the "spatial
figures", such as the square or the triangle, which produce in turn "composite figures or configurations". For Greimas (1976: 147-151), architectural design is a process originating in a deep ideological structure
arriving at the surface organization of spatial forms preceding their actual
realization. This surface organization incorporates the above three levels
of signifiers, each of which is analysed with a different grammar (cf.
Chapter 11, Section 1). Urban organization is an extension of architectural organization in a more complex form.

Greimas' approach to architectural design incorporates a particular
view on the nature of the architectural signifier - manifestly generalizable
beyond architectural production to consumption - namely that this signifier follows Euclidean geometry, as would also be the case with the urban signifier. There is no doubt that in the course of the design process
introspective mental images are used. Consequently, the nature of the architectural and urban signifier coincides with the pictorial nature of the
signifier of these images when they refer to architectural and urban
space. Assuming, then, that the architectural and urban signifier is Euclidean amounts to considering that the introspective mental image is
shaped on the basis of Euclidean geometry, at least in certain cases.

On the other hand, Eco (1972: 175-176, 178-179, 215-216, 288-291) is
not of the same opinion with Greimas on this matter. He presents the

same geometric construction as Greimas: the "elements" of Euclidean geometry (for example, point, straight line, curve, angle) generate higher-level spatial units, "choremes" (for example, square, triangle, ellipse, parallelepiped), constituting the elements of the first articulation in respect to the Euclidean "elements" which constitute the figures of the second articulation. He also envisages the possibility of one further articulation due to the transition from two-dimensional to three-dimensional geometry, a transition explicitly ignored by Greimas in his wish to simplify his analysis. But then Eco observes that the same construction may also account for the other visual semiotic systems, such as painting or landscapes, and is thus not exclusively architectural (and urban). Hence he concludes that this construction could possibly be considered as a "'Gestaltic' code" presiding over the perception of all forms. This view, however, is not favored by Eco himself. As he sees it, this geometric construction does not deliver the elements of architectural and urban space, but only represents a convenient metalanguage on them and on other visual systems. Within the perceptual system, structured perceptual data are conjoint with sets of signifieds - the latter constituting a "recognition code" - which seem to delimit for Eco the Gestalt signs of perception, subsequently transcoded according to the graphic conventions of the different visual systems or metalinguistically interpreted by the geometric code.

For Greimas, the signifier of the mental image is Euclidean in the case of architecture and urban space, while for Eco it is a typical case of the perceptual signifier, the pictorial composition of which is probably for Eco more flexible than what Euclidean geometry would prescribe; Greimas and Eco, however, both agree that the mental image is pictorial. The review of the image debate in the previous section does not give us a straightforward answer on the nature of the signifier of the introspective image. The weaker imagery theoreticians insist on the Euclidean properties of the surface display medium, but they do not imply that the individual visual representations appertain to Euclidean geometry. On the basis of their views, we could conclude that introspective images are composed of elements comparable to "Gestalt wholes", and the views of Pylyshyn and Fodor seem to point in a similar direction. The least we can say is that cognitive psychologists do not state that images are built according to Euclidean geometry; instead, it seems to us that they understand these wholes in a manner very close to Eco's.

We can assume that the visual perceptual system is unified and does not operate in heterogeneous ways in function of its different subareas, all the more so when the latter are defined by social or scientific convention (architecture, urban space, painting, etc.). If this position is accepted, data concerning regional space should be pertinent in the discussion of the nature of the introspective signifier. Having this in mind, we asked our subjects what is the shape formed by all the built areas and all the roads of their involvement region. The results from this question lead to eight different types of description of the introspective signifiers, which can be grouped into three cases. We shall present below these types and classes together with their statistical frequencies for the whole sample; the first frequency presented is calculated on the total number of descriptions of all types, which is greater than the number of our subjects given that certain subjects offered more than one description, and the second frequency is calculated on the total number of subjects (the maximum number of descriptions by a subject is four, and the average is 1.25).

The first class (47%/58%) of descriptions includes two types: descriptions mentioning *simple Euclidean geometric figures* (i.e., circle, isosceles triangle, square with radii; 28%/34%) and descriptions using *simple empirical geometric figures* (i.e., round, oblong, flat spread, egg-shaped, half-moon; 19%/24%). We shall call this class the *geometric* class.

The second class (37%/47%) includes four types. The descriptions of the first type of this class refer to the built and/or natural space without attributing to it any particular form, i.e., they approach space as an *unclear form,* but show that it is experienced with a *feeling of order* (i.e., amphitheatre, map-like; 8%/11%):

> From above. Well, I see the mountains all around, and it's like it's in a sheep-fold, our village ... the plain below, all around are the mountains. When you see it from a high place that's what it looks like. Like the houses are a bunch gathered together, like.

The descriptions of the second type have the same referent and show the same approach to space as an *unclear form,* but also show that the subjects experience space with a *feeling of disorder* (mosaic, heterogeneous; 15%/18%): "Nothing definite at all". The third no longer communicates any feeling related to the opposition *order* vs. *disorder,* but shows that the subjects experience only an *unclear form* (1%/1%). The fourth type can be reduced to the previous type. In this cace, the subjects stated that they do not conceptualize any form, which amounts to stating that they are faced with what they consider as an *unclear form* (13%/17%). We called this class the Gestalt class, for reasons that we shall explain below.

The last class (10%/13%) consists of two types, both of which include *metaphorical* descriptions. Their difference lies in that the descriptions of the first type are based on metaphors inspired by the *animate* world (egg, butterfly, spider; 3%/4%), while those of the other type use metaphors inspired by the *inanimate* world of everyday objects (frying-pan, sauce-pan, sausage, lace; 7%/9%). Finally, 6%/8% of the descriptions were negative ("I don't know").

Probably the key for the interpretation of these descriptions is the Gestalt class. It shows that in this case the form of the introspective signifier of the spatial mental image is such that it cannot be described with clear, unambiguous, and systematic terms. The subjects experience a global but unclear form and possibly also its overall connotative character (ordered/disordered), that is, they experience a complex, non-Euclidean Gestalt form. This Gestalt experience of macro-space is corroborated by the metaphorical class, covering connotative descriptions. In fact, this class shows that the subjects do not feel able to render their signifier with denotative descriptions, or feel that these are unsatisfactory, because of which they have recourse to metaphors. The kinds of metaphors used show that they are intended to render the overall character of a complex and unclear whole, a Gestalt whole. These two classes together cover almost half of the cases (47%).

The other half of the descriptions comprises the geometric class. It is not clear at first glance if the isolated descriptions of the second type, which are related to simple empirical geometric figures, are to be considered as an attempt at geometric schematization of Gestalt configurations - in which case the use of a fully geometric terminology would be prevented by the weight of the Gestalt nature of the configuration and/or the lack of geometric competence on the part of the subject - or as an empirical geometric description of experienced Euclidean figures, or even as compromise expressing a complex experience of the signifier simultaneously as Gestalt *and* Euclidean. Of course, this issue would not have surfaced had the Gestalt class not shown the existence of non-Euclidean signifiers. The first type of the geometric class poses a similar problem. 28% of the descriptions are Euclidean in nature. An isolated description of this type could be due to subjects actually imagining space in Euclidean terms. On the other hand, it may constitute an acquired operational metalanguage, which recuperates a Gestalt sign and signifier in geometric terms.

The descriptions of the introspective signifiers offer, at a first approach, two or even three different interpretations of their nature, a Gestalt, a Euclidean interpretation, and a mixed interpretation. If we accept all three interpretations as valid, we should conclude that certain subjects perceive and imagine space in Gestalt terms and others in Euclidean terms, the mixed form not being excluded. In this case, about one-fourth of the subjects would have a Euclidean signifier, about half of them a Gestalt signifier, 3% would experience a mixed kind of space, and for one-sixth the data are unclear. If, on the other hand, we exclude the mixed experience of space, the number of individuals with a Euclidean signifier remains constant (26%), the share of individuals with a Gestalt signifier increases to more than half (55%), and the unclear cases fall to 11%. The latter data are based on the exclusion of the non-convincing hypothesis that introspective space may be Euclidean for some people, but they are not able to verbalize it and this is why they have recourse to non-Euclidean terminology.

If we exclude the possibility of the Euclidean system alone founding the introspective signifiers, the last major possibility is that these signifiers consistently emerge from Gestalt wholes, which are described either directly in Gestalt terms, or metaphorically through the empirical metalanguage of empirical geometric figures, or with the help of the scientific metalanguage of Euclidean geometry. What should we conclude, then, on the pictorial nature of the introspective signifier? Is it Euclidean or non-Euclidean? We can attempt an answer to this problem on the basis of some bibliographical and statistical evidence.

We saw in the previous chapter (Section 5) that for Piaget, the appearance of the Euclidean representation of space is a universal stage in ontogenetic development. This position may lead us to three assumptions. The first is that before this stage the pistorical nature of the introspective signifier is non-Euclidean. The second is that this signifier is akin to the Gestalt signifiers. Finally, the third assumption is that, beginning with the Euclidean stage, the pictorial nature of the introspective signifier is actually altered, due to the knowledge of the Euclidean geometric figures. But, if Pinxten is correct, the Euclidean stage is not universal, and neither is the widespread use of geometric figures. It seems that for him, the fact that the geometric figures do not appear everywhere as an extended and systematic set argues against their universality and hence their ontogenetic origin. Pinxten's argument might lead one to conclude that what is universal are the Gestalt signifiers, and that it is possible that for certain (maybe for all) cultures a number of Gestalt signifiers are or may be altered through the knowledge of some Euclidean figures (the number of which varies with the culture) without, however, losing their Gestalt nature.

There is in our data a statistically significant correlation between education and the description of the spatial signifier. The individuals of the lowest educational level have a much feebler tendency to use geometric descriptions: of the individuals using geometric descriptions (exclusively or not), as many as 82% have an education higher than primary school, and about 60% of such individuals use the geometric class as compared to about 40% of the individuals with a poorer education. No other sociosemiotic program gives any significant result in respect to the spatial signifier. It is a fact that the knowledge of Euclidean geometry and its figures is deepened as the educational level increases. Thus, the use of the Euclidean figures increases with familiarity, but this phenomenon is not strictly linear, since the geometric class is used by about 40% of the individuals with poorer education, while it is not used by about the same percentage of the more educated.

According to these data, and on the assumption that the use of the geometric class offers evidence for the Euclidean constitution of the introspective signifier, we could proceed further than we did on the basis of Pinxten and accept that even within a culture there may be a differentiation in the constitution of the signifier according to a sociologically significant factor. But the cases falling outside the general tendency are not negligible, and thus disturbing. They are disturbing because they show that no clear-cut regularity exists that could explain sociologically the differentiation of the signifier. However, even this apparent regularity vanishes if we look more attentively at the data. There are individuals who together with geometric description(s) also use some other type or types of description, in which case it is the whole set of descriptions that gives us a clue as to the nature of their introspective signifier. For example, if a subject provides both an empirical geometric description and a metaphorical Gestalt description, we should probably conclude that he is describing a Gestalt signifier; if another subject provides a Euclidean, an empirical geometric, and a metaphorical Gestalt description, his signifier could be mixed; and if yet another subject uses a Euclidean description and a Gestalt description, he could have either a mixed signifier, or a Gestalt one if geometry is used as a metalanguage. If then we exclude these individuals from the group of the individuals possibly having a Euclidean signifier, the crosstabulation with education is no longer significant.

If Piaget were right on the universality of the Euclidean representation, we would be able to formulate an *ontogenetic* explanation for the existence of mixed or Euclidean signifiers, while on the other hand the very strong presence of solely Gestalt signifiers would remain unaccounted for. We think, however, that Pinxten's critique of the universality of the Euclidean representation - and particularly of the geometric figures - is convincing enough. On the basis of Pinxten, we would have to abandon the ontogenetic explanation and have recourse to a *cultural* explanation for the existence of mixed and Euclidean signifiers. Then, our own data seem at first sight to show that, if we accept that such signifiers actually exist, Greek culture would not be sociologically unified in respect to the nature of the introspective signifier and a *sociological* explanation would become necessary, founded in our case on the factor of education. But, after a taste of what a sociological explanation might be like, we seem obliged to attribute the experience of possible different signifiers to *individual caprice*. And this is not a satisfactory explanation when we address a phenomenon as basic as the pictorial constitution of the introspective signifier.

The interpretation of the data is much more economical if we agree with Eco that geometry is in fact a *metalanguage* on a signifier that is universally not Euclidean but Gestalt. After all, geometry is a historical product, indeed a very sophisticated one, the first systematic and coherent form of which appeared in ancient Greece. We also think that the most reasonable extension of Pinxten's argumentation is in a similar direction, i.e., that the geometric figures are no more than a metalanguage on the spatial signifiers. If we see geometry as just a more sophisticated terminology, it does not come as a surprise that the use of simple geometric terms spreads in contemporary societies in different directions and is not subject to any clear sociological determination. But also, if we thus accept geometry as a sophisticated system, we start wondering if anyone other than professional geometricians would be in a position to construct signifiers exclusively with the consistent use of geometric figures. There is also something else. All of the descriptions of the involvement region were, we found, notably general in nature. One of the most complex

Euclidean descriptions was "square with radii", but it is neither very different nor much more complex than the metaphorical description "spider". What, then, would be the psychological advantage of the Euclidean signifier?

A study by Martin Cadwallader (1979) on cognitive distances arrives at a conclusion that might be compared to our views. This author is not oriented towards the psychological nature of the individual signifier, but towards the relations of the connections between spatial signs. More specifically, he asked his subjects to estimate the distances between pairs of cities according to two different manners of estimation, in order to test the influence of the latter on the distance judgments. He also studied the issue of intransitivity by presenting six intercity connections and asking for a set of paired comparison judgments which aimed at the definition of the longest distance each time and covered all the combinations between connections. Intransitivity occurs when, having three interpoint connections a, b, and c, a is estimated to be greater that b, b is estimated as greater than c, but c is estimated to be greater than a rather than the inverse. Finally, Cadwallader studied the issue of noncommutativity on the basis of two-way distance estimates for 30 pairs of cities. Noncommutativity occurs when the distance from point a (in this case city) to point b is not conceived as equal to the distance from b to a.

Cadwallader finds that intransitivity does not really emerge at the aggregate level but is remarkably present (8% of the cases) at the individual level, and that distance estimates are often noncommutative. But transitivity and commutativity are intrinsic qualities of Euclidean space, which therefore cannot be constituted without them. The author is well aware of this fact, and this is the reason why he concludes that the cognitive representations of space are not Euclidean, do not have "the mathematical properties of metric space", and seem to be "highly complex". This conclusion contradicts the assumption of other writers. Thus, for example, Golledge and Spector (1978: 413-414) assume on the basis of Piaget that the representation of a familiar space "is at least approximately metric".

Of course, Cadwallader's findings show that the cognitive representations of many individuals do present the qualities of transitivity and commutativity, and are thus Euclidean, but the coexistence of these representations with the non-Euclidean ones requires an explanation. It seems clear that we cannot easily accept two different lines of ontogenetic development, one arriving at the constitution of non-Euclidean representations and the other at that of Euclidean representations, and that, as we argued above, we should concede that what is universal is non-Euclidean space; Euclidean space is an acquired cultural metalanguage on the former which is widely diffused in contemporary societies. This conclusion leads us to another issue. As we saw, for Kosslyn, the image constituted on his neural spatial medium is structured according to the principles of Euclidean geometry. But if this type of geometry is not universal but has a cultural origin, then the neural image cannot be Euclidean and should be simulated by other means than Kosslyn's surface matrix.

3. Regional images: The signifier

We saw in the previous chapter (Section 1) that one of the main criteria for the classification of the sketch maps is the type of their predominant element. We observed there that the classification of maps into road and spatial maps goes back to Lynch's classification of the maps effected on the basis of the classification of their unitary elements into five paradigmatic categories: paths and nodes, districts and edges, and landmarks. In the context of the conventions of the sketch map semiotic system, roads (paths) are usually rendered as winding, curved, or straight *lines;* districts mostly as irregular *planes;* and landmarks as *points*. Regional maps do include pure landmarks, but their most frequent punctual elements denote settlements, i.e., landmarks of a particular nature. As a consequence, most of the regional landmarks are *places*. Edges are boundaries of a linear kind circumscribing districts, thus constituting their extremities, or intercalated between districts, while nodes tend to disappear at the regional scale or be replaced by settlements. The landmark is an extreme case of the district-plane, which it is useful to consider as a category in its own right. This is not the case with another extreme case of the district, the narrow linear district exemplified by the rivers; rivers may also be conceived as purely linear and in both cases they may function as boundaries.

Lynch's paradigmatic categories constitute a kind of (morphological) *parts of macro-spatial* (urban and regional) *speech*. These parts of speech are expressed in the sketch maps through three paradigmatic categories of cartographic signifiers - points, lines, planes - and in such a manner that a particular category of signifiers generally corresponds to each part of speech. The concepts of point, line, and plane belong to a metalanguage on the sketch maps (as the five concepts of Lynch constitute a metalanguage on the denotative conception of space) but they also seem to be more than that, namely subjectively conceived notions.

This view is reinforced by Talmy's (1983: 229-234, 245, 258-259, 261-262) analysis of the semantics of the closed-class elements of language. In fact, according to Talmy, one main characteristic of the spatial system in natural language is that it imposes a fixed structure on any spatial scene through its closed-class elements (on these elements, see Chapter 11, Section 5). With these elements, as well as with sentence structure, language selects one part of a scene as the primary focus (the "figure" in Gestalt psychology terminology) and defines the spatial disposition of this part in reference to a second part (a "ground" in Gestalt psychology, or a "primary reference object") and even sometimes to a third part (a "secondary reference object" that either encompasses the primary reference object or is outside it), these parts being selected from the rest of the scene. The disposition of the figure is identified with its (relative) location when it is immobile and with its path when it is moving, and often with its orientation in both cases; the location, path, or orientation of the figure is defined in terms of its relation to the geometric properties of the reference object and in particular its relative distance from the latter. The figure is conceived as more moveable, smaller, and geometrically simpler that the reference object, and often as reducible to a point or a comparable simple form.

Talmy makes the hypothesis that the above structure (figure-relation-reference object) is due to an innate mode of conceiving, perceiving, and interacting with objects in space; the very notion of location follows from this mode. The geometry of the figure, that of the reference object(s), and the relation between them constitute together the geometry of the "schema" corresponding to a closed-class linguistic element. The "schemata" are composed of elementary geometric components, such as points, (bounded and unbounded) lines, and (bounded and unbounded) planes - the same components we found in the preceding discussion. Responsible for the reduction of the object's physical reality to these components is the function of idealization (see Chapter 11, Section 5), which, for example, causes a physical object with one dimension much greater than the other two (a pencil, a skyscraper) to be conceptualized as a line, or an object roughly equidimensional (a planet) to be conceptualized as a point.

Thus, if we follow Talmy, we may conclude that one of the results of the function of idealization is the paradigmatic classification by the subject of any physical object connected to any scale of space according to a small number of semantic types of a geometric nature, such as point, line, and plane, on the "fine-structural" level of language. Lynch's parts of macro-spatial speech and our comparable parts of speech were defined on the basis of linguistic material and the sketch maps expressing the spatial discursive level (related to Talmy's "macroscopic expository" level). The semantic content of these parts and their cartographic expression through the three categories of cartographic signifiers indicate that they could be further classified into three semantic types subjectively conceived: point, line, plane. The functioning of language on the closed-class elements level shows that this should be the case, and that the conception of space, as revealed either by these elements or by the cartographic mental images, can ultimately be reduced to a very few semantic types: point, line, plane, volume. Talmy (1983: 228) refers to a parallel generalization when he states that the general conceptual structure corresponding to the closed-class elements may to some degree constitute the structure of thought in general by offering a metaphorical model for the structuring of other domains.

Talmy's linguistic material, the geographical findings, and the work of one of the present authors (see, for example, Lagopoulos 1977: 74) on the conception of space in precapitalist societies, all converge to show that these semantic types are universal. These same notions are the prime material from which the spatial logics are constructed (see Chapter 11, Section 5).

The three categories of cartographic signifiers do not cover all the signifiers appearing on the sketch maps. The mental scale of these maps usually pushes the subjects to express their Gestalt images with the cartographic signifier corresponding to the semantic type in which the Gestalt image is classified. But this abstraction originates from the Gestalt image, and this image has a linguistic label. Not unusually, written language is used on the sketch maps, alone or (as on a professional topographical map) together with a graphic signifier. (cf. Appleyard 1970: 114; Evans, Marrero & Butler 1981: 88). Also, graphic signifiers may be used which do not belong to the above categories of cartographic signifiers and which represent an attempt to express the Gestalt image directly. The degree of abstraction of the latter is due to the perspective adopted. The paradigmatic categories of cartographic signifiers are derived from a bird's-eye visual angle, but certain individuals replace this or mix it with an eye-level view (cf. Lynch 1960: 88; Canter 1977: 57; Evans, Marrero & Butler 1981: 88). The eye-level view implies less abstract, naturalistic signifiers, rendered with greater or lesser skill in orthographic projection or in perspective.

The great majority of our interviewees (78%) founded their sketch maps on the three typical and abstract paradigmatic categories, producing the type of map that we shall call *semi-topographical map*. The rest of the interviewees are divided between two other types of maps: the *semi-topographical map with naturalistic signifiers* (13%), and the *naturalistic map*, which may also make some use of the abstract paradigmatic categories (9%). The variations of the statistical distributions for the social groups of the frequency programs in comparison to this whole-sample distribution are with some exceptions not remarkable. The exceptions mainly indicate an opposition between Thessaloniki and Veria. The highest percentage of semi-topographical maps (91%) occurs in the metropolis, and the lowest in the provincial city (67%), with the result that the share of the metropolis in the two other types of maps is the lowest of all groups: its share in the semi-topographical type with naturalistic signifiers is 6%, as opposed to the maximum share occuring in Veria (and for the lower middle class), and in the naturalistic type only 3%, which is the lowest, together with Axioupoli and the lower middle class, while the highest (17%) occurs in Ormylia.

The variable of these three types of maps was used for a series of crosstabulations in which the different deep static structures or dynamic models of the maps constitute the second variable (the two values of this variable are the maps having a particular structure or model and the rest of the maps). The results of the crosstabulations are not rich, and any significant results are generally limited to the whole sample. They are not, however, without a certain interest. They show that individuals drawing semi-topographical maps or semi-topographical maps with naturalistic signifiers are almost equally divided between use and non-use of the radial structure or model, but individuals drawing naturalistic maps pratically do not use this radial form at all. On the other hand, two-thirds of the naturalistic map drawers select the use of the central model. We could hypothesize that, on a general level, individuals drawing maps with naturalistic signifiers, because of which they seem to have a less abstract, more concrete and eye-level contact with space, i.e., a more personal contact, relate to space in a manner matching the ego-centered perspective of the central model, but not excluding the use of other models or structures.

The existence of naturalistic signifiers for about one-fourth of our subjects shows that regional space is not necessarily viewed in a more abstract bird's-eye manner, expressed in the sketch map system through the abstractness of its paradigmatic categories of graphic signifiers and producing the semi-topographical maps. The sketch mapping phase of our field work implicitly invited our subjects to adopt this more abstract perspective, but another, more concrete perspective was sometimes also activated. Here, the question arises if this eye-level perspective on regional space is exclusively used by the above subjects or is a more or less common ability activated when people are confronted with regional space. This question was investigated with the help of the oral questionnaire.

We already mentioned in the first section that almost one-fifth of our interviewees stated that they do not have introspective images of their involvement region. Even if we accept that all of these interviewees were exact in their statement, we are left with the great majority of the interviewees having regional images. The sociosemiotic programs show that certain social groups have a greater tendency to use images than other groups. A statistically significant use of images is found among the young in general, especially among city youth (0.01), and most of all among Veria youth (0.05), which is solidly composed of imagers. On the other hand, there are groups making use of images to a markedly lesser degree: the mature, and especially the Ormylia mature (almost half of them stated that they do not see images), and individuals with only a primary school education.

We were not satisfied with a simple statement on the existence of these images, since we wanted to corroborate the truth of the statement and further to analyse the character of the images. The basis for our analysis was a question inviting the interviewees to describe the most striking images from their involvement region, offering the possibility for any kind of semantic content. We should note, however, that we cannot be sure if all the descriptions given correspond to actual images or simply more generally to regional experiences. But our instructions to the interviewees and the nature of their descriptions tend to indicate that in general the interviewees responded in the expected manner; they provided descriptions of places and events well known to them and of manifest personal importance. In the discussion that follows we shall consider all the descriptions given as corresponding to introspective pictorial images, but we should keep in mind that it is not to be excluded that some descriptions do not have a corresponding pictorial signifier.

All the interviewees that stated that they had regional images described at least one such image. The richness of images varies from one to eight images; in one exceptional case sixteen images were described. Of the total number of imagers and for the whole sample, almost two-thirds of the interviewees are shown to be poor imagers, offering one or two images, almost one-third are average imagers since they described from three to five images; a greater number of images was given by the rich imagers (5% of the interviewees). According to the frequency programs, the inhabitants of Axioupoli are the poorest imagers (90% of them have only one or two images and the rest from three to five), in sharp contrast to the Verians, who are almost equally divided between these two categories of image richness (48% and 42% respectively) and present the greatest percentage of rich imagers (10%). No individual in the countryside is a rich imager. Another sharp contrast, though milder than the one between Axioupoli and Veria, is that between the lower middle and the middle class: the poor imagers of the lower middle class amount to 77%, while those of the middle class to 53%, and the average imagers of the former to 15% as compared to 47% for the latter.

The naturalistic maps and the semi-topographical maps with naturalistic signifiers pointed to the existence of eye-level maps and eye-level images referring to the involvement region, and through the questionnaire we found that regional images are quite common. A first characteristic of these images concerns the conceived scale of the signifier, following from the relative distance the interviewee chooses in respect to the imagined referent. Different distances imply different perspectives on space and the adoption of different visual angles. The images described show the existence of two different groups of locations in relation to the imagined referent: a *distant* location implying a rather narrow visual angle, and a *close* location implying a wide angle. As an example of description of a distant image we cite the following view of Thessaloniki as seen from the high location of the fashionable suburb Panorama:

Yes, at night we go to Panorama .... Mmm ... It's high up and you can see the ocean, a lot of houses, Thessaloniki down below is all built up, not so densely up toward the mountain. The air's very clean up there, I don't think down below it's so ... at night up there.

In contrast, the following is an example of a description of a close image:

I close my eyes. I see Kalamaria. I see greenery, and walking through trees.

Distant images seem to be more passive and to show a certain psychological distancing from the referent, since the latter is approached as something to be seen; in the case of distant images, the referent is viewed more or less two-dimensionally. On the contrary, close images seem to actively engage the subject with the imagined referent, something implying not only a much wider angle, but also a closer feeling for the referent and maybe a more or less concrete three-dimensional view of it. Sometimes close images incorporate a sense of movement, as in the example given above. For the whole sample, the individuals using exclusively close images amount to 54%, the individuals using distant images to 15% only, and those with both types of images to 31%. We see that close images are much more repounded than distant images, since the former are used by more than four-fifths of our subjects while the latter by less than half.

A similar distinction between distant and close images is referred to by Talmy in his analysis of the closed-class elements of language. Talmy (1983: 253-257) finds four largely independent systems functioning on this level, which characterize different kinds of conceived relations between physical objects, spatially or temporally approached. The first system allows the construction of geometric "schemata" (see Chapter 11, Section 5 and earlier in the present section). The second system defines the perspective point, i.e., the point where one is conceptually situated to look at the rest of a scene, specifically the location(s), distance from the scene, and mode of deployment of the scene. The third system specifies the hierarchy in the distribution of attention to be given to a scene looked at from a particular perspective point, and attributes the roles of figure and primary or secondary reference object. Finally, the fourth system indicates the "force dynamics", i.e., the conceived interrelation between objects attributed to the presence or absence of a field of physical forces. This system, for Talmy, mainly derives from the kinesthetic-somesthetic sensory modality, while the three previous systems mainly follow from the visual modality.

In the context of the perspective-point system, the author makes a distinction "between a steady-state long-range perspective point with synoptic scope of attention, and a moving close-up perspective point with local scope of attention." In the second case, a stationary scene is looked upon through a temporal sequence of close-up views, implying a spatio-temporal movement, a moving scan on the part of the perspective point. The author also mentions the inverse of the latter case, a fixing on a "snapshot" taken from the path of a moving object. The similarities between Talmy's typology, following from the perspective-point system revealed by the closed-class elements of language, and our own typology of regional images are evident, and point to the existence of a general and fundamental conceptual framework establishing our visual perspectives on reality.

The sketch map analysis showed us that the map-like conception of regional space is not the only one possible, that the corresponding *abstract bird's-eye* perspective on space is not exclusive, and that a more concrete perspective is also used, if only to a lesser degree. This perspective may be used for the whole of regional space or in respect to specific locations within it. Such locations may be extremely limited spatially, in which case the corresponding regional representations should be understood as regional in the very general sense of being attached to the involvement region and not in the strict sense of referring to the whole or organic parts of this region.

The oral questionnaire helped us, first, to establish that the use of concrete regional representations in the above sense is repounded in the form of introspective pictorial images. Secondly, it revealed the existence of two different concrete perspectives on space. The one perspective is the *distant* perspective, constituting the abstract extreme of the concrete perspective. The other perspective is a wholly *concrete close* perspective. A more close analysis of the naturalistic maps reveals that the distant perspective may be an *eye-level* perspective (Figure 17a) or a helicopter, *diagonal* perspective (Figure 17, b and c); the view from the eye-level perspective can be identical to that from the diagonal perspective if the viewer is conceptually located on an existing height (Figure 18b; see below, Chapter 13). The same division between an abstract perspective and more concrete perspectives is ascertained by Hardwick, McIntyre and Pick (1976: 6-7, 49-50). The aim of the authors was to study the accuracy of the locational information in the spatial representations (of a large room) among three age groups (two groups of elementary school children and one group of college students), and the manner in which these groups mentally manipulate their spatial representations. The authors show that the adult representations of space are composed of two different levels, a general and a specific.

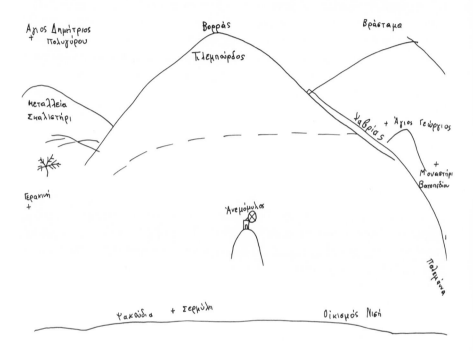

Figure 17a. Sketch map signifiers following from an eye-level view.

The first level includes "a single coordinated representation of the ordinal relationships" between objects and the second level "a series of smaller representations which are associated with particular points of view", representations which are "perspective maps" and correspond to "a single view from a single location in the environment". The authors arrive at the conclusion that that the general coordinated representation corresponds to a view that is never realized and that its formation may be due to a process of abstraction over time.

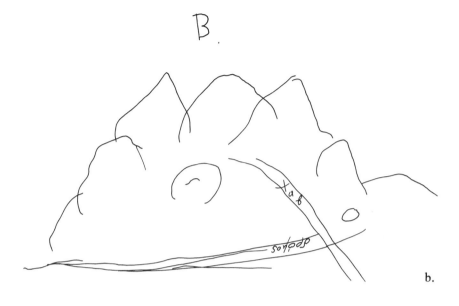

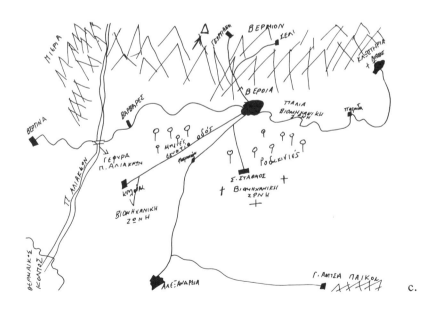

Figure 17, b and c. Sketch map signifiers following from a diagonal view.

4. Regional images: The signified

If we momentarily ignore the details, regional images can be classified as *general* or as *specific* in content. The general images are a conception of non-individualized objects, persons, or events, or even individualized objects and specific persons through a kind of composite image, a conception which is of a general nature and shows an unfocused approach to the scene conceived, for example: "Images... it's so green!"; "The most typical [images] are in Epanomi and Panorama [...] uuh ... with people and, like, landscapes." The specific images are a specific conception of individualized objects, persons, and events or patterns relating to specific persons, which shows a focused approach:

> From all of Thessaloniki? If you sit down and imagine, lots of things come to you, but some particular image comes to mind when you're far away and the one that came to my mind is the one I told you about with the [Cafe] Aigaio and the sea....

For the whole sample, the individuals with exclusively general images are one-fifth of the total, the individuals with exclusively specific images are just above half, and those reporting both types of images just above one-fourth; thus, the individuals reporting specific images amount to four-fifths of the total, while those reporting general images to just less than half. We see that the use of specific images is significantly more repounded than the use of general images.

If we compare these figures concerning the classification of images according to their general content - i.e., a semantic classification - with the figures for classification on the basis of relative distance from the imagined referent - which is a syntactic classification - we observe that they are very similar for the pairs of close and specific, and distant and general images, as well as for the last pair covering the combinations of both types of images. The two semantic types of images can be combined with the two syntactic types of distant and close images to produce four mixed types, which show different degrees of psychological attachment to the scene pictured. The two extreme degrees of attachment are represented by the distant general images and the close specific images: the former are rather passive and psychologically flat, while the latter, which Pocock (1975: 39) calls experiential images, presuppose an active psychological involvement.

With a close specific image a person can express his/her deepest feelings and attain a condensation and peak of his/her experiences, as in the following example from a middle-class man from Ormylia:

> Another very vivid image which comes to me very often is that while I was going to secondary school in 1949, I was twelve, on the road going to Polygyros - we'd walk to school - as I was running with the other kids, it was a footpath, I stumbled on a guerilla fighter, a Partisan, who had been wounded and had come down as far as the road so that somebody would find him and save him, and I stumbled on the dead body of that guerilla fighter. And that image is so vivid that it hasn't left me even today. Even today when I drive through that area at night, even in the daytime, through that area, it comes to my mind.

In the above discussion of the broad semantic types of regional images, we mentioned that their referents are objects, persons, and events. If we look closer at the objects pictured, we observe that they are of two kinds: built space and natural space; these two can also appear in combination. The distant images including these themes produce cityscapes, landscapes, seascapes. Distant images of people were not reported. The close images of built space or nature give urban views ("I might think a bit of the street [of Helioupoli], the central street, the shops all around"; "Apartment buildings come to mind, cars, noise, colors ...") and architectural wholes ("I might think of the school, which is a very nice building, I've got lots of memories from there") or natural micro-environments. Pocock (1975: 39) calls the images isolating an object in focus from its environment *non-contextual*. Non-specific persons may appear in general or specific images, always of the close type ("...crowds for the festival and things like that are going on"; "I might think a bit of the street, the central street ... further on in the evening there's a lot of life, people get together"). They may monopolize the whole image or give life to their inanimate surroundings.

A final theme of regional images is a particular person or even the interviewee him/herself. Sometimes this specificity is neutralized with the use of a composite image of a symbolic character to which corresponds an unfocused set of pictorial descriptions, as in the following example:

> Yes, if I close my eyes I see some images from Fanos, where I spent quite a few years - up to the age of 22 I used to spend every summer

there, my father had a job there. I have all kinds of images from there, from when I was a kid that is, we were there all summer, every Christmas and Easter. They're leisure images, not so much of the village as of me myself in the village, of what I'm doing in that particular place, in other words it's more myself I remember at that age and in that place.

Other times, the unique image of a person is again replaced by a set of pictorial descriptions, but they follow a common pattern which reestablishes the specificity of the image, as in the following example:

The secondary school. While I was going to secondary school [...] It's that when I was little I used to take my bike and try to get away from Axioupoli, to find something different, in the other villages, some place where they didn't know you, I was just a kid, sixteen ... fifteen ... sixteen years old, like; another movie theatre ... something different, a different environment, I wanted to get away from the routine you might say of Axioupoli and so I'd go to those places.

The thematic typology of regional images is closely akin to the typology of painting, and the specific images of particular persons are nothing less than conceptual portraits.

We divided our subjects between those including among their images at least once the theme of built space and the rest of the subjects. Then, we correlated the variable composed of these two cases with complexity of discourse in the context of the semiotic programs. The result was a significant correlation between the two variables for the whole sample, very significant for the cities. The tendency found was the same in both cases: the individuals picturing this theme show by more than 60% a higher complexity of discourse, and more than three-fourths of the individuals with higher complexity use the theme (in the cities it is as high as 97%). On the other hand, the individuals not picturing the theme show mainly average complexity of discourse. In the context of the sociosemiotic programs, different variables related to the presented typology of regional images were correlated with the sociological factors of the programs. Only the above thematic variable of built space gave significant - indeed generally very significant - results. Certain social groups, mainly the cities and Thessaloniki men (almost in their totality), have a marked tendency to picture the built-space theme, while the preferences of other groups are more divided, or incline towards the other theme group, as is the case especially with the country middle class and women in Ormylia; in general, countryside people do not have any particular preference for the built-space theme.

The themes of regional images show that, although not all regional images are regional in the strict sense (they may cover the full range from regional images in the strict sense through urban views and architectural wholes to specific spots which have been invested with personal experiences), they are nevertheless representative of *regional* experiences and constitute a particular whole with its own regional specificity, not extending beyond the thresholds prescribed by that whole. We saw in Chapter 6, Section 3, that the involvement region is generally a subjective and self-referential creation, and (in Section 1 of the same chapter) that in certain cases the involvement region was coextensive with the settlement, while in all cases the settlement represents a strong place of the involvement region. The unity of the involvement region and the role of the settlement in it show that the use of urban images as regional should not come as a surprise. But whether they are regional in a stricter or looser sense, regional images are a genuine vehicle of regional experiences.

Chapter 13. Geographical accuracy

1. The regional point of view: Orientation and perspective

In Chapter 1, Section 2, we were critical of the biologistic approach to what is usually called cognitive mapping in geography. This approach is firmly connected to behaviorism in psychology, on which behavioral geography was founded. As we saw, for behaviorism the relation of the organism to its environment is such as to allow the organism to adopt to the environment, which will be conducive to survival. The argument is that the process of cognitive mapping, by allowing the subjective representation of the external environment and generally acting as a mediator between man and his environment, partakes of the organism's survival mechanisms. The end product of this process is the so-called mental map, a representation of space with greater or lesser coherency and accuracy. This representation is subjective in two different senses. In the first sense, "subjective" is a contradictory characterization. The reason is that, as we saw, the introspective image is the result of a process of semiosis, it is a meaningful and interpreted pictorial representation, and meaning and interpretation presuppose the involvement of the whole conceptual apparatus. The latter, however, has not developed in a vacuum, but is the result of social intercourse and thus of a dialectical interaction between individual and society, during which the individual is constituted both as *subjectivity* and, above all, as a participant in a specific culture. In this way, the introspective image cannot be considered as "mental" in general, referring to "human" in general, but as *subjective* and deeply *cultural;* it is a *conceptual*, hence *ideological* representation.

In the second sense, "subjective" implies the involvement of the individual in his/her pictorial representation, an involvement manifested both in its construction and in its use. During use, though the individual is physically external to his/her representation, he/she conceptually places him/herself inside it. Since one practical reason for the use of a pictorial representation is to orient oneself in space, the individual situates him/herself in the image in a location corresponding to his/her actual location, and relates it to the rest of his/her conceptual representation. Inversely, the very denotative construction of the representation is largely due to orientational clues learned during actual practices evolving in space. Orientation is thus an integral part of our conceptual "cartography" and if we were to follow the biologistic-psychologistic interpretation of "cognitive mapping" we should conclude that it fulfills a survival function by allowing adaptation to the environment.

Lynch's central concept of legibility may be used to show the indissoluble connection between orientation and the whole of the spatial representation: for him, a legible urban image, i.e., a strong urban cartographic image, is also a coherently structured image, and in a structured image all the elements are in the right, or at least in a well-defined, relative location, i.e., they have a clear orientation in respect to each other, a complex network of relative orientations partially built upon the orientational achievements of the bearer of the image.

The function and meaning of any orientational activity are not uniform, but depend on the social practice which the orientation serves. Orientation comes closest to a survival device in the biological sense in cases such as the orientational practices of the Australian tribes - which, we should note, are not orientational for their own sake but attached to wider practices - or the Polynesian navigators - who again manifestly did not have the habit of navigating in order to practice their orientational skills, but put them in the service of the purposes of their expeditions.

In both these cases orientation is not isolated from a wider context of religious preocupations. But the relation of religious practices to orientation becomes truly prominent in cases such as the orientation of many precapitalist settlements towards the four points of the compass, an orientation which brings the settlement and its inhabitants into contact with the cosmic forces and rythms and creates for them a place in the very desirable center of the world. One could argue that the collective connection to the universe and its deities acts as a guarantor of social cohesion and reproduction, and thus that its aim is after all survival. But then orientation no longer serves the biological survival of a person or group, but the symbolic survival of a community. Finally, if we, members of Western society, miss a supermarket recommended to us in a foreign city due to our lack of the proper orientational competence, we will undoubtedly find ourselves by chance in front of some other supermarket and thus secure our survival, and if we miss an exclusive shop selling the latest in Italian shoes, or the movie theater showing *Emmanuelle*, well, we shall by all accounts survive! Survival is neither sufficient nor satisfactory as a sociological or geographical explanation of orientation.

Orientation is of course active in the structuring of our denotative spatial representation, but it begins to operate *after* the most fundamental choices have been made and in the context of these choices: *what* to represent and *how* to look at it. This is what is indicated by the great relativity in size of the involvement region, the great variation in code structuring, and their sociological determinants. It is regional meaning following from social practices, denotative meaning certainly, but also connotative meaning or otherwise regional symbolism, which guides the operations of orientation in the conceptual representation. Orientational behavior and the clues used during orientation, which underlie the construction of the conceptual map, are not necessarily the same for every person.

We studied the different modes of orientation using both the sketch maps and the oral questionnaire, and we shall first present the findings from the former. We saw in the previous chapter (Section 3) that different perspectives may be used in the representation of regional space. The difference between perspective and orientation is that a given perspective on an object also implies a particular orientation towards it, but the same orientation is valid for any kind of perspective on this object, whether a bird's-eye or eye-level perspective, distant or close, or a perspective on the front or the back of the object. Thus, if we imagine the object as the center of an infinity of concentric spheres, every line of vision pointing to that center and originating at any point in space and thus at any distance from the center, i.e., any radius of any concentric sphere, theoretically represents a different perspective on the object, but all have the same orientation towards it. For example, the prominent bird's-eye perspective of the semi-topographical maps and the semi-topographical maps with naturalistic signifiers also implies an overall orientation towards the involvement region as a unified object.

The study of the sketch maps also reveals another kind of conceptual orientation. A person as we saw uses perspective in order to represent regional space to him/herself and present it to others. In the case of the semi-topographical maps and the semi-topographical maps with naturalistic signifiers, this use follows from the decision to orient him/herself *towards* this space. But all sketch maps show that there is also an opposite orientation away *from* the involvement region and thus *outwards*. The existence of this orientation can be seen from the privileged sign or signs in the upper part of all sketch maps. This upper part is defined in function of the normal orientation of the letters and words accompanying the maps when natural language is used, as happened in 98% of our cases (cf. Pocock 1975: 62). We can also determine the upper part of the map by observing the subject during the drawing of the map: the upper part of the map is the furthest away from the subject and on an axis corresponding to the axis of the line of vision adopted, which both belong to a vertical plane perpendicular to the subject's chest. All our subjects placed the sheet of paper given to them in such a way as to bring two of its sides (the shorter ones in 91% of the cases) parallel to the above axis, following cultural convention; thus, even if we did not observe the subject while drawing the map, we can generally know a priori that the upper part is one of the four sides of the paper (Pocock 1975: 62 also mentions a very limited tendency to place this axis diagonally on the paper).

Frequently there are indications on the sketch maps of one or more cardinal points, or these points are located on the maps when the subjects are asked to do so. In both cases, the cardinal points are situated on or define the above axis (51%), the axis perpendicular to it (11%), or both (26%). In 12% of the cases, we observe a diagonal orientation of the axis or axes, while the map is still drawn parallel to the sides of the paper. The cardinal points are indicated with simple letters (39%), arrows (2%), or a combination of letters and arrows or marked lines (59%); in a couple of cases, where east is stressed, a symbolic figure of the sun is drawn. Almost two-thirds of the subjects use the conventional cartographic location of north in the upper part of the paper, while 9% inverse this location. North as the marked cardinal point may also appear on one of the two other sides of the paper (11%) or follow the diagonals of the latter (8%). In the rest of the cases, east or west replaces north in these locations. We see then that in most cases we can define the upper part of the paper by referring to the cardinal points.

The upward orientation of all sketch maps is not accidental. We just saw that the upper part of the drawing paper is the most distanced from the subject and connected to the line of vision. It thus becomes manifest that the subject attempts to draw a map that is *homologous* to the involvement region by conceptually aligning the line of vision used to see the drawing with a conceptual representation of a line of vision oriented towards what is considered as the edge of the region; i.e., the subject simulates in drawing an outwards conceptual orientation and uses the line of vision as a common axis of reference. It should also be noted that there is a strong cultural convention connecting "up" and "ahead", "upper" and "further" in the visual domain, established by the system of perspective in geometry and drawing as well as by photography. The edge of the region is mainly constituted by a privileged sign or signs and follows from an actual barrier (a mountain, the sea), or may be a clearly conceptual barrier (certain villages on a plain conceived as continuous), in which case no abrupt break of continuity between inside and outside is conceived. The orientation of the subject towards this edge is connected to a perspective and may be considered in general terms as one particular orientation (in spite, that is, of the fact that it does not usually aim at a point but at a whole edge).

We see, then, that in the case of the semi-topographical maps and the semi-topographical maps with naturalistic signifiers (which, as we saw, together represent more than 90% of the sketch maps) regional space is structured around the dialectical interplay of two opposite orientations, one inwards and the other outwards. This is not the case with the naturalistic maps, where the perspective comes down to eye-level or to an intermediary diagonal location. In these maps, the outwards orientation is indissolubly combined with the inwards orientation, and it is one and the same line of vision that grasps simultaneously the interior of the region and its priviledged most distant edge. This orientation may be clearly focused (Figure 18a) or diffused in the manner of a wide-angle lens (Figure 18b). It may also be a pseudo-orientation, in which case a unifying general framework is created independent of any actual visual possibility, but giving a sense of reality, into which a series of different and partial orientations are crowded (Figure 18, c and d). The naturalistic maps are subject to the same inwards/outwards dialectics as the other maps, but it is achieved in the context of one single orientation.

In his study of Durham, Pocock (1975: 62, 64) found that less than 40% of his subjects used in their maps the conventional orientation to the north, the objective orientation as he calls it, and the rest oriented their maps according to their travelling experiences and most importantly their entry route, an orientation that he calls "ego-centric". At the regional level, the edge is not selected in function of some entry point, but is the result of a broader regional experience. As we saw, almost two-thirds of our subjects used the conventional orientation for their maps, but not in all these cases was north the privileged sign; it just happened that the privileged sign was located to the north and this may also happen with the other cardinal points. As privileged signs of the sketch maps, together with the sign or signs of orientation, we also sometimes included the diametrically opposite sign, when it was judged that the subject was

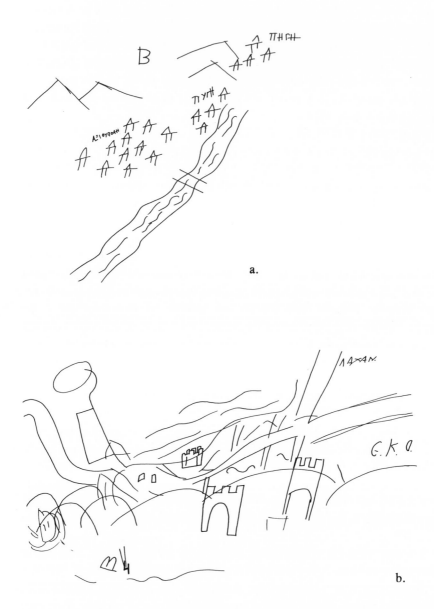

Figure 18. Orientation in the naturalistic sketch maps: a. Focused. b. Diffused.

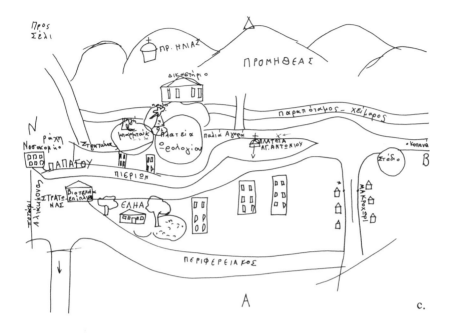

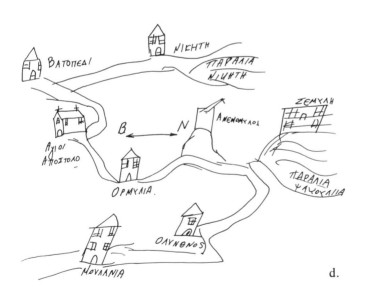

Figure 18 (continued). Orientation in the naturalistic sketch maps: c and d. Pseudo-orientation.

simultaneously "viewing" with the back of his/her head. This double orientation is rather common, for instance, in Thessaloniki, where the region is enclosed between the mountain and the sea.

We conclude on the basis of the orientation of the sketch maps that the conceptual edges of the involvement region may be grouped into two major types: the natural type that includes regional and therefore relative edges, and the astronomical type that is of an absolute nature (see also Pocock 1975: 62, and cf. Gärling, Böök & Lindberg 1984: 14); there was also an unimportant number of cases in which the edges were composed of an artificial object (a road) or seemed to be fortuitous. For the whole sample, the conceptual orientation towards a natural edge amounts to 71% of all orientations located (which are, as we just saw, greater in number than the number of subjects) and 75% of the total number of subjects, while astronomical orientation to the cardinal points does not exceed 27% and 39% repsectively. The natural orientational clues selected by our subjects were: mountains (34%/49%), the sea (21%/31%), plains (11%/16%), and rivers (5%/7%). Thus, in almost three-fourths of the cases a relatively distanced feature of the landscape attracts the attention to such a degree as to be used as a reference point.

The social groups of the frequency programs do not diverge greatly from this distribution in respect to the number of cases of orientation, with the exception of the four settlements. In fact, Veria shows the lowest percentage of astronomical orientation (5%) and the highest of natural orientation (90%). Of natural orientations, the city shows the highest percentage of orientation to a mountain (63%) as opposed to Axioupoli that shows the lowest (21%); it shows the second highest percentage of orientation to a plain (24%), comparable to Axioupoli (28%), and in contrast to Thessaloniki and Ormylia that show no such case; like Axioupoli, it does not show any case of orientation to the sea (both these settlements and their involvement regions are inland), as opposed to Thessaloniki and Ormylia where this case is dominant (around 36%). Finally, in Axioupoli the cases of orientation to a river by far exceed those of any other group (19%).

Clearly, the presence of actual geographical features in the regional landscape is a significant factor in these differences. But just as clearly, it is not in itself a sufficient explanation: Mount Païkon above Axioupoli is as impressive geographically as Mount Vermion above Veria, and the Aliakmon river that runs by Veria is comparable in size and importance to the Axios river outside Axioupoli. As with the mechanisms of inclusion and exclusion of certain parts of the involvement region (Chapter 6, Section 2), it is the *socialized* significance of an ecological feature that determines its use as a point of orientation.

The prevalent cases of orientation in Veria, first towards the mountain and then towards the plain, remind us of the feeling of its inhabitants that the city has a "back", Mount Vermion, and a focal point on its facade, the "balcony", overlooking the plain below (Chapter 6, Section 2). Four-fifths of the inhabitants of the city are oriented in their region according to these two socialized ecological features, though usually the feeling of the "balcony" is overridden by the impressiveness of the "back", with the result that the mountain becomes the object of conceptual orientation at the regional scale. All social groups of Veria tend to orient themselves to one or both of those two features of the landscape, but this tendency is stronger among the middle class (where it is exclusive) and the lower middle class, men, and the mature. Contrary to the Verians, the Ormylians tend to use astronomical orientation somewhat more than orientation to the mountain, and the groups having the strongest astronomical tendency are the workers, men, and the mature.

The general orientational (macro-orientational) clues provided by the sketch maps were complemented with the more particular clues used to specify location within the region (micro-orientational clues). The issue was studied with a question in the oral questionnaire inviting the interviewees to define "which way" were located the five settlements of their involvement region closest to its limits. For the whole sample and all cases of orientation found, it is now the astronomical type that comes to the foreground (50%/80%). The second most frequent type of clues refer to the main road leading to a settlement (22%/34%), an orientation that no longer follows the straight line of vision but locates the place aimed at on a known path: "on the road to Chalkidiki"; "towards Edessa". We encountered in Axioupoli an extreme case of road orientation in a working-class woman, the naive spontaneity of which is rather delightful: "You go to the bus station, and then you go to Thessaloniki." The third most frequent type of clues are the topological clues (18%/25%), which are topological or projective notions used to refer the place aimed at to some element (a place, a natural geographical feature, or even a road) or set of elements known to the interviewee and supposedly also to the interviewer: "*above* the Castle"; "*up above* Panorama"; "*outside* Thessaloniki"; "along the coast *toward* Phinika"; "*over there* where you can see the mountains"; "[coming] from Thessaloniki Taramoni and Patrida are to your *right*"; "from downtown left at the seashore and *over there*". Finally, the fourth type uses landmarks (10%/16%) which correspond to natural geographical features or even settlements: "to the east, on [Mount] *Chortiatis*". The micro-orientational clues add two modes of orientation not found among the macro-orientational modes, namely the path mode and the topological mode.

It is again in Veria that we find the lowest percentage of astronomical orientation (40% of all the cases of orientation) and the highest percentage of orientation toward landmarks, a type of orientation not used at all in Axioupoli. Among all the subjects, in Veria the tendency to use landmarks is characteristic of the working class. The use of landmarks is - for the whole sample, all workers (0.01), women, and the young (0.01) - incompatible with the use of introspective signifiers of the geometric class. It is again the Veria working class, together with employees in general, which has a tendency to use path orientation. No social group has any specific tendency to use astronomical orientation, but women have in comparison to men a significant tendency to use topological orientation.

It is interesting to compare the orientational modes obtained by Ward, Newcombe and Overton (1986) with our findings. One of the aims of these authors was to examine if there is any difference between genders in the use of cardinality, i.e., if use of cardinality by women is more limited than use by men, and if so, whether this difference is due to a lack of competence among women in the use of a coordinate system of reference, or simply to a "stylistic preference", by which they mean the selection of direction-giving clues which aim at communicating the feeling of a journey. A second aim of the authors was to study the types of these orientational clues. The authors observe that in fact women tend to use the cardinal directions less than men, and that this tendency is due to a stylistic selection. As to the second issue, they mention four types of clues, usually in the following order: relational clues (left/right), landmarks, cardinal directions, and metric terms, which however relate to distance and not to orientation. They thus arrive at a classification not far removed from our own.

The orientational modes we located, which can be combined in all possible ways by the individual subjects, are the following:

a. *Direct orientation*

i. *Astronomical* orientation in respect to the cardinal points, i.e., remote orientation according to a Euclidean construction.

ii. *Landmark* orientation, which is distant but not remote orientation. This orientation may be either:

ii(1). *Natural* orientation, when the element aimed at is a natural feature of the landscape, or

ii(2). *Built landmark* orientation, when the element aimed at is artificial.

b. *Indirect or mediated orientation*

i. *Topological* orientation. In this case, the place aimed at may be referred to the subject through topological or projective notions either directly (in which case the orientation is direct) or indirectly through the mediation of a third element surrounding the subject; most commonly it is referred by the subject to some element or connected elements as landmarks, to which he/she may conceptually relocate him/herself. Thus, usually topological orientation is a mixed landmark and topological orientation.

ii. *Path* orientation, which is a case of dynamic orientation. Here, there is no static definition of the element aimed at, nor is this element considered in isolation, but it is defined on a path leading dynamically to the element and to the end of the path. The path becomes the element of reference; its end, normally a settlement, is technically a landmark whose importance, however, recedes in comparison to the path. The abstract straight line of vision is replaced by the concrete tracing of the road, and the subject no longer refers the target place egocentrically to his/her position - which is the case with the other orientational modes - but refers to or even conceptually moves in an ec-centric line of movement.

2. Orientational and metric geographical accuracy

The two remaining sections of this chapter will deal with the favorite theme of the geographers, the issue of accuracy, or otherwise the degree of identification of the spatial representation with actual spatial arrangement. We shall inspect different forms of accuracy, starting with *orientational accuracy*.

In responding to the question of "which way" were located the five settlements closest to the limits of their involvement region, the interviewees when they used astronomical orientation (which is the case for 80% of them, as we saw) did not use finer astronomical distinctions than the cardinal points and the intermediary points of the compass. The result is that the points of the compass used by them correspond to a distribution of directions on the compass rose such that each direction diverges from each of its two neighboring directions by 45 degrees. We estimated that on both sides of the actual orientation of a settlement there is a margin within which we should consider the orientation as practically accurate. We defined this margin as 22.5 degrees, half of the angle between neighboring directions. We used the double of this margin, i.e., the angle of 45 degrees, as the standard unit for the measurement of orientational divergence, a unit allowing quick calculation of divergence given the number of directions mentioned by the subjects and the angle of 45 degrees between them. An answer is not considered as being practically precise if it gives for a settlement an orientation, astronomical or other, diverging from that of the actual settlement by more than 22.5 degrees. We considered that, if this divergence is no more than 1.5 times our unit of measurement, it could be considered as corresponding to one unit, and as corresponding to two units if it is greater than 1.5 times but lesser than 2.5 times the unit, and so on. This calculation could be somewhat more precise, but has the advantage of allowing for adequate and quick results.

On this basis, we calculated for each subject the average orientational divergence, and from the data obtained we arrived at the definition of four grades of accuracy: important accuracy (average divergence less than 1 unit); fair accuracy (1 unit); inaccuracy (from about 1.2 to 2 units); and great inaccuracy (from more than 2 to 4 units). For the whole sample, the subjects having important accuracy amount to 44%, the fairly accurate subjects to 19%, the inaccurate to 24%, and those showing great inaccuracy to 13%. If we group the grades of accuracy into two classes, according to the dichotomous classification *accuracy* vs. *inaccuracy,* we observe that almost two-thirds of the subjects correspond to the first class, a ratio that points to fairly high orientational accuracy on the part of our subjects. With some exceptions, the frequency-program groups do not depart much from this distribution. These exceptions are mainly Veria and Ormylia, which are in sharp contrast to each other: the share of the accuracy class in Ormylia is as high as 78% and important accuracy is represented by 61% (a degree of accuracy approached only by the middle class), while in Veria the corresponding percentages are about half; thus, the inaccuracy class rises to 57% in Veria as compared to 22% in Ormylia, and great inaccuracy represents more than half of this perceptages, being six times higher than in Ormylia.

There is a significant correlation between orientational accuracy and astronomical orientation. In fact more than half of the individuals showing important accuracy also use astronomical orientation in their sketch maps and a comparable proportion of the individuals using this orientation have important accuracy, and this is true for the whole sample (0.01), the middle class, and women (0.01). If we use for the crosstabulations the whole accuracy class instead of the two separate grades of accuracy, the results are comparable: the accuracy class is closely connected to astronomical orientation, since more than half of the accurate individuals also use astronomical orientation, and more than four-fifths of the individuals with this orientation are accurate in their orientation. Individuals in the inaccuracy or great inaccuracy grade are represented to a very low degree among the individuals using astronomical orientation. This second series of crosstabulations, in addition to the social groups already mentioned, also holds for the countryside and the two age groups, something showing that the regularity found is more or less of a general national character.

The above correlation between orientational accuracy and astronomical orientation extends to the orientation elicited from the oral questionnaire. For the whole sample, the middle class (0.01), and the countryside (0.01), the very accurate individuals use almost exclusively astronomical orientation, and this orientation is also used by more than 70% of the individuals in the fair accuracy grade; however, these crosstabulations show that some individuals in the inaccuracy or even great inaccuracy grade may also use astronomical orientation. The classification in three groups gives comparable results and shows that the regularity also holds for men and the young. On the other hand, as can be seen from the whole sample, the cities (0.01), and the mature, the individuals with great inaccuracy have a marked tendency to use landmark orientation, and they are followed by the inaccurate.

We can conclude from the above that the individuals accustomed to the use of astronomical orientation have an advantage over others in matters of orientational accuracy, whether the latter is achieved with astronomical orientation throughout or mixed orientational schemes. This conclusion, however, can be further refined. The crosstabulations between map orientation and oral orientation are in general not significant and show that there is no systematic use of astronomical orientation by the same individuals. With these data in mind we should restate our conclusion, in the sense that greater orientational accuracy occurs among the individuals who are able at least under certain circumstances to have recourse to the compass rose, i.e., to a coherent system of reference; that is, greater accuracy is achieved by those who have some ability to operate with this Euclidean construct.

The location of a point in space is commonly described through the combination of its direction and its road distance from a reference point. The issue of direction was just examined, and we shall now discuss the issue of distances. With this last factor we are at the very heart of behavioral geography. Geographers calculate accuracy on the basis of the divergence of the spatial representation from topographical reality, something quite reasonable. However, they do not reconstitute this representation through the definition of the subject's knowledge of the specific location of each and every spatial element. Instead, they work with the subject's estimates of the absolute or relative distances between two elements, frequently a pair of cities, and they elicit a set of such judgments. This set is either used in its written form, without any graphic representation being involved, or it is transformed into a graphic representation that is compared to topographical reality. In the second case, the degree of accuracy is calculated as a function of the distance between the places on the representation and the corresponding places on the topographical map. Thus, the calculation of accuracy may involve a graphic representation, which is considered to be a "mental map", and in which the location of each element is not defined in itself but relative to the locations of a set of other elements. In both cases, the often sophisticated calculation of accuracy cannot take place if the distances provided by the subjects are not crow-flight distances (see on the above, for example, Cadwallader 1979: 566; Golledge & Spector 1978: 411-413; Brown & Broadway 1981: 319-320). In fact, the most natural reaction of the subjects is undoubtedly to estimate the road distances, and the geographers impose a serious constraint on them that we criticized earlier in this book (see Chapter 2, Section 1). But the use of road distances does not allow for the reconstruction of a "mental map", due to the free (not straight-line) tracing of the roads between settlements.

For our part, we were not interested either in straight-line distances or in their use to map conceptual representations. We elicited from our subjects estimates of actual road distances, on the basis of which we calculated their *metric accuracy*. More specifically, the degree of accuracy was defined as the ratio of the sum of the absolute values of the differences between estimated and actual distances (from the home settlement to the settlements defined by the subjects as being closest to the limits of their involvement region) to the sum of the actual distances from the home settlement. For example, a ratio of 10% means that the answer given diverges as a whole from the sum of real distances by 10% of the latter.

Our data led us to the definition of four degrees of metric accuracy: great accuracy (ratio from 1% to 12%); accuracy (13%-28%); inaccuracy (29%-55%); and great inaccuracy (from 56% to more than 100%). For the whole sample, the subjects with great accuracy are one-fourth of the total, the less accurate and the inaccurate represent around one-third each, and the very inaccurate are almost 10% of the total. When we group these degrees into two classes, *accuracy* vs. *inaccuracy,* as we did with orientational accuracy, the accurate amount to almost 60%, a percentage just lower than that of the corresponding class of orientational accuracy.

This distribution is on general lines valid for the frequency-program groups, with the main exception of Veria and Ormylia, as was also the case with orientational accuracy. There is a sharp contrast between these two settlements, replicating their contrast in respect to orientational accuracy: the accuracy class in Ormylia amounts to more than three-fourths of the total and the great accuracy degree to almost half, while the share of the first class in Veria is half that in Ormylia and the share of the great accuracy category one-third; thus, the inaccuracy category rises to 53% in Veria as compared to 20% in Ormylia, percentages quite similar to those for orientational accuracy in these settlements. The isolated contrast of the two settlements, however, does not lead to a statistically significant correlation when the two settlements are integrated into the settlement hierarchy network, i.e., when they are compared to the metropolis, as is also the case with orientational accuracy. But, contrary to the latter case, the city-country program gives a significant correlation and shows that the contrast between the two settlements is representative of a wider contrast between the urban and the rural in which the metric accuracy of city inhabitants is less than that of rural people: in the cities, the center of gravity is in the inaccuracy degree, while in the countryside it is in the accuracy degree and tends to extend to great accuracy.

3. Topological and configuration accuracy

As we already mentioned (Chapter 11, Section 5), for Piaget the fundamental structure of the most primitive type of spatial representation, topological space, is the neighboring relation between spatial elements. In order to study the comparative accuracy of people in dealing with this fundamental spatial structure, we used the verbal questionnaire. Topological accuracy was analysed through a question asking for the settlements *closest to the limits* of the involvement region. This question indirectly invites the interviewees to scan the whole extent of their region and select the settlements believed to be closest to the conceptual regional limits defined by them. In order to achieve this selection, subjects have to represent to themselves all the neighboring relations between the settlements known to them and the regional limits, and compare these relations as to the closeness of their elements; it is probable that in the search for these neighboring relations some successions of settlements were taken into account and comparative judgments relating succession and closeness to the limit were made. Thus, the task demanded of the subjects, though based on their knowledge of the neighboring structure, is in fact more complex in that it also requires comparative judgments.

As index of *topological accuracy* we used the ratio of the number of inaccurate judgments to the total number of relations mentioned. Four degrees of accuracy were defined: absolute accuracy (index 0%); accuracy (10% and 20%); inaccuracy (30% and 40%); important inaccuracy (50%, 60%, and 100%). What strikes us in the whole sample is that two-thirds of the interviewees have absolute topological accuracy and in addition more than one-fifth are accurate, that is, the accuracy class amounts to almost 90% of the total, a percentage much higher than those for the same class of orientational and metric accuracy. The distribution of the shares of the above categories in the whole sample is quite typical for the frequency-program groups, but there are certain exceptions once more related to the settlements. It is again in Ormylia that we find the highest level of accuracy, since the Ormylians with absolute accuracy represent four-fifths of the settlement inhabitants and almost all the rest of the inhabitants are in the accuracy class. But this time the contrast is not with Veria but with Axioupoli, in which the accuracy class as a whole is not far from the general average, but the absolute accuracy degree is by far the lowest of all groups (45%).

We might think that the measurement of topological accuracy in Ormylia and Axioupoli concerns spatial arrangements of a different complexity, with the result that the indices obtained reflect the complexity of the involvement region rather than the aptitude of the inhabitants. We can check this possibility by assuming that the surface of the involvement region is a satisfactory index of its complexity. In this case, we have only to remind the reader of our observation, in Chapter 6, Section 2, that these is no differentiation for the four settlements of our study in respect either to the size of the involvement regions or to the distribution of their size categories. There is also a further indication that this hypothesis does not hold. There is a very significant correlation between topological accuracy and involvement region surface, valid for the whole sample and the countryside, according to which absolute accuracy is strikingly lower for individuals with small regions. The individuals with medium regions have the highest absolute accuracy, while the individuals with very large regions show a higher absolute accuracy than those with large regions, who do not diverge much from the individuals with medium regions. We see, then, that there is a relation between topological accuracy and environmental complexity, but it is far from being linear.

Surely spatial knowledge does not deal only with neighboring relations between pairs of elements and the comparison (i.e., relation) of these relations. The drawing of a sketch map incorporates not only these relations and other topological relations, such as the order of succession, but also projective relations, such as right or left, and metric relations. The sketch maps may be judged from the point of view of the accuracy of their general configuration, but also as to the accuracy of the specifics of this configuration. We shall first deal with the accuracy of their general configuration, where by this concept we mean their topological organization as a complex set of multiple neighboring relations between spatial elements and the general directional arrangement of these elements, judged against a kind of compass rose with four successive diameters forming between them an angle of 45 degrees, but independent from the cardinal points; orientation is not at issue in respect to general configuration.

With this definition, the general configuration of a map is a set of spatial elements maintaining between them specific relations of neighboring, succession, and general direction, and the accuracy of this configuration reflects the accuracy of the subject's spatial representation in matters of the general location of the spatial elements, which is why we shall call it *location accuracy*. Unlike topological accuracy, location accuracy does not refer to the degree of closeness of spatial elements, but to a more complex neighboring knowledge. On the other hand, it is connected to the same directional complexity as orientational accuracy, but it was evaluated in a more rough and qualitative way, due to the emphasis given to *general* location knowledge.

Location accuracy was calculated on the basis of the location accuracy of each settlement depicted on the sketch map, judged against its actual geographical location, after considering a first settlement of the map as correctly located (as first settlement we understandably selected that settlement the location of which implies the greatest number of accurate locations). As inaccurate was considered a location inaccurate in terms of neighboring, or in directional terms, i.e., a location which is clearly in the wrong direction. The location accuracy ratio is equal to the ratio of the sum of accurate answers to the sum of possible answers - which in turn is equal to the ratio of the total number of settlements, i.e., both the actual and the sketch map settlements related to an accurate location on the sketch map, to the total number of the actual and map settlements.

Five degrees of location accuracy were defined: identity of the sketch map with the actual spatial organization in terms of general configuration (index greater than 90%); fidelity of the sketch map as to spatial organization (76%-90%); acceptable accuracy (61%-75%); divergence of the map from topographical reality (40%-60%); and discrepancy from reality (up to 39%).[47] In comparison to the forms of accuracy previously discussed, acceptable location accuracy should thus rather be grouped under the heading of inaccuracy. More than half of all our subjects are in the identity degree and more than two-thirds in the accuracy class, composed of the first two degrees, while the rest are divided between the three remaining degrees of the inaccuracy class. The highest figure for identity occurs in Thessaloniki (70%) and the lowest in Veria (37%); and the highest figure for the accuracy class again in Thessaloniki (82%), while the lowest in Axioupoli (56%). Compared to topological accuracy, location accuracy is on the whole considerably lower.

We checked if there are any significant relations between the location accuracy of the sketch maps and their surface and deep structures. The results - which were based on the classification: accuracy (the two higher degrees of accuracy), acceptable accuracy, and inaccuracy - were generally negative. There are only two exceptions to this general rule, both related to the deeper level of the maps, the one to the deep static level and the other to the deep dynamic level. At the deep static level, accuracy is strongly connected to the presence of the biaxial structure, since for the whole sample and the countryside, around four-fifths of the individuals using the biaxial structure have location accuracy, while inaccuracy is extremely limited among these individuals. Accuracy is also found among the individuals not using this structure, but in the whole sample less than two-thirds of them have this kind of accuracy (a share that falls to less than half in the countryside), while they represent the great majority of cases of acceptable accuracy (and especially in the inaccuracy class, where they exceed 85%). At the deep dynamic level, accuracy is related to the pendulum model in a crosstabulation replicating the one just discussed for the whole sample: the individuals using this model are practically never inaccurate, while the rest of the individuals are related mainly to the accuracy class, but also to the inaccuracy class. These regularities are not systematically repeated for the groups of the socio-semiotic programs and mainly represent trends on a general level; given that they concern only two among the fifteen deep structures, we can conclude that generally the degree of location accuracy is not influenced by the conceptual mode of structuring space.

4. Geometric accuracy

The last form of accuracy we shall examine is *geometric accuracy,* by which we mean the accuracy of a more detailed aspect of the configuration of the sketch maps than the aspect to which location accuracy corresponds. Geometric accuracy renders the resemblance of the sketch map to the actual regional organization from a point of view more complex than, and incorporating, location accuracy and more or less all the other forms of accuracy studied. Geometric accuracy refers to the accuracy of the geometric features of the sketch map, i.e., the relative locations and distances of all spatial elements, proportions, and general geometric shapes.

Geometric accuracy was evaluated as a whole according to five qualitative degrees corresponding to the degrees of location accuracy, namely: adequate rendering, the highest degree of accuracy, in which the sketch map presents close similarities with reality as rendered on a topographical map; realistic rendering, a case in which there are important similarities of the sketch map with reality but also certain differences; acceptable rendering, for which, though there appears a noticeable divergence from reality, the sense of similarity is not lost; divergence, where there are only few similarities with reality; and discrepancy, where the relation of the sketch map to reality is remote, as is for instance the case with a pure diagram. The classification of the sketch maps according to these degrees

was not achieved through exact measurements but only with rough estimates, because it was considered that this method corresponds to realistic
research exceptations based on actual social practices.

The statistical distribution of geometric accuracy in these degrees is
quite different from the distribution for location accuracy; indeed, if we
consider the distribution between the accuracy (first two degrees) and the
inaccuracy classes it is the inverse of that for location accuracy. In fact,
the share of the accuracy class is 24% for the whole sample and that of
the inaccuracy class 76%; in the latter class, discrepancy prevails with
37%. The highest figures for discrepancy occur in Veria and among
women (approximately 50%).

Geometric accuracy is significantly correlated to certain other variables
in the context of the semiotic programs. As was the case with location
accuracy, it is related to certain deep structures of the sketch maps. More
precisely, it is related to the static biaxial structure for the whole sample
and the countryside - as was also the case with location accuracy - when
three classes of accuracy are used: high accuracy (the two higher degrees), acceptable accuracy, and inaccuracy. This correlation shows that
the individuals using this structure tend to show both accuracy and inaccuracy, but are on the whole more accurate than the others, who are
markedly connected to inaccuracy. Geometric accuracy is further related
very significantly to the pendulum model, as is location accuracy, but in
a more systematic manner, since the relation holds for the whole sample
as well as for the cities, the lower middle class, men, and the mature.
What we see is that the individuals using this model tend mainly to be
accurate and then acceptably accurate, while those who do not tend
markedly to inaccuracy.

We see that on the general level of the whole sample the individuals
using the biaxial pattern and the pendulum model have higher location
and geometric accuracy. These regularities are not found systematically
among the social groups of the semiotic programs, with the exception of
the influence of the use of the pendulum model on geometric accuracy. It
seems then that the conceptual reconstruction of space through the use of
a Euclidean system of coordinates (i.e., the biaxial pattern), and even
more through zig-zag scanning, offers greater advantages than other patterns for the achievement of complex forms of accuracy.

The fact that the same sketch map patterns are correlated with both the
above forms of accuracy indicates a possible correlation between these
two forms. This is in fact what holds for the whole sample (0.01). The

individuals who are locationally inaccurate are practically all also geometrically inaccurate, and those with acceptable location accuracy occasionally achieve an equal degree of geometric accuracy though by more than four-fifths they are inaccurate. It is only the individuals with location accuracy who are able to achieve better geometric scores, and again almost half of them are geometrically inaccurate; but the one-third of them who have geometric accuracy represent practically the whole of the geometric accuracy class.

There is a very strong relation between the sophistication of the sketch maps and their geometric accuracy, a relation that systematically characterizes most social groups of the semiotic programs. More than four-fifths of the individuals who have produced less sophisticated maps are also inaccurate in their mapping, and the same is true for more than half of the individuals with maps of simple sophistication, although more than one-fifth and up to one-third of these individuals are accurate. On the other hand, more than half of the individuals with more sophisticated maps have accuracy, and the rest are divided between acceptable accuracy and inaccuracy.

We already had the occasion to point out (in Chapter 11, Section 2) that the sophistication of a sketch map, one of its stylistic aspects, depends on the graphic ability of its drawer, and we can now follow the impact of graphic ability on the geometric accuracy of the map. The case of individuals with more sophisticated maps points to the obvious conclusion that developed graphic ability may allow the precise pictorial transcoding of an accurate conceptualization of regional space, but it cannot by itself create such an accurate representation; it is limited to the role of expressing with fidelity an existing (accurate or inaccurate) regional representation. Average graphic ability may allow the transcoding of accurate representations, as can be seen from the individuals with maps of simple sophistication, but its close connection with inaccuracy seems to indicate that it tends to degrade the accuracy of certain representation in transcoding. This impression is corroborated by the individuals with the less sophisticated maps, i.e., of low graphic ability, for the very great majority of whom there is no reason whatsoever to think that they necessarily have inaccurate representations, and a part of the results for whom should thus be attributed to their awkwardness in drawing. In other words, the only possible meaning of a correlation of accuracy with graphic ability is that the latter is able up to a point to influence the former. Since topological accuracy is not subject to the same influence, we should accept that the statistical distribution in its different degrees reflects more exactly the actual distribution of conceptual accuracy. Thus, actual conceptual geometric accuracy is higher than that shown by the sketch maps.[48]

In Section 1 of Chapter 11 we divided the static surface structure of both the road and the zonal sketch maps into four categories, in ascending order of complexity of coherency: discontinuous, schematic, realistic, and elaborated; the two lower degrees of coherency compose the simple topological maps and the other two the complex topographical maps. Location accuracy is not correlated to this categorization of the static surface structure, something showing that it is independent of map coherency; only in the cities does this form of accuracy increase with complexity. The situation is totally different with geometric accuracy, which is correlated with static surface structure, generally very significantly, for all the social groups of the semiotic programs with the possible exception of the countryside. According to the form of this correlation in the whole sample, as well as in the cities (and the countryside), the discontinuous maps, although occasionally accurate, are usually inaccurate, and the schematic maps are more closely related to inaccuracy than to accuracy (four-fifths of the individuals with schematic maps are inaccurate). On the other hand, although more than half of the realistic maps are inaccurate, more than one-third of them are accurate, and more than half of the elaborated maps are also accurate, while more than one-fourth are acceptable; among the acceptable maps, the schematic maps predominate (43% - Table 12).

In a first group of variants of this regularity, the discontinuous maps are mainly or exclusively associated with acceptable accuracy (for the lower middle class and the mature) and accuracy does not occur; or exclusively associated with accuracy (middle class). In a second group of variants, the realistic maps are more closely connected than in the whole sample to accuracy (workers, women, and the young); or to the inaccuracy category (men). The overall picture from the regularity of the whole sample and its variants is that the correlation of geometric accuracy to map coherency is far from linear. Schematic maps are more closely connected to inaccuracy than the discontinuous maps that show the lowest complexity. The realistic maps are related both to inaccuracy and to accuracy but are rarely of acceptable accuracy, while on the whole the elaborated maps are usually accurate, though they may also have lower degrees of accuracy.

Table 12. The correlation of geometric accuracy with map coherency (for the whole sample, significance level .0000).

Map complexity		Geometric accuracy			
		Inaccuracy class		Accuracy class	
		Inaccuracy	Acceptable		
					Total
Discontinuous maps		**50%**	25%	25%	100%
		2%	5%	3%	3%
Schematic maps		**81%**	13%	6%	100%
		64%	**43%**	12%	48%
Realistic maps		**52%**	13%	**35%**	100%
		30%	28%	**52%**	35%
Elaborated maps		16%	**26%**	**58%**	100%
		4%	**24%**	**33%**	14%
	Total	61%	15%	24%	100%
		100%	100%	100%	100%

We should like to repeat at this point our argument (in Chapter 11, Section 1) that we should avoid confusion between map coherency and accuracy since these concepts represent two theoretically different aspects of the sketch maps, a stylistic aspect and a comparative aspect respectively. The data above corroborate our position, showing that although these two aspects are not unrelated, their overall relation is not strictly linear and when we look at the details of the relation we even discover an occasional reversal of the general trend. Thus, map coherency and geometric accuracy should be kept apart and not be confused.

On the other hand, the influence of a stylistic aspect such as coherency on accuracy brings once more to the foreground the issue of graphic ability that we encountered previously with the impact of map sophistication on geometric accuracy. Map complexity does not necessarily follow from graphic ability but may certainly be influenced by it. While, then, the diverging aspects of the regularity ruling the correlation of accuracy with complexity point to the independence of these two variables, the converging aspects appear to reveal the impact of graphic ability on accuracy.

We are now in a position to discuss certain general issues of regional accuracy. To summarize, we studied five different forms of accuracy on the basis of both linguistic and graphic material. We first presented the results for two Euclidean forms of accuracy, namely orientational (directional) accuracy and metric (i.e., distance) accuracy. We then analysed one form of topological accuracy, founded on the most primitive topological structure, the neighboring relation, and probably also involving the succession relation and reflecting relative distance knowledge. Next, we passed to location accuracy, which no longer refers to the comparative closeness of the spatial elements but does involve neighboring relations, indeed more complex than those founding topological accuracy, as well as succession relations. The association of a directional Euclidean framework with these topological relations is due to the fact that these three factors together account for the general location of spatial elements, i.e., their general configuration. Strict directional measurement should be avoided when we want to evaluate the accuracy of the knowledge of this configuration, in order to keep the evaluation within the limits of the knowledge of the general lines of the configuration. The last form of accuracy studied was geometric accuracy, which is based on the geometric resemblance of the sketch map to reality; geometric accuracy was also evaluated with rough criteria.

In sum, the forms of accuracy selected allow crucial insights into regional accuracy by referring to aspects of regional knowledge that are different and of differing complexity. Our measuring criteria and the labelling of the accuracy categories were founded on common social knowledge and not on professional map-making requirements. Thus, for example, the common man operates in orientational matters with no finer tool than a compass rose divided in eight equal parts, and it is exactly this rose that we used as the criterion for the measurement of orientational accuracy. There is no reason to doubt that language was able to render adequately the accuracy of the regional representation with reference to the forms of accuracy elicited by the questionnaire. The independence of location accuracy elicited on the basis of the sketch maps from map sophistication depending on graphic ability shows that in this case also, ability in the manipulation of the medium of expression does not interfere with semantic content. But, as we saw, geometric accuracy *is* influenced by graphic ability, with the result that the overall accuracy defined through the maps is *lower* than the actual accuracy of regional representations. Since we are mainly interested in the latter, as well as in the comparative discussion of the forms of accuracy, some means of re-dressing the geometric accuracy defined through the maps should be found in order to approximate more closely to actual geometric accuracy.

A common characteristic of the forms of accuracy studied is that they generally do not vary significantly with the social groups. The only important variations we encountered concern the settlements, especially Ormylia, the inhabitants of which show higher accuracy, and Veria, where accuracy is low. Even this isolated contrast, however, is neutralized when the two settlements are integrated with the third settlement (Thessaloniki) in the context of the settlement hierarchy network. We may speak in general lines about a national standard of accuracy. But factors other than social groups may have a direct impact on accuracy, such as the use of the compass rose in the case of orientational accuracy or that of the biaxial pattern and the pendulum model in the case of location and geometric accuracy. It is not sufficient to limit ourselves in these cases to the statement that the influences take place within an exclusively semiotic context, in the sense that some semiotic variables have an impact on some other semiotic variables, because these influences are realized within certain social groups and do not appear for other groups. Thus, such intersemiotic correlations reveal another form of the foundation of the semiotic in the social dimension.

Just as accuracy is not the privilege of particular social groups, it does not seem to be that of particular individuals. This can be seen from the lack of correlation between the forms of accuracy orally elicited and those found in the sketch maps. A probable exception are the individuals showing simultaneously the same high degree of location and geometric accuracy.

We shall end this chapter with the comparative evaluation of the forms of accuracy, but this presupposes the definition of actual geometric accuracy. We already observed that only developed graphic ability can allow the exact transcoding of the geometric properties in regional representations, while a lesser graphic ability tends to degrade geometric accuracy. Let us then assume that the statistical distribution of the actual geometric accuracy of the more sophisticated drawers, which is reflected with precision in the correlation of accuracy with sophistication, is in fact indicative of the accuracy capabilities of the whole of our subjects, capabilities that the graphic ability of the rest of the subjects did not allow to surface on their maps. In Table 13 we present together the distributions in the degrees of the different forms of accuracy for the whole sample, including the redressed geometric accuracy that should replace the accuracy delivered by the maps.

Table 13 gives a general image of the overall accuracy ranking, but some further insights may be gained from the study of the frequency-program groups. For most of these groups, the highest degree of overall accuracy is achieved in the context of the topological form and is followed by location accuracy. Nevertheless, sometimes the second rank is occupied also by, or only by, orientational accuracy, in the second case followed closely by location accuracy. Orientational accuracy is usually in the second or third rank. Metric accuracy appears with almost the same frequency in any rank from the second on. And geometric accuracy may appear in any rank from the third on, but mainly occupies the last rank. In certain groups, proficiency in stricter geometric and especially orientational matters may equal proficiency in topology, while generally proficiency in orientation is higher than that referring to distances, and the lowest degree of proficiency concerns geometric accuracy.

We observe from Table 13 that the distributions in the accuracy and inaccuracy classes do not vary much, with the exception of topological accuracy for which overall accuracy is much higher than for all the other forms of accuracy. People are more accurate in their judgments when simple topological relations are concerned. But when even simple Euclidean relations are at issue, as happens with orientational and metric accuracy (evaluated with different degrees of precision), the share of the accuracy class falls drastically from around 90% to around 60%. The distributions for these two Euclidean forms of accuracy are quite comparable.

Proficiency in matters of location accuracy holds an intermediary position between proficiency in topology and proficiency in stricter geometry. The general location of spatial elements is a rather complex representation integrating topological and Euclidean relations, but the high percentage of accurate individuals and the marked percentage of the identity category show that people appear to be able to cope with rather complex spatial realities, provided that we evaluate their knowledge of the general lines of these realities. The study of location accuracy from the regional sketch maps leads to conclusions similar to those formulated by Lynch (1960: 87) on the basis of the urban sketch maps:

> However distorted [the image], there was a strong element of topological invariance with respect to reality. It was as if the map were

Table 13. Statistical distributions for the forms of accuracy (whole sample).

Form of accuracy	Accuracy			Inaccuracy			
Orientational	important 44	accuracy — fair 19	total 63	inaccuracy 24	great inaccuracy 13		total 37
Metric	great 25	accuracy 34	total 59	inaccuracy 32	great inaccuracy 9		total 41
Topological	absolute 66	accuracy 22	total 88	inaccuracy 7	important inaccuracy 5		total 12
Location	identity 53	fidelity 16	total 69	acceptable 13	divergence 10	discrepancy 8	total 31
Geometric (map)	adequate 11	realistic 13	total 24	acceptable 15	divergence 24	discrepancy 37	total 76
Geometric (actual)	adequate 25	realistic 29	total 54	acceptable 25	divergence 13	discrepancy 8	total 46

drawn on an infinitely flexible rubber sheet .... But the arangement was usually correct, the map was rarely torn and sewn back together in another order. This continuity is necessary if the image is to be of any value.

Geometric accuracy relates to an even more complex configuration co-inciding with the topographical profile, and the overall results for it are poorer than those for location accuracy, while the percentage for the highest accuracy category is less than half of the corresponding percent-age for location accuracy. On the other hand, the statistical distribution for geometric accuracy is comparable to the distributions for orientational and metric accuracy. Thus, we discover that more or less accurate knowledge of a complex Euclidean reality is rather widely accessible to the common man, provided that realistic criteria are used for the mea-surement of accuracy. With this condition, proficiency in complex but looser geometric matters competes with proficiency in stricter though simple geometric matters.

However, the geometric proficiency of the common man should not be confused with professional proficiency. Once more, Lynch (1960: 87) is right when he observes:

The image itself was not a precise, miniaturized model of reality, re-duced in scale and consistently abstracted. As a purposive simplifica-tion, it was made by reducing, eliminating, or even adding elements to reality, by fusion and distortion, by relating and structuring the parts. It was sufficient, perhaps better, for its purpose if rearranged, distorted, 'illogical' .... directions were twisted, distances stretched or compressed, large forms so changed from their accurate scale projection as to be at first unrecognizable.

Part VI. Conclusion: The social semiotics of space

Of the different approaches allowing the analysis of a topological object as complex as a city, application of the model of communication seems to be among the most productive. Within the framework of this elementary structure, consisting of a sender-producer and a receiver-reader, we can inscribe the city as an object-message to be decoded .... the city can be considered as a text whose grammar we will have, at least partially, to construct.

A.-J. Greimas, "For a topological semiotics"

Chapter 14. Society and spatial semiosis

1. Social regulation and sociospatial groups

Not unfrequently, not to say usually, the implicit assumption in spatial semiotics is that spatial semiosis can be studied each time as a unified phenomenon and that a single semiotic structure can be defined corresponding to the external spatial system under study. There is a strong tendency in general semiotics, as also in the theory of subjectivist geography, to bypass social and even cultural divisions and search for semantic structures and processes of a universal nature. The theoretical interests of both humanistic and behavioral geography revolve to a marked degree around the issue of human and spatial universals, and this issue is quite common in the semiotic bibliography as well.

More modest is the claim of two theoretical constructs that have been very influential in semiotics, namely *épistémè* and the *culture text*. *Épistémè* is the concept used by Michel Foucault (1966:11-13) for the unreflecting epistemological knowledge and experience of a culture, which he considers to be supra-subjective. The concept of culture text, on the other hand, derives from the semiotics of culture of the Tartu-Moscow group of semioticians (see Winner & Winner 1976: 101-109, 132-141). Texts are for this approach the primary units of culture and may be either verbal or nonverbal messages, generally composed of signs. Culture is seen as analogous to a collective mechanism for the storage and processing of information, as a hierarchically structured system of semiotic systems, and as a dynamic and unified semiotic whole.

Thus, both *épistémè* and the culture text turn the attention of semiotics away from the universal and toward the cultural, and both have in fact contributed to an increased awareness among semioticians of the cultural and historical relativity of semiotic phenomena. Nevertheless, what is each time defined as a cultural whole is too wide as a framework for the study of semiosis, and sometimes exceedingly wide. The Tartu-Moscow school in conceiving culture as a unified whole assumes cultural homogeneity at the expense of internal differences, and Foucault's study of the *épistémè* of various periods of "Western culture" deals with this overgeneralized and internally heterogeneous whole in a manner which frequently tends to privilege dominant ideology to the point of reification.

But as we already pointed out in Chapter 3, semiosis is forged in the context of everyday experiences and these experiences vary with the structural positions and functions of different social groups. There are reasons to believe that the semiotic dynamics in the consumption (i.e., representation) of a spatial reality do not necessarily coincide with the dynamics of its production. We also noted in the same chapter that the spatial representations in the consumption process itself are not uniform but diverge. In fact, our own study has been focused on the semiotic consumption of social groups. This asymmetry between production and consumption, and the internal asymmetries of both, escape even Eco's (1972: 279-281) attention, in spite of the fact that he is well aware of the historical transformations of the meanings of one and the same architectural work, notably its desemantization and resemantization; at this point Eco strangely enough isolates historical relativity from sociological relativity. Sociological relativity is as a general rule forgotten both by spatial semiotics and behavioral geography, and is recuperated by the latter only at the case study level, i.e., in an ad hoc manner.

In our case, our point of departure has been a sociological theory - historical materialism - of social groups, mainly social classes, and of the processes of semiosis attached to them. Our findings corroborated this starting point throughout, but also led us beyond it. Corroboration can be found in the fact that in almost all cases the semiotic variables were found to be regulated by sociological factors. The influence of the latter appeared in both the sociosemiotic and the semiotic programs. In the sociosemiotic programs the influence mainly originates directly or indirectly from the three major sociological factors used, social class, gender, and age group, and sometimes from secondary sociological factors such as education. The many statistically significant correlations of a semiotic variable with one or more sociological factors show that the modes of meaning are not haphazard but sociologically regulated. In some cases, this collective regulation is absent and then we are obliged to have recourse to individual idiosyncrasies. Thus, sociological regulation is the rule, but sometimes the explanation of the semiotic should be sought for at the psychological level - though of course it may be due in these cases to social factors that were not taken into account in our own study.

But the influence of the sociological dimension is also inherent in the semiotic programs, since the framework of the semiotic variables that are correlated in these programs is always constituted by a particular social group. The widest of these groups is the group constituting the whole sample, which is in the narrow sense representative of Greek Central Macedonia, but may be considered as representative of Northern Greece and even the country as a whole. But the generality of this latter group should not be intepreted as implying some kind of entity escaping sociological regulation.

What led us beyond the sociological theory initially used was the specific composition of the sociological component and the relative importance of the sociological factors included therein. We had recourse to social classes, a prime mover in Marxist theory, and the city-country opposition, another Marxist concept, and from the beginning we considered that the theoretical extension of this opposition led to a third sociological factor, the settlement hierarchy. The importance of the social division into genders has not been noticed by orthodox Marxist theory, but has been pointed out - much later, it is true - by contemporary Marxist-inspired feminist studies. On the other hand, age groups are given no structural role in the Marxist theory of contemporary societies, though together with genders they figure prominently in Marxist social anthropology (as in the rest of anthropological research). Our data show that the genders and the age groups are not only active in the making of spatial meaning, but are at least equally important with the social classes. On the other hand, they also show that a whole series of other social factors play minor roles in the shaping of regional representations: education, socioprofessional categories, the degree of control over labor and the means of production, regional mobility, residential mobility, and the degree of familiarity with the region.

An equally important observation leading beyond current Marxist premises is that, though classes and genders (and age groups) shape the universe of spatial meaning, they do not do so either necessarily or usually in a direct manner. Class, gender, and age groups are general social groups, the definition of which explicitly ignores their particular geographical distribution; the assumption of orthodox Marxist theory is that class and gender will be everywhere the same (age generally not being taken into account at all). But what we found was that the influence of these groups is currently mediated by the specific character they acquire in particular places or areas.

This observation brings us to the issue of the relatively autonomous sociospatial groups. Of course, among the traditionally used general groups figure the city and the countryside, which both represent cases of sociospatial groups. But in our study we also witnessed the emergence of more specific and restricted groups, which either represent a first subdivision of the above groups (such as the metropolis, city workers, or countryside women) or relate to the specific settlements studied and thus to a second-degree subdivision (as is the case, for example, with the workers of Veria or the women of Ormylia). It was shown that any one of the sociospatial groups theoretically defined can in practice acquire autonomous status, at least in respect to the particular semiotic phenomenon studied. The significance of the presence of these more specific sociospatial groups and their importance in shaping spatial meaning can scarcely be exaggerated.

We analysed in Chapter 10, Section 1, the correlations between the use of spatial codes and social groups, and observed then that the statistically significant tendencies of the general social groups to use or avoid certain codes, or the lack of such tendencies, do not at all prescribe the tendencies of the sociospatial groups derived from them. The complementary sociospatial groups (that together constitute a general group) usually tend to both similar and different codes, but when they are related to the same codes the patterns of use differ to a greater or lesser extent. As to the parallel sociospatial groups that together form the same geographical unit, they tend to importantly overlapping sets of codes, though the patterns of use of the same code usually diverge. From this we can conclude that though the spatial discourse of parallel groups may not be identical due to the different degrees of use of the same codes, it is nevertheless comparable, since it is characterized by the significant use or avoidance of a particular code.

Our conclusion in the above section was that the geographical units present a greater homogeneity than the general social groups. This homogeneity does not necessarily imply identity, since it may well correspond to opposed semiotic tendencies (discourse on topics included in the code vs. keeping silent about them). On the other hand, the data in Chapter 8, Section 3, pointed to the possibility that disaggregation is not the only reality of the general groups, but that they may also retain their own character.

Sociospatial groups are not well accomodated by Marxist theory, but their presence has recently been noticed by geographers. For example, Richard A. Walker (1985: 186) points out that the very construction of classes is sociospatial and that "classes are necessarily constituted in and through the use of space", concluding that such a view "implies a somewhat weaker concept of class".

Three factors in the present study may have reinforced the effects of the sociospatial groups. The first is our emphasis on the differences rather than the similarities between groups. The second factor is the wide field of the semiotic phenomena studied. And the third factor is our particular orientation toward spatial ideology, for certain aspects of which we could hypothesize that they are relatively independent from the core ideology of the groups. It might even seem reasonable to suppose that spatial ideology, because of its very nature, would be crucially determined by geographical rather than social factors. This, however, does not appear to be the case. We found that the general groups are not replaced by the settlements as social units, because, in spite of the fact that the settlements comprise homogeneous groups (in the sense explained above), these groups clearly have different particular semiotic tendencies. Of course this homogeneity establishes something like a common local background. But real autonomy is indicated for a settlement only if it emerges as a unit in the sociosemiotic programs, and this has rarely been the case.[49] Neither do the general groups seem to be replaced throughout by the sociospatial groups, and thus they are apparently still able to provide a direct explanation for semiotic phenomena.

The fact remains, however, that sociospatial groups to an important degree replace the general groups as the custodians of a particular semiotic characteristic, an observation that is both theoretically and practically challenging. But it is also a fact that the sociospatial groups owe their very existence to the general groups from which they derive. Classes, genders, and age groups are spatially particularized and due to this particularization they acquire a social existence of their own *in situ*. The sociological explanation of the new character of the sociospatial groups must have recourse to the group in which they are macro-socially integrated, but the social character of the new groups may differ to a greater or lesser extent from that of the initial (macro-) social group, a difference due to the same local conditions which are also reflected in the phenomenon of parallel-group homogeneity. Under these circumstances, what is at issue is the *degree of cohesion* of the general groups and not their explanatory power. It is also clear that, if the sociospatial groups surpass orthodox Marxist explanation, they simultaneously emphasize its actuality to the extent that they show on a more local scale to what degree consciousness arises from actual experiences and everyday practices.

On the whole, the study of the processes of spatial semiosis reveals both that Marxism is a valid sociological theory and that it is in need of further elaboration.

In Chapter 5, Section 1, we opposed all the social groupings discussed above, considered as "sociological subjects", to the "semiotic subjects", i.e., sociosemiotic groupings defined (according to the law of pertinence) internally to the corpus under study. Our choice inclined emphatically towards the first approach, and this choice differentiates our *social semiotics* from Greimas' *socio-semiotics*. In fact, Greimas (Greimas & Courtés 1979: 355) believes that:

> ...les critères utilisés pour établir la stratification sociale de nos sociétés industrielles (tels que les "modes de vie": comportements vestimentaires, culinaires, habitat, etc.) paraissent relever, pour le sémioticien, de pratiques signifiantes qui appartiennent à ce qu'il considère comme le vaste domaine des sémiotiques dites non linguistiques: leur mise en corrélation avec les pratiques linguistiques est alors, pour lui, une question d'intertextualité sémiotique et non d'interdisciplinarité sociolinguistique.

> ['...the criteria used to establish the social stratification of our industrial societies (such as "lifestyles": behaviors in respect to dress, cooking, housing, etc.) seem, to the semiotician, to be related to those signifying practices which belong to what he considers as the vast domain of so-called non-linguistic semiotics: to correlate them with linguistic practices is thus, for him, a question of semiotic intertextuality and not of sociolinguistic interdisciplinarity.']

Thus, the conjuncture of semiotics with sociology is transformed, in the name of pertinence, into a purely endosemiotic issue.

On the other hand, Greimas (1986: 51) in practice makes reference to the reading of the city on the part of "tourists" and the "architectural elite":

> We can go still further, by introducing new variables and multiplying the number of possible readings of the city: we can oppose, for example, along the category *external* vs. *internal,* the reading of the user of the city to that of the visiting guest, we can distinguish a particular reading proper to the social category of tourists, even make a

typology of it, examine the aesthetic attitudes of "elites": architects or interpreters of their aesthetic aims, etc.

In spite of the semiotic terminology used, the semiotic nature of these groups is not defined and they seem to us rather as ad hoc groupings derived from a commonsense sociological approach.

Aside from the reasons already discussed for the selection of sociological subjects, there is a basic difficulty with the general use of the concept of a purely semiotic subject. This difficulty surfaces if we examine more closely the nature of our semiotic programs. In these programs two semiotic variables are correlated, and each variable includes at least two groups that might conceivably be considered as sociosemiotic groups. Let us take as an example the correlation between relevance of discourse and total code richness. There are four groups of relevance: the group of subjects with low relevance, the group with average relevance, that with high, and that with too high relevance; and four other groups of code richness: the group using many codes, the group showing an average use of codes, that with a low code use, and lastly the group using few codes. From the moment there is a significant correlation between these two variables, we may assume that each one of these eight groupings may be considered as a kind of sociosemiotic group in the Greimasean sense. We might say, for example, that the low relevance group has the characteristic of high code use, or inversely that people with high code use tend to low relevance. This reversibility may confuse the issue of which is the pertinent sociosemiotic group and which is its attribute. It would be possible to delimit a relatively autonomous sociosemiotic group if we found persistent correlations of one and the same semiotic variable with a number of other variables, which would indicate the greater stability of the groups defined by the first variable. But as we saw, this was not the case with our own data.

However, whether the data delimit an unstable sociosemiotic group or a relatively autonomous one, the fact remains that it takes shape *within* the context of a particular social group, which would seem to prevent it from being truly autonomous. Thus, in the case of relevance and code richness, the correlation is only valid for the whole sample, the cities, and the mature; it does not hold, for example, for the countryside and youth. In many such cases, even if the groupings included in these variables are promoted to the status of sociosemiotic groups, they are constituted as such only if certain exo-semiotic sociological conditions are fulfilled, a fact arguing against their autonomy.

The sociosemiotic groups Greimas has in mind are probably not found among our semiotic variables, but even if they were, by their very nature they would be sociologically delimited. Let us assume that in our case one of the two correlated variables defines the groups that Greimas himself would select as corresponding to his concept of sociosemiotic group; that this variable is actually correlated with a number of other semiotic variables, themselves connected to the representation of regional space; that we ignore the significant correlations for the other social groups and concentrate on the whole sample; and that we accept that the latter is representative of the whole of Greece. Even with this Greimasean setting and these extreme assumptions, the conclusion cannot but be that the sociosemiotic groups are actualized internally within Greece, and since we can safely assume that in any case the selection of Greek society as a unit of study would be made primarily on sociological grounds, any sociosemiotic groups derived from it cannot be considered as autonomous.

The sociological component is decisive for the study of semiosis, and because of that semiotics cannot be constituted without a sociological foundation. This same foundation should be able to account also for psychosemiotics, to which we should refer the semiotic variables that escape the lower threshold of sociological regulation. There is, however, also another exception to this conclusion, which would indicate the possibility of the constitution of sociosemiotic groups beyond social boundaries and hence of universal validity. We encountered in this book a case that might fall beyond social regulation, this time its upper threshold, and this is related to the possible existence of spatial universals in the form of the spatial logics.

If such universals actually exist, and if there are universal sociosemiotic groups and universal semiotic regularities related to them (see next section), we should search for their roots not in social conditions but in the ontogenetic field, and in this manner a bridge between spatial semiotics and biology would be created via psychology. But even if this is the case, we would be far from the current geographical approach which anchors spatial representations epistemologically in biology. Biology would be encountered at the end of the road, not at its starting point, and a mixed sociological and biological foundation would be needed in order to account for spatial representations. A mixed foundation, we might add, in which sociology would have the lion's share.

2. Social regulation and the relative autonomy of semiosis

The regulation of semiosis by social factors may theoretically follow three different models. According to the first model, sociological regulation takes the form of a general and strict regulation, in the context of which the fact that any particular semiotic trait is elevated to the rank of a significant trait or reduced to statistical insignificance, as well as the precise value of this trait, are all directly explainable sociologically. This explainability may be achieved either on a priori grounds and thus take the form of prediction, or a posteriori on the basis of the statistical data. We shall call this first model of sociological regulation, according to which the semiotic *reflects* the social, *generalized determination.* In the context of this model the social groups determine semiosis wholly and directly. If this model corresponded to the actual reality connecting the semiotic with society, the intervention of sociology in the explanation of the semiotic universe would be dominant and the main job of the semiotician would be to systematize a sociologically defined universe.

There is a second model which represents the opposite of the above model. For this model, the traits of the semiotic systems again depend on social groups, but this regulation is valid only as a general principle, which by its very generality is not usually able to explain directly the specific semiotic traits of a group. If such were the case, a general and loose logic would connect the semiotic systems with the social groups, and in general no deductive reasoning based on sociological wisdom would be in a position to lead directly from the social to the semiotic. We may call this model *loose regulation.*

It goes without saying that for such a model direct social influence is not absent, since any trait found is not a trait in general, but an attribute of a particular group. What happens is that a semiotic trait is shaped by another semiotic trait, or some such traits, and so on, but at the end of the road a social factor will be operating which anchors the semiotic in society. On the other hand, the filtering of social influences through successive semiotic levels gives the latter a continuously greater independence from the initially determinant social factor, with as a result the *relative autonomy* of the semiotic system. This oblique path leading from the social factor to the semiotic trait resists the current epistemological view of hypothesis making. It shows the need to complement this way of operating with the more general principle of *question formulation,* according to which a question is formulated without being accompanied by any positively stated hypothesis whatsoever. For this model, though so-ciology would epistemologically found semiotics, it would offer the latter only a loose framework, and the deciphering of the semiotic universe would be left almost exclusively to the semiotician.

For the third model, social regulation is not generalized but is never-theless extensive; i.e., certain semiotic traits are directly explainable so-ciologically either a priori or a posteriori as in the first model, while oth-ers are not. This model, which occupies an intermediary position be-tween the two previous ones, shall here be called *selective regulation*. This model may theoretically appear in two variants. For the first vari-ant, the socially determined semiotic traits are a series of unconnected traits, while for the second variant certain of them constitute separate sets of closely related traits, which correspond to broader structuring axes of the semiotic universe. This latter variant would indicate that a *structural regulation* unites semiosis with society. In the case of selective regula-tion, there is a continuous dialogue of semiotics with sociology, a dia-logue in which the sociological work is foundational, but the semiotic work central.

Which one of these three patterns underlies the constitution of the semiotic universe and rules its structuring? We concluded in Chapter 7, Section 3, and Chapter 10, Section 1, that there is a complex logic lead-ing from particular social groups to specific semiotic variables. In fact, in the sociosemiotic programs variables closely akin may be influenced by partly or even wholly different groups, and very heterogeneous variables by the same groups; it is implied in the first case that a group may influ-ence one variable but not its related variables. It may also happen that one and the same semiotic variable may be influenced by a series of dif-ferent sets of groups. The semiotic programs too may deliver a compa-rable image, since the same regularity between two semiotic variables may characterize some social groups, but not most of the rest of the groups. The dynamics of the sociology of semiosis does not follow a simple mechanistic model, but a highly complex one. This complex model offers the framework within which the pattern looked for is integrated.

In order to clarify which is indeed the pattern of regulation, we shall take as a test case the social group of women. According to the semiotic programs, in which the social group of women is not further disaggre-gated, women have their own regional ideological model. The nucleus of this model, composed of the toponymic code, overlaps with that of the male model, but apart from this nucleus the two models represent two radically different approaches to space. The women's model focuses on the experiential code and on urban matters. The sociosemiotic programs show that city women have a notable tendency to refer to their personal experiences, which is not the case with city men and not at all the case with country men. In the same programs, women are also shown to totally avoid in their spontaneous discourse issues concerning the social (including ethnic) origin of people, and (like men) generally avoid evaluations when referring to social differences; this attitude could be interpreted as a desire to avoid controversial issues and confrontations. Women almost totally abstain from references to political issues, a point where they differ from men, not so much city but country men. The lesser political involvement of women can also be seen from their low representation in comparison to men among the individuals feeling that they participate in, and willing to continue to offer their services for, the course of their involvement region. City women are not much interested in any kind of historical references and this is even more true for country women, in contrast to city men.

On the basis of the intertextual study of code persistence, we observed that the personal (experiential and aesthetic) codes, the set of the economic codes, and the toponymic code are significantly connected to the women's group irrespective of the particular context. Since by connection we meant in this case both the significant use and avoidance of a code by a group, code persistence reflects the persistence of a common background and not a particular semiotic tendency. The persistence of the two sets of personal and economic codes is not a particular characteristic of women, but a general characteristic of all the groups studied and was thus considered as a national trait. This is not the case with the toponymic code, which thus is shown to be another mark of female regional discourse.

Country women are significantly not concerned with the public aspect of leisure. This is not surprising, since in the Greek countryside the life of women traditionally revolves around the private domain, the public domain being male-dominated. Things are different in Thessaloniki, where there is a certain focusing on leisure, and especially with the women of Veria. The attitude of women towards economic issues is equally heterogeneous. The interests of the Thessaloniki women do not markedly comprise issues of economic development, but women in Veria hold the opposite attitude and the Ormylia women an intermediate position. The tendency of Thessaloniki women in respect to the other economic code, that of economic activities, is not statistically significant, but significant use of the code appears among women in Ormylia and is stronger in Veria. The Veria women are thus interested in economy, but they are not at all involved with ecological issues, which attract some interest on the part of the male population of Veria.

On the whole, then, the most pronounced interest in economy among women is shown by the Veria women, and they are followed by the Ormylia women. A reasonable a priori hypothesis would be that women in Greece are not interested in economic matters, as proved to be the case with politics. The metropolitan women would verify this hypothesis, but not the Veria and the Ormylia women. We believe that there is a sociological explanation also for these two groups, which however has to do with the particular nature of the two settlements and not their rank in the settlement hierarchy: this is the wealth of Veria and the economic wellbeing of Ormylia, which are felt by their inhabitants and which may be considered as providing a context encouraging economic discourse. If this explanation, which goes back to the nature of the settlements and not to that of the particular groups of women, is correct, then the groups of men in the two settlements should have tendencies comparable to the groups of women. This is what actually happens: both Ormylia and Veria men are interested in economy, and the former have the greatest involvement of the gender groups of all three settlements. What cannot be easily explained is why men in Veria are less interested in economy than women.

To these discursive tendencies of the genders we may add richness in the use of codes related to economy and society. Women tend to use fewer codes related to economy than men. In respect to the codes related to society, metropolitan women and men are respectively richer in code use than provincial or rural women and men, while in each settlement, independently of settlement rank, the female discourse is poorer in codes than the male discourse. This lesser richness of the female discourse is a trait that can be generalized to all discursive contexts.

As we saw in Chapter 9, Section 4, the correlation between the total number of codes and the number of evaluated codes in the same context, i.e., the context set by any particular question, are so persistent for the different social groups studied that it may be considered as systematic. They all reflect the same regularity: a greater number of codes is accompanied by a greater number of evaluated codes, and a more limited number of codes by fewer evaluated codes. This is equally true for men and women, as well as other groups, and may be considered as a national characteristic and as a candidate for further generalization. The correlations between the total number of codes appertaining to two different contexts are less systematic and appear especially for the whole sample, but they also follow the pattern just described. Both men and women show this pattern, but especially women, and never both for the same pair of contexts. Even less systematic are the correlations between the number of evaluated codes corresponding to two different contexts. In these correlations neither women nor men figure. Comparable in frequency are also the correlations between the number of codes in any particular context and the total number of codes in the whole interview, but they are very systematic in respect to the number of codes in the functional context; this is the only case in which they are valid for women (and also for men). If the number of all codes is replaced by the evaluated codes, practically no correlations appear.

We see that the relations deriving from pairs of different kinds of code richness do not characterize women only but also other social groups. When such a relation is valid for women, it is also valid for other groups, and it is thus never exclusive to them: it represents a characteristic of women which they share with other groups. All these relations follow the same general pattern, which is the tendency for richer or poorer code use of one kind to be associated with richer or poorer code use, respectively, of another kind.

Semiotic experience could suggest to a semiotician this hypothesis as an attribute of any social group. But this a priori general semiotic hypothesis is not able to explain why the use of the number of all codes in the crosstabulations leads to richer results than the use of evaluated codes; why the use of evaluated codes gives not only rich but the richest results when they are correlated with the number of codes in the same context; and why the correlations between the number of codes in different contexts and the total number of codes are most frequent for the functional context. Any correlation referring to code richness may be a priori expected to hold for women, but which ones are actually valid is a matter for further semiotic investigation.

The actualization of such a correlation may be due to something like a set of sociosemiotic groups of general validity if the correlation may be considered as universal. If it is widespread but not universal, the correlation may be of national validity, in which case there would be an indirect relation of the semiotic to the social, since this particular type of correlation by its nature cannot be explained directly from the social practices of the Greeks. A similar rationale covers the cases in which the correlation appears for only a few groups. An example of a persistent regularity of this kind is the case we encountered in Chapter 9, Section 3, where we studied the correlation between the frequency and the order of appearance of codes belonging to the same context, a regularity that is probably of a universal nature.

In Chapter 9, Section 5, we studied the relations between the complexity of discourse and the codes elicited in response to the question on differences within the involvement region, the question on characteristics, and the associational question. We found a whole series of significant relations, which however only concerned the context of differences. All these relations follow the same pattern: the use of a code is mainly related to high or fairly high discursive complexity, whence we concluded that particular codes may function as indices of discursive complexity. In the case of women, these codes are the economic code and set of codes, the urban code, the social codes (functioning as indices of complexity also for men), and the topological codes. Why and how these codes interfere with the complexity of female discourse is a matter for further investigation, but the fact that these regularities are shown by women points to the existence of indirect social regulation. It also holds for women that their discursive complexity is linearly related to their total code richness, something semiotically expectable, while the unexpected is that this relation does not hold for men. It is, on the other hand, sociologically expectable that women show a much lower discursive complexity than men.

City women, and especially Thessaloniki women, tend to have larger maximum diameters of the contour of the involvement region, contrary to country women who tend to small diameters. On the next two spatial scales, the sizes of the conceived wider and widest regions are linearly related for women, but this regularity also holds for men and for many other groups, and is so generalized that it can be considered as a national regularity. City women hold an exceptional position among the gender groups in that they to a very high degree conceive of their settlement as an exclusive pole. In the tendency to consider the settlement either as an exclusive or a strong pole, it is again city women that come to the foreground, followed in intensity of the tendency by city men, country men, and country women. In addition, Thessaloniki women have a strong tendency to conceive their settlement as central, and from this point of view they are comparable to city men. This trait of city people to attribute to their settlement a central regional role is an expected result of the actual function of the settlement, but the relative intensity of the trait among the spatial gender groups cannot always be directly explained sociologically.

The city-country gender groups are divided in their evaluation of the regional role of Thessaloniki. The positive attitude towards this role is mainly due to country men, who have benefits from the market and the services of the metropolis; it is echoed by country and city women. But city men do not have such a positive attitude, and the reasons may vary between Thessaloniki and Veria: there could be in the metropolis a sense of the negative effects of overcentralization of the economy and services, while the economic development of the provincial city may have established the conditions for the appearance of a feeling of competition with the metropolis.

We could, on the other hand, hardly find a sociological explanation for the fact that in terms of the spatial sign ratio of conceptual spaces (see Chapter 8, Section 2), country women and men have richer social spaces than other groups, and city men poorer functional spaces than city women. But it might be semiotically expectable that individuals with a rich or poor space of one type will also have a rich or poor space, respectively, of some other type. This regularity in fact appears, but not for the pairs of global and economic or global and functional space, and with different frequencies in the various groups for each of the other pairs of spaces. Women show this regularity only in the case of the pair of social and functional space. They show a comparable regularity for the same pair, and also for the pair of economic and functional space, in respect to the coverage ratio, which, in spite of its close connection to the spatial sign ratio (see again Chapter 8, Section 2), is much more systematically realized. Once more, then, as in the case of code richness, we encounter with conceptual spaces a phenomenon which may be attributed to an exclusively semiotic regulation, and/or to an indirect social regulation.

We shall end this presentation of the female representation of regional space with the results from the analysis of the sketch maps. While the ratio in the whole sample of simple to complex maps is 1:1, it is 2:1 in the case of women, something that seems to show that the female representation of the region is rather poor. This poverty becomes even more striking if we take into account that the corresponding ratio for men is not far from the inverse. We should of course not forget the lower degree of sophistication in comparison to men of the maps drawn by women, and that this lessened graphic ability has an impact on the complexity of the maps. In spite of this factor, however, it seems probable that there is a difference in the complexity of the structuring of the region between women and men. This conclusion is reinforced by the fact that women also show another kind of poverty: they use significantly fewer signs in their maps than men; in respect to this variable, country women show the poorest maps.

Women, contrary to men, make minimal use in their maps of the biaxial structure, which is a rather sophisticated structure. On the other hand, women as men in Veria tend to use the radial model. For women, the radial structure goes together with road maps and the central structure with zonal maps, but these relations are not exclusive to them and also hold for many other groups (indeed the first relation is shown by all the groups). For women, the use of the pendulum model goes together with higher sophistication and richness of map signs; once more this regularity is quite systematic and valid for all groups except the working class. The data above point to a relation between sophistication and richness, and this in fact proved to be the case for all groups. While the pendulum model tends to be associated with rich maps, the central structure is associated with poor maps, a regularity holding for women and also certain other groups, and the radial structure especially with medium richness maps, a regularity characterizing only women.

Women tend to use topological orientation. When they use landmarks, their introspective signifiers do not belong to the geometric class and vice versa. For women, as well as for the whole sample and the middle class, a more accurate orientation in regional space is connected to the use of astronomical orientation in the sketch maps. There is a relation between the sophistication of women's maps and their geometric accuracy, which also holds for men and many other groups. There is finally a not strictly linear relation between the complexity of map coherence and the same form of accuracy, which is shown by all the groups including women.

What, then, does the structuring of the female regional representation reveal to us in respect to the pattern of the social regulation of the semiotic? Certain main axes of structuring appear, which bring together separate observations and are sociologically explainable and thus predictable. Women are not oriented toward political discourse and the historical discourse connected to it, and tend not to be psychologically involved in sociopolitical participation; unexpectedly, however, country women are more reluctant to discuss history than city women. Women are more sensitive than men to the issue of ethnic differentiations, which they avoid in their spontaneous discourse. Their discourse is poorer than the male discourse in the codes referring to economic matters, and the metropolitan women are not at all interested in these matters. The less diffused economic environment of Veria and Ormylia, in combination with their economic wellbeing, focuses female discourse on economy, but unexpectedly more markedly in the provincial city than in the rural village. Women are not only poorer than men in economic codes, but also in social codes and that for each different settlement rank.

On the whole, female discourse is not extroverted and is not oriented towards the public domain. On the contrary, city women show an orientation towards the experiential sphere of the ego, family, and friends. The attitude of country women who are not concerned with leisure outside the private domain is a comparable trait. Country women are also preoccupied with the services provided to them and their families, an issue neutralized for city women and generally for urbanites by the availability of urban facilities. We may thus conclude that female discourse is *introverted* and *oriented to the private sphere*.

The complexity of female regional discourse is less than that of male discourse. This lower complexity is accompanied by the tendency of women towards a simpler structuring of regional space. The richness in signs of the female regional representation cannot compete with the richness of men. Women also do not make much use of the relatively elaborated biaxial structure, a point on which they differ from men. If *discursive introversion* was proved to be one of the main axes of female spatial representation, the *relatively poor structuring* of this discourse and of the geometry of the region is another such axis. Both these nuclei tend to be opposed to the corresponding nuclei of the male representation: in fact, the latter tends to revolve around the *public domain* and exhibits greater discursive and spatial complexity.

We saw that city people, as one might expect, tend to attribute to their settlement a central role and also that Thessaloniki women lead in this tendency. But, while in the cities this trait is stronger among women than among men, in the countryside the opposite is true, and no direct sociological explanation can easily be offered. Contrary to country women, Thessaloniki women show a certain interest in recreational matters, as could be expected, by why is the tendency of the Veria women towards these matters even stronger? Why, on the other hand, are Thessaloniki women richer in social codes than the Veria and Ormylia women? Why do women in general have a specific relation to the toponymic code and why do they show a tendency to use topological orientation? Why do certain particular codes function as indices of female discursive complexity? Why do country women and country men have richer social spaces in terms of the spatial sign ratio, and city women richer functional spaces than city men? It does not seem plausible that it would be possible to answer all these questions directly on sociological grounds. If this is the case, we are here confronted with semiotic data that seem to escape direct sociological explanation and determination.

The semiotic regularities delivered by the semiotic programs reveal three modes of regulation. The correlation between the radial structure and the road maps, or map sophistication and richness, is quite reasonable and valid for all ten semiotic programs, hence it can be considered as a national regularity. This regularity is shown by women, but it is also shared by all other social groups. There are two possibilities relative to it. Either it is valid only for Greece and is not further generalizable, in which case its explanation is sociological - since it is limited by the social context of Greece - and in all probability indirect; or it is generalizable, which seems quite plausible, in which case we are here dealing with a universal mechanism of semiosis which would be connected to a set of sociosemiotic groups of general validity, and the form of regulation would be semiotic. A similar case is encountered in the relation between the sizes of the wider and widest regions, or map sophistication and geometric accuracy, though here the relation is not valid for three of the ten semiotic programs. This means that it is reasonable to expect that this relation should occur in all groups, and thus also among women (as actually happens), but also that certain groups may fail to realize it in a statistically significant manner, due to some social or a combination of social and semiotic factors - or perhaps even to chance.

Far more volatile is the reasonable, but too broadly formulated, expectation that there should be a significant relation between the richness of different kinds of codes. It revealed as we saw extremely intricate paths of realization and nonrealization, and some broad patterns the understanding of which needs further research in all directions. Usually, the frequency of realization among the social groups of any particular form of this relation is low. Such low frequencies may also appear in respect to other isolated relations, which may in such cases be regulated directly or indirectly by the group where they appear.

We are now in a position to draw our final conclusions on the social regulation of semiosis. Many individual semiotic variables are socially determined. Whole sets of such individual variables are grouped together, constituting semiotic axes derived directly from the social. Other variables escape direct social determination. There are mixed cases in which the general tendency of a trait is due to a social factor, but its relative intensity cannot be socially explained. In these cases, while the general lines of the semiotic phenomenon are sociologically explainable, its specific form cannot be. When, finally, two semiotic variables are significantly related, the interpretation of their pattern is, depending on the case, indirectly or directly social, or purely semiotic. Thus, the regulation of semiosis by society does not follow either the model of generalized determination or that of loose regulation. Leaving apart purely semiotic regulation, it is a selective regulation and especially a structural regulation, accomodating both determination by the social and (relative) autonomy of the semiotic.

3. Semiotics of the region

According to Greimas and Courtés (1979: 66-67, 139, 183), the context of a text is a another text preceding or accompanying this text and influencing its meaning. The context may be linguistic, or may be extralinguistic and situational, i.e., the pragmatic conditions of enunciation. In our case, the linguistic context activates the referential function of the text and acts as a constraint, since it is a request for information on a particular topic proposed by the interviewer. Eco (1972: 57) includes in the context the knowledge of the individual creating the text. But whether Greimas, Eco, or M.A.K. Halliday (1978: 188-189, 191), they all analyse context as a purely semiotic reality. The social regulation of semiosis extends the concept of context and reveals the existence of a social context, wider than the semiotic, which operates through the mediation of the ideology of the creator of a text. It is only in the case of universal semiotic structures that it is possible to bypass the social context and operate exclusively on an ideological level rooted in biology.

The result of the existence of social regulation and the social context is the group sensitivity of the semiotic message, a sensitivity noted in

Chapter 10, Section 2. We also pointed out in this section the occurence of the opposite phenomenon, group insensitivity, which may in extreme cases be due to universal semiotic structures. The semiotic context appears in our research primarily in its referential effects, since it essentially coincides with the different questions of the questionnaire. In the cited section we noted the existence of certain context insensitive codes, but also the very widespread phenomenon of context sensitivity. On the whole, group and context sensitivity are the cause of the proliferation of regional micro-discourses. There is not one single regional discourse in Greece, but a complex network of different discourses, complementary and opposed.

Context sensitivity has an impact both on the structure of regional micro-discourses and on the value judgments it includes. As we saw in Chapter 6, Section 5, when the subjects are invited directly to pronounce holistic value judgments, their evaluations are as a whole far less shaded and more polarized. This explicit context draws an involved judgment and this kind of judgment is sentimental, warm. On the other hand, the implicit call for judgments sets off a relatively unemotional response accompanied by a much subtler cool judgment. Warm and cool judgments represent the two judgmental extremes between which oscillate personal evaluations - and they oscillate quite freely. We should not, however, equate cool judgments only with realism and warm judgments with subjectivity, but should accept the possibility of cool subjectivity and of sentimental realism.

As there is no one unified regional discourse, there is also no single and unified conceptual space, as we saw in Chapter 8. There are probably as many conceptual spaces as there are spatial codes, and the study of the economic, the social, and the functional spaces showed us that these spaces may diverge markedly for the same person and that non-isomorphism is their usual pattern. We considered that this situation upsets the established wisdom in the field of the semiotics of space, which is founded on the hypothesis of the existence of one unified space, and necessitates the concept of the semiotics of *spaces*. But then the next epistemological issue is the question whether such a semiotics can remain unified, or whether it would fragment into a series of parallel, semi-independent semiotics.

We called these spaces - each defined in the context of a different code, i.e., according to a (narrow) pertinence - analytical spaces and we elicited them on the basis of particular questions inviting our subjects to hold a micro-discourse on the pertinent level. All these spaces, then, represent partial aspects of what one would innocently consider as *the* regional space, different components of the "social environment". One of these components presents the peculiarity of being general in its partiality. We are referring here to what we called global space, which was elicited without placing any constraint on the pertinences to be selected by the subject. This space proved to be richer in codes than the analytical spaces, but not in the number of signifiers or in its other characteristics.

The signifiers of the active global and analytical spaces do not cover the whole of the spatial representation of an individual. If our essential contact with our research subjects was not limited to the interview time, but extended to permit a better acquaintance with them, they would undoubtedly have offered us complementary information on their regional knowledge. We do not think, however, that this lacuna is damaging to our findings. Regional performance may be considered as having two aspects: one active aspect, concentrating regional experience par excellence, and one passive aspect, relating to the encyclopedic knowledge of a subject. There is every reason to believe that the clearcut contexts offered to our subjects and the spontaneity of their responses liberated a mechanism known in linguistics and psychology, which is that the aspects of a topic which are most significant to a subject are mentioned first in his/her discourse; an empirical corroboration of this mechanism was given in the present study by the systematic relation between the frequency and the order of appearance of the codes of regional representation. This would give the resulting active performance something of an exemplary character, presenting what the subject him/herself would consider as *the* proper conception of the region. Under these circumstances, much of the complementary information that a longer period of exposure might have given us would come under the heading of encyclopedic knowledge of space, not active regional representation.

The complexity of the composition of the signifiers of the spatial representation parallels the complexity of the code structuring of regional micro-discourses and that of the fluctuation of value judgments. Through this intricate structuring and variability of the universe of regional representations, certain stable points of reference nevertheless emerged. One such stable point is represented by the grid of the 32 regional codes located, for which our data showed that it encompasses the fundamental semantic components structuring the discourse on the regional environment. This grid functions as the cultural pool which the social groups and subjects draw on in their regional discourse. The important overlapping of this grid with the code grid ruling urban discourse in contemporary France allowed us to conclude (in Chapter 9, Section 1), first that the semantics of the macro-environment, regional or urban, is ruled by a unified spatial language, and second that the language delivered by our data approximates the language of contemporary Western culture in general. This concept of a general spatial language of Western culture belongs to the level, to use a Foucaultean term, of a spatial *épistémè* of this culture. Manifestly this level of analysis cannot be ignored, but its discursive structures should not be used to neutralize the variety of and discrepancy between the regional, local, and generally group spatial discourses.

We discussed in the previous section the eventuality that regularities found in Central Macedonia could belong to a stock of universal mechanisms of semiosis; the possibility of this extrapolation was founded on the specific content of these mechanisms and it is in this manner that the social and geographical limitations of the data were bypassed. In the case of the above cultural grid, our views were more moderate and we claimed for our grid the status of a Western spatial language. Could we advance one more step and claim for it a universal status? The answer is definitely no. Even such an overgeneralized concept as that of the spatial *épistémè* of precapitalist societies allows us to observe that in these societies the dominant spatial codes are the mythico-religious, the cosmological, the anthropomorphic, the temporal, and frequently the social and political codes, which presuppose an approach to the environment radically different from that of Western culture. Internally to this broad precapitalist spatial *épistémè,* there are in addition important differentiations as a function of structurally different types of society (see Lagopoulos 1983: 280-284, 288, 291-292 and 1977: 58).

The fact that the Western spatial language offers a framework for both regional and urban discourses poses the epistemological issue of the continuity between regional and urban semiotics. Are they to be conceived as two different fields of spatial semiotics or do they together constitute one unified area of spatial semiotics? The same issue is possed by the analysis of the sketch maps, to the extent that it demonstrates the possibility of using the same concepts for both regional and urban maps. And the same happens with spatial logics, which apply equally to the region and the settlement. There is a general tendency among the semioticians of space to consider the conception of space in general as constituting a single epistemological object, a tendency which does not differentiate between architectural, urban, and regional semiotics, and may arrive at the extreme of including in a single semiotics even cosmology or drawing. What for these semioticians unites all these heterogeneous fields is manifestly the formalist criterion of the visual spatial extension of the signifier. But this tendency ignores the obvious structural and functional differences between many of these systems, differences that go back to their social conditions of production and consumption. If the formalist criterion brings together these different fields, the social dynamics separate them, and perhaps create more organic grouping with other systems not falling under a single formal semiotics (we might think, for example, of the relations between cinema and literature).

Greimas (Greimas 1976: 129-136, 141, 147-150; Greimas & Courtés 1979: 132-134, 281-282) is more cautious than other semioticians in his epistemological construction of the semiotics of space. Initially, he warns the reader that he restricts his proposal to the visual dimension. Then he classifies the *"sémiotique de l'espace"* as one of the two branches of visual semiotics, differentiating it from the other branch, planar semiotics. The semiotics of space or topological semiotics studies three-dimensional "topological" objects (we would say objects relating to geographical space), while planar semiotics deals with two-dimensional planes including graphic representations. Finally, Greimas rightly makes a new distinction, this time internal to the semiotics of space, between urban and architectural semiotics, and considers the former as a particular semiotics concerned with a particular class of topological objects, cities; he also considers architectural semiotics as only an auxiliary aspect of urban semiotics.

It could be argued that a similar distinction should be maintained between urban and regional semiotics. In spite of their connection, the settlement and the region are different as exo-semiotic social realities, and these differences point to the possibility of a different appropriation on the part of the subject. As a consequence, practical wisdom advises us to keep regional and urban (or more generally settlement) semiotics apart. On the other hand, the spatial language and the spatial logics, as well as the analysis of the sketch maps, create a strong bridge between regional and settlement semiotics. The actual differentiation between an urban and a regional entity is not always clearcut, and, as we saw, conceptually the involvement region studied was revealed to refer to a micro-region, more or less directly connected to the settlement. We may thus conclude that, at least concerning micro-regional semiotics, it has such links with settlement semiotics that the two together may be treated for the time being as a loose whole.

A second stable point in the midst of the complexity of regional micro-discourses is the pair of opposed modes and models of apprehending the region, the descriptive objectivist and the expressive subjectivist. As we saw in Chapter 9, Sections 2 and 3, these models are persistent, since they appear in two different but complementary aspects, as aggregate models on the general level of the abstract collective text and as internal models of the concrete individual texts. They are also persistent in that they characterize all social groups, something showing that they form part of their semiotic competence. The substance of the objectivist model revolves around social and economic issues and the built environment, and its nucleus consists of a preoccupation with economic activities, the natural environment, and lifestyle; while the substance of the subjectivist model has at its core personal experiences and on the periphery social and economic issues, and the nucleus of this model extends from a similar core to the natural environment, leisure, aesthetics, economic activities, and lifestyle. The objectivist model may be accompanied by multi-codal or oligo-codal discourse, while the subjectivist by an oligo-codal discourse in the hierarchical structuring of which the importance of the experiential code produces a tendency toward the mono-codal. As we observed in Chapter 9, though the two models are contrasted, they are not polarized and exclusive: they present an overlapping from which they tend in opposite directions. The objectivist model marginalizes subjective experience without rejecting it, and the subjectivist deals with the outside world without centering on it. The focus of the overlapping of the two models is the preoccupation with the natural environment. Thus, both models follow from the grid of the 32 spatial codes, but they differ radically in the hierarchical structuring of their codes.

The contrast of these two models reminds us of the two poles of the field of value judgments, the cool and the warm judgments, and this similarity is not accidental. The subjectivist model is, as we saw, founded on the experiential code. As we observed in Chapter 9, Section 2, on the basis of the analysis of code evaluations, this code is oriented toward warm evaluations, indeed of the positive type. On the contrary, in the objectivist model, not only is this code underrepresented, but also its orientation varies greatly. We also noted the same connection of the warm evaluations with the experiential code when we studied, in Chapter

7, Section 1, the themes connected to the former. On the whole, two profound modes of experiencing the region emerge, the cool and the warm mode, showing that the experience of space is not monolithic, but contextually adaptable and flexible.

A third stable point contrasting to the variability of regional representations are the possible universal semiotic structures, to which we already made reference in this chapter and among which the spatial logics present the greatest interest for our research. These spatial logics (studied in Chapter 11, Section 5) are the fundamental patterns according to which space is conceptually structured. They cover a field from the most primitive pattern, the central pattern, through the concentric, the radial, the serial, and the axial patterns to the most sophisticated biaxial pattern. We saw that these spatial logics incorporate elementary semantic relations presiding over spatial representations in ontogenetic development, and are described by elementary geometric concepts. To the same spatial logics belong the models of spatial organization used by precapitalist - historical and "primitive" - societies.

It goes without saying that another stable point is offered by the very framework that allowed us to study the variability of regional representations. This framework is built into in every corner of our study and consists of the *semiotic variables* selected and the values into which each variable is articulated, or otherwise the *semiotic typologies*. Such a typology is produced, for example, by the classification of the grades of evaluations, discursive complexity, or the surface static structures of the sketch maps, or the classification of the latter according to the nature of their signifiers as abstract or naturalistic.

The focus of our research, which allowed us to pursue the social dynamics of regional representations and the universe and structuring of these representations, has been the involvement region, the region considered as intimately connected to the home settlement. Region and settlement were each conceived in very different ways by our subjects, something on the one hand showing their relativity in conception, and on the other leading to spatial delimitations frequently running against professional standards. We discovered in Chapter 6, Section 3, that the involvement region is linked directly to the individual and is thus self-referential and ego-centered, while the wider and widest regions outside it tend to be referred by the subjects to their settlement as a depersonalized point of reference. The involvement region is a subjective creation, while the conception of the other two regions is more strongly constrained by actual spatial organization. The construction of these two regions seems to take place through the mediation of indirect information and social stereotypes. Thus, the wider and the widest regions are more abstract spatial entities than the involvement region.

The strong involvement of people, on the other hand, with their involvement region is shown by their strong attachment to it, indicated by the positive evaluations they use for this region. The involvement region competes with the settlement in respect to positive evaluations, which fall lower the further we get from the involvement region (see Chapter 7, Section 1). This valorization of the involvement region reveals an identification with it, a feeling of belonging to it and being integrated into the local collectivity. In this manner, the involvement region is existentially recuperated as the space par excellence, the *place*. Of course, this is the dominant trend and other modes of evaluation of the involvement region are possible, either more distanced and abstract, or disillusioned and even, occasionally, hostile.

The conceptual construction of the involvement region is an active semiotic construction. It is crucially founded upon socialized personal practices. These practices underlie regional semiosis and are the cause of the semantization or non-semantization of the regional landscape in the broadest sense. In other words, it is the socialization of this landscape that makes possible the emergence of the semiotic universe. Regional practices are various; one such practice is regional trips, which as we saw in Chapter 6, Section 2, explain up to a point the formation and the geometry of the involvement region. Even remote visual contact may be related to this complex of practices and contribute to the semiotic articulation of the involvement region. Though the involvement region is an experienced region, it is not uniformly semantized throughout its whole extent, but is the field of an interplay between meaningfulness and voids of meaning.

4. Poetics of the region

In the previous section we had occasion to mention the referential function of regional semiosis. The referential function in one of the six functions of language identified by Roman Jakobson (1963: 213-220) and related by him to various aspects of the model of communication. Semioticians have often noted that these six functions are not limited to natural language but may occur in other semiotic systems as well, and it is of some interest to examine to what extent thay appear in the semiotics of the region.

Our study was designed to explore a spatial semiotic system, the conception of regional space, through the use of two other semiotic systems - natural language and sketch maps - more amenable to manipulation by the subjects. We thus need to distinguish rather carefully between the functional properties of these two auxiliary systems, and the functional properties of conceptual regional space itself as a semiotic system, and it may not always by possible to determine with exactitude whether we should ascribe a particular functional effect to regional discourse, to the iconic system of the sketch maps, or to conceptual space as such.[50]

We already noted the occurrence of the referential function, clearly in evidence both in regional discourse and in the sketch maps, and evidently also a function of conceptual space itself, since our subjects systematically constructed their conceptions of the region through the use of signs with real-world referents. They represent it with greater or lesser accuracy (see Chapter 13, Section 4), which reflects a higher or lower ability to reconstitute internally the external environment. Of Jakobson's other functions, the phatic and the persuasive (or conative), when they occur in our interview material, seem to be aspects of the linguistic system of the interview (i.e., following from the interactions between subject and interviewer) rather than aspects of regional semiosis. It is true that Eco (1972: 271) finds all six of Jakobson's functions in architectural semiotics, and it might perhaps be possible to think of a conative function of regional space - the awareness of the presence of a mountain persuading us to choose another route, for instance - or to see the home settlement as expressing a phatic "I am here" message. However, the fact remains that these functions were not much in evidence in our material.

A metalinguistic, or rather metasemiotic, function is built into the research framework itself, since two semiotic systems, natural language and the sketch maps, are used to "speak about" - to signify - another semiotic system, the region in conception (cf. Greimas 1976: 155-156). Metalinguistic or metasemiotic references are also common within each separate system: the subjects explain "what they mean" by something they have already said, or use written labels to identify graphic elements of the sketch map. More marked, on all levels, is the expressive or emotive function, the function corresponding to the emotional attitude of the subject vis-a-vis his/her region. In regional discourse, the vehicle of this function is the set of personal codes, primarily the experiential code but also the aesthetic, and the function predominates precisely in those contexts which elicit discourses where the experiential code is prominent, i.e., the associational question (Chapter 9, Sections 2 and 3). There can be little doubt that the emotive function is a function of conceptual space itself (and not just of regional discourse). It is clearly part of the pattern of evaluation of space, notably the warm judgments on the settlement and the involvement region (Chapter 7, Section 1).

Of particular interest is also the poetic function of regional space, an aspect that has commanded our attention repeatedly in this study. The poetic function has always held a special attraction for semioticians, since it is the function which concentrates on the message itself, not to express or inform but to explore its possibilities as a semiotic phenomenon, as a set of signifiers linked to a set of signifieds. Jakobson himself (1963: 218-219) was the first to point out that the poetic function is by no means limited to the socially recognized aesthetic forms of discourse - i.e., to art - but occurs in many different uses of language. Nonetheless it was something of a surprise to us to discover just how repounded the poetic function is in such a seemingly commonplace and practical semiotic system as that of regional space.

The complex semiotic universe of the regional environment is not a hypothetical construction made by us in the name of our subjects, nor does it correspond to conceptions held by intellectuals or specialists - theoreticians or managers - of space. On the contrary, this universe is constructed by real social groups, composed of common men and women, who invest part of their psychology in what they consider to be their region. We saw that this universe is not some sort of mirror image, mechanically produced by contact with an outside reality. It is a universe not reflected but created; created by ordinary people, and created not through what we usually valorize as noble experiences - such as the heroic, the aesthetic, or the unique - but eminently through the everyday experience of a usually commonplace reality. The conception of the region is the locus of an encouter between external reality (people speak about existing settlements, inhabitants, and ecological features), the specific character of social groups (deriving from their practices), the social dynamics of semiosis which they create, and probably the dynamics of semiosis as such (universals). The conception of the region is literally an *interpretation* of reality, a semiotic *re-construction* of it.

This reconstruction forms part of the wider world view of a group; it actually constitutes its world view of its intimate environment. It is not simple, naive, chaotic, or unpoetic, but a structured and largely coherent whole. It synthesizes two contrasting and complementary approaches to the region, the "cool" and the "warm" approach, the *ratio* and the *anima*. The poetic function of regional conception becomes possible precisely because this conception is a *text,* a complex construct investing the world with meaning. Every aspect of regional representation is not necessarily obviously aesthetic or markedly complex, but on the whole the poetic function of the regional text, including the aesthetic view of the region, is as evident as is the general complexity of the structure of regional representations and regional space.

The most obvious place to look for the poetic function of regional semiosis is perhaps in regional discourse. We have already noted (in Chapter 9, Section 5) the not infrequent use of metaphor by our subjects. Metaphors in regional discourse are generally not a purely discursive phenomenon; quite typically, it is precisely a *spatial* element that is picked up by language and invested with a multiplicity of meanings which are also generally spatial in nature. The use of metaphor produces a semantic density, both in the discourse and in the regional conception, very exactly comparable to the concentration of meaning achieved in poetry, and was, as we saw, considered in our study as one of the main forms of semantic complexity. But we should note that it is not only subjects with high discursive complexity who use metaphor. The use of metaphor is quite repounded among our subjects, and instances of it may occur in discourse which is in other respects of rather low complexity. Richness of code use (Chapter 9, Section 4) is another area in which the poetic function may emerge, multiplying the kinds of meaning invested in regional space and creating a rich texture and depth of regional experience. Neither complexity nor richness are the exclusive characteristics of a semiotic elite: our subjects tended to show rather high values for both of these, and (with the exception of men) no privileged group emerged as possessing these qualities to an exceptional degree, though certain individuals in all groups apparently do.

The poetic function is also inherent in certain aspects of the sketch maps, notably in those aspects which (Chapter 11, Sections 1 and 2) may be considered as stylistic. These features - choice of predominant element, mode of development, richness, complexity of coherence and sophistication - are the ones which determine the "look" of the maps, their visual appearance; we compared some of them to analogous features of literary style, such as the use of dialectal elements, narrative technique, or realism. The sketch map, like the regional discourse, is a coherent text susceptible of elaboration according to aesthetic criteria; it is not a mechanical reproduction but a dynamic recreation. With the exception of complexity of coherence and sophistication, which as we saw depend on graphic ability, the other stylistic aspects of the sketch map seem to derive from the poetic function of actual regional representation. Once again, there were few significant differences between groups in the use of these features; with the exception of those which are dependent on graphic ability, where men were systematically superior to women, the ability to work with spatial features to produce aesthetic effects is apparently evenly distributed among social groups.

We found that our subjects used a set of different perspectives on the region: the abstract bird's-eye perspective and the concrete eye-level or diagonal perspective. The use of bird's-eye perspective is prominent in the semi-topographical maps and the semi-topographical maps with naturalistic signifiers, conveying a regional space conceived in an abstract, maplike manner. Some of our subjects, however, conceive of their region predominantly through the use of naturalistic signifiers seen from an eye-level or diagonal perspective, rather in the manner of a naive painting. When our perspectives on space are integrated into a painting or a film, they imply aesthetic choices; the same should manifestly be the case when they form part of our regional representations. The combination of a close perspective with the focused approach of a specific regional image (Chapter 12, Section 4) can incarnate a profoundly emotional personal experience. But regional images can also produce cityscapes and architectural wholes; landscapes, seascapes, and natural micro-environments; crowd images and portraits. Regional images are thus closely related to classical themes of the visual arts, painting and photography certainly, but probably also film, television, and advertising.

A particularly intriguing emergence of the poetic function occurred when, in Chapter 12, Section 2, we argued for the Gestalt nature of the introspective signifier. We then saw that quite a few of our subjects rendered the overall shape of their region in terms of metaphorical descriptions. Some of these are poetic in a conventional sense: the peninsula of Chalkidiki with its fragmented coastline is thought of as lace, or the city of Thessaloniki spreading out on either side of its central axis is imagined as a butterfly - or, in a more pessimistic mood, as a bat. Other descriptions make use of marked traditional elements: to see your village surrounded by mountains as a sheepfold conveys a familiar and rather charming symbolism of enclosing and protecting warmth. But there is much to be said for the poetic quality of less conventional metaphors. To think of your region as a frying pan or a sausage may not be sanctioned by traditional aesthetics, but it does draw attention in a startlingly effective manner to the form of the signifier (focusing on the message for its own sake, as Jakobson defines the poetic function). It also juxtaposes two widely heterogeneous categories - kitchen utensils or foodstuffs with an entire geographical area - that nonetheless are found to be similar in some aspect, thus momentarily forcing us to reorganize our semantic universe in a manner often held to be one of the essential qualities of art. There is no reason to feel that the poetic metaphors used by ordinary men and women should always be conventional, or to promote the Romantic school at the expense of Surrealism in regional poetics.

This is not the first time it will be observed that the distinction between the aesthetic and the ordinary, between art and non-art, is a matter of social convention.[51] One of the advantages of a semiotic approach to conceptual space is precisely its built-in awareness of the textual nature of this space (an awareness not shared by geography or psychology, which habitually ignore symbolism, sentiment, and aesthetic values in their analysis of spatial meaning). This approach to the elements of space as part of a *text,* the concept of text implying that of *context,* is the theoretical framework which makes possible an awareness of the presence of the poetic function in many different forms, frequently surpassing the ones conventionally recognized as aesthetic. The semiotics of the region is inseparable from a poetics of the region, a poetics of the ordinary. The poetic is part of the ordinary, and thus its analysis is part of any semiotic analysis.

A poetics of the ordinary also implies a poetics available for the use of ordinary people. Just as the conception of space is not the privileged domaine of professional geographers, so the symbolism of space, its emotional significance, and its aesthetics are not the exclusive province of trained intellectuals. Though obviously the wider exposure and the intellectual exercise of professional training has an impact on the semiotic abilities of conceptualizing and rendering - linguistically or graphically - space, it is evident that such training is not the only way in which an individual may have access to the semiotic universe of space. In fact, the semiotician or geographer is haunted by the metasemiotic function at the expense of more immediate forms of experience of space. To the extent that the semiotic consumption of space remains an active and creative process in which anyone can engage - and does not become an essentially passive acceptance of ready-made models produced by the mass media - it will apparently be one of the fields in which members of all social groups may develop and demonstrate their creativity, forming their general as well as poetic understanding of the world around them, and sharing it through communication with others. All of society is the richer thereby.

Notes

1. By American semiotics we do not mean here semiotics in the United States in general, a large part of which grew out of the French tradition, but the specific American tradition in semiotics which took shape under the influence of the other major source of contemporary semiotics, the American philosopher Charles Sanders Peirce (1839-1914), whose pragmatism included *semeiotic* as the study of logic.
2. The roots of the concept of geosophy are to be found in Wright's views as far back as 1925 (Koelsch 1976: 63).
3. In fact, phenomenology would be interested in the subjective experience as achieved after the purification of the subject of knowledge from all a priori assumptions. One does not need to be a Popperian to realize that this is manifestly impossible.
4. For a critique of the transfer of the approaches of the natural sciences to geography, see Relph (1981: 135-136), who labels the resulting geography "scientistic", and Ley (1981: 212-214).
5. Lynch also makes reference to the possible existence of "a series of public images" (Lynch 1960: 46), but does not develop this remark further.
6. We have focused in the presentation of our theory of space on modern societies, but we believe that it is applicable *mutatis mutandis* to all societies, though this is not the place to discuss the efficacy of Marxism for the study of precapitalist societies.
7. There are various ways of transliterating Greek place names when using the Latin alphabet. We have chosen transliterations very close to modern Greek pronunciation, but have indicated in parenthesis alternative forms which may appear on some maps (for example, Veria is also found spelled Beroia, the Aliakmon river sometimes appears as Haliakmon, etc.). An optional final -s or -n, or final -e instead of -i, were felt to be no serious obstacle to recognition of a place name.
8. This discussion of the geography and history of Macedonia is based primarily on Sakellariou 1982, Vakalopoulos 1969, and Jelavich 1983; the reader who wishes more detailed information is referred to these sources, and to the extensive bibliographies which they contain.
9. These concepts refer to the social process of production, which should be distinguished from the technical process with its corresponding technical division of labor, i.e., the division of tasks in the interior of the productive unit, a division belonging to the productive forces. While the technical division of labor refers to the relation of society with nature, the social relations of production refer to the relations among social beings.
10. The sketch maps correspond to the visual sensory modality and manifestly this modality is not the only one through which regional or any other kind of

space, or indeed the world in general, is apprehended (see also Greimas 1976: 139; Greimas & Courtés 1979: 133; Pocock 1975: 11). But undoubtedly this modality holds a dominant position in respect to the others, at least after an early stage of biological development.

11. From now on, the relations presented will be significant at the 0.05 level of significance if not otherwise indicated. When they are significant at the 0.01 level, this will be indicated by (0.01), or by expressions such as "very strong relation" or "very significant".

12. Evans, Marrero and Butler (1981: 88) use a similar procedure: they calculate for each sketch map of their sample the number of signs belonging to the three paradigmatic categories (paths, landmarks, and nodes) into which the signs of the maps were classified.

13. Grouped categories were used, namely categories 1 and 2; 3 and 4; 5; and 6 for the second region; and categories 1; 2 and 3; 4 and 5; 6 and 7 for the third - see Table 5.

14. National characteristic or tendency should here be understood not in a statistical but in a structural sense, since our sample is not proportional.

15. This recognition of a settlement as a center, the notions of polarizing and being polarized, the multiplicity of centers, and the double function of a settlement as polarizing and polarized are also acknowledged by Pellegrino et al. (1983: 27, 69, 107, 134).

16. The frequency distributions for all variables used were calculated for fourteen social groups (the whole sample; the cities and the countryside; the four settlements; the three social classes; the two genders; and the two age groups), which when discussing these distributions we shall refer to as frequency-program groups.

17. This is a rather unorthodox procedure in semiotics, since semioticians usually stay within the semiotic pertinence and ignore the referent, i.e., the real world, in their analysis. We would concede that semiotics must be constituted on the basis of the law of pertinence, that is, the epistemological definition of its point of view, but we are reluctant to isolate it in positivist fashion from either its sociological context - as we made clear from the very start of this study - or its relations to the real world. This is not to imply the belief that it is possible to have an absolute knowledge of reality, but we do think that a relative, historically bounded knowledge is possible by using metalinguistic means.

18. We did not attempt to elicit evaluations concerning the widest region since, given its remoteness, we felt we would be inviting our interviewees to a rather abstract exercise. Instead, as we shall see immediately below, we suggested an equally remote spatial entity, Northern Greece, on the grounds of its socially sanctified and historical character.

19. Some statistical data will help in understanding the relation of the predefined entities to the organic spatial entities. On the basis of the whole sample, there

is a very limited identification (5%) of the nomos with the involvement region, i.e., only 5% of the involvement regions are of the size of the nomos, and the nomos generally follows the involvement region as a spatial entity, as the wider region also does. If, however, we compare the wider region with the nomos, for 28% of the interviewees (36% of those for whom there exists a wider region) the wider region coincides with the nomos; the rest of the wider regions are divided between smaller and larger sizes. As for the comparison of Northern Greece with the wider regions, the wider region can in some cases be identical with Northern Greece or even (in 6% of the cases) exceed it in size.

20. In Chapter 2, Section 2, we saw that Osgood's semantic scales include seven grades (Osgood, Suci & Tannenbaum 1957: 28-29, 83). If x and y are the two polar terms of a semantic scale, the first position in the scale equals "extremely x", the second "quite x", and the third "slightly x"; next comes "neither x nor y", which is grouped together with "equally x and y"; then follow, in a manner directly opposed to the first three positions, "slightly y", "quite y", and "extremely y". We used a similar scale for the characterization of the non-holistic evaluations.

Between the polar terms of positive or negative evaluation, we include eight grades. The first three grades (in order of intensity: positive orientation; positive tendency; and positive synthesis of opposites) and the last three grades (negative synthesis of opposites; negative tendency; and negative orientation) correspond closely to the six grades of Osgood's opposed pairs. In the center of the scale we place the synthesis of opposites, corresponding to Osgood's "equally x and y". Our eighth grade is also in the center and concerns evaluations which are neutral or tend to neutrality. We mean by neutral the lack of value judgments and a discourse of purely descriptive statements. Oddly, this term is used by Osgood and his collaborators for the case we called synthesis of opposites. Apart from the misinterpretation of synthesis as neutrality, the authors wrongly equate it typologically with complete irrelevance ("neither x nor y").

As is apparent, we replace the adverbs of Osgood and his collaborators, which appertain to holistic judgments, with descriptive terms. The reason is that our scale was constructed for composite evaluations, which were derived from a preexisting set of holistic evaluations. These were formulated as a function of a set of codes corresponding to the spatial entity each time under study, on a five-grade scale, again with descriptive terms (very positive evaluation; positive; neutral; negative; very negative).

The evaluations elicited by the direct questions were formulated by the interviewees according to a six-grade scale, closely related to that of Osgood and his collaborators. In the case of the evaluations of Northern Greece, one scale has five grades and develops between the two terms of Northern Greek and Greek, which are not necessarily opposite but may be experienced as such. The other scale is a three-grade one and its middle grade overlaps to a certain degree with the second and fourth grades of the previous scale.

21. We redressed distribution 2 of evaluations for the settlement by using the percentage for the neutral position of distribution 3 and distributing the difference (considered as people who would have expressed value judgments if they had been asked to do so) proportionally among the percentages in the other positions. A similar technique was used for the wider region, though here the data for the neutral position were defined by subtracting and proportionally distributing the percentage of people who do not pronounce value judgments if not asked, which we estimated at approximately 15 %.

22. For example, in the spring of 1981 a front-page article appeared in a Thessaloniki newspaper. One of the players on a local football team had been approached by another Thessaloniki team (called Heracles) and offered a bribe. He reported the incident to the regulatory board, and the Heracles team was demoted to a lower league. This event was presented by the local newspaper, in strongly sentimental language, as treason: the Thessaloniki teams, instead of maintaining a united front against their common enemy in the South (regulatory board and Athenian teams), had engaged in fraternal strife, and the one brother, younger and more inexperienced, had betrayed the other to the Athenian athletic establishment (see Boklund-Lagopoulou 1982).

23. Each one of the three analytical spaces was constructed almost exclusively on the basis of the information provided by the corresponding question. However, information pertinent to one space was occasionally given in the context of one of the two other questions, and was then included in the analysis of the appropriate space.

24. For global and economic space this was usually the total number of signifiers used by the interviewees in all four questions. On the other hand, the denominators for the two remaining spaces were sometimes derived through the subtraction from this total of the signifiers that we considered as resisting semantically the social and functional codes. Though it is possible, for example, to imagine a functional meaning attached to a mountain, we did not feel it was to be expected of our interviewees, and thus we subtracted such possible signifiers, when they occured, from the pool of potential signifiers capable of semantization in the social code.

25. These categories are: 6%-23%, 25%-50%, 51%-75%, and 76%-100% for global space; 6%-31%, 33%-48%, 50%-75%, and 78%-100% for economic space; 8%-33%, 34%-47%, 50%-75%, and 77%-100% for social space; and 6%-33%, 36%-63%, 67%-75%, and 78%-100% for functional space. The conclusions from the frequency programs were based on the same classification for the four spaces, but the classifications used in the crosstabulations are organic, i.e., adapted to the distributions specific to each space.

26. On the classification of the sets of codes and the codes included in each set, see Chapter 9, Section 1.

27. The percentages for partial isomorphism in the divergence class for the social-functional, economic-functional, and economic-social pairs of spaces are 25%, 22%, and 17% of the total cases respectively.

28. Kelly's personal constructs and Osgood's experiential continua are in fact unstructured semantic axes akin to the semic categories and thus to elementary isotopies. These axes, like the key concepts used by content analysis, are as a rule defined a priori by the researcher, which from our point of view is a considerable drawback.

29. This is the term we have used throughout this study for the semantic components found in our material. To some extent it exaggerates the depth of our analysis, which delimited isotopies more than it defined codes. We have retained it, however, in preference to the less familiar isotopy, since it is the current term in the semiotic literature and more easily accessible to the reader.

30. Not infrequently, in a question concerning economic activities ("what do people there do for a living?") the interviewees answered by referring to a profession ("they're farmers"). We considered in these cases that the interviewees were using both the code of economic activities and the code of social groups.

31. Due to the geographical orientation of our study, topological and toponymic semantic units were usually overrepresented in the corpus. In order to avoid an undue statistical emphasis on these two codes, we counted them as present only when they had a significant function in the discourse.

32. The demographic code does not really belong with the codes of the built environment. It was included on the one hand because of its relationship to the regional code, and on the other because it is of such low frequency that it does not justify the creation of a separate set and does not alter the statistical status of the built environment codes.

33. The correlations appear at least for the first three ranks of order and frequency, although not in the same degree for all three ranks or all social groups.

34. When a pair of tables of this kind gives rise to significant crosstabulations, the order of the codes in the two tables tends to coincide, with as a result that the definition of the importance of a code is more or less unambiguous. When, on the other hand, it does not, the importance of a code is frequently defined as a mean.

35. The distribution for the whole sample is as follows: up to 11 codes, 4%; 12-14 codes, 16%; 15-20 codes, 67%; 21-26 codes, 13%.

36. There are also certain similarities between our degrees of discursive complexity and the individual conceptual structures built in psychology upon the repertory grid protocols inspired by Kelly's personal construct theory. One of the approaches to these structures is the study of the "topographical organization of constructs", which is based on the patterns of correlations in the repertory grid. This study has revealed two major types of structures. The

first is the articulated structure, in the context of which several clusters of interrelated constructs are related with "linkage constructs", i.e., constructs that are correlated with constructs in two or more different clusters. This structure is considered as typical of normal adults.

The second type of structure, considered as more current among obsessive-compulsive neurotics, is the nonarticulated structure, which includes two different subtypes: the "segmented" structure composed of a series of unconnected clusters, and the "monolithic" structure comprising one main large cluster and possibly an unconnected secondary cluster as well as certain isolated constructs. The monolithic structure corresponds to what has been called in psychology "cognitive simplicity" or "unidimensionality", in opposition to the more complex multidimensional conceptual construction of social behavior (see Adams-Webber 1979: 54; Bannister & Fransella 1986: 52).

This psychological approach, then, defines conceptual complexity on the basis of the existence of statistical links between clusters of correlated constructs, the foundation of the defined structures being the concept of the construct. In our case, the foundation of our definition of discourse complexity is the concept of code, and the links are the qualitative semantic relations between codes. Thus, our semantic complexity has a very different content from the cognitive complexity of the psychologists, but nevertheless the two are structurally more or less comparable: our category of poor overall complexity corresponds to the monolithic structure, rather poor and average complexity to the segmented structure, and fairly high and high complexity to the articulated structure. Needless to say, our structures only apply to semantic complexity of discourse and have no extension whatsoever into the field of psychopathology. Lack of articulation between codes is indicative of poor overall discourse complexity, or a mono-codal or oligo-codal response may be an example of subjectivist, experiential discourse in an appropriate context, as we saw in Section 2.

37. In our discussion of the different spaces in Chapter 8, Section 2, we used the global space delimited by the question on differences and not that of the question on characteristics. This choice may imply a loss in representativeness, but has the advantage of referring to a systematically defined space which is directly comparable with the three analytical spaces, also defined on the basis of internal differences within the region.

38. Code persistence was studied on the basis of selected individual codes, the number of which represents one-third of all the spatial codes located; all the sets of codes were examined.

39. At least the nine first codes and frequently the twelve first codes of each one of the ten groups of the semiotic programs are represented in the thirteen codes selected. This does not of course imply that they appear in each group with the same rank or frequency of appearance. The frequencies in the series

of first codes included in the selected codes vary from around 55% to around 25%.

40. A parallel structural aspect of the sketch maps has been studied by Gary Moore, who is interested not in the specific contents of the maps, but in the structure of the frame of reference for the representation of space that they incorporate (see Evans, Marrero & Butler 1981: 85-86) - we shall return to the matter of this frame of reference in the last section of this chapter.

41. The sequence of the colors was: red, orange, pink, purple, turquoise, light blue, olive green, dark blue, brown.

42. The results for the middle class (significance level 0.01) and the countryside are comparable.

43. The term "code" is not used here in the narrow sense in which it has been used so far, but in its broadest sense of the systemic aspect of a language.

44. We would like to remind the reader of our discussion in Chapter 5, Section 2, on the neurological specialization of the cerebral hemispheres. We there presented Harris' view according to which the left hemisphere is specialized in language processing and the right in visuospatial coding. It is obvious that the dual-code model can be directly linked to such a view.

45. Similar views are held by Ronald A. Finke (1980: 113-115, 124-125, 129). For him, the visual system includes a variety of levels of information processing and there are three types of such levels. In respect to the first type, there is a functional equivalence, i.e., manifestation of similar behavioral effects, between perceiving an object or event, forming its mental image, and recalling facts about it. This kind of equivalence occurs in the highest stages of information processing within the visual system and the corresponding levels are frequently cognitively penetrable. At the second type of level, corresponding to the lowest stages of information processing only, the perception of an object does not have effects comparable to those produced when the object is imagined or thought about, and thus imagery is not functionally equivalent to perception. For these levels information processing is assumed by processing mechanisms, not cognitively penetrable, of a specific structure and function. At the third type of level, the perceptual and the mental images of an object result in comparable effects, which are different from those produced when the object is only thought about. This type both shows an important degree of functional equivalence between imagery and perception, and demonstrates that mental imagery activates many levels of the visual system that are not penetrable by tacit knowledge. For this type too, functional equivalence should be attributed to special processing mechanisms.

   A physiological account of imagery, to which Finke's views may be compared, is given by D.O. Hebb (1968: 466, 471-476). Hebb believes that an essential feature of perception are the primary or first-order cell assemblies, including simple cells (on each of which converge a number of retinal cells) directly excited by sensory stimulation. Groups of first-order assemblies stimulate the lower level of the higher-order assemblies, the second-order assemblies, and the latter in their turn stimulate the third-order assemblies. Perception activates both first- and higher-order assemblies, while mental images consist only of these two higher-order kinds of assembly, which support both less specific imagery and non-representational conceptual processes. It is the lack of the first-order assemblies that deprives these images of the completeness and vividness of perceptual images, a phenomenon also noted by Shepard (see below).

46. A useful review of the psychological views on imagery, addressed to the geographical community, can be found in Lloyd 1982.

47. The location accuracy ratio concerns the locational overlapping of the settlements of two configurations, the sketch map configuration and the actual configuration, and thus refers to a phenomenon similar to the divergence ratio used in Chapter 8, Section 5, to measure the overlapping of any pertinent signifiers of two different configurations. The two ratios, however, were not formulated in the same manner, as can be seen if we compare them; this is reflected in a pure technicality, the form of the denominator, and is due to the argumentative content, which is reflected in the numerator. In Chapter 8, divergence was at the heart of the argument and the numerator was the sum of the non-common signifiers, but now we are interested in the accuracy of our subjects and the numerator is the total number of settlements related to an accurate location, i.e., of the settlements with a more or less common location. The categories defined on the basis of the two ratios can easily be brought into correspondence, since this is mathematically possible for the two ratios, and the correspondence is qualitatively the following: the discrepancy degree of the location accuracy ratio corresponds to the autonomy category of the divergence ratio; the divergence degree of accuracy of the first ratio includes strong divergence plus the most divergent part of noticeable divergence of the second ratio; acceptable accuracy includes the less divergent part of noticeable divergence and the lowest convergence part of the convergence category of the second ratio; the fidelity degree of accuracy corresponds to the medium part of the convergence category; and the identity degree to the highest convergence part of the latter category.

48. In the case of this correlation we aimed at the apparent map accuracy, but our general concern is with actual accuracy. Thus, with this exception and manifestly with the exception of the correlation revealing the impact of graphic ability on sketch map geometric accuracy, the rest of the correlations discussed with this form of accuracy may seem out of context. All these correlations, however, show that map and location accuracy are characterized by similar tendencies, something expectable given the inclusion of the latter in the former, and we thus preferred to present them, if only in an indicative manner.

49. We should not confuse the autonomous character acquired by the inhabitants of a settlement in the context of a significant correlation - which in turn presupposes a meaningful context, such as the settlement hierarchy - with a tendency of the settlement to diverge importantly, positively or negatively, from the average established by the whole sample. Such divergence, of which we have presented many cases in this book, may be statistically significant when the diverging settlement is placed in its meaningful context or - as was usually the case - it may be devoid of statistical significance.

50. We consider the introspective regional image as part of the semiotic system of conceptual regional space.

51. This has in fact long been one of the tenets of both structuralist and Marxist approaches to art and literature (see, for example, Eagleton 1983: 194-217).

References

Adams-Webber, J.R.
    1979   *Personal construct theory: Concepts and applications.* Chichester: Wiley.

Anderson, John R.
    1978   "Arguments concerning representations for mental imagery", *Psychological Review* 85 (4): 249-277.

Appleyard, Donald
    1970   "Styles and methods of structuring a city", *Environment and Behavior* 2: 100-116.
    1979   "The environment as a social symbol: Within a theory of environmental action and perception", *Journal of the American Planners Association* 45: 143-153.

Bachelard, Gaston
    1969   *The poetics of space.* Boston: Beacon Press.
    [1958]   [Original French edition Paris: Presses Universitaires de France.]

Bannister, Don & Fay Fransella
    1986   *Inquiring man: The psychology of personal constructs.* (3rd edition.) London - Sydney - Dover, NH: Croom Helm.

Barthes, Roland
    1964   "Éléments de sémiologie", *Communications* 4: 91-135.

Bernstein, Basil
    1971   *Class, codes and control, Vol. 1: Theoretical studies towards a sociology of language.* London - Henley - Boston: Routledge and Kegan Paul.

Blaut, James M.
    1984   "Modesty and the movement: A commentary", in: Thomas F. Saarinen, David Seamon & James L. Sell (eds.), 149-163.

Boklund, Karin & Alexandros Ph. Lagopoulos
    1984   "Social structures and semiotic systems: Theory, methodology, some applications and conclusions", in: Tasso Borbé (ed.), Vol. I: 431-438.

Boklund-Lagopoulou, Karin
    1982   "I synchrones methodi analysis logotehnikon kimenon" ['Contemporary methods for the analysis of literary texts'], *Filologos* 29: 145-162.

Borbé, Tasso (ed.)
    1979   *Semiotics unfolding: Proceedings of the second congress of the International Association for Semiotic Studies, Vienna, July 1979.* Berlin - New York - Amsterdam: Mouton.

Bourdieu, Pierre
1977   "The economics of linguistic exchanges", *Social Science Informa-tion* 16(6): 645-668.
Brenner, Michael, Jennifer Brown & David Canter (eds.)
1985   *The research interview: Uses and approaches*. London: Academic Press.
Brown, Marilyn A. & Michael J. Broadway
1981   "The cognitive maps of adolescents: Confusion about inter-town distances", *Professional Geographer* 33 (3): 315-325.
Bunting, Trudi E. & Leonard Guelke
1979   "Behavioral and perception geography: A critical appraisal", *An-nals of the Association of American Geographers* 69 (3): 448-462.
Burnett, Pat
1976   "Behavioral geography and the philosophy of mind", in: Reginald G. Golledge & Gerard Rushton (eds.), 23-48.
Cadwallader, Martin
1979   "Problems in cognitive distance: Implications for cognitive map-ping", *Environment and Behavior* 11 (4): 559-576.
Canter, David
1977   *The psychology of place*. New York: St. Martin's Press.
Canter, David V. & Kenneth H. Craik
1981   "Environmental psychology", *Journal of Environmental Psychol-ogy* 1: 1-11.
Carlstein, Tommy, Don Parkes & Nigel Thrift (eds.)
1978   *Making sense of time*. New York: Wiley.
Cassirer, Ernst
1955   *The philosophy of symbolic forms, Volume 2: Mythical thought*. New Haven, NH: Yale University Press.
Castells, Manuel
1975   *La question urbaine*. Paris: Maspero.
Chomsky, Noam
1965   *Aspects of the theory of syntax*. Cambridge, MA: MIT Press.
Cox, Kevin R.
1981   "Bourgeois thought and the behavioral geography debate", in: Kevin R. Cox & Reginald G. Golledge (eds.), 256-279.
Cox, Kevin R. & Reginald G. Golledge (eds.)
1981   *Behavioral problems in geography revisited*. New York - Lon-don: Methuen.
Desbarats, Jacqueline M.
1976   "Semantic structure and perceived environment", *Geographical Analysis* 8 (4): 453-467.

Diodorus of Sicily
  1952   *Diodorus of Sicily.* English translation by C.H. Oldfather. (Loeb Classical Library.) London: William Heinemann and Cambridge, MA: Harvard University Press.
Downs, Roger M.
  1981   "Cognitive mapping: A thematic analysis", in: Kevin R. Cox & Reginald G. Golledge (eds.), 95-122.
Downs, Roger M. & David Stea
  1977   *Maps in minds: Reflections on cognitive mapping.* New York - Hagerstown - San Fransisco - London: Harper and Row.
Eagleton, Terry
  1983   *Literary theory: An introduction.* Oxford: Blackwell.
Eco, Umberto
  1972   *La structure absente: Introduction à la recherche sémiotique.* Paris: Mercure de France.
  [1968]   [Original Italian edition Milano: Bompiani.]
  1976   *A theory of semiotics.* Bloomington, London: Indiana University Press.
Eliade, Mircea
  1959   The sacred and the profane: The nature of religion. New York: Harcourt, Brace & World.
  [1957]   [Original German edition, Rowohlt Taschenbuch Verlag.]
Evans, Gary W.
  1980   "Environmental cognition", *Psychological Bulletin* 88 (2): 259-287.
Evans, Gary W., David G. Marrero & Patricia A. Butler
  1981   "Environmental learning and cognitive mapping", *Environment and Behavior* 13 (1): 83-104.
Finke, Ronald A.
  1980   "Levels of equivalence in imagery and perception", *Psychological Review* 87 (2): 113-132.
Firey, Walter
  1945   "Sentiment and symbolism as ecological variables", *American Sociological Review* 10: 140-148.
  [1961]   [Reprinted in: George A. Theodorson (ed.), 253-261.]
Fodor, Jerry A.
  1975   *The language of thought.* New York: Thomas Y. Crowell.
Foucault, Michel
  1966   *Les mots et les choses: Une archéologie des sciences humaines.* Paris: Gallimard.

Gärling, Tommy, Anders Böök & Erik Lindberg
1984   "Cognitive mapping of large-scale environments: The interrelationship of action plans, acquisition, and orientation", *Environment and Behavior* 16 (1): 3-34.

Godelier, Maurice
1973   "Modes de production, rapports de parenté et structures démographiques", *La Pensée* 172: 7-31.
1978   "La part idéelle du réel: Essai sur l'idéologique", *L'Homme* 18 (3/4): 155-188.

Goldmann, Lucien
1970   *Marxisme et sciences humaines.* Paris: Gallimard.

Golledge, Reginald G.
1976   "Methods and methodological issues in environmental cognition research", in: Gary T. Moore & Reginald G. Golledge (eds.), 300-313.
1978   "Learning about urban environments", in: Tommy Carlstein, Don Parkes & Nigel Thrift (eds.), Vol. I: 76-98.

Golledge, Reginald G. & Gerard Rushton
1976   *Spatial choice and spatial behavior: Geographic essays on the analysis of preferences and perceptions.* Columbus: Ohio State University Press.

Golledge, Reginald G. & Aron N. Spector
1978   "Comprehending the urban environment: Theory and practice", *Geographical Analysis* 10 (4): 403-426.

Golledge, Reginald G. & Robert J. Stimson
1987   *Analytical behavioural geography.* London - New York - Sydney: Croom Helm.

Goodchild, Barry
1974   "Class differences in environmental perception: An exploratory study", *Urban Studies* 11 (2): 57-69.

Gottdiener, M. & Alexandros Ph. Lagopoulos (eds.)
1986   *The city and the sign: An introduction to urban semiotics.* New York: Columbia University Press.

Gregory, Derek
1978   *Ideology, science and human geography.* London: Hutchinson.

Gregory, Derek & John Urry (eds.)
1985   *Social relations and spatial structures.* New York: St. Martin's Press.

Greimas, Algirdas-Julien
1966   *Sémantique structurale.* Paris: Larousse.
1976   *Sémiotique et sciences sociales.* Paris: Seuil.

Greimas, Algirdas-Julien & Joseph Courtés
1979   *Sémiotique: Dictionnaire raisonné de la théorie du langage.*
         Paris: Hachette.
Gurvitch, Georges
1966   *Études sur les classes sociales.* Paris: Gonthier.
Halliday, M.A.K.
1978   *Language as social semiotic: The social interpretation of language and meaning.* London: Edward Arnold.
Hardwick, Douglas A., Curtis W. McIntyre & Herbert L. Pick, Jr.
1976   "The content and manipulation of cognitive maps in children and adults", *Monographs of the Society for Research in Child Development* 41 (3), Serial No. 166: 1-51.
Harris, Lauren Julius
1978   "Sex differences in spatial ability: Possible environmental, genetic, and neurological factors", in: Marcel Kinsbourne (ed.), 405-522.
Harrison, John & Philip Sarre
1971   "Personal construct theory in the measurement of environmental images: Problems and methods", *Environment and Behavior* 3 (4): 351-374.
1975   "Personal construct theory in the measurement of environmental images", *Environment and Behavior* 7 (1): 3-58.
Hebb, D.O.
1968   "Concerning imagery", *Psychological Review* 75 (6): 466-477.
Heise, David R.
1969   "Some methodological issues in semantic differential research", *Psychological Bulletin* 72 (6): 406-422.
Hjelmslev, Louis
1961   *Prolegomena to a theory of language.* Madison - Milwaukee - London: The University of Wisconsin Press.
[1943]   [Original Danish edition Copenhagen: Ejnar Munksgaard.]
1971   *Essais linguistiques.* Paris: Minuit.
Hudson, Ray
1980   "Personal construct theory, the repertory grid method and human geography", *Progress in Human Geography* 4 (3): 346-359.
Hymes, Dell
1974   *Foundations in sociolinguistics: An ethnographic approach.* Philadelphia: University of Pennsylvania Press.
Jakobson, Roman
1963   *Essais de linguistique générale.* Paris: Minuit.
Jelavich, Barbara
1983   *History of the Balkans. Vol. I: Eighteenth and nineteenth centuries. Vol. II: Twentieth century.* Cambridge - London - New

York - New Rochelle - Melbourne - Sydney: Cambridge University Press.

Jonassen, Christen T.
1949   "Cultural variables in the ecology of an ethnic group", *American Sociological Review* 14: 32-41.
[1961]   [Reprinted in: George A. Theodorson (ed.), 264-273.]

Kafkalas, Grigoris
1977   "Kinoniko periechomeno tou diktyou ton hellinikon ikismon" ['Social content of the network of the Greek settlements'], in: Alexandros Ph. Lagopoulos (ed.), E:1-66.

Kelly, George A.
1963   *A theory of personality: The psychology of personal constructs.* New York - London: W.W. Norton.

Kinsbourne, Marcel (ed.)
1978   *Asymmetrical function of the brain.* Cambridge: Cambridge University Press.

Koelsch, William A.
1976   "Terrae incognitae and arcana Siwash: Toward a richer history of academic geography", in: David Lowenthal & Martyn J. Bowden (eds.), 63-87.

Kosslyn, Stephen M., Steven Pinker, George E. Smith & Steven P. Shwartz
1979   "On the demystification of mental imagery", *The Behavioral and Brain Sciences* 2 (4): 535-548, 570-581.

Kosslyn, Stephen M. & James R. Pomerantz
1977   "Imagery, propositions, and the form of internal representations", *Cognitive Psychology* 9 (1): 52-76.

Kousidonis, Christos
1983   Litourgiki periferiopiisi: Efarmogi sti dierevnisi tou hellinikou chorou ['Functional regionalization: Application to the analysis of Greek space']. [Ph.D. thesis, Aristotle University of Thessaloniki.]

Lagopoulos, Alexandros Ph.
1977   "L'image mentale de l'agglomération", *Communications* 27: 55-78.
1983   "Semiotic urban models and modes of production: A sociosemiotic approach", *Semiotica* 45 (3/4): 275-296.
1986   "Semiotics and history: A Marxist approach", *Semiotica* 59 (3/4): 215-244.
1988   "Über die Möglichkeit einer materialistischen Soziosemiotik", *Zeitschrift für Semiotik* 10 (1-2): 9-17.

Lagopoulos, Alexandros Ph. (ed.)
1977   Defteri fasi dierevnisis tou diktyou astikon ikismon stin Hellada ['Second phase of the research project on the network of urban

settlements in Greece']. [Research Report, Technical Chamber of Greece and Chair B' of Urban Planning, School of Engineering, Aristotle University of Thessaloniki.]

Ledrut, Raymond
1973 *Les images de la ville.* Paris: Anthropos.
[1986] [Partly translated as "The images of the city" in: M. Gottdiener & Alexandros Ph. Lagopoulos (eds.), 219-240.]

Lefebvre, Henri
1971 *Au-delà du structuralisme.* Paris: Anthropos.
1974 *La production de l' espace.* Paris: Anthropos.

Lévi-Strauss, Claude
1958 *Anthropologie structurale.* Paris: Plon.

Ley, David
1981 "Behavioral geography and the philosophies of meaning", in: Kevin R. Cox & Reginald G. Golledge (eds.), 209-230.

Ley, David & Marwyn S. Samuels (eds.)
1978 *Humanistic geography: Prospects and problems.* Chicago: Maaroufa Press.

Lloyd, Robert
1982 "A look at images", *Annals of the Association of American Geographers* 72 (4): 532-548.

Lowenthal, David
1972 Environmental assessment: A comparative analysis of four cities. Publications in Environmental Perception 5. New York: American Geographical Society.

Lowenthal, David & Marquita Riel
1972 Environmental assessment: A case study of New York City. Publications in Environmental Perception 1. New York: American Geographical Society.
1972 Structures of environmental associations. Publications in Environmental Perception 6. New York: American Geographical Society.
1972 Milieu and observer differences in environmental associations. Publications in Environmental Perception 7. New York: American Geographical Society.
1972 Environmental structures: Semantic and experiential components. Publications in Environmental Perception 8. New York: American Geographical Society.

Lowenthal, David & Martyn J. Bowden (eds.)
1976 *Geographies of the mind: Essays in historical geosophy in honor of John Kirtland Wright.* New York: Oxford University Press.

Lynch, Kevin
1960 *The image of the city.* Cambridge, MA: MIT Press.

Lyons, Elizabeth
   1983   "Demographic correlates of landscape preference", *Environment and Behavior* 15 (4): 487-511.
MacKay, David B., Richard W. Olshavsky & Gerald Sentell
   1975   "Cognitive maps and spatial behavior of consumers", *Geographical Analysis* 7 (1): 19-34.
Marx, Karl
   1976   *Le capital.* Vols. I - II. Paris: Éditions Sociales.
Marx, Karl & Frederick Engels
   1975   *L'idéologie allemande.* Paris: Éditions Sociales.
Medvedev, P.N. & M. M. Bakhtin
   1978   *The formal method in literary scholarship.* Baltimore - London: Johns Hopkins University Press.
   [1928]   [Original Russian edition Leningrad: Privoi.]
Moore, Gary T. & Reginald G. Golledge (eds.)
   1976   *Environmental knowing: Theories, research and methods.* Stroudsburg, PA: Dowden, Hutchinson and Ross.
Mostyn, Barbara
   1985   "The content analysis of qualitative research data: A dynamic approach", in: Michael Brenner, Jennifer Brown & David Canter (eds.), 115-145.
Murray, Debra & Christopher Spencer
   1979   "Individual differences in the drawing of cognitive maps: The effects of geographical mobility, strength of mental imagery and basic graphic ability", *Transactions of the Institute of British Geographers* NS 4 (1): 385-391.
National Statistical Service of Greece
   1972   *Population de la Grèce au recensement du 14 mars 1971.* Athens: Office Nationale de Statistique.
   1977   *Apotelesmata apografis plithysmou - katikion tis 14is Martiou 1971, T. III.* ['*Results of the population-household census of March 14, 1971, Vol. III*'] Athens: Ethniki Statistiki Ypiresia tis Hellados.
   1982   *Population de fait de la Grèce au recensement du 5 avril 1981.* Athens: Office Nationale de Statistique.
   1984   *Résultats du recensement de la population et des habitations effectué le 5 avril 1981, Vol. II.* Athens: Office Nationale de Statistique.
   1985   *Résultats du recensement de la population et des habitations effectué le 5 avril 1981, Vol. III (Fasc. A).* Athens: Office Nationale de Statistique.

Osgood, Charles E.
1952   "The nature and measurement of meaning", *Psychological Bulletin* 49 (3): 197-237.

Osgood, Charles E., George J. Suci & Percy H. Tannenbaum
1975   *The measurement of meaning.*(9th edition.) Urbana - Chicago - London: University of Illinois Press.

Paivio, Allan
1965   "Abstractness, imagery, and meaningfulness in paired-associate learning", *Journal of Verbal Learning and Verbal Behavior* 4: 32-38.

Park, Robert Ezra
1936   "Human ecology", *American Journal of Sociology* 42: 1-15.
[1961]   [Reprinted in: George A. Theodorson (ed.), 22-29.]

Pearce, Philip L.
1977   "Mental souvenirs: A study of tourists and their city maps", *Australian Journal of Psychology* 29 (3): 203-210.

Pellegrino, Pierre, J.-C. Ludi, G. Albert, C. Castella, A. Lévy, K. Klaue & J.-P. Martinon
1983   Identité régionale et représentations collectives de l'espace. (Research Report no. 25.) CRAAL, School of Architecture, University of Geneva and FNSRS.

Piaget, Jean
1972   *L'epistémologie génétique.* Paris: Presses Universitaires de France.

Pick, Herbert L., Jr. & Linda P. Acredolo (eds.)
1983   Spatial orientation: Theory, research, and application. New York - London: Plenum.

Pickles, John
1985   *Phenomenology, science, and geography: Spatiality and the human sciences.* Cambridge: Cambridge University Press.

Pinxten, Rik
1976   "Epistemic universals: A contribution to cognitive anthropology", in: Rik Pinxten (ed.), 117-175.

Pinxten, Rik (ed.)
1976   *Universalism versus relativism in language and thought.* The Hague: Mouton.

Pocock, D.C.D.
1972   "City of the mind: A review of mental maps of urban areas", *Scottish Geographical Magazine* 88(2): 115-124.

1974   The nature of environmental perception. (Occasional Publications NS 4.) Department of Geography, University of Durham.

1975   Durham: Images of a cathedral city. (Occasional Publications NS 6.) Department of Geography, University of Durham.

Pocock, D. & R. Hudson
   1978   *Images of the urban environment.* London: Macmillan.
Pylyshyn, Zenon W.
   1973   "What the mind's eye tells the mind's brain: A critique of mental imagery", *Psychological Bulletin* 80 (1): 1-24.
   1981   "The imagery debate: Analogue media versus tacit knowledge", *Psychological Review* 88 (1): 16-45.
Rapoport, Amos
   1976   "Environmental cognition in cross-cultural perspective", in: Gary T. Moore & Reginald G. Golledge (eds.), 220-234.
Relph, Edward
   1981   *Rational landscapes and humanistic geography.* London: Croom Helm - Totowa, NJ: Barnes and Noble.
Rossi-Landi, Ferruccio
   1983   *Language as work and trade: A semiotic homology for linguistics and economics.* Massachusetts: Bergin and Garvey.
   [1968]   [Original Italian edition Milano: Bompiani.]
Saarinen, Thomas F. & James L. Sell
   1980   "Environmental perception", *Progress in Human Geography* 4 (4): 525-548.
Saarinen, Thomas F., David Seamon & James L. Sell (eds.)
   1984   *Environmental perception and behavior: An inventory and prospect.* Chicago, IL: Department of Geography, University of Chicago.
Sack, Robert David
   1972   "Geography, geometry, and explanation", *Annals of the Association of American Geographers* 62 (1): 61-78.
   1980   *Conceptions of space in social thought: A geographic perspective.* Minneapolis: University of Minnesota Press.
Sakellariou, M.V. (ed.)
   1982   *Macedonia: 4000 years of Greek history and civilization.* Athens: Ekdotike Athenon.
Saussure, Ferdinand de
   1971   *Cours de linguistique générale.* Paris: Payot.
Sebeok, Thomas A.
   1975   "Zoosemiotics: At the intersection of nature and culture", in: Thomas A. Sebeok (ed.), 85-95.
Sebeok, Thomas A. (ed.)
   1975   *The tell-tale sign: A survey of semiotics.* Lisse: Peter de Ridder.
Shepard, Roger N.
   1978   "The mental image", *American Psychologist* 33: 125-137.

Shepard, Roger N. & Susan Chipman
    1970   "Second-order isomorphism of internal representations: Shapes of
            states", *Cognitive Psychology* 1: 1-17.
Spencer, Christopher & Jill Dixon
    1983   "Mapping the development of feelings about the city: A longitu-
            dinal study of new residents' affective maps", *Transactions of the
            Institute of British Geographers* NS 8 (3): 373-383.
Spencer, Christopher & Marie Weetman
    1981   "The microgenesis of cognitive maps: A longitudinal study of
            new residents of an urban area", *Transactions of the Institute of
            British Geographers* NS 6 (3): 375-384.
Stokols, Daniel
    1978   "Environmental psychology", *Annual Review of Psychology* 29:
            253-295.
Talmy, Leonard
    1983   "How language structures space", in: Herbert L. Pick, Jr. &
            Linda P. Acredolo (eds.), 225-282.
Theodorson, George A. (ed.)
    1961   *Studies in human ecology.* Evanston - New York: Harper and
            Row.
Tuan, Yi-Fu
    1977   *Space and place: The perspective of experience.* Minneapolis:
            University of Minnesota.
Vakalopoulos, Apostolos E.
    1969   *Istoria tis Makedonias, 1354-1833* ['*History of Macedonia, 1354-
            1833*']. Thessaloniki [No indication of publisher.]
Volochinov, V.N.
    1977   *Le marxisme et la philosophie du langage.* Paris: Minuit.
    [1929] [Original Russian edition Leningrad, no indication of publisher.]
Walker, Richard A.
    1985   "Class, division of labour and employment in space", in: Derek
            Gregory & John Urry (eds.), 164-189.
Ward, Shawn L., Nora Newcombe & Willis F. Overton
    1986   "Turn left at the church, or three miles north: A study of direc-
            tion giving and sex differences", *Environment and Behavior* 18
            (2): 192-213.
Whittaker, James O. & S. J. Whittaker
    1972   "A cross-cultural study of geocentrism", *Journal of Cross-
            Cultural Psychology* 3 (4): 417-421.
Winner, Irene Portis & Thomas G. Winner
    1976   "The semiotics of cultural texts", *Semiotica* 18 (2): 101-156.

Wright, John K.
    1947   "Terrae incognitae: The place of the imagination in geography",
                 Annals of the Association of American Geographers 37 (1): 1-15.

Index

Milton Singer

Semiotics of Cities, Selves, and Cultures

Explorations in Semiotic Anthropology

1991. xiv, 380 pages. Cloth.
ISBN 3 11 012601 X
(Approaches to Semiotics 102)

This volume makes empirical applications of Charles S. Peirce's general theory of signs to the areas of the cultural role of cities, the relation of personal identity to social identity and the comparison of cultures and civilizations.

In addition, it traces the intellectual sources of the new paradigm represented by a semiotic anthropology to Radcliffe-Brown's and Levi-Strauss's use of a "genuine structuralist" analysis deriving from Russell and Whitehead's logic of relations, and to Malinowski's use of Peirce's triadic relation of sign, object, and interpretant.

Each of these applications can stand on its own, but, taken together, they suggest an interrelationship and unity that comes in part from the method of semiotic analysis and in part from the results obtained by the application of the method.

This work, a sequel to the author's 1984 book, thus applies a new paradigm and theoretical model for the analysis and interpretation of cultural symbolism and behavior, which deemphasises the models of mechanical causality and biological funtionalism. Two historical chapters trace the sources of the new paradigm for a logic and language of relational structures and a pragmatic contextual theory of meaning.

mouton de gruyter

Berlin · New York